THE ART
OF
BEING RULED

and they make
A doctrinal and witty hieroglyphic
Of a blessed kingdom.

Chapman : from ' Charles Duke of Byron.'

THE ART
OF BEING RULED

BY

WYNDHAM LEWIS

CONTENTS

PART IV

VULGARIZATION AND POLITICAL DECAY

PART V

' NATURES ' AND ' PUPPETS '

PART IX

MAN AND SHAMAN

PART X

SOCIALIST THEORY

PART XIII

BEYOND ACTION AND REACTION

INTRODUCTION

THE easy assumption of Swift that his correspondents were States-girls, as he called it, since what he had chiefly to write about was matters of a public and not a private nature, was perhaps the best way out of a difficulty. To write to a girl incessantly about such matters as that ' I was this morning soliciting at the House of Commons' door for Mr. Vesey, a son of the Archbishop of Tuam, who has petitioned for a bill to relieve him in some difficulty about his estate,' or ' The Secretary turned me out of his room this morning, and showed me fifty guineas rolled up, which he was going to give some French spy,' shows little sense of apropos. The author of a book, it is true, is lifted above the dilemmas of the letter-writer. But his advantage is perhaps more apparent than real.

Most writers to-day, far from making Swift's light-hearted assumption, measure, with a sense of realities that is even less flattering, the calibre of their reader. But their pessimistic calculations will, where we are concerned, be neglected. Most books have their *patients*, rather than their *readers*, no doubt. But some degree of health is postulated in the reader of this book. Its pages are not intended to supply the figurative equivalent of Kruschen Salts or an enema. Nor is it the intention of its author to open a clinic or a nursing-home, or an institute for the half-witted, nor yet a beauty-parlour. Understanding on that point with the reader at the start will be an advantage.

Proudhon in a letter (May 21, 1858, quoted by Sorel) says: 'How many readers are required to make the theoretic conviction (of socialism) pass into the general consciousness ? A few dozen, not more. The rest will get hold of it as best they can. What they get from science will make up for what they have missed elsewhere.' The few dozen readers are the hard-worked *corps d'élite* from whom eventually all authority comes. But it is perhaps a more special audience that ultimately gives the true response. A book's audience is not, in any case, this professional critical *corps d'élite*.

A book of this description is not written for an audience already there, prepared to receive it, and whose minds it will fit like a glove. There must be a good deal of stretching of the receptacle, it is to be expected. It must of necessity make its own audience; for it aims at no audience already there with which I am acquainted. I do not invent (or if that was not an invention, then I am not happy enough to know) a class of *esprits libres*, or ' good Europeans,' as Nietzsche did. I know none.

PART I

REVOLUTION AND PROGRESS

'*Michel Bakunin . . . porte en lui une force . . .
c'est le principe de l'éternel mouvement qui gît au
fond de son âme.*'   Bielinski.

'*This new phase of organism, which has been
introduced with man into the mundane economy, has
made him a very quicksand for the foundation of an
unchanging civilization . . . every century the change
in man's physical status . . . is greater and greater;
he is a shifting basis on which no equilibrium of
habit and civilization can be established; were it
not for this constant change in our physical powers,
which our mechanical limbs have brought about, man
would have long since apparently attained his limit
of possibility; he would be a creature of as much
fixity as the ants and bees. . . . If there were a race
of men without any mechanical appliances we should
see this clearly.*'   Note-Books. Samuel Butler.

'*It is quite true that, if Progress be understood with
its only intelligible meaning, that is, as the continued
production of new ideas, scientific invention and
scientific discovery are the great and perennial
sources of these ideas. Every fresh conquest of
Nature by man . . . generates a number of new ideas.
. . . (But) experience shows that innovating legislation
is connected not so much with Science as with the
scientific air which certain subjects, not capable of
exact scientific treatment, from time to time assume.*'
                Popular Government. H. S. Maine.

'*That view involves both a right and a wrong . . . are
there indeed, or are there not, the two views, that and
this? They have not found their point of correspond-
ency which is called the pivot of the Tâo. As soon*

as one finds this pivot, he stands in the centre of the
ring (of thought) where he can respond without end
to those affirming, and without end to those denying.'
Khî Wû Lun.   Kwang-tze.

' Man is, either in the good or bad sense, the infinite
animal.'
Democracy and Leadership.   Irving Babbitt.

CHAPTER I

REVOLUTION

S OCIAL reform is to-day a very fluid, mercurial science.
That is only to say, however, that it is a science : for
what is there more fluid and constantly changing than
science ?   And all varieties of political belief, the more
outwardly they seem violently to differ, inwardly grow
alike.   They agree to differ in order to resemble each
other, so that the more they ostensibly change, the more
they are the same thing.   And all serious politics to-day
are revolutionary, as all science is revolutionary.   If you
stop to consider it, this must be so ; for since politics and
science are to-day commutative, it would be impossible
for one of them to have this revolutionary character and
not the other.

Every one to-day, in everything, is committed to revolution.   But when unanimity on the subject of revolution
—of one type or the other—has become complete, then
there will be no more revolution !   When every one agrees
to be, or is forced to be, a revolutionary, then a new
equilibrium will have been reached.   At present there are,
however, very many people, exerting great personal
authority, who refuse so to regard politics and science as
one and refuse to be revolutionary.   And the mass of the
people are, of course, as non-political as they are unscientific.   They are essentially conservative and not revolutionary.   That man is ' a political animal ' is of course
completely false ; it is as false as Hobbes' remark that he
is ' a fighting animal.'   He is neither.   It is only the
wealthy, intelligent, or educated who are revolutionary or
combative.   The political battle to-day is between those
political leaders who are ' political animals,' and those
who are not (as prominent and successful men they are of
course both ' fighting animals ').

The revolutionary state of mind is then, to-day, instinctive : the *all that is is bad, and to be superseded by a better*
attitude.   In this attitude there is an inherent falsity :
but it has the advantage of stereotyping a revolutionary
state of mind.   When we say ' science ' we can either mean

any manipulation of the inventive and organizing power of the human intellect : or we can mean such an extremely different thing as the *religion of science,* the vulgarized derivative from this pure activity manipulated by a sort of priestcraft into a great religious and political weapon. In which of these senses we are employing this word we must generally leave it to the reader to determine.

The word ' revolution,' like ' civilization,' is a big reverberating one. In most people's minds it is associated with the rolling of the tumbrils and the baying of the mob. It invariably also suggests the overthrow of the rich by the poor, or of a tyrant or oligarchy by the populace. It must of course have a much wider interpretation than this to include many things that are certainly revolutions, and often referred to as such.

' Revolution ' can be used to describe even the superseding of one parliamentary party by another : it is commonly applied to any marked and important change, political, scientific, or religious, involving to some extent a break with the past, as though something had been *skipped.* The Reformation was, for instance, a great revolution. In the Canisius Encyclical it is described as a ' rebellion,' which is popularly synonymous with ' revolution.' That, thanks to the energy of Luther, was a bloodless revolution as far as Germany went. The same religious disturbance in France was very bloody. Again, Sorel quite justly describes the *affaire Dreyfus* as a revolution. It was a great political event, marking a great change of ideas. People thought and felt after it quite differently from what they did before it. Therefore it was a revolution. The Great War was of course not a war, strictly speaking, in a nationalist or dynastic sense, but a revolution. It was a gigantic episode in the russian revolution. From one end of the world to the other there was nothing that was not changed by it.

Therefore, when the big reverberating word is used, armed proletarian revolt is not necessarily intended nor fascist violence. If the theory of the armed insurrection of the masses occupies our attention a good deal, that is because socialist theory deals so much with that : and any revolution to-day, just as it must be involved with science, must to some extent start from and be modelled on socialist practice. This applies as much to a fascist movement or putsch, as to anything else. Socialist theory is the school in which we all graduate. Mussolini was, to start with, a socialist agitator. And all *change* to-day is rooted in science : and in science and its imperative of change, all active political creeds meet and to some extent merge.

Armed proletarian revolt is, then, the archetype of the dramatic and militant aspect that the change we term ' revolution ' takes. Sorel defines so happily the true nature of ' revolution,' that I cannot do better than quote him rather fully. The following passage is from *La révolution dreyfusienne* :—

> In revolutions, two distinct periods should be distinguished.
> The first comprises : the disturbances which have accompanied the overthrow of the old order—battles engaged, without quarter and sometimes of a sanguinary nature, between the parties struggling for power, a legislation *de circonstance* and often ferociously partisan, designed to abolish completely the power of the vanquished. At this point an accumulation of episodes of a type familiar to professionals of political history are met with. These are far more exciting than those met with in ordinary times. Consequently, men adroit in the art of extracting from documents stories calculated to interest a wide public, in such a time find golden opportunities for exercising their address. It is quite natural that so many authors should be attracted by events enabling them to employ their talents in a profitable manner.
> Next comes the period of calm, of repression, of dictatorship. This appears so colourless, contrasted with the preceding phase, that often it has been asked whether the national genius had not exhausted itself in the superhuman effort required of it to suppress the old order. These times when political life seems so flat, do not interest the chroniclers of great feats. Even they find it difficult to believe that these times can belong to the same *ensemble* as the times of violent disturbance. It is consequently to these latter that commonly the name of ' revolution ' is affected, because they alone seem to bear the imprint of the genius of innovation. . . .
> So one must not expect to find necessarily bloody adventures analogous to those of 1793. In 1848, everything might have passed off peacefully enough, if, in June, the parisian proletariat had not believed itself strong enough to put into practice the theory of *the right to work*—which,

the publicists of the time say, was to be the basis of the new order. The workman succumbed in the ensuing struggle ; and the republicans thought it politic to treat them like the *grands ancêtres* had treated the nobility.

Historians attach an exaggerated importance to the acts of violence by which, often, a time of popular upheaval closes. The description of these events relieves them of the necessity for seeking out the true causes of the change that has occurred. The vanquished denounce, with fury, the *méchanceté* of the greedy, ambitious, unscrupulous people who have broken the laws to satisfy their passion for domination. The victors contend that they have saved the country from the most terrible disasters, and appropriate the title of *pères de la patrie*. In this way it happens that the true meaning of these events becomes obscured.

What is really essential is the transformation occurring in *the ideas* of the community. . . .

There always arrives a time when the people no longer are moved by the absurd hopes that had filled the hearts of the first makers of the revolution. These hopes, even, in the end, are denounced by all sensible people as ' dangerous illusions, likely to mislead.' So from hopes directed to the regeneration of mankind, one passes to a consideration of the practical methods required to realize some quite limited social amelioration. The day on which a considerable number of the principal actors in the revolutionary drama consider that their interests, their passions, their prejudices have received a reasonable satisfaction, any statesman who has a taste for wielding power can try his luck, with the best prospects of success.

That is a very good description of the phases of a violent political revolution : and there Sorel emphasizes the fact that an *exaggerated importance* is attached to the *acts of violence*. He shows throughout this curious essay how the revolution is always a revolution of ideas. So what Fouillée (*Humanitaires et libertaires*) says disapprovingly of the ' *hommes à la cocarde* ' or ' *les violents*,' does not in every sense apply to the author of *Réflexions sur la violence*. At all events, in the essay from which I have just quoted, it is for him *a change of ideas* that constitutes a revolution.

But an ' idea ' is a very great force, or an *idée force*, as Fouillée would call it. And one idea cannot overcome another without violence, though it may not be the stupid

violence of physical force. Where the society is very
materialized or brutalized, and ideas have to plough their
way too much, it is no doubt difficult not to resort to
surgical means. Besides, a very brutalized society is not
amenable to ideas at all, in the way that the French, for
instance, as a nation have shown themselves to be. Personality takes the place of thought, and physical things
of spiritual.

> Every idea (Fouillée says) is the conscious form taken by
> our feelings and impulses ; every idea covers not only an
> intellectual act, but also a certain direction of the sensibility
> and of the will. As a consequence of this, in a society, as in
> an individual, every *idea* is a *force*, tending more and more to
> realize its individual end. Thus with the idea of race . . . (1)
> a certain conscience of itself which a race develops and which
> gives it a sort of specific self in each of its members : (2) and
> a tendency to affirm more and more this (general, racial) *self*,
> at the expense of other races and in dominating them. *The
> idea of race* envelops, in other words, a conscience of race.
> Undoubtedly, for instance, a white man has the *idea* of the
> white race.

This is a summary by Fouillée of his well-known theory
of the *idées forces*. Each white man has a ' white '
ideological seed, so to speak, as part of his make-up. Those
seeds can on occasion expand till they fill the whole creature,
the white man becomes nothing but ' white.' It is then
that he is *a walking idea*, and his force is the force of his
idea. But classes of every sort, as well as races, produce
these *idées forces*. And it is such an *idée force* that Marx
recommended the world to exploit in order to emancipate
itself. Or he recommended the development almost of
a class ' complex.' What he said was that people should
fill themselves from head to foot with the idea of class, of
the under-class, swell with the idea of its numbers, its
power, and its wrongs. And he believed that this mighty
ideologic engine, once primed and ready, would necessarily
explode in an immense gesture of violence. That is the
marxian theory of the ' catastrophe.'

But this ' catastrophic ' conclusion to the ' revolutionary ' process is not only inessential ; it distorts, and I think
degrades as well, the notion of revolution. To say that
people cannot change their souls (or a good part of them)

without destroying their bodies, is a very material doctrine indeed.   If people are only ' walking ideas,' you can make them parade one as well as another.   ' Dying for an idea,' again, sounds well enough, but why not let the idea die instead of you ?   If people insist on dying with their ideas (as people have been known to insist on succumbing with their pets), in the hope, of course, of surviving, in some mysterious way, through them, they cannot be prevented from doing it ; and it is difficult to advance any very good reason why they should be restrained, except that it must probably lead to an undesirable confusion of the mind and the body, which has already gone so much farther than is comfortable.

CHAPTER II

REVOLUTION ROOTED IN THE
TECHNIQUE OF INDUSTRY

'THAT it (science) grows fast is indeed its commonest boast,' Prof. Santayana says. It changes too quickly for the normal mind to keep abreast of it and retain its independence. But any creative mind—and science is one of its products—is devilish in that sense.

Kautsky, in a passage I will quote at length, gives expression to the normal feeling of the danger and damage there is for the human mind in this obsession of a mechanical *betterment*—especially where it is misapplied :—

> The economic revolution prepared by the epoch of discovery was perpetuated by the introduction of the machine into industry. From that moment our economic situation has been submitted to a continual changing. Everything ancient is rapidly disappearing, novelties succeed one another at short intervals. The old, the traditional, is ceasing to pass for guaranteed, respectable, intangible. It is becoming a synonym for the imperfect, the insufficient, the superannuated. This way of looking at things extends beyond economic life, to art, to science, to politics. If formerly we held to the ancient without examination, to-day we are willing to reject it without examination, simply because it is ancient ; and the time required to age and put out of fashion a machine, an institution, a theory, a tendency in art, becomes ever shorter and shorter. And where formerly we worked with the consciousness of working for eternity, with all the devotion which this consciousness gives, to-day we work for the fugitive effect of a moment. We know this, and the work is lightly done. Also our products are not only quickly out of fashion, but they are in a short time effectively out of use.
>
> The new is what we notice first, what we study most thoroughly. The traditional . . . seems quite natural. (*The Social Revolution. K. Kautsky.*)

' This way of looking at things,' Kautsky says, that is, the revolutionary way, that regards anything that *is* as provisional, for the day, and anything that belongs to the

9

past as part of the *bilan* of error and failure that is human history, ' extends beyond economic life, to art, to science, to politics.' Of these four things that he mentions, it is only the first really that has any particular meaning. For it is surely science that is responsible for this revolutionary attitude, not it for that of science. In the case of art, on the other hand, far from this spirit extending to our way of regarding it, it is quite the contrary. It is only to contemporary movements in art that it could apply. They, it is true, are subjected to the mechanical betterment and the time valuation. It is really the fact that it is impossible to apply these mechanical betterment and time standards to pictures and architecture, that provokes a certain hostility and contempt where the arts are concerned, at least on the part of the small popularizing practitioners of science, and the superstitious public. And so politics to-day are revolution, quite simply.

Nevertheless, there remains some truth in the statement : for loosely, vaguely, and in the form of a habit, the mechanical betterment and time valuation (in which the new and not the antique is the thing possessing prestige) is applied *à tort et à travers* indiscriminately, where it is logical to do so and where it is not.

In a book, recently translated, of Edo Fimmen (*Labour's Alternative*), how revolution, in the widest sense, flows from modern technical progress is well brought out ; he shows how the movement of unification is due to it. ' An important impulse towards the concentration of capital,' he says, ' originates, nowadays, from the technical side. The methods of production are continually being improved, and, as a result of such improvements, extant machinery has to be scrapped and replaced by new.'

He then quotes from the first volume of *Das Kapital* to support his description of the ' revolutionizing influence exerted by technical advance.' I will reproduce this excellent summary by Marx :—

> Modern industry never looks upon and treats the existing form of a process as final. The technical basis of that industry is therefore revolutionary, while all earlier modes of production were essentially conservative. By means of machinery, chemical processes, and other methods, it is

continually causing changes, not only in the technical basis of production, but also in the functions of the labourer, and in the social combinations of the labour process. At the same time, it thereby also revolutionizes the division of labour within the society, and incessantly launches masses of capital and of workpeople from one branch of production to another.

Fimmen then proceeds, on this text from Marx, to show how the system of commodity production was made possible by the invention of machinery ; how machines have made individual energy and capacity unnecessary : how the earliest machines were resisted by those workmen rendered superfluous by their invention : and how to-day the employing class is as much affected by the drawbacks from a general human point of view of the scientific technical *ramp* as the employed.   The methods of sabotage, the suppression of some new invention temporarily to slow down this ' killing pace,' and so forth, he examines. Finally, he points out how nothing but an absolute elimination of competition, and gathering of the control into the hands of *one* vast concern, can appease this force, and remove its inconveniences.

What he does not say is that, once this were effected, the pace would certainly slacken. Sabotage and slow-down would be the rule, the happy rule, not the anomaly. The senseless and outstripping speed of the merely mechanical and ingenious side of science would terminate, once its commerical utility had vanished with the disappearance of competition, either in a vast capitalist system or a vast socialist system.

The foregoing examples will suffice to show how *revolution*, as we understand it to-day, is in origin a purely technical process. It is because our lives are so attached to and involved with the evolution of our machines that we have grown to see and feel everything in revolutionary terms, just as once the natural mood was conservative. We instinctively repose on the future rather than the past, though this may not yet be generally realized. Instead of the static circle of the rotation of the crops, or the infinitely slow progress of handiwork, we are in the midst of the frenzied evolutionary war of the machines. This affects our view of everything ; our life, its objects and uses, love, health, friendship, politics : even art to a certain extent, but with less conviction.

That so much restlessness and dissatisfaction can be a matter of congratulation, as we began by saying, does not seem at first so obvious.   The average man feels that he was not designed, as far as he can understand the purposes of his ' noble machine,' to live in the midst of a fever of innovation.   He may even momentarily entertain a doubt as to the perfectly beneficent character of science.   It is conceivable that he may mutter to himself, on rare but ominous occasions, that *plus ça change, plus c'est la même chose* ; that it ' all leads nowhere ' : that to live in a world where nothing matures, but everything is technically nipped in the bud, as it were, where everything shines like polished nickel and pretends to superhuman *pep,* is an outrage on his ' noble machine.'   The complaint of Lord Tennyson's Lotus-Eater about 'for ever climbing up the climbing wave,' ' Why should I toil alone, who am the roof and crown of things,' etc., would seem to him to exactly hit off the disgust at length resulting from his industrial experiences. As he felt the full dead weight, not of the atmosphere but of the capitalist system, pressing on his soul in the proportion of six tons to the square inch, resolutely forcing down his wages for the hundredth time, such a frame of mind might shyly peep forth.   Short of abandoning the dogma that he is the ' roof and crown of things,' he must have lapses in which such misgivings see the light.

These misgivings are without foundation.   Without this *technical* dissolvent that has come to the assistance of philosophy and religion, men would have ceased to criticize life, perhaps, and a sad stagnation would have been the result.   To be able at last to have a technique that enables men to regard life itself as something *imperfect,* like a machine to be superseded, should far outweigh any temporary inconveniences, or even murderous absent-mindedness, of science.

Science, in making us regard our life as a machine, has also forced us to be dissatisfied at its sloth, untidiness, and lack of definition, and given us in our capacity of mechanics or scientists the itch to improve it.

Our life and personality, viewed as science obliges us to, is not *humanly* true or *personally* useful, any more than is the scarified, repellent picture of our skin under the micro-scope. Science makes us *strangers* to ourselves. Science destroys our personally useful self-love. It instals a principle of impersonality in the heart of our life that is anti-vital. In its present vulgarized condition science represents simply the principle of destruction : it is more deadly than a thousand plagues, and every day we *perfect* it, or our popular industrially applied version of it.

If a new and presumably better machine should not put in its appearance to take the place of the old, then the work of science would be purely destructive. And again, unless life possesses what the author of *If Winter Comes* calls *One Increasing Purpose*, then science is a supreme mis-fortune. It is only a religious intelligence, in short, that would be disposed to favour science.

Above, science was said to have made us regard our life as scientific or mechanistic, and to have *given us the itch to improve it*. The question is evidently how far it can be *improved* without radical transformation.

But radical transformation is what the most typical modern scientific thought envisages. ' Philosophy can only be an effort to transcend the human condition,' Bergson has said : and Nietzsche proposed some sort of biologic transformation no doubt with his super-man. Do you want to be a super-man ? Do you want to be a god ? That is the question ! Does ' conscience ' make cowards of us *all*, as Hamlet asserted ?

CHAPTER III

CREATIVE REVOLUTION
AND DESTRUCTIVE REVOLUTION

THE difficulty attendant on such a task as the one here undertaken is, that to treat of anything permanent in a society with a sort of religion of impermanence imposed on it, is not easy. But there is no intention to counter (even if such a thing were possible, which it manifestly is not) that condition. To treat of permanent values and metaphysical truths is the natural, useful task of a small number of men, and one chaos is much like another to them. If they take illustrations from chaos and destruction for the things they believe never are destroyed, that is natural enough, for that is all the landscape provides.

Then there are two kinds of revolution: there is *permanent revolution*, and there is an impermanent, spurious, utilitarian variety. Much 'revolutionary' matter to-day is a mushroom sort, not at all edible or meant for sustenance. There is *creative revolution*, to parody Bergson's term, and *destructive revolution*. A sorting out or analysis is necessary to protect as many people as have the sense to heed these nuances. A great deal of the experimental material of art and science, for instance, is independent of any destructive function. Reactionary malice or stupidity generally confuses it with the useful but not very savoury chemistry of the Apocalypse.

The present is of course a particularly 'transitional' society: but the transit must take some time, as it must go all round the earth. Animal conditions, practically, must prevail while this progress is occurring. We begin already to regard ourselves as animals. The machinery of the transit is the 'revolutionary' dogma daily manufactured in tons by the swarming staffs specially trained for that work.

The virtues that we are apt to confuse in our excessive officially promoted pragmatism are the *disruptive* and the *creative* ones: or rather, katabolism comes too much to be

14

described as *life*. If I kill you, that is a different thing
from giving birth to you.

In our society two virtues are baldly contrasted, that of
the *fighter* and *killer* (given such immense prestige by nineteenth-century darwinian science and philosophy) and
that of the *civilizer* and *maker*. But the ancient and valuable iranian principle of duality is threatened. We confuse these two characters that we violently contrast. The
effort in this essay is to separate them a little. It is hoped
that certain things that have flown a grey and neutral flag
will be forced to declare themselves as Ozman or Ahriman,
the dark or the light.

Many ' reforms ' that are daily launched are deliberately
suited for the weak and staggering body for which they
are destined. Like a sort of intellectual sabotage imitating the industrial, a great deal of scientific thought is
deliberately slowed down, distorted, or even it may arrive
that stones are offered in place of bread. Under the
present system this cannot be avoided any more than other
forms of sabotage.

It is desired, with reason, that ambitious building
operations should not be undertaken. So it is that social
reform is a very fluid, ' futuristic ' science. You can be
sure that every social innovation you are witnessing will
be scrapped, probably loaded with contempt, and forgotten, to-morrow ; or, if not, the next day. It is not
there because it is pleasant, beneficent, or abstractly
desirable, but solely because it is at the moment *useful*.
It is almost always a weapon of war. Almost all our arts
of peace are to-day disguised weapons, for the good reason
that there is nowhere anything that could be described
as peace.

The popular prestige of the clinic and the laboratory is
lent to the revolutionary experiments in progress. So the
habits of the laboratory, as well as the life-history of
machines, substitute themselves for the rhetoric and play
of animal instinct. The functional conservatism of the
animal is exchanged for the revolutionary experimentalism
of research.

The decretals of the scientist are received with great
popular reverence. This is surprising, seeing how fugi-
tive and fashionable merely the fiats of the laboratories

are now proved by experience to be. This in the long run must effect a new mentality in the person submitted to these constant deceptions—a kind of fashionable attitude to his own beliefs. This alone would either turn into intelligence, or, what is more likely, a disposition to regard his personality as discontinuous—the attitude of mind that a dog who had a new master every day might get. Each new spasm of faithfulness would produce a new dog.

In such a fluid world we should by all rights be building boats rather than houses. But this essay is a sort of ark, or dwelling for the mind, designed to float and navigate; and we should all be wise, with or without covenants, to provide ourselves with some such shell in everything, rather than to rely on any conservative structures. For a very complete and profound inundation is at hand. After *us* comes the Deluge : more probably than not, however, before that, and out of its epigrammatic sequence.

Meantime, we have a duty where the *officials of the Flood*, as they might be called, are concerned. We have to serve them out with gas-masks, light navigable craft of a sea-worthy and inconspicuous type, and furnish them with instructions as to currents, winds, head-swells, maritime effluvia, Saragossa seas, doldrums, sharks, waterspouts, and sea-serpents. The complete equipment of an inspector of the Flood would be of such a technical description that it is impossible, however, to more than hint at it.

When Heine's english engineer had made his automaton, it ' gnashed and growled ' in his ear, ' Give me a soul ! ' Naturally, being an english engineer, he had never thought of that, nor was he able to invent it. Some day we shall probably be confronted with some such harsh request. And we shall probably be as ill provided as was the english engineer. We should remember what we owe to our machines, which are our creatures. ' Remember the machines ! ' would be a good watchword or catchword. We are imbuing them with our own soullessness. We only have ourselves to thank if things turn out badly as a result. We brutalize them as the Senegalese and other native troops are brutalized by contact with our ruthless and too barbarous methods of warfare. But, as I have suggested above, in all likelihood the evolution of the machine will eventually be guided into more humane channels, when the destruction phase is past.

The modern ' soul ' began, of course, in the Reformation. The most beautiful illustration of that birth (where you could almost observe it being born out of the bowels of the Venus of Milo) would be found within the anxious brain of Olympia Morata, the saintly blue-stocking of Ferrara. There the classical learning and beauty of the ancient world bred, body to body with the Reformation, this strange child.

When Luther appealed for the individual soul direct to God, and the power of all mediating authority was definitely broken, God must have foreseen that he would soon follow His viceregents. The individual soul would later on, had he been God, have known very well that when he abandoned God, he would before long himself be abandoned. The mediator should have known that too. In any case this necessary triad has vanished. The trinity of God, Subject, and Object is at an end. The collapse of this trinity is the history also of the evolution of the subject into the object or of the child back into the womb from which it came. And the section entitled *Sub Persona Infantis*, later in this essay, is a description of the raid back into the ideology of childhood of the mature ' bourgeois ' world of to-day.

CHAPTER IV

THE *PHANTOM MAN* OF DEMOCRATIC ENLIGHTENMENT

INTIMATELY associated with the notion of *revolution* is the notion of *progress*. The origin of this latter notion is traced by George Sorel to the rise of monarchy in Europe. In his very interesting book on this subject (*Les illusions du progrès*) Sorel starts by indicating the generally accepted theory which places the origin of the idea of progress in the quarrel of the moderns and the classicists occurring in the last years of the seventeenth century. He justly remarks how strange or paradoxical it must seem to any one to-day that a literary quarrel could have engendered such an idea. For no one to-day would be disposed to admit the existence of ' progress ' where art is concerned. In the one activity that in most ways is excepted from the system of mechanical betterment applied to everything else, this very idea is said to have had its origin !

' Nothing seems to us more strange,' he says, ' than the bad taste of Perrault systematically claiming for his contemporaries a higher place than that accorded to the great men of the Renaissance or of antiquity—preferring, for example, Lebrun to Raphael.'

Brunetière (whom Sorel largely follows) believed that the idea of ' progress ' originated in two cartesian theses relative to science : one, that science is never separated from *practice*; and two, that science goes on indefinitely *growing*. Indeed, from an acceptance of these two theses Sorel admits it would be natural to proceed (in applying them to the political or social world) to the belief in an *indefinite progress* for society too. But he prefers to reverse this explanation, in a sense. When the notion of ' progress ' first took shape the political world was of such very great importance, and the idea of the monarchy enjoyed such great prestige, that it is more likely, he thinks, that the idea of ' progress ' came from a contemplation of the kingly power, rather than from the notions of the stability of natural laws popularized by Fontanelle.

18

The governments of the new monarchical model, even in the time of Descartes, with their centralized power and regular administration, could give effect, with great exactitude, to all their wishes. They could realize the stipulated physical union, in fact, of theory and practice. The grandiose dreams of the political primitives of Italy of the machiavellian type had become astonishing realities. The kingly power, in its culmination in such a figure as that of *le roi soleil*, dazzled everybody so much, its success seemed so stable and assured, and it seemed automatically increasing with the predictable acceleration of a law of nature, that it must have been from that, rather than from the new triumphs of natural science, that men got their idea of 'progress.' Sorel even suggests that Galileo perhaps derived his interest in the laws of gravitational acceleration from the type of constant force presented by the monarchy, with its power swelling under his eyes every day.

Instead of the gay, 'enlightened' notion of 'progress' coming to birth in the eighteenth-century aristocratic world, such people as George Sorel or Lenin would have a gravity and pessimism much nearer to the religious mind than to the light-hearted, secular, pagan European. Their way of envisaging the problems that the idea of 'progress' was invented to meet would imply a static conception of the world, or the world's mind, rather than a 'scientific' and evolutionary one. Their 'progress' would be a discipline and adjustment. Nor would it admit the whole, unregenerate human family on equal terms, as a jolly party of friends, with the humbug ensuing from such a notion.

In the contemplation of a partly latent political power (beside which the power of a Louis xiv would seem indeed a pigmy), rather than in science, a Galileo to-day could find support, no doubt, for even more formidable physical laws.

Bound up with the idea of progress is the democratic conception of a social unification. It is this idea of *unification* inseparable from 'democracy' that Sorel, the syndicalist, is principally concerned to attack and if possible destroy.

Democracy has for its principal object (both according to the revolutionary school to which Sorel belonged, and equally according to leninism) the disappearance of the class feeling. Its idea is to *mix* all the citizens of a given society into one whole, in which the most intelligent would automatically ' better themselves ' and rise, by their talents, into the higher ranks. Such *social climbing* would be of the essence of this democratic society. The real social classes are, for the syndicalist, occupational classes or syndics, of course. ' Class ' in the bourgeois sense is an abstract abomination. In following for a little the main line of the syndicalist we shall be arriving at one of the most interesting critical points where class is concerned in recent socialism. At the bottom of the syndicalist idea is the wish for a caste system. This is not explicit in the syndicalist doctrine : nor is, I had better add, much of the interpretation I am about to provide.

Europe has had ' classes,' Asia ' castes.' The ' free ' European has always been a *gentleman* for himself, through all his intermittent slavery. His power of self-deception has been very remarkable ; all the realities of hard labour and subordination were replaced by a rosy abstraction of ' freedom.' ' Nosotros somos todos caballeros aqui ! ', mixing his chivalry with his democracy, he would exclaim. Syndicalism is non-European in that sense. It would aim at breaking up this *abstract* dream, and abstract classification based on the unreality of ' freedom.'

Against the finished product of scientific popularization syndicalism also raised itself. This neat, simplified, *abstracted* truth, prepared for the democracy, it regarded as pernicious. It is that abstract machinery that manufactures the *abstract man* of democracy, the great european make-believe.

The *bourgeoisie* who seized the power at the Revolution concocts this abstraction now (before, it was the aristocratic *salon* who concocted it, or had it concocted). And by means of it the *bourgeoisie* imposes its galb on the mind of the worker, so that he becomes a little *bourgeois*. But democratic ideals hold up to the workman images of a life that is not his, and to which he can never belong. He remains an eternal spectator — other people, the *bourgeoisie*, act his life for him, out of reach. He has no imaginative life of his own.

For this *up* and *down*, this *higher* and *lower*, this *betterment* of ' progress ' and democratic snobbery, with its necessary unification into a whole, suppressing of *differences* and substituting for them an arbitrary scale of values, with the *salon* at the top, the syndicalist would substitute an equally dogmatic egalitarian *this* and *that*, a horizontal diversity.

If you are a pro-specialist to the extent that the syndicalist is, you will naturally not regard the phenomenon of vulgarization with favour. This *abstract* of truth or knowledge, this thin miniature pretended cosmos, over-simplified till it becomes meaningless, is a self-indulgent pretence not worth having. It makes a society of little sham gods, or know-alls (*Je sais tout* is the name of one of their organs). Every one in this sense becomes a phantom man, namely *l'homme éclairé.*

This *homme éclairé* is nothing at all—he is not a bootmaker, an engineer, a carpenter, or a doctor. He is a man-of-fashion really, if he is anything—a man of conversation. And his habitat is the *salon* or fashionable, and at the same time intellectual, dinner-table. What has the hard-working country doctor, the busy engineer or bootmaker, to do with this strange figure of aristocratic leisure, senseless ' curiosity ' and loquacity ? Nothing at all. Then why be ' vulgarized ' in that way, as though you were he and not yourself ?

The cultural, ' all-round ' personage (the ideal of the vulgarizer and of democracy) is the opposite of the narrow class-man, or, better, caste-man, the narrow *occupational* mannequin, the narrow integral self-effaced unit of the syndic. The bootmaker (for the theorist of syndicalism) must have only bootmaking thoughts. No godlike, *éclairé*, gentlemanly thoughts must interfere with his pure, sutorial one-sidedness—thoughts that in any case he would get all upside down, never have any time to properly enjoy, and which would only make him absurd and diminish his utility ; whereas, sticking to his last, he could be as ' noble ' as any noble (the ' nobility of toil '), a figure like a sistine prophet, at his best. Contrasted with him, the courtier ' skipping nimbly in a lady's chamber to the lascivious pleasing of a lute ' is far less grand, infinitely less to be respected or admired.

The majority of men should, and indeed must, be screwed down and locked up in their functions. They must be functional specialists—the doctor smelling of drugs, the professor blue-spectacled, bent, and powdered with snuff, the miner covered with coal-dust, the soldier stiff and martial, etc., etc. The only person who can be an ' all-round ' man, *éclairé*, full of scepticism, wide general knowledge, and ' lights,' is the ruler : and he must be that—that is *his* specialization. This is naturally not the way that the syndicalist puts it. But it is what is implied in the political system of Sorel and the other syndicalists.

Now, if we were dealing in dreams, in impossible people instead of people as they are found in their daily life, we could argue with success, perhaps, against the syndicalist that people are *happier* when they are (although nailed down to their technical occupation) *imagining themselves something they are not.* It is perhaps in the Madame Bovary in everybody that is to be found the true source of human happiness. People like to have a dream or hope : to think they can ' rise in the world,' become a ' Bourgeois Gentilhomme,' or even perhaps, with very great luck indeed, a little noble. If you told them that this was very absurd and snobbish, they would perhaps reply that it was no more absurd than anything else in life, than remaining boxed down, for instance, in the specializations of some trade. Most men, again, do not really love their ' shop ' so much that they *never* want to get out of it.

In this way you could represent this abstract region of useless but enlightened, sceptical, romance (to which democratic vulgarization admitted *everybody*) as the organization of a happiness that is a permanent, invariable factor in the human make-up. The ' gentleman,' the superb, unreal invention of the European, might seem worth preserving. It might even seem that the European must sink politically when he gave it up.

If people needed discipline less than they do, not more ; if they were not so disposed to take advantage of these godlike conditions offered, even, only vicariously, and all wanted to be gods more than the resources of human life, and the patience or jealousy of men, will support (and so on with the tale of the reality of life and human nature) : then, perhaps, these arguments would be true. But unfortunately they cannot meet these hostile requirements, forced on every one by experience.

CHAPTER V

THE OPPRESSIVE RESPECTABILITY
OF 'REVOLUTION'

IF ours is an 'already revolutionized society,' it is very imperfectly so. We are in the position of impatient heirs, waiting for a long-expected demise, torn between pious concern for the poor sufferer, and anxiety, since now nothing can avert the catastrophe (which we hope will be a 'peaceful end'), to get on with our business.

This situation accounts for the fact of a certain anomaly where the 'revolutionary' tendencies in this 'revolutionized' but still formally traditional society are concerned. 'Revolution' is accepted everywhere, the battle is everywhere won, and yet nothing happens. When it does happen, as in Russia or Italy, no one can pretend that things are changed enough to meet our expectations.

'Revolution' to-day is taken for granted, and in consequence becomes rather dull. The Heir of all the Ages (as every one is quite ready to admit that he is, and indeed it would be quite impossible to deny that he is an *heir*) stands by the death-bed — *penniless*. The immensely wealthy society, at its last gasp, lies gazing listlessly across the counterpane, staring at a Pom, which stares back at him. The evening comes, the day has been spent in idleness. The Heir of all the Ages retires to his garret at the neighbouring inn. The bulletin is issued, *No change*.

Revolutionary politics, revolutionary art, and, oh, the revolutionary mind, is the dullest thing on earth. When we open a 'revolutionary' review, or read a 'revolutionary' speech, we yawn our heads off. It is true, there is nothing else. Everything is correctly, monotonously, dishearteningly 'revolutionary.' What a stupid word! What a stale fuss!

A really good, out-and-out 'reactionary' journal is, at first, like a breath of fresh air in the midst of all this turbulent, pretentious, childish optimism. A *royalist* publication is worth its weight in gold. Catholicism, we feel, is essential to our health. We fly to the past—anywhere out of this suspended animation of the so smugly 'revolutionary' present.   Out of the detestable crowd of quacks —*illuminés*, couéists, and psychologists—that the wealthy death-bed has attracted, and who throng these antechambers of defeat ; from all the funeral - furnishers, catafalque-makers, house-agents, lawyers, moneylenders, with their eye on the Heir of all the Ages, we fly in despair.

But the 'Reactionary' (a sort of highly respectable, genteel quack, as well, with military moustaches and an 'aristocratic' bearing) is even more stupid—if that were possible—than the 'Revolutionary.'   We listen to him for a moment, and he unfolds his barren, childish scheme with the muddle-headed emphasis of a very ferocious sheep. He lodges in the garret next to us at the inn, and is in arrears with the rent.   The servants (who are all the reddest of revolutionists, of course) hate him.   The Reactionary, in the long run, does not add to the cheerfulness of the scene.

This aspect of 'revolution,' its increasing respectability, is well brought out by Kautsky in *Social Revolution*. He contrasts the difficult position of a 'revolutionary' formerly, in the *salons* of the *bourgeois*, and the very different position to-day.   The 'revolutionary' of yesterday would at present find himself in the tamest situation, surrounded by a benevolent welcome everywhere he went, Kautsky shows.   Indeed, he would find nothing but 'revolutionaries' everywhere.   At the millionaire's table, in the millionaire's press, as in the cabman's shelter or the labour journal, he would find nothing but the most respectable and discouraging conformity to his eager beliefs.   If he were incorrigibly desirous of experiencing the 'revolutionary' thrill and of tasting the rude delights of the outcast, it would be—oh, strangest of paradoxes !— in being *unradical* alone that he could hope to find it.

'Formerly, it is true, when, even with the majority of cultivated people, socialism was regarded as a crime, as a madness, a *bourgeois* could only embrace socialism by breaking with the whole of his world.   The man who under these circumstances abandoned the ranks of the *bourgeoisie* to join the ranks of the socialists had to be possessed of an energy, a passion, and a revolutionary conviction much more intense than that required by a workman engaging in the same revolutionary path.

' It is a very different thing to-day : socialism is accepted in the *salons*, there is no longer any need of any particular energy, it is no longer necessary to break with *bourgeois* society, in order to bear the name of " socialist." '

That is ' official ' revolution, as it could be called. It is to-day everywhere obligatory—just as evening dress has become more or less obligatory, at the same time, in our society. Every one who has money enough is to-day a ' revolutionary'; that and the dress suit are the first requisites of a gentleman. There are also a great many unemployed who naturally also are revolutionaries, sharing to the letter their revolutionary opinions with their prosperous brother iconoclasts. It is this that perhaps it would be well to break with a little, unless we are going to die of *ennui*. Things have gone so far with ' Revolution,' it is becoming so palpably, dogmatically, wearisomely, and insolently ' top dog,' that it may some day even have to be rescued from poor old ' Reaction.'

CHAPTER VI

THE NON-IMPERSONALITY OF SCIENCE

IN Chapter IV we saw how vulgarization is not the indiscriminate scattering of *truth*, but the organizing and adapting of certain chosen *truths*, or discoveries, of philosophy or science, to an ultimately political end. The ideology of a time (*ideology* is Napoleon's word for the metaphysics of government) is that of the contemporary ruling class. So the finished product of scientific vulgarization is not an inhuman, objective bundle of pure scientific truth, but a personally edited bouquet or bundle, with a carefully blended odour to suit the destined palate.

But here we arrive at one of the most significant delusions of the present time, to which in passing we must devote some attention. The popular notion that science is ' impersonal ' is one of the first errors we are called on to dispel. The *non-impersonality* of science should at all cost be substituted for the idea of its impersonality.

Science in itself, to start with, when it first began its revolution, was a force of nature sure enough : a thing and not a person. But this impersonal thing men have now got hold of and harnessed, to a great extent. So pure science is one thing ; its application another ; and its vulgarization a third.

One of the most ridiculous effects of the vulgarization of science and the application of its methods, *à tort et à travers*, to human life, is what could be defined as *the belief in anonymity*. From this many absurdities result. First of all, the man of science himself begins to believe in it. He believes that he is *not a person*, that he is *not human*, that he is in some way a part of nature. Then, through admiring this ' scientific detachment ' and ' impersonality ' so much, Tom, Dick, and Harry begin to believe that *they*, too, are not *persons*, not *human*. A man (a quite ordinary man, not a man of science) will stand in front of another man (who knows him quite well and all about him) and pretend that he is not himself, that he is ' impersonal,' that he is incapable of any emotions, appetites, or prejudices : that

26

he cannot be angry, partial, offended, jealous, or afraid. And the strangest thing is that he *is believed*.

This delusion of impersonality could be best defined as that mistake by virtue of which persons are enabled to masquerade as *things*.

A simple belief in the ' detachment ' and ' objectivity ' of science, the anxiety of a disillusioned person to escape from his self and merge his personality in *things* ; verging often on the worship of *things*—of the non-human, feelingless, and thoughtless—of such experiences and tendencies is this delusion composed.   Its godlike advantages from the point of view of a hundred different classes of people are obvious.

A book that I have just read (*Bolshevism and the West*, by Bertrand Russell) suggests to me the best manner of educing this point in my argument.   A detailed scrutiny of it will serve that end, I believe, extremely well.

I will preface my remarks on Mr. Russell's contribution to this debate by a word or two as to the beliefs of his opponent.   The book is the account of a debate organized in 1923, in America, to decide whether the soviet principle might be expected to meet with success if applied to western countries.   Mr. Bertrand Russell was chosen to try it out from the english liberal standpoint.   It was his task mildly to oppugn the militant americanism of a representative there of the bolshevik idea, Mr. Nearing. The debate resolved itself into an orthodox statement of the militant communist ideal on the part of Mr. Nearing ; and a characteristic counter-statement of Mr. Russell's attitude in these matters.

As regards Mr. Nearing's beliefs, I find more to agree with in the soviet side of the argument than in Mr. Russell's. I am not a partisan, but an independent observer of these events.   I am not a communist ; if anything, I favour some form of *fascism* rather than communism.   Nevertheless, when two principles are opposed, and one of these is that of english liberalism, in most cases I should find myself on the other side, I expect.   In my comment on this debate it is rather as another opponent of Mr. Russell, than as an ally of Mr. Nearing, or of bolshevism, or of communism, that I take my place.

PART II

AGRICULTURAL THOUGHT AND INDUSTRIAL THOUGHT

' *Qui serait assez osé que de prendre un homme pour marteau, un autre en guise de pelle ; d'employer celui-ci comme crochet, celui-la comme levier ?* '
Idée générale de la révolution. P.-J. Proudhon.

' *The good men in the world are few, and those who are not good are many : it follows that the sages benefit the world in a few instances and injure it in many.*' *Khü Khieh. Kwang-tze.*

' *A keeper of monkeys, in giving them out their acorns, once said, " In the morning I will give you three measures and in the evening four." This made them all angry, and he said, " Very well, in the morning I will give you four and in the evening three." His two proposals were substantially the same, but the result of the one was to make the creatures angry, and of the other to make them pleased. . . . Therefore the sage man brings together a dispute in its affirmations and denials. . . .*' *Khi Wû Lun. Kwang-tze.*

CHAPTER I
'BOLSHEVISM AND THE WEST'

THE industrial system (of which the communist state would be the appropriate flower) is still in its infancy, said Mr. Russell; for a century is too short a time for a social system to grow up in. The gist of his argument throughout, in fact, turned on the slowness of all real ' progress.' If with Mr. Russell you believe in ' progress,' you must be prepared for any amount of *slowness*. He asserted, on the other hand (not in disparagement but as a point to remember), that contemporary man still thought agriculturally : in terms, that is, of the growth of crops, of the processes of plant and animal life.

His opponent he represented as an orthodox marxian ; and going to the fountain - head, he found the following arguments against the marxian position. Since Marx thought and wrote his economist bible, a lot of water had flowed under the London bridges, and the blood of many terrible tyrants had flowed too. Marx's thought matured, he said, before the darwinian revolution—that is, before the change occurred leading us from the logical to the vitalist approach. That thought (on which bolshevism is built) is a fish out of water in our present world ; or shall we say that it is a land animal, whereas we are fishes—accustomed to a fluid medium? *We* have plunged into the element controlled by a Great God Flux of whom M. Bergson is, or was, a powerful hierophant : whereas Marx lived in a formal hegelian world, in which ' it was all a matter of hard outlines, sharp, rigid outlines, such as you get in logic.'

Mr. Russell had been introduced to his american audience as ' this great logician,' and they may some of them have been a little confused subsequently by witnessing this great logician freely using the arguments of a vitalist position to sustain his argument against the introduction of bolshevism into western communities. They should perhaps have been told that Mr. Russell has a different mind as a politician to that he has as a philosopher. Or it would be more accurate to say *to that he began with* as a philosopher. For the emotional impurities of the facile liberalism he inherits have gradually invaded his philosophy, and emolliated the logical erectness with which he set out, by admixture with the *vase* of vitalist-pragmatical theory. Or it could be said that Mr. Russell had and has a first-class intellectual machine ; which is, as is sometimes the case, independent of his personality. The ' great logician ' is a *machine* : but Mr. Russell, the person, is not a great logician. He is a conventional, not very far-seeing, routine english liberal. The great logical machine scorns to associate itself, apparently, with the mildly dramatic activities of this ' sentimentalist.' This is what the chairman should perhaps have said. The audience would then have been able to follow the proceedings more easily.

The words in which Mr. Russell explains Marx's unfortunate position on the hither side of the darwinian flood are as follows : ' Later on, after Marx's thought was fully formed, came the biological outlook which is associated with Darwin, a habit of viewing human society as a thing that grows, a thing that develops like a tree, a thing that has a life by itself, a thing that moves in a certain manner not prescribed by the laws of logic or reason, but prescribed by the law of life.'

A kind of retrograde movement is suggested by these two statements. We are retrograde (as Mr. Russell sees it) because ' our thoughts are still agricultural, not industrial.' But what is an ' industrial thought ' like ? (An agricultural thought is like a tree or a cabbage, we have already said.) Roughly, it would seem, and without examination, that the ' biologic ' welter of sensationalist ' life,' said by Mr. Russell to have been inaugurated by Darwin (of whose evolutionary doctrine Bergson, crossed with Plotinus, is the emotional metaphysical expression), would be the equivalent of the *agricultural* type of thought ; and that the logician would be more in sympathy with the *industrial.* So, either in one case or the other, the cart looks as though it were before the horse ; or that mankind were in one sense ascending the hill, and yet simultaneously descending it.

If we return to the ' industrial thought ' to find out what may be meant by that, we shall probably discover where the ' logic ' comes in in this contradictory movement. It is natural, we learn, for a logically minded man to regard

human society as ' a thing that develops like a tree ' ; that
grows irrationally according to a law of its own.   But that
is also the way that the agriculturally minded man would
regard human society, at first sight, it would seem.   The
cultivator, thinking of his pigs and trees, would instinctively think of human institutions autonomously maturing
and withering on such a plan.   The ideal industrialist, on
the other hand, who had participated in the manufacture
or creation of everything he saw and handled, would regard
his man-made world as more within his control—just as the
logician would.   Yet, as we have seen in Mr. Russell's
account, the phase in our industrial society that has superseded the, according to him, immature logic of Marx and
Hegel, is the biologic phase inaugurated by Darwin.   This
is responsible for the following strange situation : that the
farther men get away from nature, and their former
agricultural pursuits, from trees and pigs, the more they
employ the imagery of nature, of the growth of pigs and
trees, to define the irrational, fatal, evolution of human
societies.   This at least is Mr. Russell's account of how it
works out, and this no doubt unconscious paradox can
now be examined more closely.

Agricultural thought, or the mentality of the cultivator,
will naturally regard every process brought to its notice
in terms of plant and animal growth.   But industrial
thought will be disposed, on the other hand, to regard all
processes, or creative possibilities, offered to its notice, in
terms of manufacture.   It will substitute the will of man
for the more mysterious will of nature.   In place of the
living growth of organisms, it will be apt to reduce everything literally *to a dead level.*   In its way of envisaging
events and processes, a dead ' raw material ' will be what
is to be acted on, and shaped by man for his particular
purposes, infinitely docile and with no limits to its rapid
adaptability.

But for such a man as this latter one—the ideal *industrial·*
man—the ' logical ' world of Hegel—that world in which,
as Mr. Russell puts it, everything ' went by sharp transi-
tions from this thing to that thing and then to the other
thing, and it was all a matter of hard outlines, sharp, rigid
outlines, such as you get in logic '—the logical world would
be much more to his taste than the ' biologic ' world of

Darwin. So is it not unfortunate that Darwin should have
come later in time and superseded Marx and Hegel, instead
of the reverse ?   This seems to be a mistake—these personalities reached us, owing to some oversight, in the
wrong order, perhaps ?   But Mr. Russell evidently regards
this as quite in order, and in logical sequence. And I think,
in consequence of this inattentiveness of his, that he has
created for us, in reading the account of his american
debate, a little confusion in the heart of his argument
that requires clearing up.

In passing, it may be as well to say that Darwin's particular evolutionary doctrine was responsible for an ' industrial ' type of thought rather than an ' agricultural.'
As it tended to reduce all intelligent organisms to *things*,
men's thoughts and wishes to stones and sticks, it was easy
for its followers to substitute motor-cars and aeroplanes
for sticks and stones. So it came about that, although it
is true it dealt with a ' growth,' since that ' growth ' was
a mechanical growth it easily passed into the category
of manufacture. Bergson's ' invisible arms ' and ' *élans
vitals* ' came later.

But the industrial age itself is historically not a little
contradictory, and would, by itself, encourage such confusions as those in which Mr. Russell-the-politician light-
heartedly engages. For the european community which
participated at the great change-over from the predomi-
nantly agricultural to the industrial age presented us with
the French Revolution, which was made possible by the
super-agriculturist dreams of Rousseau. While these
people bustled into factories, or were driven into them,
building themselves more rigidly and irretrievably into a
mechanical urban life, they exploded in dreams of bucolic
' freedom.' Pictures of the ' freedom ' of the noble savage
and the child of nature excited them to a great outburst
at the very moment when (as they must from their own
point of view have regarded it had they not been so full of
a false and exotic emotion) they were enslaving themselves
more thoroughly to men. So it has been in the name of
nature always that men have combined to overthrow the
natural in themselves.

For their instinct to be so fallible, where, it would seem,
so much is at stake for them—for them to proclaim so

ardently that they wish to be ' free ' and nature's children, and yet, in effect, to carry through great movements that result in an absolute mechanization of their life,—can only mean one thing. It must mean that they do not really know what they want, that they do not, in their heart, desire ' freedom ' or anything of the sort. ' Freedom ' postulates a relatively solitary life : and the majority of people are extremely gregarious. A disciplined, well-policed, herd-life is what they most desire. The ' naturalistic ' form that eighteenth-century revolution took was because all violent revolution is saturnalian. A rare saturnalia is necessary for most people, but it exhausts their passions, and the rest of the year they are anything but their saturnalian selves. The few years of youth is such a saturnalia : but youth, in that case, is not synonymous with life.

That men should *think* they wish to be free, the origin of this grave and universal mistake, is the (usually quite weak) primitive animal in them coming into his own for a moment. It is a restless, solitary ghost in them that in idle moments they turn to. The mistake can be best appreciated, perhaps, by examining a great holiday crowd. How can these masses of slowly, painfully, moving people find any enjoyment in such immense stuffy discomfort, petty friction, and unprofitable fatigue, you may ask yourself as you watch them. They ask themselves that, too, no doubt, most of them. That is the saturnalian, libertarian, rebellious self that asserts itself for a moment. But if they *have to choose* between what ultimately the suggestions of the ' free' self, and the far steadier, stronger impulse of the gregarious, town-loving, mechanical self, would lead to, they invariably choose the latter. So to be ' free ' for one person is not what to be ' free' for another would be. Most people's favourite spot in ' nature ' is to be found in the body of another person, or in the mind of another person, not in meadows, plains, woods, and trees. They depend for their stimulus on people, not things. So inevitably they are not ' free ' nor have any wish to be, in the lonely, ' independent,' wild, romantic, rousseauesque way. In short, the last thing they wish for is to be free. They wish to pretend to be ' free ' once a week, or once a month. To be free all the time would be an appalling prospect for them. And they prefer ' freedom ' to take a violent, super-real, and sensational form. They are not to the manner born where ' freedom ' is concerned ; and so invariably overplay it, when they affect it.

This point is well brought out by Ford, the motor-magnate, in his interesting autobiography. He there affirms, with an admirable candour, that a great deal of humanitarian sentiment is wasted on the ' terrible mechanical conditions' under which his employees work. He insists that from long experience he is convinced that they ask nothing better than to be given a quite mechanical and ' soulless ' task. He himself, he says, could not bear it for a week ; he finds it difficult to understand how *they* can bear it. But they not only can bear it, they like it, he is convinced. The testimony of such a very humane and intelligent man as Ford, with his vast experience of industrial conditions, cannot be disregarded.

But the ' sentimentalist ' in the average man, the emotional spot that is a greater or smaller ' worst enemy ' to him, will not let him quite alone : and such a statement as Ford's would always be used by this sentimentalist minority in his make-up to cause trouble. No consistency can be expected with such an irresponsible factor always at hand and so easy to inflame. The agricultural life, for instance, offers more chances of ' freedom ' than the town life. Libertarian enthusiasts are constantly pointing to it. But most men hate it.

The so-called ' free cities ' of the feudal age were contrasted with the neighbouring villeinage of ' the land.' But it was a ' freedom ' for the trade magnificos, and not for the technically enfranchised slave who had escaped into this ' free ' urban commonwealth. The notion conveyed by the expression ' free city ' is still effective. The industrial slave looks down on his agricultural brother-serf vegetating among his pigs and erops. To be anchored to a plot of land like a tree is much the same thing as being tied for life to a machine, only the former is healthier. But this is not how most people regard it. To be anchored amongst people is their true heart's desire ; to *share* their life and responsibility, to be a blind, dependent, obedient cell of a crowd organism.

It is characteristic of Mr. Russell that, still further

entangling himself in his political web, he should draw a
picture of the industrial revolution ending as it began—if
it is *too* violent and bolshevik !—in rousseauism.

> If the leading nations all at the same time are engaged in a
> cataclysm . . . (a bolshevik revolution coming after a great
> war) there will be no one to help them out. . . . A vast
> percentage of the population will die. The rest will grow
> savage through the difficulty of keeping alive. . . .
> You will have a state where we shall have to return
> probably to hunting animals with bows and arrows, where a
> few of us will lead a precarious existence upon the wild fruits
> of the earth. . . .

Mr. Russell can imagine nothing more unpleasant than
pursuing the bison and the wild horse with his little bow
and arrow : in that he is properly orthodox.

There are people, of course, who can imagine occupations
less congenial (although far less industrial) than a healthy
life on the savannas of Mr. Russell's horrified imagination
beyond the coming cataclysms. But Mr. Russell is from
any point of view not justified in curdling the industrial
blood with this wildly agriculturist nightmare. Is it, on
the face of it, at all likely that this wild-west holiday would
be encouraged by the revolutionary authorities ? Surely
the expensive and perilous wildness and freedom either of
the cowboy type, or that of the world of the migration-
period, is hardly likely to suit anybody's book. The urban
and industrial organization so suitable to the communist
programme, and so popular with the mass of men, is
certainly in no danger from revolution, which Mr. Russell
persists in talking about as though it were a ' cataclysm '
of nature and not of man.

The essential mistake of Mr. Russell, to go no farther
than him, and still remaining within the radius of this
particular debate, is that engendered by the confusion I
started by considering ; or else the confusion is due to it.
It is precisely the biologic way of looking at these things
that is the absurd mistake. Revolutions, like wars, do not
grow. None of the things with which men supplement and
perfect animal life grow : but often things are put down
to some alien natural force of fatal *growth* which are really
less anonymous. All art, as it is found in science, painting,
politics, literature, is based on this illusion of the natural

miracle. The pleasure we derive from a poem or statue is that we have no sensation of manufacture, but of anonymous growth.

> It is no use to try things until people are more or less ready for them. You have got to *develop*, you have got to *grow*, people's thoughts have got to come up to the point where the thing is possible . . . that is a matter of appealing to people's intelligence. It is a slow matter, because people's intelligence is not so great as we could wish.

These remarks of Mr. Russell's suggest a further fallacy for which the ' biologic ' attitude is responsible : namely, that in a human society people's notions develop freely and naturally as a tree grows from the soil. Nothing could be more opposite to what is actually the process of their development : for, as we have seen, the machinery of education, of the press, cinema, wireless, and social environment, is directed to preventing them from doing that. And their happiness actually is found in having all ' biologic ' responsibility taken out of their hands. They do not like to *grow*, to feel, think, and suffer for themselves. They far prefer having it done for them. This position could actually be put in this way : they are not unlike the young man of Leghorn, on the whole, when first confronted with the major difficulties of life. If they could go back and *not be born*, they would. But the creative biologic life-instinct has them in its grip, and they have to go on. Now, at this moment any one who can show how they can at once live and not live, get through life, and get through it as a child gets through childhood, without responsibility, because so helpless, will be welcomed as a saviour.

The miracle of Education answers this purpose, only it forestalls the event. It provides them with a system of habits which agree with their neighbour's habits, and from this coma they seldom wake. This is the kindest thing that can happen in the usual human life.

The bolshevik standpoint—that of the necessity of violent upheaval to terminate the present system of exploitation—is confronted by Mr. Russell's theory of biological ' gradualness.' The bolshevik belief in the necessity of a dictatorship over an eternally shiftless mass of *inapertiva* mankind—the standpoint advocated by Mr. Nearing, with whom this ' battle of wits ' was fought—is, Mr. Russell says, ' based upon too pessimistic a view of human nature.' Whether you prefer the bolshevik pessimism or Mr. Russell's optimism depends on the quality and extent, no doubt, of your political intelligence. The humanitarianism of liberal England was characterized by an unruffled optimism, the result of a spoilt and heedless prosperity which is no longer there. It was also an effect of that natural race egotism and ' aristocratism ' to which reference has been made. Mr. Russell inherits this liberalism in every sense along with his playful high spirits. It is a condition of mind, however much graceful good humour and superior indulgence it takes with it, that must arouse more impatience every day.

As to the masses to be either educated up to the point where they become both good and wise, or dictated to, as they would be under a revolutionary dictatorship, Mr. Russell, then, announces himself an optimist. But these same people when they become a *government* (as in the case of the soviet rulers) arouse nothing but distrust in Mr. Russell. About them he is a pessimist.

' Mr. Scott Nearing,' he says, ' suggested that one of the great things about the russian revolution was the attempt to introduce justice and equality as between man and man.' This, however, was not ' realized in the early days of the soviet revolution, nor is it one which can ever be realized by methods of violence and by methods of force. . . . You did not have any degree whatever of political justice. Certain men held political power, and certain others did not. And it rested with the men who held political power whether they should rake to themselves a larger share of the economic goods than other people, or whether they should not. That is to say, the form of government which was provided contained no safeguard whatever against economic exploitation, except the personal integrity of the politicians who ran it.

' Well, we know something about the personal integrity of politicians. (Laughter.) And, although I do not like to say it, I believe that politicians are politicians in one longitude as in another.'

How Mr. Russell justifies his distrust of ' politicians ' and his belief in all the rest of the world, he did not inform his listeners. Politicians as a rule seem of much the same

stuff as the people they legislate for.   That may be, in the
western countries to-day, because they have as little to do
as the rest of the people with the legislation of which they
are the humble instruments.   Yet it is presumably to these
politicians (with whom he and his hearers are supposed to
be a little bitterly acquainted—the ' politician ' is a similar
joke to that of the ' lawyer ' or the ' mother-in-law ') that
he is referring.   With such open power as that possessed
by the soviet leaders (' greater power than any government
has ever had before in the world's history,' he says),
Mr. Russell, like the rest of us, can have little acquaintance
enabling him to gauge what changes, for better or for worse,
the possession of such great power over others can effect
in the average man.   Yet in the future an even more
absolute power, extending from one end of the world to
the other, will certainly be possessed by some group of
men or other.   In another pamphlet Mr. Russell has himself forecast this situation, and described the power that
will be so exercised as ' beyond the dreams of a Jesuit.'
Between the present soviet dominion and that ultimate one
—through whatever vicissitudes the present revolutionary
ideologies may pass—why should there be a break ?   Any
' cataclysm ' that may arise this young power is to-day
competent to control, and is already able to provoke or
suppress such ' cataclysms ' at will.   Of what use to that
power, as has been said above, would the european masses
be, running about with bows and arrows, labouring to
secure a lark-pie for their dinner, gathering nuts in may,
or collecting a basket of edible mushrooms ?   Should not
Mr. Russell's own conviction of the early collapse of
western society, his socialism, make this future a thing
that it requires no second sight to foretell ?   So why, it is
natural to ask, is he stopping to playfully argue whether
we should become bolsheviks or not, discussing alternative
propositions of a *very gradual* development and education
of mankind (fitted to the slowness of their intellectual
processes), so that perhaps in two thousand years they
might be ready for a *little* rational freedom—his benevolent
' politicians ' watching this gradual progress meanwhile, age
after age, with kindly, though perhaps a little sleepy, eyes ?
    In this debate, contrasted with his less intelligent but
single-minded antagonist, he exhibits all the weaknesses

of the society that he conventionally represents.   He
accuses Mr. Nearing and his masters, the bolsheviks, of
being unscientific.   The domination of the bolsheviks in
Russia is imbued with a theologic and not a scientific
spirit, he says.   By that remark he thinks he can discredit
them.   ' The man of science as he should be is a man who
is careful, cautious, piecemeal . . . who is not ready with
sweeping generalizations,' etc.

' The man who is scientific is tentative.   He is cautious '
(is this even true ?   for does that really describe a great
discoverer, or does it only fit ' the man who is scientific ' ?) ;   ' the real progress of the world is a more patient
thing, a more gradual thing, and a less spectacular thing '
than the conditions provided by violent revolution, he says.
This ' tentative ' and ' cautious ' creature is the kind of
man of science who was so well described by Nietzsche, the
man who was no longer able to will anything, even in his
sleep ;   whose resolution had become entirely absorbed by
his cautions and hesitations.   That on the face of it does
not seem ' scientific ' either, if by scientific you mean such
creative imagination as was released in the case of Faraday
or Newton.   But this tentative and cautious spirit certainly is the spirit in which Mr. Russell attacks—or plays
with—the social questions of this time.   It leads him into
those limp and hesitating, half despondent and half bright,
generalizations;   and the mental confusion, too, which of
all things you would not expect from this great logician.

The function of science to-day is a very significant one—
and in this definition of its uses no criticism of it is implied,
for everything is science, in one sense, that is effective.
Science is often described as the religion of industrialism.
It is said to have provided man with ' a new world-soul.'
Its public function is actually, however, as was suggested
in the preceding chapter, to conceal the human mind that
manipulates it, or that manipulates, through it, other
people.   For in its *impersonality* and its ' scientific detachment ' it is an ideal cloak for the personal human will.
Through it that will can operate with a godlike inscrut-
ability that no other expedient can give.   It enables man
to operate as though he were nature on other men.   In
the name of science people can be almost without limit
bamboozled and managed.   When in our opening statement

we examined what was meant when the *agriculturist* mentality was contrasted with the *industrialist*, we showed how nature was the power that the agriculturist was concerned with, and to whose processes, owing to his environment and occupations, he referred everything as a matter of course. Then we saw how the industrialized man was taught to believe—and it is through the agency of the propaganda of science that he is principally brought to this belief—that it was still nature that was functioning in this new and different social evolution. And it was pointed out how this contradicts what you would expect of the industrialist mind. For surely the analogy most natural to that mind would not be the *biologic* imagery of growth and of living organism, but rather the analogy of a man-made, dead, manufactured thing. So, we said, it was in reality *man* who had taken the place of *nature* in the industrial world—the soul and will of man in the machine, and not the foreign element we describe as ' nature ' through the phenomena of crops, plants, climate, and the reproduction of animal life. And except in so far as man is certainly no longer subject to its irrational impulses, that it is certainly no longer true to describe our immediate destiny as being in nature's hands—or in the lap of the gods : and that therefore, whatever happens to us, we can only say : ' Well, it is decreed by nature that such and such a line of evolution—strange, unnecessary, and against all our interests as it may seem—must be followed, and there's an end of it.' There are, on the contrary, responsible human wills to-day, conscious and deliberate as formerly, and more powerful, responsible for all this mysterious natural growth that Mr. Russell compares to the irresponsible growth of a tree. The ' pitiless ' and ' inhuman ' character of nature has been overdone. We should have to look elsewhere, and nearer home, for ' inhumanity.'

One of the greatest innovations, and the most beneficent, of the sovietic rule has been the check it has begun to put on the popularization of science. That will be like handing back the soul to the machine, and guaranteeing by means of science, no longer evident but occult, the smooth running of that machine.

In conclusion, to give an example of a more obvious technical sort of contradiction afforded by these discoveries of Mr. Russell's, I will quote two statements that almost face each other on pages 40 and 41 of this book :—

Pp. 89-40 : (1) He (Mr. Nearing) spoke of a centralized dictatorship by delegates from peasants and workers, dominated by the communist party. Well, these delegates from peasants and workers do not really count in the government.

Pp. 40-41. I should like to associate myself most whole-heartedly with the words of the chairman in regard to the recognition of the russian government and the right of the Russians to choose their own government as they like.

What is meant by 'the Russians' here ? Presumably the 'dictatorship by delegates from peasants and workers,' which he says is a farce ; though from the point of view of the worker it cannot be as cruel a farce as that it has superseded, and would turn into more of a farce if the workers 'counted more in the government.' So Mr. Russell's 'whole-hearted association with the chairman' on the right and proper sentiment that 'the Russians' should be allowed 'the right to choose their own govern-ment as they like' is likewise a farce, only a stupid and ineffective one.

Then, last, comes the question—which was the main issue in this debate—of the *gradualness* (advocated by Mr. Russell) as contrasted with the method of sudden and violent revolution advocated by the other debater. The answer to this is involved with the question with which we started ; or rather it would be answered differently by (1) the *agriculturist*, and (2) the *industrialist*. Mr. Russell, as a logician, should give the bolshevik answer, the *logical* answer of the industrial man. But as a politician he is very retrograde—he is an agriculturist : so as a politician he gives the answer of Hodge.

The industrialist, living in an abstract world akin to that of the logician, accustomed to the intensive manufacturing of things rather than to the gradual growth of living organ-isms, would be more disposed to believe in a 'catastrophic' method than the farmer would. He would say : 'You can change all that is useful or important in a man in an afternoon, or at any rate from one generation to the next.' I think he would be right. (Whether it is desirable to change him, and into what, is a different question.) But

the agriculturist would be slow, cautious, and tentative—
' at least in a couple of thousand years you could grow a
new man, with all the resources of scientific agriculture
at your command,' he would say dubiously, scratching
his head very slowly indeed with the point of his horny
forefinger.

But revolution is, in any case, as we have seen already,
also not a ' catastrophic ' thing in itself, or necessarily
' catastrophic ' at all.

Mr. Russell's true mind in this matter is very clearly
shown in the following passage :—

> . . . I am not at all sure that the world is going to develop
> on the lines which Marx laid down, lines of schematic sim-
> plicity more simple than any human affairs ever are. After
> all, we know that one individual is different from another
> individual. Two men will grow up in exactly the same
> environment and yet they may differ very profoundly.

In the first place, if the rulers of the world wished it to
develop on marxian lines, which ultimately is not at all
likely, it would develop like that.   Were these rulers world-
rulers, either an open or unavowed centralized government,
or a confederacy of closely knit international interests,
they would have the power to impose any orthodoxy they
chose from China to Peru.   They would be able to make
the matron in Yokohama and Dublin simultaneously
appear in a dress of lotus leaves, a vest of mail, a ballet-
dancer's skirt, or a crinoline : to shave her head, or dangle
her hair in plaits ; to see that she had seven lovers, or to
see that she confined herself to her husband : to decree that
she only had sexual intercourse on prescribed days ; that
in the grip of *fashion*, so much more effective than that of
law, she was a confirmed vegetarian one week and a hearty
beef-eater the next.   Every thought and action of both
herself, her husband, and her family could be rigidly controlled without her knowing it, actually, if it amused them
to leave her in ignorance of her puppet-like servitude.
And she would be quite happy.   All these things in any
case can be observed around us in an imperfect, primitive
form to-day.

Already the standardization coming in the wake of the
compounding of local national interests has made our
civilization very uniform ; sport, the cuisine, the central-

ized fashion-control, and so forth, imposing this unity more thoroughly every day. Without insisting on this tendency, the evidences of which are so accessible and universally recognized, it is legitimate to say that those differences between individual and individual in our community, or between the various western nations, the differences to which Mr. Russell refers, are potentially a matter of the past. That past was truly nationalist and regional. To-day neither the motive nor even the possibility of these differences between nation and nation exist. And the change has not been ' gradual,' like biologic growth ; but swift, like the effect of the appliances of the human will precipitating the leisurely habits of nature.

With individuals it is the same thing. As the opportunities for individual business enterprise diminish, the great trusts relieving the individual of any particular initiative or energy more thoroughly every day, and as the mechanical pressure of public opinion, aiming at a highly organized uniformity, makes any personal irregularity increasingly prohibitive and not worth while, the differences between individuals, either in mentality, or personal appearance, or individual habits, disappear. They were the exuberant marks of a disordered age, before the doctrine of an economic uniformity had become also a social law. The ' individual ' tends rapidly to disappear, as do national characteristics. In this, too, Mr. Russell is using an argument for ' gradualness ' depending on conditions that no longer have any reality. For the pace, even, at which this standardization and drawing together is proceeding is in itself one of the most excellent arguments against his theory of a leisurely, conservative growth.

This *uniformity* is the object of much abuse and protest on the part of the stereotyped regionalist reactionary. But does he not contradict the reality responsible for his protest ? China for the Chinese, for instance, is the regionalist cry. But when China was actually for the Chinese, a Chinaman never saw, from year's end to year's end, anything but a Chinaman. Did he complain of this ' uniformity,' then ? Regionalism, Merrie England, etc., is in reality a movement to substitute one uniformity for another : a small one for a big one. The really fanatical regionalist, confining himself entirely to Puddletown and

its parish pump, would be surrounded by an absolute
'uniformity' of puddletownians.

Every argument that Mr. Russell uses throughout his
two addresses is open to the same criticism, namely, that it
testifies to a very poor sense of the realities in the midst
of which we live. 'Revolution,' he says, for instance, 'is
applicable to societies at a certain elementary stage of
development. But when they become so organic as our
developed industrial societies have become, revolution
means too much destruction.' It is as though the war
had never occurred to enlighten him, for that meant
destruction enough, and every wiseacre said it would be
'impossible,' just as Mr. Russell says revolution will be.
Or he says 'the struggle for existence during the cataclysm'
(a war followed by a revolution) 'would be so terrible that
men would not be in the mood for any organized or rational
form of government.' That, however, was the state the
Russians were in (agricultural or industrial), but their
'mood' was taken very little notice of by their new rulers.
Neither they nor any future people in the same conditions
would be encouraged to have any 'moods.' Or he says
'the cataclysm . . . can only be brought about by unsuccessful war.' He still thinks in nationalist terms, as
though *all* wars were not unsuccessful to-day for all but
the private individuals who promote them, whichever side
technically wins or loses.

The rather distressed amiability or puzzled apathy which
would describe the state of mind of the average 'enlightened' english or american public is one that it is kind to
encourage ; and the sort of discourse that Mr. Russell can
be relied on to provide is excellently suited to maintain
those publics in that bemused condition. There they sit
and are soothed by the thought of the 'gradualness' of
the change demanded of them. It is perhaps kindness that
induces Mr. Russell to occupy himself in that way.

There can hardly be any other reason for it. The
communist revolution can be trusted to take as much
notice of the 'gradualness' and 'caution '—so typical of
both nature and science, Mr. Russell says—as an avalanche
would of other natural phenomena whose transformations
are slower than its own. And this applies to it either as a
'catastrophic' or a 'non-catastrophic' one.

CHAPTER II

DIFFERENT SOLUTIONS OF THE
PROBLEM OF THE YAHOO

IN the debate dealt with in the last chapter Mr. Russell
attempted to confront the ' catastrophic ' dogma of
Marx with the ' gradualness ' of nature and its processes.   I am not a ' catastrophist ' either from the side
of fascism or of leninism, but I do not believe that any
help against the doctrine of violence is to be found in the
supposed indefinite periods of time required to modify a
society.   Men are not cabbages, and, perhaps unfortunately, are infinitely teachable.   Caught very young, a new
mankind almost could be made from one generation to
the next.   This is highly desirable ;   only two questions
remain, with various solutions—one as to the pattern to
be chosen, and the other that of the necessity of violence
and force.

Of the various patterns of a new mankind on the market
to-day, the sovietic cut, when brought in juxtaposition to
the untidy liberal ' genre ' of Mr. Russell, seems to me to
show up very well.   The question of the ' catastrophe,'
and all its insane violence, is more difficult to deal with.
The best answer to that, if you dislike it, is to be found, I
think, in the very fact (if it is a fact, or if you accept it as
such) that men are so easily and also more effectively
changed by other methods than those of force ;   in the
instantaneousness attributed by Mr. Russell to the soviet,
rather than in the ' gradualness ' preferred by him.   For
if it is true that you can train men so easily into something
else, so quickly (and without the ' gradualness ' demanded
by Mr. Russell), then why bludgeon them into it, it is
possible to contend.   That is the best answer to the
catastrophist.   The war, the blood, and the ' catastrophe '
is the method of the capitalist, not the method of the socialist, nor necessarily of the fascist.   The quarrel at present
engaged between the Vatican and fascism is directed
naturally to this question.   Cardinal Gasparri is reported
as writing that licence on the one hand and violence on the

other are the extreme positions into which our society
has been driven : violence, he says, that ' last expedient
for the maintenance of any kind of order when moral
strength has ceased to exercise its beneficent influence.'
' Moral' persuasion can be as violent as any physical
régime.   But the ' catastrophe,' where it is not necessary,
has an air of weakness, actually, that is disquieting for any
one disposed to favour the ends symbolized by it.

Failing the ' scientific' contention of ' gradualness,'
Mr. Russell or Mr. Shaw, in their desire, which in itself is
a praiseworthy one, to avert all the misery of wholesale
violence, would fall back on that english humanitarianism
that, unbalanced by political power (as it is in the anglo-
saxon world to-day), is such a sad mockery.   It will be
useful at this point to examine a little two recent and
characteristic pronouncements of Mr. Shaw and Mr. Russell.
The preface to *Back to Methuselah* is Mr. Shaw's latest full-
dress summary of his view of post-war conditions : and a
short essay, *Icarus*, is a characteristic summary of what he
thinks the future has in store for us, by Mr. Russell.

After having reviewed, in a chapter dealing with ' The
increase of organization' that science has so wonderfully
promoted, all the dangers to democracy lurking in this
great efficiency and enhanced power to govern, Mr. Russell
ends by going over what he regards as the ' hopeful element
in the problem.'   I will reproduce this passage as it stands.

The planet is of finite size, but the most efficient size for
an organization is continually increased by new scientific
inventions.   The world becomes more and more of an economic unity.   Before very long the technical conditions will
exist for organizing the whole world as one producing and
consuming unit.   If, when the time comes, two rival groups
contend for mastery, the victor may be able to introduce that
single world-wide organization that is needed to prevent the
mutual extermination of civilized nations.   The world which
would result would be, at first, very different from the dreams
of either liberals or socialists ; but it might grow less different
with the lapse of time.   There would be at first economic and
political tyranny of the victors, a dread of renewed upheavals,
and therefore a drastic suppression of liberty.   But if the
first half-dozen revolts were successfully repressed, the vanquished would give up hope, and accept the subordinate
place assigned to them by the victors in the great world-trust.

As soon as the holders of power felt secure, they would grow less tyrannical and less energetic. The motive of rivalry being removed, they would not work so hard as they do now, and would soon cease to exact such hard work from their subordinates. Life at first might be unpleasant, but it would at least be possible, which would be enough to recommend the system after a long period of warfare. Given a stable world-organization, economic and political, even if, at first, it rested upon nothing but armed force, the evils which now threaten civilization would gradually diminish, and a more thorough democracy than that which now exists might become possible. I believe that, owing to men's folly, a world-government will only be established by force, and will therefore be at first cruel and despotic. But I believe that it is necessary for the preservation of a scientific civilization, and that, if once realized, it will gradually give rise to the other conditions of a tolerable existence.

My answer to those remarks is as follows. That 'single world-wide organization' that Mr. Russell desires, and that he truly considers is the only guarantee of peace on earth and the cessation of wars, is taking shape beneath his eyes —only, apparently with such unexpected rapidity that (looking for 'gradualness') he cannot see it. That peace which, like anybody else, he desires, could be had to-morrow. By the agreement of the workers of the world, through their accredited representatives, to align themselves with the sovietic and fascist power, that unity would immediately be achieved. But if it is not done voluntarily, it will undoubtedly be achieved by compulsion and violence.

'I believe that, owing to men's folly, a world-government will only be established by force,' Mr. Russell says. More pacific than Mr. Russell, I believe it could be established without any force or violence at all. Further, the obstruction offered by such theorists as Mr. Russell, of a quite pointless and unreal 'gradualness,' is the likeliest way to ensure a catastrophe. This ill-starred procrastinating theory, joined to the senseless bellicosity of the reactionary groups of the *Action Française* type, may certainly result in far more violence, before long, than any one is able to measure.

The warfare of the african nations, as we hear of them in the earliest accounts, as those of Mungo Park, was far more civilized, because more flexible and intelligent, than ours.

Where two armies came face to face, either at once or after a little significant sparring, the weaker party laid down its arms. The battle was finished. There were, it is true, no financial interests to compel them to ' get on with the war ' in order to continue to supply them with expensive muniments and weapons and to lend them money at crushing interest. Nevertheless, they displayed an excellent *savoir vivre* in their methods. All the European seems to understand is a *savoir mourir*. That he has to unlearn, as so many people have remarked lately. It is not altogether the fault, it must be conceded, of the people who benefit greatly by this pugnacity of his ; the white races seem almost incurably brutal, and always ready, after the regulation press provocation, to slaughter themselves. The breaking of that traditional spirit in them is the most hopeful possibility.

Mr. Russell's solution of this difficulty—namely, that of inherited, or ' injected,' military ferocity—is ' kindliness.' He says : ' And so we come back to the old dilemma : only kindliness can save the world, and even if we knew how to produce kindliness we should not do so unless we were already kindly. Failing that, it seems that the solution which the Houyhnhnms adopted towards the Yahoos, namely extermination, is the only one ; apparently the Yahoos are bent on applying it to each other.'

The white European, in this instance, is Mr. Russell's Yahoo. ' Kindliness ' cannot be taught or injected into the Yahoo : therefore the Yahoo must die. That is Mr. Russell's verdict. But why even pause to consider a solution which he admits (sadly) to be out of the question ? By making melancholy faces at the Yahoo he will not turn him from his deep heredity. The possibility of ' kindliness ' becoming sufficiently prevalent for it to have any influence on the human race would never have occurred to any one except an individual injected not with ' kindliness ' at all, necessarily, but with liberalism. And as to idly taunting the Yahoo with what he can never hope to possess, that is again a proceeding of the same political complexion.

A quite practical solution—a thing in a different world altogether to the fanciful generation of a quantity of ' kindliness ' or anything positive, too positive, of that sort—is, I believe, in process of being applied to this european pugnacity. Nature—let us give her credit for it—has come to the help of her children, and exactly in the way that would suggest itself to Mr. Russell's physiologist, by way of the *glands*, namely.   I believe that (in one form or another) castration may be the solution.   And the feminization of the white European and American is already far advanced, coming in the wake of the war.

CHAPTER III

VIOLENCE AND 'KINDLINESS':
MR. BERNARD SHAW
AND MR. BERTRAND RUSSELL

IN a general way Mr. Russell has a habit of discussing things that are in full swing to-day as though they belonged to a very distant future. Thus he says that *some day* it may be possible, in place of violence, for the ruler to attain his ends by means of other forms of coercion.

It is not necessary, when we are considering political consequences, to pin our faith to the particular theories of the ductless glands, which may blow over, like other theories. All that is essential in our hypothesis is the belief that physiology will in time find ways of controlling emotion, which it is scarcely possible to doubt. When that day comes, we shall have the emotions desired by our rulers, and the chief business of elementary education will be to produce the desired disposition, no longer by punishment or moral precept, but by the far surer method of injection or diet. The men who will administer this system will have a power beyond the dreams of the Jesuits, but there is no reason to suppose that they will have more sense than the men who control education to-day.

By 'sense' here Mr. Russell means—what? That these rulers, with governmental power infinitely magnified, will still wish to *rule*; get all they can out of their fellows, in short, rather than live, and use the power they have seized, ' for the good of ' mankind. ' Sense ' does not mean anything more than that, however : it would show very little ' sense ' if they applied themselves to these good works, instead of enjoying their power. The words he uses, such as ' kindliness ' and ' sense,' are characteristically weak and modest. Such graceful modesty will not to-day meet the case. And the ' kindliness ' of Mr. Russell or Mr. Shaw has an unpleasant sound of moral charlatanism, of the virtue *à bon marché* of the immensely prosperous old liberal England; that again will not answer the case. No one but a great saint can tread that road to-day and be respected. Vegetarianism and geniality are a mockery for our present danger and need.

In seeing Mr. Shaw's play, *St. Joan*, it was difficult to resist the suggestion that the cast had been furnished by the anglican clergy. The 'kindliness' of the Earl of Warwick, the 'kindliness' of the Bastard, the 'kindliness,' in different ways, of everybody on the stage (with the exception of the admirable actor who took the part of the bishop of Beauvais) was overwhelming. It could have been produced by no machinery except that of anglo-saxon protestantism, livened up a little bit for the occasion by irish charm. The poorness of the language (when such things as 'green fields' had to be mentioned by Joan of Arc, who booed cheerlessly the thin journalese with which she was provided, this was forced on the attention)—the incessant rattle of stale, clever argumentation—the heartiness and 'kindliness' pervading everything—the chill of a soulless, arty, indefatigable 'rational' presentation of the theme—must have an increasingly depressing effect on the audience it seems destined to attract, if it is not softened or otherwise modified in new interpretations. It is the swan-song of english liberalism staged for the post-war suburbs of London. The 'kindly' twinkle in Mr. Lyall Sweete's eye, his massive gladstonian jaw and bulky person, is the symbol of that strange thing, part humbug, part fierce possessiveness, part real gentleness and goodness, that has served the white race so ill.

Why it is necessary to expose and condemn this humanitarianism, with the especial local colour conveyed for us in the word 'kindly' ('kindliness' having such a different sense to 'kind'), is because it is a sort of spiritual nineteenth-century vulgarization of the great fanatical compassion of which it is a degenerate, genial, tepid form; a half-measure, embalmed in rationalistic discourse.

It is always 'on the right tack': it never reaches any effective position. *St. Joan*, for example, has for its theme a very noble understanding of the unhappy situation of the saint. But Mr. Shaw, in spite of himself, desecrates it with his weak-minded, chilly worldliness, which is *plus fort que lui*. He seems to 'give away,' to betray, at least

artistically (which in a play is naturally everything),
his heroine. He is resolved to show the world this situation, but he has not the power. He laughs, twinkles,
and cackles to hide his incompetence where this task is
concerned.

In the preface of *Back to Methuselah* there is similarly a
fine humane motive at work. But what happens at the
end ? Well, of course, the play. But Adam and Eve are
in the same predicament as Joan of Arc where their pre-
sentment by Mr. Shaw is concerned. They speak the
jargon of the city tea-shop ; as you read you fancy them
in bathing drawers, a London bank clerk and his girl, great
Wells readers, extemporizing in a studio the legend of the
creation, prompted, mephistopheles-fashion, by Mr. Shaw :
and the preface remains the play.

' Nobody noticed the new religion in the centre of the
intellectual whirlpool,' he says, referring to the master-
work of his maturity. He now reveals this latent ' new
religion,' which turns out to be Bergson's *élan vital*. He
writes : ' Darwinism proclaimed that our true relation is
that of competitors and combatants in a struggle for mere
survival, and that every act of pity or loyalty to the old
fellowship is a vain and mischievous attempt to lessen the
severity of the struggle and preserve inferior varieties from
the efforts of Nature to weed them out.' But in the surplus
life in which he suggests, as human creatures, we should
live, he has nothing very positive to offer, except his ' new
religion,' that is, Bergson's *creative evolution*.

He misrepresents his hero Nietzsche, whom he interprets
as follows : ' Nietzsche, for example . . . concluding that
the final objective of this Will was power over self, and
that the seekers after power over others and material
possessions were on a false scent.' This sense is certainly
not obtained from a reading of Nietzsche's works. ' Power
over others ' came very vividly into the programme of that
philosopher. Again, as a persuasive engine the exhortation to ' self-control ' does not seem the best ; it smacks
of the Y.M.C.A. straight talks to young men. All his
persuasiveness is haunted by this sort of vulgarity of mind :
almost less than any famous english writer has he what
Arnold would call a ' celtic ' tact. He incessantly (when
his criticism is finished and his persuasion begins) suggests

the sunday school, or the 'straight and hearty, man to man ' talk.

How, finally, these things can be summarized, is that both Mr. Shaw and Mr. Russell fail as artists, they have no dramatic sense above the rhetoric of the anglican pulpit. Although they can convince us of their sincerity, they would not be able to convince a stranger from some other system of things, because there is no vibration in their words or universal significance in their gestures. They are just words, opinions, that they have been unable to fuse, and which they have not the force to dramatically present. And their humanitarianism is a poor, prosaic food, meant for a cruder animal existence, and a much easier and more fortunate one, than ours.

CHAPTER IV

VEGETARIANISM AND CAPITAL PUNISHMENT

THE eating of meat and the execution of criminals are the two acts that bring out more intensely than any others all our perplexities as ' human animals.' It is difficult to come to any decision about them without appearing either a brute or a humbug.

At the root of both of these questions it is advisable to place the not necessarily inhuman proposition that life is in itself not important. Our values make it so : but they are mostly, the important ones, non-human values, although the intenser they are the more they imply a supreme, vital connotation.

To attach, as the humanitarian does, a mystical value to *life* itself, for its own sake, is as much a treachery to spiritual truth as it is a gesture of ' humanity.' We execute a criminal for a variety of frivolous reasons, and often kill the wrong one. The manner of the administration of our law is thoughtless and brutal usually. But the theory of capital punishment (if the ' punishment ' of the *too-just god of the law* could be abstracted from it) is as humane as possible. A higher value than all he can allege in his favour—namely, the fact that he is *alive*—we consider is threatened by the most violent and extreme criminal. It is his ' violence ' that we are seeking to eliminate by destroying him. It is the principle of non-violence that he menaces by his existence : which is a superhuman one. We know that to improve our conditions as animals we must banish violence from life. We put a ' value on life,' a *violence value*, as it were. The assassin or poisoner cannot plead that he should live *because he is alive*, when it is *life*, and in addition the only thing that gives life a supernatural value, that he is attacking.

' It is sometimes necessary to kill men, as it is always necessary to kill tigers,' Mr. Shaw admits in the preface from which I have already quoted. And many people hold that it is very often necessary to kill men as it is necessary to kill sheep in prodigious numbers. (Shaw is saved by his vegetarianism from extending his permission to massacre.) But are the tiger-men untamable ? Or could they not all be trapped and put in a Zoo, where the humane crowds could examine them at leisure ?

One of Mr. Shaw's principal intellectual weaknesses is his optimism where the success of taming is concerned. That is the liberal's old and terrible mistake. The permission to slay the tiger-man is belated. And the ' kindliness ' shown to the man-eating tiger-man has accounted for the slaughter of more sheep-men than any simple brutality could ever have done : the theory is so humane, but in practice it is so inhuman. So the point is reached at last when all the liberal men can say is what we have heard Mr. Bertrand Russell saying: ' Failing that ' (the world being saved by ' kindliness '), ' it seems that the solution which the Houyhnhnms adopted towards the Yahoos, namely extermination, is the only one ; apparently the Yahoos are bent on applying it to each other.' This is a rather bloodthirsty point of bitterness for the liberal (surveying the sanguinary chaos for which he is responsible) to have reached !

The intricate problem of capital punishment cannot be dealt with, of course, here, in a few passing observations. For my purpose, however, it is enough to say that the rhetoric of death and of the law, devised as a ' punishment ' and a deterrent, is one thing, and the question of regarding the loss of life itself (apart from the needless tortures of trial and execution) as inhuman or not, is another.

In general, it can be asserted that the characteristic humanitarian attitude reposes on an exaggeration of the importance of crude and concrete *life* itself. Life, *tout court*, plays too great a part in that attitude.

The cruelty of the law, on the other hand, errs in assuming a sensitiveness that is certainly absent in the majority of violent criminals. That accounts for the ' deterrent ' notion. In general, men seem disposed to think that other men are greater cowards than in fact they are. Animal courage is the most underestimated of common facts. It seems that people are not as a whole so attached to life as they are supposed to be, or they are attached differently. About the animal world of Darwin's ' struggle for existence,' with which Mr. Shaw's preface to *Back to Methuselah* principally deals, men must be even more mistaken. Many of the situations observed by Fabre and other entomologists can only be accounted for in the way that Weismann, to Mr. Shaw's horror, accounts for them. Here is the passage in which he discusses this point :—

> And the darwinians went far beyond denying consciousness to trees. Weismann insisted that the chick breaks out of its egg-shell automatically ; that the butterfly, springing into the air to avoid the pounce of the lizard, ' does not wish to avoid death, knows nothing about death,' what has happened being simply that a flight instinct evolved by Circumstantial Selection reacts promptly to a visual impression produced by the lizard's movement. His proof is that the butterfly immediately settles again on the flower, and repeats the performance every time the lizard springs, thus showing that it learns nothing from experience, and—Weismann concludes—is not conscious of what it does.

Battle itself, or murder even, is probably not horrible for living creatures, only *thinking about* those things. Action, mechanical functional activity without reflection, probably leaves no room for the conception of death. Although it is disputed, it is still a widely held belief that primitive men did not understand or reason about death, as they were ignorant of the circumstances of their coming into the world.

We have the well-known statement that the horse in the burning stable is very difficult to get away. He moves into the flames if left alone : he does not wish to leave the fire, which he does not understand and which fascinates him. He is like the child who has never burnt his fingers, but likes and is attracted by the pleasant flame. Without accumulating instances or going farther into this, it seems likely that the bird being fascinated by the snake is having what we should call a ' fascinating ' experience, perhaps unique in its life. Until it is killed, which naturally terminates its pleasure, it is having ' the time of its life.' The snake, it is true, is an artist, and that Mr. Shaw would hardly understand. But many insects develop mesmeric head-dresses and symbolize their destructive purposes with emblems of terror and power that probably make the insect-world, for their victims, a place of delight.

To take two of the homeliest examples : it is probable that the mouse enjoys its half-hour with the cat when it is caught very much. Then who can doubt that the spinster or susceptible widow with a small bank account enjoys every minute of the time during which she is being destroyed by some homicidal impostor for her money ? And the soldier, except when he is inactive and has to think and imagine instead of act, is no doubt usually having a most enjoyable time. He likes acting better than thinking, habit is strong ; and he will find ways of acting even when thrown on his own resources, and in a situation more favourable for thought.

To conclude, the vast mistake, exemplified so well by Mr. Shaw, is that he does not realize that men are tigers, wasps, and wolves, or parrots, geese, sheep, and asses, or the humdrum monkey, rather than men. He is, in short, too anthropomorphic. For all his lifetime of raillery and scolding he has not realized quite what sort of animal he has been talking to. ' The creatures that we see around us are not men : there is some perversion, the cause of which we cannot penetrate,' Rousseau would have told him. I think that his is a creditable and amiable mistake ; but it puts him (and those of his persuasion) in a weak position where the science of life is concerned.

Sometimes, of course, he will pretend to understand, as when he is describing the embarrassments of the ruler :—

> Good-natured, unambitious men are cowards when they have no religion. They are dominated and exploited not only by greedy and often half-witted and half-alive weaklings who will do anything for cigars, champagne, motorcars, and the more childish and selfish uses of money, but by able and sound administrators who can do nothing else with them than dominate and exploit them. Government and exploitation become synonymous under such circumstances ; and the world is finally ruled by the childish, the brigands, and the blackguards.'

That statement is full of confusions, because he has only half come out of his shell into the light of reality. For example, he admits that even ' able and sound administrators ' can find nothing better to do with ' unambitious men ' than *dominate* them. (' Exploit ' is only an emotional redundancy : for who ever heard of a ruler not getting something out of his rule ?) But then he winds up with his ' children and blackguards,' immediately forgetting his admission of the ' able and sound administrators ' into the picture. Yet (if such people exist, and he says they do) these ' able and sound ' personages would surely have something to say to their ' childish and blackguardly ' rivals, and not necessarily leave them to have the last word and the world to be ' finally ruled ' by them ?

What Mr. Shaw does not add, but should, is that ' unambitious men ' would far rather be ruled by a ' brigand ' or a ' child ' (whom they can understand) than by Mr. Shaw. For that would require a measure of ' ambition ' that is unfortunately by no means common. That is the fallacy of the philosopher-king that we are brushing against.

Mr. Shaw has been a sort of mocking and ' mischievous ' conscience to middle-class England for a good many years. People have put up with him because (in his capacity of ' a conscience ') he was such a respectable thing to have. He has been the one thing that has saved their face—while all the time he has been persuaded that he was putting them dreadfully out of countenance ! But he has often been angrily accused of treating the public with contempt. The mistake emphasized above shows him, of course, in an opposite light—the mistake in virtue of which, bursting with optimism and friendliness, he approached the public brimming innocently with highly intellectual conversation, as though cheerily exclaiming, ' Ah, you old villain, I 'll make a philosopher of you before I 'm done with you ! ' The public has smiled and smiled—and remained a villain. Horatio wrote in his tablets in vain where Mr. Shaw is concerned.

In the nursery in which the ' blackguardly ' children (who ' will do anything for cigars, champagne, and motor-cars ') rule the unambitious children (whose appetites do not aspire to these exciting luxuries), and in which Mr. Shaw has sat like a very genial uncle, a ' kindly ' twinkle in his eye, humorously recommending the unambitious to revolt, there is a great deal of bloodshed. The game of government goes on, and it is a game that no philosopher has ever been able to interrupt seriously for a moment. The

children die in shoals, the philosopher is aghast. But they
hardly know they are dying—in the way, at least, that the
philosopher understands it. The villains of the play (namely,
the children fond of champagne and cigars) are as intent on
the game, and as childlike, necessarily, as the others. The
presence of a grown-up (a philosopher like Mr. Shaw) is
useful; it enables them to be more ferocious than ever.
The ' freedom of speech ' in which he is able to indulge is
their sanction, it gives an air of *fairness* to anything that
happens. (Mr. Shaw especially, would give an air of *fairness* to almost anything. His mere presence at the most
disgraceful spectacle would confer a certain respectability
on it.) The philosopher stands wringing his hands, and
the bloodshed redoubles in violence. A paroxysm of
slaughter supervenes. When it abates, the voice of the
philosopher is heard imploring the children not to cut off
the tail of a mouse that they have caught : ' Ever since
(Darwin) set up Circumstantial Selection as the creator and
ruler of the universe, the scientific world has been the
very citadel of stupidity and cruelty. Fearful as the tribal
god of the Hebrews was, nobody ever shuddered as they
passed even his meanest and narrowest Little Bethel or
his proudest war-consecrating cathedral as we shudder
now when we pass a physiological laboratory.' In the
listlessness and exhaustion ensuing on what was perhaps
the biggest beano that has ever occurred, the voice is heard
exclaiming : ' Neither the rulers nor the ruled understand
high politics. They do not even know that there is such a
branch of knowledge as political science ; but between
them they can coerce and enslave with the deadliest
efficiency, even to the wiping out of civilization, because
their education as slayers has been honestly and thoroughly
carried out. Essentially the rulers are all defectives ; and
there is nothing worse than government by defectives who
wield irresistible powers of physical coercion.'
The scandal of these childish sports is, however, probably
about to receive the attention of a more efficient principle
of order than that of the irresponsible philosopher. Instead of the ineffective sporting ' fairness ' of moral
authority, there will be the justice of force. Let us suppose
that that turns out worse than things have always been.
At least the attempt is on novel lines, the old factors of

failure are as far as possible eliminated. And at least the power engaged has shown from the start a sympathetic understanding of the adage, ' Boys will be boys!' which commutatively could be expressed, 'Animals will be animals!', which is more than can be said for the author whose views I have been discussing, who wishes that all the children would grow up, which is impossible. Animal life would never support the strain of his too ambitious programme.

Death and blood and all the problems arising in connection with them are, then, the central difficulty with us as ' progressive' animals. No one could object to wars for an instant if they were like the Valhalla wars, in which the dead rose up and rode home to a good dinner once the battle was over. It is the fact that they are supposed, rightly or wrongly, to be *real* that makes them objectionable. And I have just indicated what lines the solution of that secular problem would take here. A few further remarks of a general nature may define a little more the answer intended.

The philosopher at all times is opposed to violence : at least, it is very seldom that he is not, Sorel and Nietzsche being exceptions. The philosophic man inveighs against violence ostensibly on other people's behalf. Really he is speaking for himself : not only has he no mandate, but he would be found on careful investigation not to have the sanction of life, for his humane contentions. As in the play or novel, drama or violence is a highly prized ingredient, so it is in life, which the majority of people do not take so seriously as the philosopher. The philosopher is apt to regard life (*tout court*) as precious and full of mysterious power and sanctity, because his own is so full of interest and vitality. That is probably not the general view : most people cannot develop any such flattering conception of their personal existence.

The faith and conviction of the philosopher imposes itself on them when they come in contact with it. But when they get out of touch with this influence—which tends to attach so much *importance* to everything—they naturally pitch their tone much lower, and a fatalism or frivolity where life and death are concerned is the result.

' (Shakespeare) developed that curious and questionable art of building us a refuge from despair by disguising the cruelties of Nature as jokes,' says Mr. Shaw. If this is a true account of shakespearean humour, then it was not Shakespeare who invented it. The popular mind is at one with Shakespeare in that respect. And it is actually a characteristic of philosophy that enables it to reach this ' questionable ' condition, if Schopenhauer's definition holds, namely, that the true philosopher is to be recognized by a constant sense of the *unreality* of the things by which he is surrounded.

How then is bloodshed or violence to be regarded ? Essentially as an excess, nothing more : for if you see life not in compartments, but unified as one appetite, violence is a sadism merely, a degeneration the powerful ruler would ban. The roman mortuary games, and their eventual overwhelming extension into an official blood-bath, were the sign of the decline of authority and power.

No ' moral' or ethical value can stand for a moment against the intoxication of death, and such values are of no service except in secure and peaceful times. Nothing but the most dreadful force can deal with a licence of that sort that has got its head. Therefore there are times when any resolute ambitious force must be supported.

Where violence is concerned the æsthetic principle is evidently of more weight than the ' moral,' the latter being only the machinery to regulate the former. One is an expedient, whose pretensions can easily be exploded : the other is the thing itself. As measure is the principle of all true art, and as art is an enemy of all excess, so it is along æsthetic lines that the solution of this problem should be sought rather than along moral (or police) lines, or humanitarian ones. The soberness, measure, and order that reigns in all the greatest productions of art is the thing on which it is most useful to fix the mind in considering this problem. The blood of the roman circus ; the cheap pastry of stuffy and sadic romance, with its sweet and viscous sentimentalism, which was manufactured with such success by Proust ; the highly spiced incestuous pastry of Freud ; the *exaggeration*, emphasis, and unreality of all forms of common melodrama, are all in the same class, and are vulgar first, and evil because of that : the ethical canon must ultimately take its authority from taste. It is a higher form of the appetite that leads to excess, that leads to the measure of æsthetic delight. Sadistic excess attempts to reach roughly and by harshness what art reaches by fineness.

PART III

THE ‘SMALL MAN’

‘ *In all these things they . . . resemble beasts, saving that beasts are better than they, as being contented with nature. When shall you see a Lion hide gold in the ground, or a Bull contend for a better pasture? When a Boar is thirsty, he drinks what will serve him, and no more; and when his belly is full, he ceaseth to eat, but men are immoderate in both. . . . And doth it not deserve laughter to see an amorous fool torment himself for a wench; weep, howl for a mis-shapen slut, a dowdy, sometimes, that might have his choice of the finest beauties? Is there any remedy for this in physick? I do anatomize and cut up these poor beasts, to see these distempers, vanities, and follies, yet such proof were better made on man's body, if my kind nature would endure it. . . . And here being interrupted by one that brought books, he fell to it again, that all were mad, careless, stupid.*’
    The Anatomy of Melancholy.   Robert Burton.

‘ *(The people of) neighbouring states might be able to descry one another; the voices of their cocks and dogs might be heard (all the way) from one to the other . . . yet all their life they would have no communication together. In those times perfect good order prevailed. Nowadays . . . their footsteps may be traced in lines from one state to another, and the ruts of their chariot-wheels also for more than a thousand lí.*’   *Khü Khieh.*   *Kwang-tze.*

‘ *To arrange our systems with a view to the greater happiness of sensible, straightforward people—indeed, to give these people a chance at all if it can be avoided—is to interfere with the greatest happiness of the greatest number. Dull, slovenly, and arrogant people do not like those who are quick, painstaking, and unassuming; how can we then, consistently with the first principles of either morality or political economy, encourage such people when we can bring sincerity and modesty fairly home to them ?'*

Notes for Erewhon Revisited.   Butler.

CHAPTER I

THE TWO GREAT RIVAL POLITICAL PRINCIPLES TO-DAY : LIBERALIST DEMOCRACY AND AUTHORITY

A WORLD-WIDE accommodation of ideas is going forward in which the european system is only one factor no longer possessing an ascendency. Behind the scenes a novel adjustment of the world-consciousness is in preparation. The 'democratic' european idea is one that is undoubtedly being strangled off the stage. One day a messenger may appear and announce in solemn tones its pathos.

By their superficial idea of ' freedom,' by their insistence on the individual *(any* individual, that is), every northern or white community, from the Greeks to the present Europeans, have made it impossible for the white race to combine and consolidate itself. Each individual, when he got the chance, became a little universe to himself of exclusive personal life. The spectacular, in fact rather flashy, strength, but also the deep weakness of the white man has been his ' independence.' Even his physical prowess is a weakness. His exclusive reliance on the physical has been made nonsense of by a physical thing, his greatest asset —namely, science.

The white man has not in his imagination been able to look all round the world and see it as one large mud-ball with certain possibilities. Its possibilities of unification have escaped him, in spite of all his mechanical opportunities for becoming himself a unifier. He has only been able to propel his body laboriously round it, not his mind. So he made a better globe-trotter and buccaneer than an organizer, or civilizer.

Again, as good brains have been born in the West as in the East, no doubt : but they have been less used and exploited by the over-materialized western rulers. Matthew Arnold's ' barbarian ' oligarchs, for instance, the english aristocracy, with their ' fine fresh appearance ' and ' fondness for outdoor sports,' but who ' for thinking and reading

have no great turn,' were hardly the people to rule the
world.   So it is always important to remember what is
currently meant in the West by ' freedom ' or ' independence.'   The western democratic principle has always been
too anarchic to be sensible.   It sees things in pieces.   It
even sees life in pieces : its personality is unstable and easy
to isolate.   Such are some of the capital causes for the
rapid eclipse of european power.   Its character of ' independence,' its pretended franchises, its ' nationalisms,'
make it unable to organize itself as *one* white race ; and
politically, organization is everything :   talent, martial
qualities, nothing.

The parliamentary system is the great characteristic
european institution that to-day has on all hands lost its
meaning.   There are no doubt worse things for the people
than parliaments.   But the humbug involved in such a
transparently one-sided assembly makes it impossible to go
on with it once a certain point of enlightenment or ex-
asperation has been reached.   All the liberal tricks are
seen through and known now by heart.   So, for better or
for worse, parliamentary rule is finished.

The liberal ' hero ' of the farce staged in the english
parliament, and the tory ' villain,' can no longer ' draw '
the electorate.   The day of that pantomime is past.   But
the liberal ' hero ' has *pris son parti* ; he was not the great
' professional ' (that he always has been) for nothing.   So
he transformed himself into a *reformist socialist* or *fabian* or
social democrat : and there he is—in the person for instance
of Mr. Ramsay MacDonald—still going strong, still with
the noble bearing and rather long hair of his old liberal
days !   But slowly he is becoming the *villain* of the piece.
It is very complex and we need not go into it very much :
but the communist left wing has stolen his thunders.
His *reform*, beside communist *reform*, appears very insipid.
His high respectability and professional scruples would
not allow him to compete with this ultra-radical, desperate,
ungentlemanly interloper.   So he is gradually being forced
into the rôle of the Tory—the villain of the political piece.

The competition in the matter of *liberal* or *radical* principles having become so hot, and all the personnel having
moved bodily into the *Left* (the sham fight meantime
having become a *real* one), all political struggle is well

over the dexter line of social revolution, every one to-day is *somewhere* on the Left : all except fascism, which is a faction of the extreme and militant Left who have burst round and through to the Right, as it were—circumnavigated, boxed the compass.   But from whichever side he is attacked and whether geographically he is on the ‘ left ’ or the ‘ right ’ of his immediate opponent, the liberal (in whatever disguise) henceforth will remain the villain of the piece.   He will always popularly be in the wrong.

The principal conflict to-day, then, is between the democratic and liberal principle on the one side (of which Kautsky is a typical continental exponent), and on the other the principle of dictatorship of which Lenin was the protagonist and first great theorist, proving triumphantly in action what he had arrived at speculatively beforehand. He discarded all the confusions that the legacy of a century of liberal thought involved, and all the concepts of democracy and mass-control were rooted out of his system. Thus purged, it presents itself as something highly abstract and elemental.

An extreme version of leninist politics—although, making its entrance from the opposite end, it is still weighted with a great many impure elements of an opposite order to those impairing sovietism—is fascismo.   Or, if you like, it is leninism adapted to an ancient and intelligent population.   Very roughly it can be said that in a country where the chief resistance to be overcome is in the aristocratic class, the revolutionary dictatorship must appear dressed as a moujik : in a democratic country like Italy or France, it would probably effect its purpose best in a nationalist and slightly aristocratic uniform.

But there can be no arbitrary rules ; only regional and racial expediency can count in the particular colour given to these adjustments.   They must all ultimately reach the same objective.

Under the heading ‘ Kautsky versus Lenin,’ in Lansbury’s *Labour Weekly*, April 25, 1925, the general socialist opinion of Kautsky (and with him is associated Ramsay MacDonald as the chief representative of democratic opinion in England) is clearly expressed.   It is very exactly the position of Sorel as regards such people as

Kautsky, or would be the attitude that Lenin would have advocated :—

> This book is his (Kautsky's) admission that his marxism has been vulgarized into a creed of *petit-bourgeois* opportunism and liberal go-slow.
>
> But what is important for us at the moment is that Kautsky is not an isolated phenomenon, and kautskianism not a purely german creed. The doctrine preached in this book is but typical of the whole outlook and historical rôle of the Second International. In this country we have macdonaldism, flesh of the flesh and blood of the blood of kautskianism : and to-day many of our best workers in the labour movement are still tied by bonds of tradition and personal loyalties to those who preach this very creed.

Those, then, are the opposing principles in the non-revolutionized countries to-day. (All other issues are negligible : the façades of the old party systems still left standing you can walk behind and find nothing there but a few underpaid officials holding them up.) On the one side is the principle of democracy, parliamentarianism, or ' liberal go-slow,' as it is called above. On the other is the policy of dictatorship, or leninism. The first of these two policies is pacific and non-' catastrophic.' The second, leninism, is orthodoxly marxian in that it is ' catastrophic.'

CHAPTER II

THE DEMOCRATIC STATE AND ITS
MONOPOLY OF INDIRECTNESS

IN Part I the term 'revolution' was defined in a sense
that gave it the widest interpretation. And indeed
to-day it has to cover more things than most people
suppose. 'Revolutionary' is, as I said, a sensational,
reverberating word. But it applies to many of the most
respectable things already officially established amongst
us. Much recent tory and liberal legislation is as 'revolutionary' as any sovietic enactments : only, as it occurs
under an ostensibly old-fashioned parliamentary régime,
it is not recognized as such. The spectacular violence
of the reds or communists attracts our eye like a fiercely
gesticulating puppet : meanwhile the tory legislator is
quietly drawing up, behind a heavy, respectable, official
screen, communist measures : also *anti*-communist measures. His left hand imposes on the nation a communist
measure : his right hand signs a decree consigning a batch
of communists to prison. In the press of all parties we
have a *close-up* only of his *right* hand, covered with
'capitalist' jewellery, with exquisitely manicured nails.
All these automatic hands, whether painted red or painted
white, are doing the work of *revolution*, in the sense of that
radical spiritual revaluation to which we are all committed.

What is this revolution that can take here one form,
there another : that is as far removed from the primitive
humanitarian notion of the rising and reigning of the *sans-
culotte* as it is from that of a limited *bourgeois* brotherhood : that does not aim merely at a passing revenge of
the unfortunate on the fortunate, but envisages rather
the purification and ordering of the world from top to
bottom ? That it is not my task on this occasion to show.
I have set out only to clear a little space in the midst of
the ruins of our society, where a few of the advantages of
the future society (that everything so clearly prognosti-
cates, and whose outlines, in the aspirations of a few
political thinkers, artists, and scholars, are distinctly

seen) can be enjoyed by those who care to avail themselves of certain facilities here specified. But in order to
arrive at this slight clearance, it is necessary to some
extent to give an answer to that question.

The political ferment expressed by the fierce opposition
of the principles of democracy or liberalism on the one
hand, and dictatorship on the other, resolves itself into
the secular question of the One and the Many : of a unification of the world or of a plurality of control : of the rule
of the minority or the majority ; rule by a show of hands
or rule by the most vigorous and intelligent.

On one side and the other there are many schools of
thought.   Some, for instance, believe that a vast staff of
people should be maintained to live parasitically on and
exploit the stupidity of the general mass.   Others are of
opinion that things can work out in such a way that half
the world can take in the washing of the other half ; and
that mutually these two sleepy halves can live (and *sleep*)
on each other.   Another school of thought contends that
very gradually this mass can be wakened to a sense of
responsibility ; but that under no circumstances must it
be *brusqué*. (This is the school to which Kautsky, Mac-
Donald, Russell, etc., belong.)

Frederick the Great of Prussia, that famous ruler,
thought that in condescending to rule, with the assistance
of his *heiduques* and grooms, he had gone as far as could
be expected of a man of his calibre.   There is a story that
he astonished some one attempting to represent him as
a kind and much-loved *father of his people*, by suddenly
and dramatically delivering himself of the following
quotation :—

> Croyez-moi les humains que j'ai trop su connaître
> Méritent peu, monsieur, qu'on daigne être leur maître !

That snub expressed his sentiments more truly than his
treatise *Antimachiavel*.

Henry iv of France can be regarded as an early ideal
liberal, certainly one of the greatest.   He also represents
the highest reach of gallic statesmanship.   He was as
humane, tolerant, and rational a ruler as it is possible to
get, in combination with great vigour.   He never revenged
himself ; he was at once thrifty, and fond of life ; he was

a courteous, just, and amiable prince, and he was, of course, stabbed in the stomach at last for his pains.

Machiavelli showed, and no one has ever been able seriously to dispute it, that government must be carried on, and can only be successful, if the nature of the governed is thoroughly taken into account, and regarded extremely coldly in an extremely matter-of-fact way. The citizens of Plato's republic are hypothetic ; they do not exist, but are optimistic phantoms of philosophy ; and you cannot make bricks without straw. Yet his republic is humanly desirable, if there is any sense in the word ' humanly,' since there are so few creatures who answer that description. In this way it is inevitable that you should arrive at the notion of the *will of the greatest number*, the dogma of *What the Public Wants*.

What the ' will ' of the greatest number may be is consequently the capital question of statesmanship. And it is discovered, at first with a certain surprise, that nothing that can properly be called *will* exists for anything except a series of things that can conveniently be catalogued under that famous catchword, *What the Public Wants*. These resolve themselves into a simple series of disconnected appetites. But far more than this has always been forced on people : a luxurious, hypothetical surplus.

As a result of the dogma of *What the Public Wants*, and the technical experiences of the publicist, a very cynical and unflattering view of what the Public *is* is widely held to-day. And, indeed, the contemporary Public, corrupted and degraded into a semi-imbecility by the operation of this terrible canon of press and publicity technique, by now confirms its pessimism. It has learnt to live up to, or down to, its detractor. So in speaking of ' the Public ' we must speak of that sad product of publicity that we see around us.

It is inevitable that men who had escaped or resisted the general dementia should, surveying the fruits of liberal enlightenment and press control, at last formulate a counter-doctrine. ' Why turn yourself into the eternal servant of an imbecile,' they then exclaim, ' or (in the christian idiom) of the halt and the blind ; or condemn yourself to teach the alphabet in an infant class for ever ? Why not *rule*—would not that be simpler ? ' That is the

natural reaction of the best contemporary statesmanship
to the fruits of *What the Public Wants.*

Having arrived at this point, we are confronted with
two figures, who remark that *It is not worth while to
rule men*; and that *All rule is evil,* respectively.   The
first is excellently symbolized by Frederick the Great,
who proceeds, of course, to rule men as they have seldom
been ruled before.   The second would be symbolized by
Count Tolstoy, who did not believe in authority.   He considered that no man should have power over another,
and that authority in itself is evil.

It is this second type of man to which the soviet rulers
especially object : for he is casting contempt on what they
regard, rightly, as their predestined function—namely, to
be rulers : men organizing and legislating for human beings
as they are, not as they should be.   They cover with scorn,
in consequence, the 'intellectual' who 'does not wish to
stain his lilywhite hands with such a sordid thing as power.'
Power, they say, is *good.*

As to Frederick the Great, they would have more sympathy with him.   But it is unlikely that they would regard
it as essential (as he did) to shed tears after a battle on
beholding the destruction for which he was responsible :
or to protest, as Frederick did, how much he disliked
governing, how distasteful the cruel things to which
(because, alas ! he was a ruler) he was committed were
to him.   On the contrary, with a peculiar candour they
express their will to rule, their delight in power.

And here we reach a point that must often have been
observed by any one surveying at all intelligently the duel
of communism and capitalism, of fascism and democracy ;
of the East and the West, for it is roughly that.   It is a
paradox of that situation that all *the frankness* is on one
side, and that is not on the side of the West, of democracy.
All the traditional obliquity and subterranean methods of
the Orient are, in this duel, exhibited by the westerner and
the democratic régime.   It is *we* who are the Machiavels,
compared to the sovietist or the fascist, who makes no
disguise of his forcible intentions, whose *power* is not
wrapped up in parliamentary humbug, who is not eternally
engaged in pretences of benefaction ; who does not say at
every move in the game that he is making it for somebody

else's good, that he is a vicar and a servant when he is a master. It is true that he promises happiness to the masses as a result of his iron rule. But *the iron* is not hidden, or camouflaged as christian charity. He says that *one* politics in a country, *one* indisputed government, will be for the good of the average man. And when these *one*-party states are centrally organized, as Italy is becoming, who can gainsay him ?

This contrast of *directness* and *indirectness* was very patent during the war. The undiplomatic, unmachiavellian frankness of the german method of war appeared to the anglo-saxon consciousness, so used to make-believe, as diabolical. What the German was direct about, or much that fascismo or the soviet is direct about, is extremely barbarous. But much that western democracy is indirect about is barbarous as well. All I wish to emphasize is a new factor, a political openness and directness, the initiative in which democracy cannot claim.

Russian society for fifty years before the revolution was painfully confused, dragged this way and that by its liberalism and mysticism, as the great russian writers witness. The sovietic power has put an end to all that painful confusion as though by magic. The means were terrible ones : the Bolsheviks did not believe in ' gradualness ' and biologic growth, perhaps, enough. Many of the means taken to create the new state are no doubt susceptible of infinite improvement. And the most difficult task of any *real*—that is, powerful and severe—form of government is to reconcile the requirements of authority with the personal initiative that is impatient of rules, and which yet must not be crushed unless you wish to rule machines, not men. Nothing on earth to-day can overthrow such powers as the soviet or fascismo. The sovietic or the fascist chiefs, like other people, have to do the best they can with the material to their hand : and they are not perfect themselves. What they have done in a short time in the way of organization must be the admiration of the world.

CHAPTER III

NO *END OF THE WORLD* IN
SOCIAL REVOLUTION

HAVING done my best to remove the kind of general verbal misunderstanding where the sensational word ' revolution ' is concerned, I can very briefly offer an interpretation of the great cluster of movements disrupting our time. The first thing to notice about it is its implacableness, inasmuch as no local success will satisfy it. It is not any personality, nation, or even particular ruling class that is aimed at, but an entire human revaluation. That is, of course, why it is more like a religion than a rebellion. It is as though a mind had placed itself over against the world and formed the resolve to reconstitute the human idea itself. It is the whole of humanity this time that is at stake. The philosopher's dissatisfaction with the human animal expresses itself at the heart of this disturbance, rather even than the outraged prophet's disgust at the way men treat each other. The oppression of the poor by the rich is associated with the stultification of the great by the small. The *stupid* rich is the enemy ; and, strange as that might sound, it is the *small* who are the real villains of the piece. It is much more the senseless competition of a false ' independence,' the chaos of a multitude of ineffective, pretentious, and discordant wills, that it is sought to reduce to order, than the overthrow of this ephemeral plutocracy or that.

That this fanatical and grandiose conception is not necessarily tucked away inside the head of any subordinate official of this vast change, or shared even by all its promoters, is no doubt true. But nothing short of such a conception can adequately account for its scope, implacability, and power. At least I am unable to imagine any other. We are in the presence, I think, of a religious rather than a political intelligence ; or rather, as in all primitive societies these two things are one, in the presence of an unspoilt and primitive source whose will is so great that it clothes itself naturally in the form of a god.

76

That any such movement must float itself at first on some great emotional tide is plain. And it is inevitable that it should take a ' class ' form rather than a ' national ' form. The ' nation ' as a unit is not universal enough for its purposes : only the ' class ' is general enough, and the subject or slave class bulky enough—both helpless and immense—pathetic enough, and primitive enough, to answer to its requirements.

It is really an *idea*—in the sense that we have seen Fouillée interpreting a certain class of ideas for us ; that is, a forcible emotion wrapped up in an ideologic covering, fixed and, as it were, embalmed in the intellect. It is in the exactest sense ' idealistic.' As such its natural enemy is the great group of emotions of a natural order—the filial and family emotions. All the organizations and habits that attach people to *life* in its ordinary sense, those of the state and family notably, stand between it and its realization. St. Columba was the saint of a similar religious upheaval for affronting and overcoming these deepest human affections in favour of the greatest abstract love of God.

How near in many ways primitive christianity was to the present revolution has often been pointed out. It claimed of the convert the same fanatical allegiance, was ' international ' in the same way, and hostile to organized social life. Sir Samuel Dill, in speaking of the contemporary objections to evangelical christianity on this score, writes :—

And there is some of the religious literature of that period which gives a colour to part of this indictment. In the very years when the great invasions were desolating the provinces of the West, and when the hosts of Radagaisus and Alaric were threatening the heart of the Empire, S. Paulinus wrote a remarkable letter to a soldier who felt himself drawn to the higher christian life. In this epistle the ascetic ideal is expounded with a breadth and absence of qualification which shock and amaze the modern reader. The evangelical counsels of perfection are construed in the sternest and most uncompromising fashion. Christian obedience is boldly represented as inconsistent with the duties of citizenship and the relations of family life. The love of father or mother, of wife or child, the desire for riches or honour, devotion to one's country, are all so many barriers to keep the soul from Christ.

There is not a word to indicate that a christian life, worthy
of the name, could be made compatible with the performance
of worldly duties. The rich are condemned for ever, in the
words of prophet or evangelist. The soldier is a mere shedder
of blood, doomed to eternal torment. There is no possibility
of serving both Christ and Cæsar. This was the way in
which secular life was regarded by the voluntary exiles who
followed St. Jerome . . . such a movement might well seem
to an old-fashioned Roman as a renunciation, not only of
citizenship, but of all the hard-won fruits of civilization and
social life. If this was the highest form of christian life, as
its devotees proclaimed it to be, then christianity was the
foe, not only of the old religion, but of the social and political
order which Rome had given to the world. It is hardly to
be wondered at that the monks were execrated alike by the
mob and by the cultivated pagan noble. (*Last Century of the
Western Empire.*)

The ways in which these two movements differ from each
other is as easy to see as their points of comparison. The
heavenly kingdom was not essentially different to the
promise of proletarian participation in a higher terrestrial
life, because the world was to be destroyed almost at once
prior to its establishment, and its rewards and benefits
were very concrete. To-day, however, the promises on
this plane are realizable. There is no necessity to postu-
late the suppression of the world for its advent : for the
goods are there to hand over. People can manufacture
their own heaven ; the All-father or Father Christmas is
Science. But the plan does not end with this animal
bounty and static salvation. The christian otherworldli-
ness was far more worldly and limited than the present
objective. The christian heaven is *thrown in* here, as it
were, as a practical inducement to allow at last the freeing
of the human mind for tasks of a higher order. It is both
more positive and more aristocratic, to use that convenient
term to discriminate it from the usurpation of christian
altruism. That is its great and valuable difference.

THE DOCTRINE OF *WHAT THE PUBLIC WANTS* ORIGINATES IN THE PESSIMISM OF PHILOSOPHY

ON a previous page the true complexion of the incentive force of the revolutionary change proposed was said to be ' the philosophic dissatisfaction with the human animal.' But this dissatisfaction, unless its motives were felt to be rather purer than what is at the back of most complaints about other people, would with reason be resented as presumptuous. Certainly if the average stockbroker complained of the shortcomings (on grounds of insensitiveness of an intellectual or moral nature) of the plain man, the plain man would be fully justified in retorting that this censorious financier should examine the beam in his own eye first.

But there is nothing ' philosophical ' or speculative about the great business interests that control us. Therefore, if a ' philosophic dissatisfaction with the human animal ' exist, and if it is that, and the interests threatened by it, that provides the basis of social revolution, it must come from the philosopher, or ' intellectual,' not the business executive. This is in fact the case. Everything that makes revolution valuable comes from the scientific, philosophic, and discursive intelligence.

But has the most imaginative, inventive, and resourceful of human beings the right to complain of and criticize the average of his kind ? He evidently has not, although it could be conceded that he has more right probably than has the stockbroker. Also it could be conceded that probably his motives are purer : at least he does not *rob and murder* the less talented, less alive, more savage of his kind, making the excuse of his disgust at their mediocrity. That is, however, too much what the financier is apt to do.

But how is it that the financier speaks the language of philosophy, and takes over the watchwords and fiercely reformist temper of revolution ? That is, of course, the

key to our democratic society.   It is the vulgarization of
scientific and philosophic thought that provides him with
his mighty excuse to enslave and change as he likes.   That
is another thing in favour of open, direct, and avowed
rule.   The fascist and soviet governments have done with
' revolution ' : they do not rule in the name of the ' intelligence ' (they quite rightly repudiate this bastard, vulgarized article), but by right of *political* economic intelligence
and political economic power.

The philosopher has never considered it as part of his
function to flatter people.   But his most unflattering
attitude has never been so unflattering, if considered for
a moment, as is the flattery of the *What the Public Wants*
idea.   But the theory or philosophy of *What the Public
Wants* would never have come into existence without
(1) the democratic, ' enlightened ' régime of modern
Europe ; and (2) the censure of the moralist, criticism of
the philosopher, inhumanity of the scientist, and *superbia*
of the napoleonism of Nietzsche.

At the beginning of this part of my essay I have placed
a characteristic piece of hortative, moralistic censorious-
ness from *The Anatomy of Melancholy.*   But Burton can
be matched by a scientist of our day, Professor Richet,
who writes very much in the same strain of good-hearted
but rather stupid abuse.   In order to trace the philosophy
of *What the Public Wants* (with which we are now about
to deal) to its origins, I will quote a few passages from this
distinguished french liberal man of science.   It is to such
unflattering generalizations as Professor Richet's in the past
that all the insulting accommodation of *What the Public
Wants* can be traced :—

> Many people (he says) will doubtless be astonished that in
> comparing animals with men, I constantly find the animal
> less stupid.   Certainly at a first superficial examination we
> might be tempted to think that man's intelligence is incom-
> parably higher than that of animals.   But . . . stupidity
> does not mean that we have not understood, but that we
> act as if we had not understood.   To know that which is
> good, and to do that which is bad ; knowingly and deliber-
> ately to inflict pain upon ourselves ; to recognize the cause
> of unhappiness and to fling ourselves upon that cause :
> that is stupidity.

The war was what stirred Professor Richet into this declamatory little book. That terrible blow to all hopes· of civilization and a humaner, happier life apparently took him down from his professorial chair into the market-place. How few people it affected in that way ! You must admire the gesture of this old Frenchman, and the soundness of his heart—so ill served by his judgment :—

> The fitting out of an armoured cruiser (he says) is, from certain points of view, a demonstration of stupendous intelligence. (Neither rabbits, cats, nor even monkeys could do as much as this.) Powerful engines, wireless telegraphy, huge guns of increasing accuracy, electric power directing the entire mechanism, luxurious state-rooms, picked libraries, and swift hydroplanes. What perfection ! The ingenious arrangement of the whole structure enables us to sail without any risk on all seas, with all the wonders of civilization accumulated in this narrow space. How beautiful ! I am lost in admiration ! But presently, when I think it over, my admiration evaporates so completely that no trace of it remains. For when all is said and done, what is the goal of this wonderful machine ? To destroy a similar machine—therefore, to what end ? . . . It is not enough to create ingenious works. If they bring about pain, illness, wounds, and poverty, they show the stupidity of their creator.
>
> Aviation is a very fine thing, a decisive victory over gravity, that relentless gravity which seemed destined to keep us tied to earth until the end of time ; and I give it due reverence. But when we make it the essential function of aerial machines to scatter bombs and terror over peaceful towns at midnight, then at once my admiration withers, and I prefer the society of the penguins and the bisons, who know nothing of aviation.

What happens in a war? what values reign? he asks. Take the Great War as a specimen :—

> The flood of suffering caused by the war was a hundred-, a thousand-fold worse than the bloodshed. All justice scorned ; all falsehood exalted ; all pity insulted. The whole of humanity wallowing happily in blood and slime. . . . During five or six thousand years man had tried his strength in continuous, but comparatively bloodless, little wars. But these were sketchy, childish efforts, mere preludes to the magnificent work accomplished in 1914-18. Ah ! this time he has achieved success. . . . The sum of human sorrows has exceeded all forecasts, even the most optimistic.

And then he comes to the nietzschean or sorelian problem
of 'heroism.' 'The more energy, fortitude, and heroism
exacted by the war, the more glaringly it exposed our
madness, since these virtues were dedicated to destruction.'

> Humanity is like a sultan who has two wives. One is
> young, beautiful, and healthy, radiantly graceful and sweet,
> with a musical voice, dazzling charms, and eyes alight with
> tenderness and love. To her husband she gives pleasure,
> mirth, and serenity. She is Science. The other wife is a
> dirty old hag, abject, blear-eyed, a walking skeleton. She
> has only a few scanty tufts of grey hair thick with vermin,
> toothless jaws, and fœtid breath : a body ravaged by dis-
> gusting ulcers and covered with filth. She is violent, full
> of lies and fury, given to fits of frenzied rage ; she foams
> and bites. She roars instead of speaking. Even from afar
> she stinks. She is War. . . . And yet, nevertheless, she is
> the favourite wife of this egregious fool.

This is rather an emotional outburst than anything else.
It is only by intellect, not by indignation and emotionality,
any more than by geniality and jokes, that the terrestrial
paradise can be attained. He feels the same about *Homo
sapiens*, whom he calls *Homo stultus*, as does Mr. Shaw,
but he is angrier and more benevolent.

In the rather unfortunate ' sultan ' simile (after reading
which any woman's mind would be adversely affected)
he places ' Mankind ' in the position of an all-powerful
potentate, able to embrace either the paradises of science
or the loathsomeness of war. Was an image ever less
accurate ?—and of that particular sort of emotional in-
accuracy that does far more harm than good to the cause
it espouses. To picture ' Mankind ' (the ' Poilu,' the
' Tommy,' the ' Pickelhauber,' etc.) rushing wilfully on
war from sheer love of war, and hatred of the fleshpots of
peaceful life they left behind, is so ridiculous that even
the goodness of Professor Richet's intentions do not
excuse it.

In an earlier page he referred to the *asset* side of war ;
' undeniably,' he said, ' war brings great happiness to
some men ' : and he indicated the armament manufacturers and war profiteers. But do these people *wait*,
patiently and without interference, for such lucky accidents
as wars to occur ? The falsity of the Mankind-the-Sultan

notion is patent. 'Mankind' is, alas! as helpless as the animals, as the professor's penguins or bisons, and therefore is amenable to the excuses provided for the animals on the score of ignorance.

It is the abstraction 'Mankind' (the *Homo stultus* or the *Homo sapiens*, when there are men who gain and men who lose by everything that occurs, when what is one man's food is another man's poison, and what it is 'foolish' for one man to engage in it is 'wise' for another) that makes such nonsense of this book of Professor Richet's. It is a myth like *l'homme éclairé* that trips up his reason, and uses up his emotion in vain.

Why all this anger and indignation, then, with 'Mankind,' or with men in general? They are helpless, but they do not mind dying very much : in a state of nature (as Professor Perry and others have pointed out, and as the aborigine shows) they are not very violent or given to war. They are rather quiet and reasonable animals than otherwise, though of course superstitious, and addicted to the use of feathers, which Professor Richet finds very ridiculous. To describe the carnage of the war as *willed* by the majority of men, in some sadic excess, is so stupid that it is almost *too* stupid. If you tickle the sole of the foot of a sane man he temporarily loses his reason. When excited, confused, worked up, drugged, and shrieked at by the magnate and ·his press for a few weeks, 'Mankind' (*Homo stultus*) becomes ferocious, that is all.

'Mankind' is part of the machinery of the democratic flattery of democracy. Democracy is to blame for the war, also for Professor Richet and his inability to understand the war. Everything that abstraction 'Mankind' is made to do himself he is (since he 'democratically' rules himself, does he not?) responsible for; it is *he* who has willed it! ' So now you 've been and gone and killed fifteen million of yourself, have you ? ' the Profiteer might have asked him in 1918. 'Well, you are a silly fellow! still, you *would* do it, you bloodthirsty, homicidal devil!—*I* can't stop you! There 's no holding you in *when you see red*, is there ? Ah, well! you rule yourself, thank goodness for that—or you might start blaming me for it! But I suppose after all a bit of a scrap does you no harm occasionally! Boys will be boys! I 'm glad I 'm not your

father ! I shouldn't like to be responsible for such a
high-spirited, fiery, tigerish devil as you ! Straight I
wouldn't ! '

And poor ' Mankind ' in his concrete form of the plain
man—mutilated, bankrupt, and brutalized—would have
looked at that genial, ' kindly ' face, with its merry pickwickian twinkle and plausible tongue (not a bit proud !
a self-made fellow, evidently ! good luck to him !), with
a ' grim ' smile, and would think to himself, ' Yes, I am a
bit of a devil ! '

There in Professor Richet you have the enlightened,
despairing, liberal intelligence of our times : and how
futile it is !

CHAPTER V

THE VULGARIZATION OF DISGUST

THE critical dissatisfaction of the scientific and philosophic mind where human capacity is concerned is not novel. Vulgarization is the novelty. Another novelty is the vulgarity of the governing mercantile class, side by side with the extraordinary intellectual resources of the ' intellectual.' The effect of the vulgarization on the ruler is at least as significant as its effect on the man-in-the-street.

Philosophers or men of science, witnessing the popular miscarriage of their thought, are disgusted or resigned, as the case may be. The democratic ruler (who alone is responsible for the worst and most calamitous miscarriages) associates himself with them ; and in chorus they all abuse the poor plain man. What has happened is that *disgust has been vulgarized.* This is more deadly in its effects than the vulgarization of knowledge. The natural insolence and desire for a feeling of superiority of those who are superior in nothing but money and the power it gives, is thus provided. And the noble pessimism of the speculative mind is at once translated into acts, and employed as a sanction for exploitation.

The whole of this new system of governmental metaphysic can be best defined as the philosophy of *What the Public Wants.* The form that government in the western democratic countries takes being publicity (suggestion, persuasion, and ' education '), the full significance for the community of this cynical dogma cannot be exaggerated.

I will attempt to formulate more explicitly than one of its adepts would be able to do, or would care to do, probably, the principle of the dogma of *What the Public Wants.* Its similarity to the philosopher's cry of despair from which it derives will in this way be brought out.

Let us imagine, then, an adept of this dogma summarizing his principles for the benefit of some budding publicist. In the candour of the confessional, heart to heart with a secure postulant, they would run as follows :—

' Take the poorest and most abject *crétin* in the com-

85

munity (eighty per cent. of which resemble him very nearly). Say to yourself, "There is nothing too simple and inhumanly stupid—the sort of thing that gives you that empty feeling in the pit of the stomach—for this low-grade fool. It would take you five hundred centuries to teach him to frame the simplest abstract notion. He is permanently and for ever an infant ; the Infants' Class always absorbs eighty per cent. of the personnel of our famous terrestrial training school, or technical institute, which we call ' mankind.' The eternal alphabet A, B, C, D is the music that, in one form or another, would greet a visitor from another planet come to see how we were getting on. This re-partition of the fairy's gifts, leaving this vast human surplus practically *crétinesque*, you must accept. It is not your doing, you did not make the world. You can do nothing to modify it ; and even if you could, are you sure that you would not be going against Providence ? There is a possibility that a wisdom superior to yours arranged things in this way. Abandon, therefore, all those queer attempts to ' educate ' this dense throng of *inapertiva* mankind : or rather, canalize your educative efforts in such a way that only the simplest instruction is provided, nothing that will tax those truly infantile intelligences. (For they are as truly infantile as what more technically is an infant, and the same rule not to overtax and overstrain this undeveloped brain applies to them as to the child.) So, A, B, C, D : *Two and two make four—Donkey tap the door. Three and three make six— Lamps, not tramps, have wicks* (compare the american army tests of Yerkes and others) : whatever you consider it possible or desirable to impart to them, let it be on that system.

From these ineluctable premises and observations, as you will see, a vast system of government ensues. Although we have called this prodigious mass of people ' infantile,' they of course outwardly grow up. They do not call themselves infantile as a community. They claim to be treated as responsible, accomplished, intelligent beings. They want to have official bulletins every morning of all the accidents, fires, murders, rapes that have occurred throughout the night and part of the preceding day. They wish a detailed account of how their agents and ministers of state have 'fulfilled their trust,' as they call it, in the conduct of that great and sacred affair, the commonwealth. And they wish to be informed punctually of the results of all racing, ball games, paper-chases, bull-fights, and other similar events.

The *What the Public Wants* method of meeting these demands is the best and only one (see our advert.). It is run on the lines outlined above. Something in the form of the enthralling adventures of *Bo Peep and Patsy* is essential to wreathe all their rosy faces in happy smiles. Then a hush will come at the sight of a heading, *War-cloud in the East* or *War-cloud in the West*. Father will frown, exclaiming : 'I say! things look serious!' Then the Infants' Class will be let into the deepest and dirtiest secrets of the underworld of Westminster in a column of the most wildly indiscreet gossip. 'It is an open secret— among those in the know—it is freely whispered in the lobbies and closets of the Talking House—that Mr. Chamberlain will shortly make an announcement that will surprise three of his colleagues and most intimate cronies very much indeed, unless—as may of course happen—it comes to their ears : for there is always the chance that they may get wind of it.' Mr. Citizen looks very knowing at this. He has indeed got his penn'orth!

The same great principles laid down above apply to the Cinema, Wireless, and Theatre. Unless you wish to give yourself quite unnecessary trouble, involve yourself in a considerable money loss, and become very unpopular, in these occupations, as in everything else, you must follow the golden rule, namely : *You cannot aim too low.* The story you present cannot be too stupid. It is not only impossible to exaggerate—it in itself requires a trained publicist to form any idea of—the idiocy of the Public. In general it can be said that no confidence trick is too transparent to dupe them with ; no picture of life is too unreal or sugary for their taste ; no mental effort is too slight not to arouse an immediate and indignant protest from them.

That, I suppose, would be the main statement. But associated with the stupidity of the public is also its malignity. (*Cf.* Richet's 'Stupidity and ferocity are even made for each other. When you have a lot of one, you cannot have too much of the other.')

' There is a further point,' this credo can be imagined
as proceeding : ' this great mass with which you have to
live and deal as best you can is not either reliable, truthful,
possessed of the slightest magnanimity or kindness, or any
of the things that would make it easy to get on with.
However much you trick it, it will not fall short of you in
cunning, but only in ability : you will never trick it as
much as it would like to trick you.'

(*Cf.* : ' Because this is to be asserted in general of men ; that
they are ungrateful, fickle, false, cowards, covetous, and as
long as you succeed they are yours entirely, they will offer you
their blood, property, life, children, as is said above. . . .
Friendships that are obtained by payment, and not by greatness . . . are not secured . . .,' etc., etc. *Machiavelli.*)

So, ethically, even, your adherence to the doctrine of
What the Public Wants is justified by the *méchanceté* of
human nature ; just as intellectually you are forced to the
procedures laid down in that doctrine by human stupidity.
The most bitter philosopher (Machiavelli, just quoted, as
an example) would not speak very differently to this.
But the doctrine of *What the Public Wants* begins where
philosophy leaves off.   And in the case of this belief it is
not so much the truth of what it states, as of the uses to
which this discovery is put, and the spirit in which it is
held.   Nothing useful to the world was ever accomplished
as a result of such a belief steadily held—nothing at least
but a work of hatred, which has its ' creative ' uses, no
doubt, as Jaurés thought.   What on the analogy of the
dyer's hand it usually produces, except for the moments
during which it is engaged in epic destruction, is something
inconceivably common and barren.
Professor Richet or the author of *The Anatomy of Melancholy*, one a man of science and the other a divine, would
thus agree with a great prophet of *What the Public Wants*
to a large extent in their estimate of ' the Public.'   But
they would act quite differently on this information.   The
latter would rub his hands with satisfaction, and approach
the Public with an obsequious grin, and a *What can I do
for you to-day, my little man ?*   Professor Richet, his face
convulsed with angry discouragement, would rush out and
apostrophize his *semblable*, his *frère*.

Hideous and undesirable as is the caricature of the private thoughts of the philosopher contained in *What the Public Wants* theory, yet the pessimistic original cannot be neglected.

If the creative minds of the world are indeed for ever cancelled and rendered ineffective by the agency of the ' unprogressive ' mass of men, then they should be protected and rescued. This is of more importance than the gratification of the vanity of the human average : the human average would get more out of such a salvage than out of those satisfactions for which it pays the expert of *What the Public Wants* so dearly. Left at the mercy of this vast average—its inertia, ' creative hatred,' and conspiratorial habits where ' the new ' is concerned—we shall always checkmate ourselves. The more we ' advance,' the more we shall lose ground. In the ultimate interest of all of us we should sacrifice anything to the end that this most priceless power of any (the intellectual power by which, as a kind, we express and illustrate ourselves, precisely because of which we are conscious of our poor organization and the fatuity of our record up to date) be put in a position finally to be effective. . . . Instead of the vast organization to exploit the weaknesses of the Many, should we not possess one for the exploitation of the intelligence of the Few ?

Does the Public really want *What the Public Wants* ? In a sense, no doubt, it does. But it would not want to be *flattered* on such a gigantic scale if it knew what this flattery cost it.

Again, *What the Public Wants*, as it is practised to-day, must lead its practitioner into lunacy or some form of imbecility, or else, with the stronger-minded and more cynical, into a mood of *hatred* where their millions of ' little charges ' are concerned. *Hatred of stupidity* must result, where it is not succumbed to, in those whose business it is to be incessantly isolating and exploiting it. But a great specialist in stupidity (like one of the great original newspaper kings) could only become what he does thanks to the clairvoyance of hatred of some sort. The great journalist and publicity figures with which everybody is familiar probably started with an intense irritation and dislike of the stupidity out of which subsequently they

made their great fortunes. What started in hatred and
contempt, passing to mastery and fortune, has been seen
sometimes to end in madness. *Hatred of stupidity* is a
most dangerous thing to encourage in yourself or others.
It must have as a policy, or widely-indulged-in practice,
the most diabolical results.

Then, again, *to hate stupidity* is really to hate failure,
for stupidity is that. And although the christian attitude
on this point does not of necessity recommend itself, it is
better than what we are familiar with under the form of
the *worship of success*.

But *to love stupidity* would be even worse, no doubt.
Self-sacrifice in the interest of the lame, the halt, and the
blind is the extreme theoretic, christian, form of that. It
cannot be said to have *succeeded*—in that sense it has
practised what it preached.

An entirely different attitude either from that of christianity or from *What the Public Wants*, towards the majority
of mankind, having no trace of disgust or dislike, hatred or
impossible unreal ' love,' seems to suggest itself as necessary
for the new ruler of the world.

It is no doubt as unkind and as great a waste of time to
give the Public *What it Doesn't Want*, in the way of art,
literature, or science, as it is to degrade it below what it
does actually want in order to make more money out of
it. If you must treat the Public as animals in a vast Zoo,
you should at least observe the usual rule for such places :
namely, *Do not irritate the animals*. Why not be satisfied
with the Public as it is, and let it amuse itself as it pleases ?
If you yourself have other ideas of amusement, then it is
always open to you to turn from that humdrum human
fair and occupy yourself in some other way without
offending anybody.

CHAPTER VI

BOLSHEVIK 'WILL TO POWER'

MARX invited the other countries of Europe, in his time, to gaze at England; for in England they would see their own future (of fifty years thence) reflected, he said. England was already treading the path they in due course must tread: that was his theory. On the same principle, by scrutinizing contemporary Russia or Italy we to-day can see where we shall be some years hence. We can get there without ' catastrophe.'

The present rulers of Russia or Italy, we must assume, are imbued with a ' creative,' compassionate emotion for the human being. But they are intelligent enough to perceive, it seems, that he is a very helpless child, dependent on others (like a horse or dog). They realize that he finds his greatest happiness in a state of dependence and sub-servience when (an important condition) it is named 'freedom.' It matters very little, then, if you outrage often, as you must do to rule successfully, the most ele-mentary principles of ' freedom.' He will be happier with you, dependent, than with other people, *independent*. Men will always get their happiness out of *words*, whatever is popularly and scientifically said to the contrary. Put a word on him, as God put His *word* on the Israelites, and he is yours, and as happy as an enthusiastic dog.

But the wise ruler (and I am assuming that in the world to-day there is really such a ruler) would see quite well—if I am correct, has seen—that there must be a master. Some one or other has to assume responsibility for the ignorant millions. And their expression of their willing-ness and determination to assume power, even to wrest power from those who abuse it, where necessary, is the personal announcement on the part of the russian rulers, or the rulers of Italy, of their accepting this situation.

A very interesting book has recently appeared on the questions that are occupying us here. It is called *After Lenin*, and is by Michael Farbman. Mr. Farbman, I gather, is an independent, non-partisan observer. But he is undoubtedly very much in sympathy with the soviet

régime, and very well informed.   At this point I will make
a fairly long quotation from his book.   He deals with great
candour and clearness with the facts as they present themselves to him.   We could not, I think, have a better guide,
or one whose conclusions correspond more nearly with
those I am expressing throughout this essay :—

> The important point to grasp (he writes) in any considera-
> tion of the political future of Russia is the fact that a new
> ruling class is being evolved.   Russia has never been so
> fortunate as to possess a ruling class in the european sense
> of that word.   Certainly the nobility was, traditionally, the
> first order in the empire.   But the nobles never actually
> exercised real power ; though the bureaucracy was recruited
> from them, it was in fact independent of them as a class.
> It was, indeed, independent of any class, absolutely isolated.
> Certainly the monarchy and bureaucracy were accustomed
> to invoke the name of the nobility in any reform they initiated.
> But, as a matter of fact, the nobility, having no instrument
> of publicity in their hands, had never any direct or immediate
> say in such matters.   And though the monarchy was per-
> meated with the feudal ideas of the nobility, the nobility
> was in no proper sense the ruling class.   The nobles had
> many privileges but no political power.   They were the
> ' foundation ' of the state : but they could make no claim to
> ' being the state.'
> The merchants, the *bourgeoisie*, on the other hand, had
> infinitely less influence in state affairs than the nobles.
> Not even in an elementary form could they acquire the
> position of a ruling class. . . .
> The peculiarity . . . of political life in Russia has been the
> complete absence of the party system.   There were many
> groups in opposition, but a party in power never existed.
> No party, up to the creation of the Duma, ever contemplated
> the possibility of assuming power. . . . The revolutionary
> parties, too, though determined to smash all and every
> government, never contemplated the idea of assuming them-
> selves the government of the country, and indeed were
> entirely opposed to taking any part in it.
> Members of russian revolutionary parties have generally
> been intellectuals of the Dostoievsky type, idealists and
> dreamers, introspective, doubting, hesitating, diffident.
> Propagandists and conspirators, they were never men of
> action ; they never even expected to have to act, except
> perhaps in a spasmodic and impulsive fashion . . . these
> men showed themselves capable of great self-sacrifice ; but

. . . when the success of the revolution of 1917 threw them up and they were called to assume power in the state, they proved themselves not only inexperienced, as might have been expected, but timid and perverse. . . .

At the very moment when the West was looking for the arrival of the strong man who should dissolve this hopeless chaos (of the early days of the Revolution) and stem this flood of words, Lenin emerged. . . . Lenin supplied what had always been lacking in previous russian parties, a programme and a purpose. . . . The organized and businesslike persistence of the little group of bolsheviks was bound to meet with success : for they brought with them new methods of political activity and a relation to life quite unusual in Russia. . . .

What was new and really surprisingly new about (the bolsheviks) was the tenacity and thoroughness with which they went to work. The strict discipline and thorough organization of their underground party . . . the indomitable ability and energy shown in the pursuit of their aims, startled the average Russian as something not only unusual but even uncanny. These qualities were indeed so alien from the usual national laxity that they could not but suggest a foreign origin. . . .

The more the Revolution is studied, the more it becomes evident that it was Lenin's attitude to the problem of governmental power that gave him and his party the victory. Indeed, the bolshevik attitude to power, their appetite for power, their already undeviating advance to it, and their continuous exercise and successful retention of it, constituted the crucial and unpassable line of demarcation between the bolsheviks and the other socialist parties in Russia.

There, in his admirably clear account of the conditions of the success of the bolsheviks, Mr. Farbman has shown us how it was ' power,' a love of it, and determination to obtain it, that enabled Lenin and his small party to reach the pinnacle they did. And, as Mr. Farbman started by saying, the important point to remember in any considera-tion of Russia is that *a new ruling class is being formed* : and further, that it is the first thing of that sort that the Russians have had.

I will quote a few further passages from Mr. Farbman's book about the attitude of the usual russian intellectual to the problem of *power*, and Kerensky's rôle :—

The russian intellectuals had a pietistic abhorrence of power as a thing essentially evil, base, and degrading. Controlling most of the instruments of real power from the very moment of the March Revolution, the socialists were afraid not only to assume the government, but even to ask a share in it. Kerensky alone took the risk of entering the Provisional Government ; but his decision aroused a storm of indignation among his fellow-socialists, who only forgave him when he put forward the theory that he took office as a Minister of Justice, not in order to exercise power, but merely to secure the punishment of the enemies of the people—the leading members of the old régime. In accordance with this theory, Kerensky proclaimed himself a ' hostage of democracy in the first Provisional Government,' not a member of it. . . . The bolsheviks were the only party of the Left which definitely and persistently fought for power. But this thirst for power was so contrary to the traditions of russian political life that even the bolshevik rank and file had time and again to be reassured by Lenin that the assumption of power was necessary and by no means wicked or degrading.

... This clash of opinion and divergence of attitude towards power was the main if not the only cause of the conflict between the bolsheviks and the russian intellectuals ; it is no exaggeration to say that the russian intellectuals not only hated but loathed the bolsheviks for ' sticking to power.' The bolsheviks were certainly not behindhand in reciprocating this hatred. They ridiculed the intellectuals as ' too pure-minded to do the dirty work of the world ' and only concerned with keeping their ' robes unsullied ' ; and they actually persecuted them.

. . . The success of the bolsheviks is due solely to their capacity for responding to this new spirit of action, of enterprise, and of acceptance of life. The bolsheviks saw a new ruling class emerging in Russia, and were astute enough to manœuvre themselves into the position of its leaders. To define in set terms this ruling class is impossible at this stage. The bolsheviks, at any rate, were not anxious to give a very strict definition of the class in whose name they assumed the government. They proclaimed that the ' toiling masses,' whoever these may be, alone possessed political rights ; they excluded the ' exploiting elements,' an equally vague class, from any exercise of such rights ; and on this foundation they based a theory which permitted them to retain power exclusively in their hands.

CHAPTER VII

THE RULER AND THE RULED

IF the problem of ' power ' is envisaged by the Soviet as Mr. Farbman has represented it to be, and as everything leads us to believe that it is, then it is clear that from the start the soviet system must clash with ' democratic ' prejudice. So it is natural that the struggle for ascendency throughout Europe should to-day be more or less reproducing the struggle that occurred in the first months of the revolution in Russia ; and that the opposing camps resolve themselves into a set of men on the one side imbued with the notion of a rigidly disciplined obedience to a central authority with dictatorial powers, and on the other into a set of men faithful to the liberal, democratic ideal of the last century.

But let us leave these young, not fully tried, powers out of the question. We will pursue the argument independently of controversial parallels. As it takes two to make a quarrel, so it takes two categories of people to rule a state ; and however artificial at certain points the division may be, you must have a ruling caste, if only to satisfy the profound instinct and wish of the great majority of people to be ruled.

To rule is a painful, dangerous, and arduous duty. It is only when it becomes too much of a pleasure that it is a danger for other people—namely, those who are ruled. So long as it is an unpleasant duty, involving a great deal of work, it is the indispensable ideal of human life. Most young aristocracies in their first generations are kept very busy and live hard, and in consequence answer to one of the principal requirements.

This division into rulers and ruled partakes of a sexual division ; or rather, the contrast between the one class and the other is more like that between the sexes than anything else. The ruled are the females and the rulers the males, in this arrangement. A stupid, or slow-witted, not very ambitious, conventional, slothful person (what has been called aptly *homme moyen sensuel*, the human average) has necessarily a great many feminine characteristics. These involve him, too, in a great many childish ones. And the relation of the ruler to the ruled is always that of a man to a woman, or of an adult to a child. (By 'man' here is meant any ruler-like person, of whatever sex, age, or class.)

Such a division for the purposes of ruling necessitates two distinct types of life : that of the ruled must be lived on one plane, that of the ruler on another. The life of the subject will be lived concretely, stereotyped on a narrow, fashionable plan, of use for the day or time ; full of kind, protective illusions, like a screen round a child's bed ; full of nicely arranged flowers, little presents, and meaningless courtesies, a life of name-days and birth-days, mechanical work, easy bursts of animal laughter, all tied up in a little neat bundle with a comfortable personal vanity.

The life of the ruler, on the other hand, will be very unpleasant. It will be severe, full of the shock of the forces of outer vastness from which the masses are sheltered, full of incessant labour. The ruler must be completely disillusioned—a suspicion of belief and he would be lost ; the cares of his numerous duties will prevent him from sleeping very much ; he will not be able to regard life as agreeable in any way, or else, like Faust, it would be all up with him ; hearty laughter or anything that we associate with *bourgeois* relaxation would never visit him. To be a true ruler he will have paid every penalty of man's aspiring lot, a pact with the Devil included.

It often occurs (and we even have to-day a unique picture of this in contemporary western society) that the ruler becomes a confirmed practitioner of one of Haroun al Raschid's most objectionable habits, namely, that of spending his time disguised amongst his subjects as one of them. This tendency in a ruler is very much indeed to be deplored. No good has ever been known to come of it. And such an arrangement should always be resented and resisted by the ruled. The determination to have the apple and eat it too is not the sign of a very serious or pleasant person, and he should in every way be made to feel his subject's disappointment. The good ruler, like the good artist, can be recognized at once by the inflexible discomfort of his life ; isolation, further, being essential.

Here, then, we can formulate a valuable rule for the

conduct of the ruled, as follows : *The ruler should be made to pay for ruling in every possible way. He should be prevented at all cost from sharing in the pastimes or simple advantages of his inferiors.* ' Rule ! so be it ! ' (you should say to him, in your acts, if not in your words). ' Rule away, Dick Whittington, thrice Lord Mayor, Lord Chancellor, Lord King, or anything else you please, of any town you like. But if we are of different clay, then understand, Lord, that we *are* of different clay. We are foolish little people with whom you must not mix, shaming us with the superior quality of your superior clay. We will be your creatures, we will depend on you. But we will not live with you. Our respect prevents us from associating with you in any way. There must be no dropping into the nursery for a romp, into the kitchen for a cuddle, or into the garden for a nice pat-a-ball-about-a-net. No, no, milord ! I keep my distance, you keep your distance ! Go back to Jehovah on the mountain, and hobnob with your kind. We know our place. We are your servants. Recollect what is owing to your position.'

This system of reprisal for the odious fact of rule—or, if you like, it can be regarded as a discipline to keep the ruler up to the mark (just as wealthy people are so often heard observing, in generalizing about artists and men of science, that they should be *kept poor*, as this forces them to work)— should be extended to every form of superiority or excellence, political, social, or intellectual. No form of person extensively imposing his will, for their good, on others, should escape. But, of course, of all things this least of all requires formulation. For people do not require any lessons in this aspect of the art of being ruled.

But where our political rulers are concerned to-day, in western democracies, this system of ' keeping your distance ' is very little observed. When open privilege and evident power returns this can be remedied. At present that, like so many other things, is impossible. So the most valuable privilege and weapon of an *inferior* is for the time obsolete.

For the sake of the ruled—that is my argument—the ruler should be forced to rule by force, ostensibly, responsibly, as does (to the great disgust of our western liberals) the soviet or fascist government. That all your troubles come from that charming neighbour of yours, whose bald

head you see peaceably shining in the early morning sunday sun while he waters his lawn, who is always ready
with a cheery word on the weather, the holidays, the
cricket score—that is what is intolerable. Riding past
your modest dwelling in shining armour, at the head of a
brilliant cavalcade, scowling at your name-plate on the
gate, or kissing his hand to your wife as she peeps appre-
hensively from behind the respectfully drawn curtains—
Mr. Lionel Brown, your altogether too anonymous neighbour, would be better that way. You would ' know which
way to take him ' then, would you not ?

But we need not invoke this Timour-like figure of asiatic
despotism, as he, at all events, will not arrive for some
time, if ever. The harsh and ominous words, *ruler* and
ruled, although they must be used, are in practice infinitely
tempered to the shorn lamb in our educationalist era.
Education plays, and will continue to play, a much more
important part in government than physical and exterior
force. Force is a passing and precarious thing, whereas
to get inside a person's mind and change his very personality is the effective way of reducing him and making him
yours. Merely to chain him up like a dog or a slave is
the act of an unimaginative tyrant. To kill him is equally
meaningless. It is by taking him when he is young, and
educating him, that you can secure him to yourself. The
physical part of power, like the bloody part of revolution,
should not be insisted on.

The causes that made this great revolution or readjustment of power possible, namely, science, must also continue to influence the form that power takes. Without
the recent spectacular advance of science no unity would
have been possible, and small competition would have continued as the basis of social organization. The tremendous
power science confers on men in their war not only with
nature, but with other men, has made unity certain.

But what distinguishes the new revolutionary ruler from
the commercial magnate of our own democratic society is
that the former is not, first of all, a money-man, but an
open political leader. His aims, however practical, are not
entirely circumscribed by economy. The best and most
ancient material of speculative thought has gone to the
making of his economic picture,

What was it that made the brilliant groups of revolutionary aristocrats of the last century in Russia, England, and
elsewhere, revolutionary ?   Why did the Byrons, Shelleys,
and Swinburnes in England, Tolstoys, Bakunins, etc., in
Russia, become so unpatriotic and lawless all of a sudden
in the cause of universal upheaval ?   Because ' revolution '
was on the side of philosophic thought ; and also christian
thought, of course, which they had been taught as little
boys.   Without that they would hardly have turned with
so much gusto against the society in which they occupied
such an enviable position.

The state of mind of the social revolutionary is the
permanent state of mind of most philosophers.   There are
few revolutionary parties that have this *permanent* ideal
as a dogma.   The bolshevik party had apparently this
doctrine from the start ; and it is said that Lenin was
confronted with it by his old associates at the time of his
' realistic ' conversion.   But there cannot have been many
revolutionaries, ever, who possessed such a radical programme.   All the means the revolutionist takes to reach
some sort of perfection or emancipated life is only a violent
mass or group expression of what the philosopher, without
urging, and in the detachment of his contemplation,
desires for men.   Socrates did not formulate a doctrine
of *propaganda by deed*, but he was as ' revolutionary ' as
Bakunin—indeed, more so, because his mind was so much
more powerful.

But the permanent state of mind of the revolutionary
ruler will now be that of the philosopher ; a more cultivated, in addition to a more able, ruling class than Europe
has ever possessed is promised.

CHAPTER VIII

THE EUROPEAN'S *PHYSICAL* LIBERTY

BEFORE leaving the region of general principles it will be useful to examine one of the characteristic tenets of ' liberty ' as conceived of in the european world : namely, physical ' liberty.' This subject can be introduced by following a few remarks of Goethe in his conversations with Eckermann. He is discussing the libertarian peculiarities of his brother-poet :—

> All the work of Schiller (Goethe said) is dominated by the idea of liberty. . . . In his youth, it was physical liberty that preoccupied him . . . later, it was the liberty of the mind.
>
> What a singular thing is physical liberty ! According to my idea, anybody easily has enough of it. . . . For instance, you see this room here, and the one next to it, the door of which is open, and in which is my bed. It isn't big, and the space is further diminished by all sorts of furniture, books, manuscripts, *objets d'art*. It is big enough for me, however. I have lived in it all the winter, and I have hardly put my foot in the front rooms. What is the use to me, then, of any huge house, and the liberty to go from one room to the other, if this liberty is of no *use* to me ? When you have liberty enough to live safe and sound and apply yourself to your business, you have all the liberty you want. . . . Besides, we are all of us only free on certain conditions, which must be fulfilled. . . .
>
> If Schiller was in his youth so obsessed with *physical* liberty, that is partly due to the nature of his mind, and more still to the restraint imposed on him by military discipline at the Military Academy. But in his maturity, when he possessed as much physical liberty as he wanted, he then wished for the liberty of the mind : and it could almost be said that it was that idea that killed him. . . .

These very interesting remarks of Goethe, himself a particularly revolutionary figure, apply with great force to the circumstances of our life to-day : for the question of *physical liberty* is a much more burning one than it was in his day, and no effort is made to answer it or understand it. The questions of travel and domicile grow more and more urgent as the human mass grows.

To-day there is complete *liberty of circulation* every-where for everybody. . . . People without anything in particular to do avail themselves of this *carte blanche*.   In great herds they move painfully to the seaside.   Both their progress there and back, and the short time they spend on the pebbles or sand (where it is rather a sea of people than a sea of water that they behold), is so exhaust-ing that it is the power of the ' holiday ' idea alone that can sustain them. . . . Another idea, or word, could be quite easily substituted for this.

In a more continuous way this *carte blanche* to *circulate* is used and abused by great masses of women daily in the cities.   A never-ending stream of luxurious omnibuses transports them for a few pence wherever they want to go. The unequal distribution of these masses causes the same sort of disequilibrium as will the constant agitation of masses of liquid in a vessel jerked this way and that. There is no danger of the vessel upsetting, but dense congeries of beings accumulate wherever there are shops, and masses of huge vehicles cart them up and down.

All this movement, and the great staffs of men employed in the various operations connected with it (in the factories turning out the conveyances, at the garages, and on the road), is largely pointless.   For the frocks, underclothing, boots and shoes required, great suburban outfitters would answer the purpose.   If the bus ticket could not be ob-tained without a travel permit, the immense waste of labour, shattering of the roads, and stagnation of masses of traffic accompanying this ritual of shopping, would be spared.   And this would (after the first fortnight of indignation) *satisfy the shopper just as well.*   The woman whose practice it is to engage daily in this tussle in the great shopping centres would find this restriction on her physical liberty a blessed relief.   Her health would improve, doctor's bills be spared, and home-work benefit.   For the ' family,' so stoutly defended by liberal sentiment, hardly exists for these mechanically restless, half-useless indi-viduals, living in a no-man's-land half way between the extravagances of chivalry and a new economic era.

The same observations apply to the massing of people in the great cities for work.   The competitive system makes this insane clustering at a centre of exchange, and the lengthening of the lines of communication to distant suburbs, necessary. It is a great hardship for the workers, and a huge and wasteful transport system results from this barbarous lack of system and shyness where the obvious remedy of trustification and unity is concerned. People prefer to organize the necessary machinery to make this vast discomfort and waste possible, for the sake of a word.

As to foreign travel, the ' tourist ' is obviously the greatest absurdity. The masses of people who cross the three thousand miles of the Atlantic every year to do— what ? To gape at the place where a very uninteresting blackguard divorced his sixth wife three hundred years ago, or perspired at his favourite game of tennis, until he became too fat, when his courtiers also had to stop playing ; when in their own country there must be, alive and quite ready to be looked at, men who have divorced more women than Henry VIII ever dreamt it was possible to do, and perspire as much.

As to the quantities of tourists who yearly cross the Channel into England or France, attracted by a cheap holiday, were that holiday not attractively cheap and easy they would not miss the week or two spent in gazing at people who are in every respect very like themselves (and more so every day), only that they say *Oui* instead of *Yes*, which is peculiar, but must pall in the long run. Guide-book in hand, they examine some quite commonplace building where some event of no more intrinsic interest than a football match, or, at the most, a bungalow murder, happened. They are not stirred in any way—how could they be, as they have not the least idea what the event in question signified historically in any case, and the building is usually so dull that it can never have caused any emotion since it was built ? Therefore they have gained nothing in experience, only *displaced* themselves for nothing, to the great inconvenience of everybody, except an occasional hotel-keeper.

All this energy, such as it is, that has to be worked off in physical displacement could be directed into more interesting channels. They say the imaginative qualities so noticeable in the russian peasant is due to the fact that for the winter months he has spent a great part of his time, owing to the severity of the weather, lying on top of his stove. Willy nilly, he was forced to reflect a little bit about things in general. The conditions in his case were needlessly severe and forbidding.

A scholar or a student of history or architecture, or a trained painter, or a parson is interested in cathedrals, for instance : nobody else is ; and when he looks at them he feels overcome with boredom, self-reproach, hatred, sleepiness, fatigue, thirst, and absent-mindedness. But with many people with a specialist claim on their interest some of these symptoms occur, either because their technical specialization has imperfectly overcome the old slothful, unimaginative Adam, symbolized by the deep chasm of their yawning mouths : or else because the cathedral is really in no way remarkable.

Or let us take the language attraction. That, again, is really only a matter for students of language. The little sensation caused at first by seeing a lot of ' foreigners ' talking together a jargon closed to you, in the very home and fastness of these ' foreigners,' is not one that it would be a very serious thing to be deprived of. These *differences* are primitive things, that in future will be of interest to the curious student while they last. But they are, as it were, a sign of backwardness. They no longer represent either a living culture or political power. The nations of Europe are helplessly laid out side by side, each talking ' its own language ' like so many indian tribes in reservations or reductions. It is even rather indecent, to-day, to take an interest in them, or intrude on their decadence and distress. Some scientific motive—such as takes a man to the quarters of the Plains Indians or the Lilloetts—is respectable. But the tripper should not be encouraged. The French, those perfect traditional hosts, will soon hardly possess the necessary machinery to entertain on such a scale, at all hours and in all places. All the european nations have recently suffered great losses, and their privacy should be respected. If they retain their local customs and speech, it will be on sufferance and as a concession to a colony. This sad condition should no longer be exploited ; especially there should be more reserve on the part of the different tribes concerned. Visitors are not wanted.

So this matter can be left in this way : our *primitive*

characteristics (our *Oui-ouis* and *Jah-jahs*) should no longer
be made a peep-show of. For a serious student that is
another matter. But idle curiosity where these *peculiarities* are concerned (these *afflictions*, really, as they are
to-day) cannot be justified.

That in the old days the cosmopolitan aristocrat naturally travelled about, we know. But we are not, most of
us, cosmopolitan aristocrats, and most of us do not know
the elements even of any speech except our own. These
cosmopolitan aristocrats were *at home* everywhere, for
there were other cosmopolitan aristocrats everywhere with
whom they could consort. They were the ' good Europeans.' But there are no ' Europeans ' to-day.

But the real approach to the question of ' foreign travel '
and cheap-tourism is that the mass of people *do not want
it.* The remnants of the nineteenth-century Middle Classes
who have any money to spare enjoy this pastime. But
the great majority of the english or french population, for
instance, would not hesitate a moment between a free
fortnight at one of their own seaside places and a fortnight
' abroad.' The latter proposition fills them with uneasi-
ness, dislike of what is strange, remote, unrestful, out of
their routine. It is only the perpetual thrusting under
their noses of advertisements recommending cheap foreign
travel that ever induces some of them to take this disagreeable step. It is, in short, an excellent example of
how the precious liberty of free movement is not a ' liberty '
at all. But so long as people have to get money by competitive enterprise and advertisement, so long will people
be expensively dragged hither and thither, in motor-
coaches, trains, steamboats, and omnibuses, and have the
idea imposed on them that they are enjoying this displacement. Most people are born *molluscs* (there is no offence
in saying it, for it is quite true), and they are made into
sham students, artists, cosmopolitan aristocrats, globe-
trotters, philosophers, poets, mountaineers, buccaneers,
and gypsies.

PART IV

VULGARIZATION AND POLITICAL DECAY

'*Competition, that prodigious social force of which
the action is measured by political economy, is of
relatively modern origin. Just as the conceptions
of human brotherhood and (in a less degree) of
human equality appear to have passed beyond the
limits of the primitive communities and to have
spread themselves in a highly diluted form over the
mass of mankind, so, on the other hand, competition
in exchange seems to be the universal belligerency of
the ancient world which has penetrated into the
interior of the ancient groups of blood-relations.*'

Rede Lecture, 1875. H. S. Maine.

'*As we grow to have clearer sight of the ideas of right
reason . . . and to make the State more and more
the expression of our best self, which is not manifold,
and vulgar, and unstable, and contentious, and ever-
varying, but one, and noble, and secure, and peaceful,
and the same for all mankind—with what aversion
shall we not* then *regard anarchy . . . when there
is so much that is so precious which it will en-
danger!*'

Culture and Anarchy. Matthew Arnold.

'*In our common notions and talk about freedom, we
eminently show our idolatry of machinery. Our
prevalent notion is . . . that it is a most happy and
important thing for a man merely to be able to do as
he likes. On what he is to do when he is thus free to
do as he likes, we do not lay so much stress.*'

Ibid. Arnold.

'*But with the progress that science has made . . . we
cannot afford to allow Machiavelli to return. One
or two more such returns on a large scale will, under*

existing conditions, mean the end of white civilization, and possibly of the white race itself.'
Democracy and Leadership.   Irving Babbitt.

' He hath raked the truth too far, in many things,
which makes him smell as he doth in the nostrils of
ignorant people ; whereas the better experienced know
it is the wholesome savour of the court, especially
where the king is of the first head.
' He would have men prepared to encounter the
worst of men ; and therefore he resembles him to a
man driving a flock of sheep, into a corner, and did
there take out their teeth, and instead, gave each of
them a set of wolves teeth ; so that, whereas one
shepherd was able to drive a whole flock, now each
sheep had need of a particular shepherd, and all little
enough.'
The vindication of that hero of political learning, Nicholas Machiavel.   James Bocvey.

CHAPTER 1

THE COMPETITION OF THE
' SMALL MAN '

GIANT Trusts and Cartels everywhere, at the present time, as they coalesce, approach the economic pattern of the socialist state. Whether the trust-king is a highly salaried servant (as Lenin said he should be, if proved to be the most efficient organizer), or a capitalist magnate (when these chiefs become fewer and fewer, as they do every day), does not particularly matter. The enemy of unification to-day is everywhere the ' small man.' The irrepressible village *kulak* is the typical russian ' small man '; in the West the small retailer and middle-man. This small representative of the remnant of ' free ' barter and ' open competition ' in our society is the real obstacle to a radical reform of human conditions. It is he who is rightly the *bourgeois* of the revolutionary tract.

The little shopkeeper has never been anybody's darling until to-day. In the past he always has been an object of contempt and usually of derision : the little, ' money-grubbing,' mean, smooth, soft-living, over-practical pro-duct, to-day he represents ' the old order.' The ' big business ' celebrated in fiction by Zola in *Au Bonheur des Dames*—crushing out of existence the small rival in its neighbourhood—did not, in fact, do anything of the sort. Vandervelde's statistics point quite the other way. There are every day more, not less, small businesses. Their tenure is a precarious one, certainly. But they continue to spring up impassibly. They live a harassed, uncom-fortable life ; but that does not seem to discourage them from irrepressibly springing up everywhere. As soon as one has gone bankrupt, two more take its place.

It is difficult to regard the small grocer as a very sym-pathetic figure, nevertheless. He is ' human,' it is true, where the salaried slave of the big ' business,' or the bureaucrat, is ' a machine.' Whether he is ' too human,' or not quite ' human ' enough, is a dispute into which we need not enter. At all events, his humanity is of the sort

that could be spared. But if that is true of him concretely, it is very much more the case when you consider
the system that he represents. It is not even accurate to
compare him with the master craftsman, or the small
creative worker who was his own master, of the Middle
Ages. He is *toto cælo* different to that admirable figure.

What the small tradesman really represents, where his
own personal occupation is concerned, is a more recent
principle than that, or in the spiritual context of our lives
a much older one. He is the emblem of the ' small **man.**'
with his small, lawless, egotistic competition, throughout
the ages. What he competes with is not his own **kind,**
but a power superior to his own and an intelligence superior
to his own. It is the upper crust of *nature* and chaos, as
it were, *organized.* He is protected in his lawless war by
that very ' civilization ' against which he struggles, and
which he himself would have been powerless to invent.

What is it that has always brought to nothing the work
of the creative mind, and made history an interminable
obstacle race for the mind which would otherwise be free ?
Precisely the competitive jealousy of this famous ' small
man,' with his famous ' independence '—snobbish, ' ambitious,' very grasping, considering himself better than the
plain workman ; making an unreal, small *middle-world,*
or no-man's-land, from which his vanity and uselessness
can bite at and checkmate those above him, and exploit
those beneath him. He is not only the enemy of a unification of the intelligent forces of the world ; he is the symbol
of what has always held back our race, held up all that
challenged his self-sufficiency and small conservatism. It
is his small superiority, egotistic ' independence,' smugness,
assertiveness, and uselessness, preying (above and below
him) on anything that was creative, that has been the cause
of human society losing, not gaining, by its efforts. His
' little touch of nature ' does not compensate for that
record !

We do not any longer want the competition of the ' small
man.' The human race, anxious to be free to create, has
had enough of this precious ' small man ' and his small ways
for ever ! His clamour for ' freedom ' is for *his* freedom,
not ours : freedom to live on the creative work around
him, to interfere with his betters with the power he gets

from cheating his betters underneath : for he has ' betters ' underneath him, and ' betters ' above him. To be fair to him, this may not precisely be his situation to-day, very luckily for every one concerned. But he and his ' freedom,' and his small competitive instincts, symbolize an entire and very widely distributed human type, which (whatever else it does, or does not, do) the great unified machine will get rid of for us.

It is rather as a unit of spiritual life, than as a unit of economic life, that I have been considering the ' small man.' But the one is not independent of the other. In every phase of life, social, economic, or political, there is the ' small man,' with his small, hard ' independence ' that nothing about him justifies, with his small competitive push, entrenched in the forms and conventions of polite life, calling himself ' civilization,' and defying the elements on the one hand, and the human mind (that has created him for its sins) on the other.

CHAPTER II

THE DEMOCRATIC *EDUCATIONALIST STATE*

IN the democratic western countries so-called capitalism leads a saturnalia of ' freedom,' like a bastard brother of reform.   With its *What the Public Wants* doctrine it enervates the populations.   It is now, when crushed with debt and threatened with every form of danger, without and within, that the western countries are led in the great cities into a paroxysm of display and luxury. And the papers that call them to it with their massed advertisements admonish them on another page, which is quite safe, because they know it will be unheeded.

It is not that, however, that need occupy us, for this contrast between our present growing beggardom and rapidly declining assets and our increasing splendour of appointment and personal display is a commonplace of our time.   It is rather where the great system of *What the Public Wants* apes the system that is destined to supersede it, in all that wide, scientized field of ' progressive ' vulgarization, social debate, social change arriving in half measures and strangely arbitrary compromises, that it is necessary to scrutinize it.   And, to start with, the whole principle of vulgarization, on which we have already touched, must be briefly related to the ground we have already covered.

Education consists, of course, of a decade of soaking in certain beliefs and conventions.   The jesuits considered that the first six years of life sufficed.   However this may be, it is of course a soul, and not knowledge, that education signifies.   It is character-stimulus, and actually the reverse of mind-stimulus, that popular education sets out to provide.

All education begins with reading and writing : and it is principally by means of reading that the ' education ' gradually comes.   At a certain age the work is done. not where the jesuit fixed it, for character only, but somewhere in the first years of adult life,   It is rarely afterwards that the hard-working clerk, engineer, doctor, or mechanic has leisure or opportunity to supplement this basis of teaching. But even if he has, he seldom has the energy, on his own account, to modify what has been imposed on him. The contemporary European or American is a part of a broadcasting set, a necessary part of its machinery. Or he is gradually made into a newspaper-reader, it could be said, rather than a citizen.

The working of the ' democratic ' electoral system is of course as follows. A person is trained up stringently to certain opinions ; then he is given a vote, called a ' free ' and fully enfranchised person ; then he votes (subject, of course, to new and stringent orders from the press, where occasionally his mentor commands him to vote contrary to what he has been taught) strictly in accordance with his training. His support for everything that he has been taught to support can be practically guaranteed. Hence, of course, the vote of the free citizen is a farce : education and suggestion, the imposition of the will of the ruler through the press and other publicity channels, cancelling it. So ' democratic ' government is far more effective than subjugation by physical conquest.

In a very small percentage of cases better brains and good social opportunities enable a person to extricate himself from this ideologic machine. Like a mammal growing wings, he exists thenceforth in another and freer element. But this free region is not conterminous with the arts and sciences ; and free spirits do not, as is popularly supposed, inhabit the bodies of men of science or artists. For art and science are the very material out of which the law is made. They are the suggestion ; out of them are cut the beliefs by which men are governed. And the teacher is usually as much a dupe as the learner.

So what we call conventionally the *capitalist state* is as truly an *educationalist state*.

The sporting training of the Englishman and American makes him into a fighting machine. Even his military training is disguised as sport. This Robot is manipulated by the press. By his education he has been made into an ingeniously free-looking, easy-moving, ' civilized,' gentlemanly Robot. At a word (or when sufficiently heated by a week's newspaper-suggestion), at the pressing of a button, all these hallucinated automata, with their technician-trained minds and bodies, can be released against each other.   And if a war only lasts four or five years, it is something to be thankful for : since it could easily be prolonged to a hundred years, and these machines, and new ones constantly turned out on the same pattern, would never go back on the lessons they had learnt so well, until the last man fell gallantly resisting ' the enemy.'

Within ten years England would be at war with Scotland, mad as that may sound at first sight, if the propaganda and educational channels received orders to that end.   If you believe that it would be impossible to stir up on either side of the scottish border ' race ' feeling, through ten years, by acrimonious chatter in the press, frictions, small acts of violence and reprisals, appeals to history and its old feuds, patriotism and clanism, so that in the end it culminated in war, you are certainly mistaken.   The organization of suggestion and the power of education are so perfect to-day that nothing, given a little time, is impossible.

When the vast populations of Asia have been similarly organized, athleticized, introduced to ' sport,' trained as boy-scouts and asiatic ' guides,' the same will apply to them : the Japanese being for Asia what I have said Russia and Italy are for us.

All this great power in the hands of people whose intentions were charitable, not wicked, and they would instantly make, with all the resources of modern science, a paradise of the earth !   The Utopia of the philosophers would then come true.   When the present many-sided revolution is complete and world-wide, and competition no longer exists between rival groups of exploiters, that state of affairs should be a reality.   But between then and now much water will flow under the bridges of the Thames, Seine, Spree, Danube, Manzanares, Liffey, Clyde, Tiber, and Hooghly.   And unless mankind hastens to its unification under one unique control, far too much blood will flow with it.

CHAPTER III

CAUSES OF EUROPEAN DECAY

W E have given as a capital reason for the political weakness of Europe the notion of individual freedom, as opposed to the greater solidarity of a community ' working together ' under a centralized consciousness and despotic, or at all events very powerful, control. Yet in the last chapter we have shown how illusory this ' independence ' must in practice be. But the confusion is not so real as it would seem. It is rather the *notion* of freedom than the fact of freedom that is, of course, in question : and it is just that idle pretence that is so wasteful and disorganizing. It is, in short, the aristocratic temper of the achaian Greeks extended and caricatured by vast numbers of people. The aristocratic liberties of the dominant race in a small city state applied to the whole white population of Europe has led to the *impasse* of white ' democracy.' And white, european democracy is, of course, an aristocratic notion at bottom, for it is a *race* notion : all caste, of course, of that sort originating in the fact of race.

Why Europe has never had a religion of its own (and that is naturally another great source of weakness, as weakness in ' mystery ' in the long run spells political weakness) is because of the ascendency and persistence of this secular, aristocratic, græco-roman tradition that has fixed the European in a pagan, personal, non-religious mould. Let us exaggerate the circumstances of this so as to lay bare a sort of subterranean ideologic stream whose presence is usually only revealed by a sort of misty snobbishness. The nineteenth-century John Bull, we then can say, was the proud, aristocratically minded person he was because the migratory Achaian or Dorian was of divine race, or imposed himself as such on the subject population. The heroic demi-god of the homeric saga was the distant exemplar of the ' beer-drinking Briton ' who could ' never be beat.'

It may be as well to go for a moment into the relation between class and race in the formation of the former.

The *classes* that have been parasitic on other classes have always in the past been *races*. The class-privilege has been a race-privilege. Every white man until recently has been in full possession of a race-privilege where other races of other colours were concerned, which constituted the white man as a *class*. The privilege was never developed to the extent that the achaian race-privilege of the athenian citizen, for example, was. But in a general way it formed part of the consciousness of the white man. Cleanliness was next to godliness, and whiteness was the indispensable condition of cleanliness. So to be a chosen people was to be a white people.

This class element in *race* expressed itself in the application of the term ' lady,' for instance, to the most modest citizens of the anglo-saxon race. The *lady* in *char-lady* is a race courtesy-title. It is a class-title that it was possible for her to exact on the score of *race*. This rudimentary fact very few poor whites have understood. They have been inclined to take these small but precious advantages for granted, as indicative of a *real* superiority, not one resulting, as in fact it did, from the success of the organized society to which they belonged. They have confused class with race—somewhat to their undoing.

To-day race and colour are as distinctive features as ever : and it is unlikely in the future that *race* will cease to play its part in the formation of class—as, again, many simple white people will discover to their great chagrin. But the character of our civilization, as defined by the great discoveries of modern science, with their unifying effect, must tend very rapidly not only to world-wide standardization, but to racial fusion. Or rather, this must be the consequence of the new conditions, unless this process is artificially held up, and national idiosyncrasies and differences artificially preserved and fostered, as with the jesuits in the territories they controlled in South America, each tribe locked up in its tribal district or re-duction, and friendly intercourse of any sort between the various tribes prohibited.

That most fundamental of all questions for us, namely, War and Peace, is dependent on these questions of class and race. If there were not to-day communities with an exclusive race-consciousness (with or without sacred books, and the theologic paraphernalia of race), the future of *class*, too, would be much more precarious than it in fact is. The people of the United States are or have been the nearest to an egalitarian ideal because they are the most racially mixed : this in spite of all the simple jokes to the contrary.

But even if race were abolished by intermixture, it would still be possible, of course, to get your class-factor, and with it your organized war, by way of sex, age, occupational and other categories. 'The intensity of organization is increased,' as Mr. Russell points out, ' when a man belongs to more organizations.' The more classes (of which, in their various functions, he is representative) that you can make him become regularly conscious of, the more you can control him, the more of an automaton he becomes. Thus, if a man can be made to feel himself acutely (*a*) an American ; (*b*) a young American ; (*c*) a middle-west young American ; (*d*) a ' radical and enlightened ' middle-west young American ; (*e*) a ' college-educated,' etc., etc. ; (*f*) a ' college-educated ' dentist who is an etc., etc. ; (*g*) a ' college-educated ' dentist of such-and-such a school of dentistry, etc., etc.,—the more inflexible each of these links is, the more powerful, naturally, is the chain. Or he can be locked into any of these compartments as though by magic by any one understanding the wires, in the way the jesuit studied those things.

To return to the question of the race origin of caste-feeling, the notion of the ' gentleman ' as we call it to-day is a race notion, originating in such things as roman citizenship and its universal aristocratical privileges. The most absurd as well as degrading spectacle that this notion has ever provided was when the roman citizen, in fact, was in question in the time of the Empire. All the wealth and power of the roman state passed more and more into the hands of the alien freedmen. The Roman began rapidly to die out (the custom of child-exposure contributed largely to this), and grew daily more impoverished. But the client-system kept those that remained just alive. The procedure of the allotment of food for the *sportula* of the client, and all the rest of the humiliating life of charity of the latest Romans, was carefully organized. So it came about that living as a numerous class of decayed gentility in the midst of the luxury and wealth of imperial Rome were most of the true Romans.   One emperor shipped a hundred thousand or so of them off to some colony.   But there were still a good number of these proud, ragged remnants of republican Rome (or of cultivators of the surrounding land of original italian stock driven to the city by the introduction of foreign slave-labour on the *latifundia*) remaining.

Class always takes with it the idea of race, then, and of some distant or recent conquest.   How the notion of political personal freedom has spelt *weakness* in the end for Europe (so that it is not at all too much to say that that is the principal cause of its present decline) is that it is by way of this notion, through this gate, that all the disintegrating tendencies have entered.

CHAPTER IV

THE MISUSE OF THE INTELLECT

THE great men of science of China, Babylon, or Egypt thought their thoughts and proceeded with their researches in spite of an entire absence of such conditions as makes Einstein's name, ten days after an astronomical success, broadcast all over the world, and his relativity theory painfully popularized for the toiling, tired, unleisured millions. What's in a name, if a workman is allowed to work ? All any true scientist or true artist asks is to be given the opportunity, without interference, indifferent to glory, to *work*. And it is just the popularization and vulgarizing of art that is responsible for the innumerable swarms of dilettante competitors who make of every art a trifling pastime, so that it is impossible for the rest of the world to regard that occupation as a serious one, seeing into what sort of hands it has fallen. So it would certainly be the redemption of art, and it would no doubt have the effect of protecting, and actually of encouraging, science, if they were both removed from the wide, superficial, ' democratic ' (that is, aristocratic) playground, and reinstated as a mystery or a craft.

You could not get a better example than this of how much of the intelligent organization of the soviet authorities, because of its novelty and challenge to the old playful ' democratic' notions of the European, is misrepresented. They have taken in this respect the wisest and sanest step where both art and science are concerned, in curtailing the impossible freedom of art, and discouraging the people from gaping incessantly for new and disturbing novelties of science. For this they are blamed—by the playboy of the western world, not by the true man of science or the artist.

The ' freedom ' of the last century or so has from any point of view been of a very remarkable nature. There was something about it that should have aroused misgivings in those, sometimes with too little measure or reticence, naïvely benefiting by it. For it was surely, from their point of view, 'too good to be true.' It certainly contrasted very strongly with the conditions under which people lived at the time of the religious struggles of the Renaissance and Reformation.

The opinions and discoveries of the most ' advanced ' of mankind, of the learned and splendid few, were thus made available for a mass of people (whom these opinions and discoveries reached in a garbled, sensational, and often highly misleading form) who were themselves, as they still are to-day in mental equipment and outlook, savages— only, savages degenerating rapidly under the influence of their own ' civilization.'   They very naturally made of this mass of (for them, unequipped and unprepared) highly exciting, dangerous, and difficult matter what they had formerly made of the teaching of Christ.   These theoretic, purely scientific, and aloof researches they transformed into some sort of weapon or tool at once, to get at food with, or sanctimoniously rip up their neighbour : the most disinterested idea became, in their hands, a pawn in the practical system of their life.   As a doctor's scalpel might make an excellent dagger, or the axle of a car a good enough club, so most of these discoveries suggested some violent and destructive action to them, just as in Christ's teaching they found nothing but a sanction to kill and oppress.

How was it, under these circumstances, that any government in its senses allowed this orgy of revolutionary heresy to be published and broadcast ?   Evidently because they were either too weak, too ill instructed, or too heretical themselves to stop it.

It is a safe prediction, and one that it is by no means to the discredit of the russian rulers to make, that the time will soon come when a copy of Tolstoi's *War and Peace* will be read by the person possessing it, if at all, *en cachette*; in the same way that a pornographic book is read to-day.   It was a book written to rouse the consciousness of the oppressed : and from that point of view, when all that can be done for the moment has been done for that oppressed humanity, there is no further point in mechanically exciting it.   The great beauty and truth of the book in other respects make it natural to preserve it, for the interest of those whose minds are not ignorantly inflammable, and whom it would not pervert to lawless actions. It should only be placed in the hands of those who are in a position to understand it. The people who read such books, after all, should be the rulers.

CHAPTER V

NIETZSCHE AS A VULGARIZER

WHEN we are considering nineteenth-century vulgarization, Frederick Nietzsche at once comes to the mind as the archetype of the vulgarizer. His particular vulgarization was the most flagrant of all, and certainly the strangest. For what he set out to vulgarize, the notion of aristocracy and power, was surely the most absurd, illogical, and meaningless thing that he could have chosen for that purpose.

Nietzsche's lifetime saw the beginning of the heyday of the literary vulgarizer. By what elliptical and peculiar roads this vociferous showman arrived at his ends would be in itself a very interesting study. And the society in the midst of which such a proceeding was encouraged would certainly lend itself to a first-class farce. However that may be, in a frenzy of poetic zeal he alternately browbeat and implored the whole world to be *aristocrats*. They were naturally enchanted. Such flattery was unique in their experience of such popular events. Nietzsche, got up to represent a Polish nobleman, with a *berserker* wildness in his eye, advertised the secrets of the world, and sold little vials containing blue ink, which he represented as drops of authentic blue blood, to the delighted populace. They went away, swallowed his prescriptions, and felt very noble almost at once.

If we consider for a few moments some of the characteristic phases of this great vulgarizer's thought, we shall get in touch with the working of the most paradoxical nineteenth-century system.

The intellectual opportunism of Nietzsche associated him with the ' pragmatism ' of the psychologists and philosophers who immediately succeeded him. The hollow, ' stagey,' mephistophelean laughter of his *Joyful Wisdom* was directed principally against ' truth.' He would say, for instance :—

We now know something too well, we men of knowledge : oh, how well we are learning to forget and *not* know as artists !

120

And as to our future, we are not likely to be found again in the tracks of those Egyptian youths who at night make the temples unsafe, embrace statues, and would fain unveil, uncover, and put in clear light everything which for good reasons is kept concealed.   No, we have got disgusted with this bad taste, this will to truth, to ' truth at all costs,' this youthful madness in the love of truth ; we are now too experienced, too serious, too joyful, too singed, too profound for that. . . . We no longer believe that truth remains truth when the veil is withdrawn from it : we have lived long enough not to believe this. At present we regard it as a matter of propriety not to be anxious either to see everything naked, or to be present at everything, or to understand and ' know ' everything. ' Is it true that the good God is everywhere present ? ' asked a little child of her mother : ' I think that is indecent '—a hint to philosophers ! (*Joyful Wisdom*.)

(Nietzsche's reproof could be addressed with some point to Freud, that more recent vulgarizer : for he located *le bon Dieu* in that very spot, and there only, which aroused the outburst of modesty that Nietzsche records.)

There you see Nietzsche not only unveiling Truth, but attempting to drug and rape her, after having, ' futurist ' fashion, made her live. For if his words mean anything, they mean that we should seek Truth by avoiding it, or flying from it. Court the Lie, and we shall find the Truth. But that is only another, and more or less (as presented in *Joyful Wisdom*) Bergson's way, as it happens. It is all extremely reminiscent of Christ's strategy of salvation and power : 'he who humbleth himself shall be exalted '—'the last shall be first,' and all those precepts that could be described as the *strategy of humility*.

So Nietzsche's ' Fly Truth and you shall find it ' is a stratagem only, taken literally. But the passage I have quoted above is a very dramatic incitement to a certain attitude ; although it is advice, needless to say, for others, and not for the philosopher himself. He had delved far enough, and anatomized, or otherwise in any case his words would have had no meaning.

Nietzsche was in fact himself, where philosophy is concerned, a sort of Christ. Under the pretence of a doctrine of *aristocracism* (with that attractive and snobbish label ARISTOCRACY) he went out into the highways and byways and collected together all the half-educated, anything but aristocratic, student and art-student population of Europe. There was no small attorney's son or small farmer's daughter who had been to a school where their parents had to pay, or had studied painting or music, who did not imagine themselves barons and baronesses, at least, on the spot. A few years after his dramatic exit from the stage he became the greatest popular success of any philosopher of modern times.

The character of his action as a philosopher, then, was not unlike that of Christ with regard to the religious heritage of the Jews. Both threw wide open the gates— Christ those of salvation, and Nietzsche those of Truth— to the ' publicans and sinners,' the ' barbarian ' strangers. And the doctrine of aristocracy arranged by Dr. Nietzsche, for Tom, Dick, and Harry, was a snobbish pill very violent in its action.

Had Nietzsche cared, in the passage quoted above, to be candid, he would perhaps have added : ' You poor little beast (how unlike my big blond one !), whoever you are, who are not fit to touch the hem of the garment of *my* goddess, Truth. So go away and amuse yourself in your characteristic way. You couldn't *stand* the truth, in any case. It 's not for the likes of you. So there 's no use in your gaping around this exclusive pavilion. *I* can hardly support her embraces. Just look what she 's done to me ! So what do you suppose is likely to happen to you ? Better make yourself scarce. No ? Very well. It doesn't matter. Here 's a permit for the holy mountain. Say the great Nietzsche gave it you—they 'll let you pass. But they don't much care who you are, as a matter of fact, any more than I do. Don't forget to look off the top—the view is splendid. Be careful not to slip ! It 's very *dangerous*. It 's terribly *high* ! Try and understand the *privilege* of such a glimpse : and remember *who* it was procured you that privilege. (*Sotto voce*) I hope the stairs are well greased ! Tra-la-la ! '

What he said instead was :—

Oh, those Greeks ! They knew how to *live* ; for that purpose it is necessary to keep bravely to the surface, the fold and the skin, to worship appearance, to believe in forms, tones, and words, in the whole Olympus of Appearance ! And are we not coming back precisely to this point, we dare-

devils of the spirit, who have scaled the highest and most
dangerous peak of contemporary thought and have looked
around us from it, have *looked down* from it !

Had Nietzsche from the first followed these instructions
himself, should we ever have heard of him ? Yet his
advice was not wholly perfidious. For it was not unlike
a miner arriving at the surface from a very deep and
uncomfortable pit, and saying, ' Ah ! how pleasant the
sun is ! Give me the good old surface of this rotten earth.
Never you go down *there* ! ' Or, if you like, it was
Descartes' advice to people ' never to read a book.'

The influence of Nietzsche was similar to that of Bergson,
James, Croce, etc. He provided a sanction and licence,
as the others did, for LIFE—the very life that he never
ceased himself to objurgate against ; the life of the second-
rate and shoddily emotional, for the person, very unfortunately, smart and rich enough to be able to regard
himself as an ' aristocrat,' a man ' beyond good and evil,'
a destroying angel and cultivated Mephistopheles. If you
read the following passage carefully it will be at once
apparent how that, with his particular method, came
to pass :—

> Oh, how repugnant to us now is pleasure, coarse, dull, drab
> pleasure, as the pleasure-seekers, our ' cultured ' classes,
> our rich and ruling classes, usually understand it ! How
> malignantly we now listen to the great holiday-hubbub with
> which ' cultured people ' and city-men at present allow
> themselves to be forced to ' spiritual enjoyment ' by art,
> books, and music, with the help of spirituous liquors ! How
> the theatrical cry of passion now pains our ear, how strange
> to our taste has all the romantic riot and sensuous bustle
> which the cultured populace love become (together with
> their aspirations after the exalted, the elevated, and the
> intricate) ! No, if we convalescents need an art at all, it
> is *another* art—a mocking, light, divinely serene, divinely
> ingenious art, which blazes up like a clear flame, into a
> cloudless heaven ! Above all, an art for artists, only for
> artists !

Many great writers (and Nietzsche was of course a very
great one) address audiences who do not exist. Nietzsche
was always addressing people who did not exist. To
address passionately and sometimes with very great wisdom

people who do not exist has this disadvantage (especially when the imaginary audience is a very large one, as was the case with Nietzsche) that there will always be a group of people who, seeing a man shouting apparently at somebody or other, and seeing nobody else in sight, will think that it is they who are being addressed. Nietzsche was sufficiently all-there to realize that this must happen. And most that is unsatisfactory in his teaching was a result of that consciousness. Nietzsche imagined a new type of human being—the Superman ; and to ' supermen ' he poured out sometimes his secret thoughts, and sometimes what he thought they ought to know of his secret thoughts. But he lived in a Utopia, and wrote in and for a Utopia, hoping to make Europe that Utopia by pretending that it was. He had a very great effect on Europe : but an opposite one to what you would have anticipated from his creed, as was only to be expected. For a message getting into the hands of the many, or of people opposite to those for whom it is destined, has usually an opposite effect to that it is intended to have by its sender. Nietzsche was much too astute not to know that this is what would probably happen to his message : and, as I have said, you are constantly aware of this consciousness.

Imagine, for a moment, the average ' pleasure-seeker ' of our ' cultured classes,' as he excellently describes a numerous class, reading the above passage. They would be very annoyed while reading about the ' pleasure-seekers of the cultured classes ' and their ' coarse, drab. and dull pleasures.' But they would have read above that after an illness you were apt to be of a much ' merrier disposition,' ' more wicked,' and ' more childish,' ' a hundred times more refined than ever before.'

They clap their hand ecstatically and ' childishly.' A HUNDRED TIMES MORE REFINED THAN EVER BEFORE ! Just think of it (though was there so much room for improvement ?) !

In the first place, every word written would be *applied to themselves*, inevitably and at once. It would be *they* who had had the illness : they who were now convalescent, and feeling so naughty and devilish. For had they not just been in a nursing home with a nervous breakdown, for a cosmetic operation, or hæmorrhoids, for a fortnight ?

Yes, it was extraordinary how well you felt after being ill!
It was almost worth it, to feel so well.

Having, with some pain, got through the part about
the 'rich and ruling classes' and their 'coarse, drab
pleasures' (and having with a gulp passed over 'spirituous
liquors'), they would arrive at WE CONVALESCENTS (by
this time they would have completely forgotten, or absorbed, the 'coarse and drab'): WE 'need another art!'
(How true! how divinely true! that's just how I feel!,
they will think.)   Then they come to MOCKING, LIGHT,
VOLATILE, DIVINELY SERENE, etc.   *Could* a better description have been found of what *they* liked, of what *they* were?
It was all so true!   'Above all, an art for artists, only for
artists!'   Were not *they* artists?   Was not Nero an
artist?   Were not *all* people of the best stamp (except
Lady This or Mrs. That, of course) artists?

So it is easy to imagine them (interrupted at this point
by the visit of a friend) going off and being more *mocking,
light, volatile, and divinely serene*, all at once, than ever
before!   With little wistful looks, a little 'sad and far-
away,' thrown in from time to time (to show that it was
in reality a *mask*—the *latest* mask, or only a crust above
plutonic fires!).

But it is in Nietzsche's Will to Power conception, the
central feature of his thought, that we get to see most fully
what it means to be a vulgarizer in such a world as his.
If we wish to understand the penalty of such a function,
it is there that we shall discover it.

Nietzsche, like his contemporary Von Hartmann, belongs
to the *Will-school*, as it might be called, of which Schopenhauer was the founder.   As such he was of course opposed
to the evolutionism of Darwin, though very much influenced by the latter's notion of a hopeless and meaningless struggle.

Nietzsche repudiated the world of positivist knowledge,
which is essentially a world of disillusion and pessimism:
and substituted for it a world of affirmation (his *Yea!*)
and of ACTION.   What he really proposed was that people
should turn their backs on the *procès* made against illusion
by the examining and cataloguing of the senses, and plunge
back again into ignorance—or the world of will and of
illusion.   Schopenhauer's pessimism was the pessimism of

thought and knowledge. Action—and the will to action —was necessarily paralysed by that. So up against thought and the intellect Nietzsche wished to raise ACTION, with all its innocent light-heartedness, ignorance, and superficiality. He was as much a believer in crude, undifferentiated. action as the behaviorists of to-day. Only, his was emotional action, where the behaviorists' is *unemotional*, i.e. ' behaviour.'

Again, really, his *will to power* was not so fundamental a doctrine with him as what could be called his *will to action*. And his will to illusion was based on the theory (advanced by Lange and many near and remote philosophic predecessors) of ' falsification.'

The difference between the lyrical strategy of Nietzsche —despairing as it was—and the strategy of defeat of the *mondain* type, was that Nietzsche saw the surplus—because, of course, he *felt* it in his own organism—left over from the darwinian ' struggle for existence.' He thought that Darwin's struggle for existence, his mechanical brand of evolutionism, was too drab, utilitarian, and spiritless a picture. There was, for him, a *margin* in this struggle (like Peirce's ' chance ') which caused it to assume more the character of a struggle for something *marginal and over and above* too—a super-something. And this he described as the Will to Power.

In this idea of a superfluity of energy, enabling the warring organism to aim beyond mere destruction—higher than equilibrium or ' balance of power '—there was a beneficent effectiveness which was spoilt by one thing, but that a very fundamental one. Before coming to this heroical decision, he had become so used to the idea of a fierce utilitarian struggle, that what he did (or suggested that other men should do) with their superfluous, creative energy, was *to go on fighting and struggling* : just as though, in short, they had not been provided with a margin for play or a superfluity of energy at all.

Any criticism of Nietzsche must rest on that point: that of his suggested employment and utilization of this superfluous energy *to go on doing the same things that we should be doing without it*. And his will requires to see this precious *something over* put to the same uses that many of the lowest of his helots would have put it to. He was so impregnated

with the pessimism of Schopenhauer, and his health was
so broken by his experiences in the Franco-Prussian War,
that he could not imagine, really, the mind doing anything
else with itself than what it did in post-darwinian or
schopenhauerian pessimism : to just go on contemplating
the horrors of existence.   And in reality the will to enjoy
was dead in Nietzsche, much as he clamoured for latin
light-heartedness.   He had plenty of Will left : only, it
was Will to struggle merely, not Will to live.   Fine artist
as he was, he passed his life in a nightmare, and was, I
think, unable to benefit by his own falsification theory.
Schopenhauer probably was a wiser man, and came to
better terms with life than Nietzsche did.

The average, worldly man does not, on the other hand,
get beyond the conception of ' the struggle for existence.'
He has no creative surplus at all.   His strategy is as much
a state of war as was Nietzsche's *will to power*.   But with
him it is a defensive war ; and he is only aggressively cunning, not in the heroic ' dangerous ' fashion suggested by
Nietzsche.   He disposes his forces very prudently and
strategically.   He is by nature what is called ' pessimistic ';
he sees nothing but *defeat*, in the sense of horror and
struggle.   This bloody struggle he is determined to subsist
in the midst of, and yet keep it at a distance.   He outwardly, like Nietzsche, has a powerfully developed ' falsification ' theory and ' will to illusion.'   Only (naturally)
he is much more successful in the use of it than Nietzsche
could be.   He is, in short, that person disliked by Nietzsche to such a great extent—the ' cynic ' against whom
he directed such eloquent invective.

Of his ' power ' complex, as the Freudian would call it,
and his bellicose dogma, I shall leave the discussion until
at a later stage I return to these questions.

CHAPTER VI

GEORGE SOREL

EORGE SOREL is an even stronger vulgarizer in some ways than Nietzsche, of whom he was a follower of sorts : he vulgarized aristocracy (as seen through the eyes of Nietzsche) for the labourer and mechanic.

George Sorel is the key to all contemporary political thought. Sorel is, or was, a highly unstable and equivocal figure. He seems composed of a crowd of warring personalities, sometimes one being in the ascendent, sometimes another, and which in any case he has not been able, or has not cared, to control. He is the arch exponent of extreme action and revolutionary violence *à l'outrance* ; but he expounds this sanguinary doctrine in manuals that often, by the changing of a few words, would equally serve the forces of traditional authority, and provide them with a twin evangel of demented and intolerant class-war.

If he must be given conventionally a ' class,' he has that chilliness that you associate more with the official class than with that of the artisan or servant. In this he is the opposite of Péguy. Yet in his criticism of the class he attacks, he displays sometimes so much fierceness and acuity that it is difficult to doubt his sincerity on such occasions. But ' sincerity ' hardly enters into the question.

George Sorel is a mercenary who is devoted to his profession—that of arms—and is willing to fight without pay, since in easy circumstances. The ' cause ' matters very little to him—the ' battle ' is everything. And yet in the midst of this detachment you have to allow for some deep, and indeed rather mysterious, sectarian passion. And intellectually he is a sensitive plate for the confused ideology of his time. He is a semitaur who sees red both ways, the bull-nature injects the human eyes with blood. He is, in brief, a symptomatic figure that it would be difficult to match.

As to his standing in the world of letters and politics (and in that as in everything else he is a fabulous hybrid, attacking himself, biting his own tail, kicking his own heroical chest, contunding his own unsynthetic flesh, and

128

showing his wounds with pride—self-inflicted, *self* in
everything) he has an enviable position. ' Sorel,' says
his English translator, Hulme, 'is one of the most remarkable writers of his time, certainly the most remarkable
socialist since Marx.' (Introduction, Eng. translation of
Réflexions sur la violence. T. E. Hulme.)

So this strangest of ' socialists ' is described ; no one
would dispute such a claim : '. . . quintessence, extré-
misme, individualité, différenciation élite, c'est du sorelisme
intégral. Par l'héroïsme, et par l'hétérogénité, M. Sorel
est le grand excitateur du monde moderne.' (*Itinéraire
d'intellectuels*. R. Johannet.)

That is the man, as he appears to many of his contemporaries, with whose ideas we are dealing. M. Johannet,
the writer I have just quoted, believes that his ideas are
ultimately of more use to reaction than to social revolution.
I do not share that view, but I think his *practical* work of
incitement to revolt must be considered apart from his
more speculative work—though it enters into that, of
course, and often causes some confusion.

M. Johannet prefers to leave Sorel as ' an enigma,' an
' insoluble problem.' ' Always enigmatic and reserved,'
he writes of him, ' a master of obsessional ideas, and
generator of the maximum of tension, always fleeting and
unstable—so he appears to us—even in the depths of his
confidences. Why ! are we dreaming after all ? The
Sorel *individualist*, then the Sorel *socialist* and *traditionalist*,
are they after all only attitudes of a curious student ?
Insoluble problem ! . . .'

' The faith in socialism,' says Le Bon (*Psychologie
politique*, quoted approvingly by Sorel), ' gives back to the
simple-hearted the hopes that the gods no longer provide,
and the illusions that science has taken away from them.'
Sorel has certainly the attitude of a lonely traveller who
has gone into the comfortable atmosphere of a rustic inn,
for whose appointments he has a superior townsman's
contempt, just to be out of the *néant* for the brief period
of his life. Once there, he seems to have been moved to
entertain and excite his simple hearers with accounts of
blood-curdling and quixotic adventures. He thought he
would supply them with the *epic* and heroic material they
had lost at the same time as they lost the comforts of

religion and their ' simple faith.'   That is the Sorel of the
Réflexions sur la violence.

Fourier, with his *papillone,* started revolutionary
thought on a course of psychological exploitation.   The
child's ' love of dirt ' (*les immondices*) was to be utilized to
get the scavenging work of the phalanstery done with the
efficiency of gusto.   Sorel would apply the *papillone*
system to humanity's noble instinct for blood and carnage ;
very different, he is at pains to point out, to the rather
despicable notion of Jaurés, by which their envy and
hatred should be exploited (*la haine créatrice,* as he called it).

Genuinely *violent*—about that there is little doubt—he
applies the nietzschean ' warlike ' idea to the crowd, with
a great deal of jugglery which it is not difficult to penetrate.
He steals the philosophy of ' war,' in short, and passes it
quickly to the ' slave ' *against* whom the romantic Nietzsche
had designed that it should be used.   But he does not at
the same time fail to abuse the ' slave ' with a few aristocratic airs that he has stolen, along with the ' war '—
especially if the ' slave ' does not snatch at his beautiful
present eagerly enough.   It is not surprising that at times
it is difficult to tell where the stolen packet has got to, and
in whose hands, at the moment, it is supposed to be.

His taunts with regard to the ' mediocrity ' of his curious
protégés never slacken.   This crowd - master and this
crowd are the most strangely assorted pair, in fact.   He
takes his revolutionary blessings to them ' whip in hand,'
with a girding pedagogic intolerance.   Coriolanus could
not be more contemptuous asking for their ' voices.'   (Only,
he has no wounds to show, although very martial and
possessing a fine patriotic vein.)   He approaches his
' proletariat ' with the airs of a missionary among ' natives,'
with an armed colonizing government behind him.   His
colleagues also feel the weight of his lash.   For example :—

The transformations that marxism has undergone illustrate
very well the theory of *mediocrity.*   The social-democratic
writers, who have pretended to interpret, apply, and extend
the doctrine of their so-called master, were men of a surprising
vulgarity . . . The great mistake of Marx was to under-
value the enormous power of mediocrity as displayed throughout history.   He did not understand that the feeling for
socialism (as he conceived it) was extremely artificial.

The production of the *hero*, and of the *heroic*, was his constant preoccupation. It is that, as M. Johannet says, that took him to catholicism. He interrogated in turn Proudhon, Marx and Isaiah, Pelloutier, in search of this illusive phantom of a past world. Only in social revolution did he see possibilities of the old grandeur and vigour. His ' proletariat ' is really the people of the ' Germania ' of Tacitus :—

> Greek christianity (he says) is very inferior to Latin christianity, every one is agreed, because it had not at its service men spiritually trained, rushing to the conquest of the profane world. The exceptional value of catholicism comes from its monastic institutions continually providing the conditions for the formation of such heroes. . . . What we know of the hebrew prophets enables us to say that the judaism of the Old Testament owes its glory to religious experience. The modern Jews only see in their religion rites analogous to those of the ancient magical superstitious cults. (*La ruine du monde antique.*)

To the Bible Sorel constantly points—but of course to the Old Testament, not the New. He tells the world of the universities and the *bourgeoisie* that if they would turn to that admirably savage and moral book they would once more become sublime by dipping into that fiery source. Like Cromwell (*His Highness' speech* to the Parliament in the Painted Chamber, at their dissolution upon Monday, Jan. 22, 1654-5), he might have pointed to such passages of an invigorating description as are to be found in the Bible :—

> 1. Who is this that cometh from Edom, with dyed garments from Bozrah ? this that is glorious in his apparel, travelling in the greatness of his strength ? I that speak in righteousness, mighty to save.
> 2. Wherefore art thou red in thy apparel, and thy garments like him that treadeth in the wine-fat ?
> 8. I have trodden the wine-press alone ; and of the people there was none with me ; for I will tread them in mine anger, and trample them in my fury ; and their blood shall be sprinkled upon my garments, and I will stain all my raiment.
> 4. For the day of vengeance is in mine heart, and the year of my redeemed is come.
> 6. And I will tread down the people in mine anger, and make them drunk in my fury. (*Isaiah* lxiii.)

It will be seen that the gaudy red figure is not without its sublimity : that action is his passion if not his element (perhaps his exoticism, as it is a woman's) : and that such a man would not be likely to have great sympathy with Kautsky and his views.   The tearing of men's hearts out of their bodies, and the stewing of their eyeballs in the gravy of their bowels, or the stamping on the pulp of their entrails and making a Burgundy of their blood, or making a hole in their abdomen and winding their entrails round a tree, as Brian Boru did to celebrate his triumph, is not the type of action that appeals to me most, for reasons already set forth.   I found myself in the blood-bath of the Great War, and in that situation reflected on the vanity of violence.   So that side of Sorel seems to me too literary. But all the emotional and ' heroic ' section of Sorel is deeply romantic, and by that I understand untrue.   A truer part of him, as I see it, you get in his analysis of progress and ideas about ' class.'

PART V

'NATURES' AND 'PUPPETS'

'"*Süsse Puppe!*" *war in solchen Fällen sein Lieblingswort, so wie der Ausdruck* "*Es ist eine Natur!*" *in Goethe's Munde für ein bedeutendes Lob galt.*'
Goethe aus näherm persönlichem Umgange
dargestellt. **J. D. Falk.**

'*L'intelligence est autre chose que la Liberté; l'Amour et l'Art, autre chose que la Liberté : la Société et la Justice . . . autre chose que la Liberté.*'
De la capacité politique des classes ouvrières.
Proudhon.

'*It is better for a nation . . . to be free than to be sober. If the choice has to be made, and if there is any real connection between Democracy and liberty, it is better to remain a nation capable of displaying the virtues of a nation than even to be free.*'
Popular Government. **H. S. Maine.**

'*(There are) reasons for thinking that the love for change which in our day is commonly supposed to be overpowering, and the capacity for it which is vulgarly assumed to be infinite, are . . . limited to a very narrow sphere of human action, that which we call politics . . . men do alter their habits, but within narrow limits, and almost always with more or less of reluctance and pain . . . most of their habits have been learned by the race to which they belong through long experience, and probably after much suffering. A man cannot safely eat or drink, or go downstairs, or cross a street, unless he be guided and protected by habits which are the long result of time.*'
Ibid., **Maine.**

' There is written on the turrets of the city of Luca in great characters at this day, the word LIBERTAS; yet no man can thence infer that a particular man has more Liberty, or immunity from the service of the commonwealth, there than in Constantinople. Whether a commonwealth be monarchical or popular, the freedom is still the same.'

Leviathan, chap. xxi.   Hobbes.

CHAPTER 1

WHAT THE PUPPETS WANT

OUR problem is, no doubt, ' to perfect a larva,' but not, as that statement suggests, the larva ' Mankind,' the whole of that dense abstraction. The system of ' breeding horses for speed ' is a far better one. That is no doubt the solution. But the slowness, sloth, and commonness of the stock of *Homo stultus* would still be there when the sub-species, or the super-species, had been bred : though it would no longer be a matter of despairing concern to the Professor Richets of the future. There would be two species, there would be two worlds. There would not be the lively competition, I believe, for entrance to the *upper* world, and its rigours, that you might suppose. On the contrary, the under world, the relaxed and animal one of *l'homme sensuel*, would be the favourite, probably.

To-day there are, in fact, two species and two worlds, which incessantly interfere with each other, checkmate each other, are eternally at cross purposes. They *speak the same language* (in that they answer to Professor Richet's ideal of the universal tongue), but they do not understand each other.

Goethe had a jargon of his own for referring to these two species whose existence he perfectly recognized. He divided people into *Puppets* and *Natures*. He said the majority of people were machines, playing a part. When he wished to express admiration for a man, he would say about him, ' He is *a nature*.' This division into *natural* men and *mechanical* men (which Goethe's idiom amounts to) answers to the solution advocated in this essay. And to-day there is an absurd war between the ' puppets ' and the ' natures,' the machines and the men. And owing to the development of machinery, the pressure on the ' natures ' increases. We are *all* slipping back into machinery, because we *all* have tried to be free. And what is absurd about this situation is that so few people even desire to be free in reality.

The ideal of obedience conceived by the jesuits, so that, in their words, ' a member of their order should regard

himself as a corpse, to be moved here or there' at the
absolute discretion of the superior, has often been described
as an 'inhuman' one. But is it 'inhuman'? For is it
not what most people desire, to be dolls of that sort ; to
be looked after, disciplined into insensitiveness, spared
from suffering by insensibility and blind dependence on a
will superior to their own ?

'The more accentuated the complexity of forms or
functions becomes, the more startling the inequality,' Professor Richet remarks in his chapter on inequality. 'If
two pebbles are always dissimilar, how much more two
leaves, and, with still more cause, two ants.' How will
it be in the case of two men ? To accept and to organize
these differences is the solution of ills of which Professor
Richet speaks. And Professor Richet's classification
would no doubt serve : 'A moment's reflection will convince us that men can only be classified according to their
merits. On the one hand, those who are industrious,
upright, brave, and intelligent; on the other, those who
are lazy, dishonest, cowardly, and stupid.' That would
of course not be the way to put it, for the lazy, stupid,
and dishonest cowards would show themselves both industrious and brave, perhaps, in opposing this settlement.

A popular book of gossipy predictions that has recently
appeared, called *The Future*, will provide us with a few
further pictures of 'Mankind' from the point of view of
science. Its author, Professor Low, has the necessary
scholastic quarterings, F.C.S., F.R.C.S., etc., and is a
member of the Council of Patentees. His heart is in a
different place to Professor Richet's. In the future, he
says, 'boxers, footballers, and others who rely mainly
upon their strength for a living will be regarded as "throw
outs" of low mental capacity.' ('Money can to-day be
guaranteed for a concourse of athletes, but not for the
maintenance of a hospital.' In the future men will be
more sensible.)

The optimism of this writer about the future is at times
a little oppressive (he goes into so much detail). But his
scorn of the present 'Mankind' leaves nothing to be
desired :—

   Imagine a really *intelligent*, thoughtful man—and future
education will make men thoughtful—kicking a ball about in

a field for a living! At present one of the most popular alleged amusements is dancing. When considering this it can only be agreed that it is fortunate that the planet to which people are confined by ignorance does not contain any beings of high mentality. Imagine a really intelligent person—one who had solved the electrical problems of life, who really understood planetary movement and the actual appearance of babies into the world—suddenly entering a hot, smelly room where a nigger band shrieked and groaned the latest jazz tunes to a crowd of dancers of all ages, and in all stages of intoxication, the soulless gaiety perhaps being enhanced by paper carnival hats! They would be regarded as interesting specimens, like performing mice, and efforts would be made to explain the phenomenon. Hysteria—result of peculiar breeding—local anæsthesia—very sad!

Thus this young professor : as Descartes strolled among the inhabitants of Amsterdam as though they had been the trees of a wood, so this contemporary representative of advanced thought regards his kind, surprised at one of their characteristic occupations as performing mice. ' Human life appears to depend to a large extent on some superimposed rhythm. People are like leaves agitated by the breeze ; when the wind stops the leaf falls into rest, but does not appear to alter. The heart, lungs, eyes, and feeding intervals are all periodic happenings or modulations of some function of time.' So dancing can be a ' great relief,' a ' dope.' But this popular scientific view of the moment could be extended to everything : indeed, science is extending it, in the sense that many psychologists of the *tester* type recommend orchestras in factories.

It is certain, I think, that by far the greater part of people ask nothing better than to be ' performing mice.' And (as has already been said) they do not mind having their tails cut off by a Dr. Weismann, as Mr. Shaw thinks they do. Plato, ridiculing the mystery-poets in the *Phædrus*, says : ' What better recompense can they give to virtue than an eternity of intoxication ? ' But an eternity of intoxication is what ' the performing mice,' or, if you prefer Goethe's word, ' the puppets,' want.

When Plutarch's wife is mourning the death of her daughter, he recommends her to go and get consolation from the Dionysia. That was the advice of a kind and excellent husband. The philosopher who does not require this rhythm, recommending his own diet, the ecstasy obtained in ' the recollection of that which he has seen in a former existence with God,' is unreasonable enough.   Is that sensible advice to give to a performing mouse ?

The tone of studied contempt on the one hand, or despairing abuse on the other, for *Homo sapiens*, is unmerited probably.   It is a mistake arising from the ' democratic standards from which the subject is approached.   There is nothing contemptible about an intoxicated man (if it is nothing more than a bookful of words or a roomful of notes that he has got drunk on).   A dancing-mouse, the little favourite of Mr. Yerkes, performs its function and keeps Mr. Yerkes amused.   A corpse is even not a *contemptible* thing.   (' There 's a good deal to be said for being dead,' etc.)   It is the tone of indignation or of pedagogic displeasure that is the fault with the attitude of science towards man.   Either rage, disgust, misanthropy, or the scorn of a public examiner is displayed.   The attitude should surely be more truly scientific than that to give promise of effectiveness.   There should be no unkindness or disgust.   But all these tones are adopted by a certain class of men who from no point of view have very much right to them.

The differentiation of mankind into two rigorously separated worlds would not be on the old ' class ' lines at all, to begin with.   It would be like a deep racial difference, not a superficial ' class ' difference.   This would entirely remove the sting of ' inferiority' and the usual causes of complaint.   A beaver does not compare itself with a walrus or an antelope.   There is no ' upper ' and ' lower ' between a cat and a dog.   So it would be with the new species of men.

Under the aristocratic or feudal régime there were two worlds of thought, with amusements and so on adapted to the training and habits of these two communities living side by side.   The arrangements were at no time perfect ; they were always on a social rather than an intellectual basis, the small world of the european ' upper class' being merely a better washed, and scented, powdered, and laced, replica of the animal standard from which it had merely snobbishly removed itself.   There still were certain banalities from which this segregation protected the fortunate few.

This *aristocratic* separation of classes on the old bad model was wounding to the susceptibilities of those who were not fortunate enough, as they thought, to be born into this select and brilliant world. This was because the separation was artificial, in the sense that it reposed on the heredity principle and accident, that it was conducted and upheld (naturally) in an insolent and unintelligent spirit, and because it too plainly reproduced (in a sumptuous form) the less fortunate state—the ' third estate '—with which it was contrasted. This ' top-dog ' did all the things, with an ostentatious relish, that the poor, envious under-dog, squinting jealously at him from his kennel, would like to do. The aristocrat pretended to be ' of another clay ' to the proletarian : but the proletarian knew better. He knew that he was exactly of the same clay as himself. There was no spiritual or intellectual chasm—only a rather dirty little social ditch.

Now, instead of a separation in which a small group of people gets the upper hand, the ' power ' separates itself, builds a fence round itself, and proceeds to do with an extreme monotony, and usually without much taste or intelligence, all the animally pleasant things that all those left out in the cold, down in the basement or out in the slums, would like to do, let us imagine a separation not the result of a skin-deep ' power,' or of social advantage, but something like a *biological* separating-out of the chaff from the grain. Or to put it in another way : if, of two men, one wishes to go and play cricket, and the other wishes to go to a shed in his garden, where he has fitted up a small laboratory, and spend the day in research, neither one envies the other : they both recognize that nature has turned them out so differently that what amuses the one does not amuse the other. ' It takes all sorts to make a world,' they would no doubt both remark, if discussing it. All would be well, and harmony would reign between them.

If, on the other hand, there were two men, both of whom were passionately fond of cricket. If one, by cheating the other in business, or by arming himself and robbing the other, became extremely wealthy, and then proceeded to lay out a beautiful cricket ground, to have golden stumps manufactured, a lovely bat with a big diamond on the top, and laced pads, and left a hole in the fence so that the poor man, at whose expense all this luxury was built up, could peer at him playing the favourite game of both (not especially well, perhaps) : then we can at once understand that a great deal of animosity must result.

Such a separation as would be obtained by an examination system instead of heredity, perhaps ; or such a separation as the instinctive growth and differentiation of another type of man, heredity serving a biologic and not a social end : that is one solution of the present difficulty. There would be no stigma attached to a devotional adherence to the routine of the animal life. *L'homme moyen sensuel* would cheerfully, or 'cheerily,' confess that all 'highbrow' matters he had from the cradle disliked, and would disappear round the corner to the local bridge-club with cheery words on his honest lips, ejaculating contentedly, 'It takes all sorts to make a world.' And angry professors would not be allowed to call him *Homo stultus*. He, as much as the more creative type of person, would be *Homo sapiens*. It would be the Professor who would be convicted of *stupidity* then, if he called *stultus* after this well-satisfied, ' good-natured, unambitious ' man.

It is not by any means as an aspirant for the highest biologic honours that I am writing. But the scorn of the man of science and the rage of the philosopher have to be met. They cannot much longer be neglected, or resisted, rather—for they are now an integral part of the great system of *What the Public Wants*. As they originally appear in the speculative brain or superbly trained eye, they must be allowed some foundation in the common observation of all of us. Although personally unambitious, I am not indifferent to the interests I serve. It is in that spirit that I set out to consider how *What the Puppets Want* might differ from *What the Public Wants*, and to see if the growing hatred and contempt could not be lifted a little from these very ticklish relations. The threatening attitude of Mr. Shaw and Mr. Russell to the Yahoo tallies too much, I thought, with the suave malignity of the publicist.

Another way of regarding it would be this. The ferocious misanthropy of the adepts of *What the Public Wants* is a very compromising thing for the intelligence to be associated with. The puppets Ozymandias and Semiramis, as conceived by Mr. Shaw, have to be destroyed. But those puppets are a libel on the Public—or they would be if it were intended to identify them, and that seems Mr. Shaw's intention. In reality they are another genus of puppets, a genus of homicidal puppets, sure enough. And they bear a strange resemblance to the misanthropic masters of the doctrine of *What the Public Wants.*

CHAPTER II

'LIBERTY' IS DEAD

IT is a belief that has never been formulated, but it is at the root of a great deal of behaviour to-day, that *freedom and irresponsibility are invariably commutative terms.* The first object of a person with an ambition to be free, and yet possessing none of the means exterior to himself or herself (such as money, conspicuous ability, or power) to obtain freedom, is to avoid responsibility.

Absence of responsibility, an automatic and stereotyped rhythm, is what men most desire for themselves. All struggle has for its end relief or repose. A rhythmic movement is restful : but consciousness and possession of the self is not compatible with a set rhythm. All the libertarian cries of a century ago were based on unreal premises, and impulses that are not natural to, and cannot be sustained by, the majority of men. Luxury and repose are what most men undeniably desire. They would like to be as much at rest as if they were dead, and as active and 'alive' as passivity will allow. When action is required of them they prefer that it should be 'exciting' and sensational, or else that it should have a strongly defined, easily grasped, mechanical rhythm. The essential fatigue and poorness of most organisms, and the minds that serve them, is displayed in nothing so much as in this *sensationalism.* Every low-grade animal is to some extent born sadic, for that is the only way he can *feel.* Sensationalism and sadism are twins. The only effort that is acceptable to many people is violent, excessive, and spasmodic action. 'Simple' delights, as we call them, appear to be the privileged possession of the chosen ones of nature.

All the old libertarian claim was for a liberty involving the opposite of all this. Consciousness and responsibility are *prose* as contrasted with the *poetry* of passive, more or less ecstatic, rhythmic, mechanical life. There is, therefore, the intoxicated dance of puppets, and besides that the few *natures,* as they were called by Goethe; moving unrhythmically, or according to a rhythm of their own, which is the same thing. The conventional libertarianism of a

142

century ago envisaged this latter form of personal freedom, this *prose of the individual,* as it could be called. The libertarianism of to-day rejects with horror the idea of that 'independence.' In place of this *prose of the individual* it desires the *poetry of the mass* ; in place of the *rhythm of the person,* the *rhythm of the crowd.*

The extreme expression of this desire is the jesuit ideal of self-annihilating obedience, so that the adept becomes a disinterested machine, ecstatically obedient, delighted to find himself entirely in the power of another person, his superior in will and vitality.   The very principle of authority is his bride.   That is the release of ecstasy, absolute repose of the *will* (which, with the generality of men, require a great deal of rest) : also complete abandon of the principle of self, which is the principle of effort too, and the cause of all suffering.   The ' apathy ' of the Stoics was also intended to secure this rest.

If the traditional idea of Liberty, or what is *to be free,* is no longer satisfactory, but if really ' freedom ' is perhaps the opposite of what the *grands ancêtres* were persuaded it was, then ' revolution ' will to-morrow have a different meaning, though by no means a less ' revolutionary ' one.   If that notion of ' freedom ' were indeed imposed on people by philosophers, or by ambitious rulers—just as a very restless, active man's idea of an enjoyable afternoon's entertainment (incapable, as such active men usually are, of putting himself in other people's shoes) might be imposed on a sluggish party ; or a very ' intellectual ' person's notion of a jolly evening's relaxation imposed on a gathering of friends, snobbishly adapting themselves to his vigorous ' highbrow ' appetites— then the sooner this mistake is corrected the better : or (since this is under correction, for these ' betters ' are not naturally the object of my interest) perhaps at least that may be so.

But there is another consideration here : that is, that people have found this out for themselves—who can doubt it ?—for they certainly do not behave any longer as though they were under the old delusion.   Far from behaving in that way, they seem to have embraced the new, and much more true, idea of freedom if anything too indiscriminatingly.   It is easy to foresee that before long people

may have actually to be warned off this more recently
appreciated form of ' freedom,' which formerly they would,
under the influence of early libertarian, saturnalian excite-
ment, have described as ' slavery.'   It is possible yet that
masses of people, many of them big strong men, will have
to be warned off and driven away from the fleshpots of
feminine submission ; they may have to be prodded by
lictors to prevent them from sinking into a lascivious coma,
and told not to be such naughty little slaves !   That is at
least a situation that the responsible authorities may have
on their hands, unless the ruler is to be surfeited with sub-
missiveness, and find his occupation, that of ruling, gone,
or grown very unexciting.

What a peculiar fanatic of energy (' professor of energy,'
as Stendhal called himself) the liberty-obsessed personage
seems to-day !   The more indignantly humanitarian he is,
the more sturdily he swells his chest and points to ancient
' liberties,' and the more he whips himself into a rage at
the thought of the monstrous, disgraceful *enslavement* of
mankind, the more he almost seems like an agent and
emissary of the despot—as of course in the first instance
he was—putting a little spirit into the cattle to be ruled.
In the times when the herd was wilder and more unruly,
he had to pretend to lead them to the attack, misleading
them (back to their pens and corrals) instead.   He is
without any function to-day, but he often looks as though
it were his function to stimulate the jaded performers.

Like wildfire, since the termination of the War, the truth
about ' freedom ' seems to have flown from mind to mind
(it has not been formulated or appeared in words).   It is
a *secret*.   It is even in the nature of a rather dirty secret,
none the less, I am afraid, appreciated for all that.   With
an immense sigh of relief it has been learnt that all personal
effort, after all, is vain ; that the notion of ' liberty ' was,
by those who wished to impose it on men, a programme of
monstrous heroism, a labour of Hercules, a colossal burden,
to no purpose.   Not the word, but the thought, has gone
round, of immense *acceptance*, of the end of *struggle*.

' Liberty ' was a nightmare like death.   That at length
has been perceived.   It is a weight off every mind to-day
that it is *dead* ; for *death once dead, there is no more dying
then*.   The enemy of the human race, ' liberty,' is dead—

and men are free once more ! But at once, naturally, they begin to abuse this freedom : especially men—for women have always to some extent possessed it.

So the great revolutionary afflatus, the plough of science that has gone across the necropolis of the past, the sudden opening up of the whole earth to its children, has turned out to be something of a more prodigious nature than was at first supposed, or is yet much understood ; more truly new and revolutionary, for Europe at least, than any one would have thought, watching the first, aggressive, libertarian mobs, with their phrygian caps and cockades. Let us, now that we are acquainted with this *secret* of our contemporaries, examine it, still warm from the bosoms from which we have wrenched or otherwise secured it. We shall see that it is the first genuine philosophy of slaves that has ever been formulated. Christianity, with its aggressiveness towards authority, and its insistence on ' a new law ' as opposed to the ' old law,' was misrepresented by Nietzsche. It was, if a philosophy of slaves, a philosophy of slaves who desired to rule some day, and to discredit power. The present is very different : it consists in an exploitation of the joys of slavery and submission. ' How enjoyable to be a slave ! ' the really sensible woman must often have said, lazily awaiting her lord and master. ' How divine to have *a master*! How delightful to have everything done *for* one, and everything done *to* one, and have to do nothing oneself! *Dolce far niente!* How happy I am ! ' That (sometimes minus the sensuality, and sometimes with it) is what the new discoverers of freedom have said. It has led, of course, to inversely libertarian excesses. But the mind of the world is easier to-day than it has been for a long while—I am speaking of the european world.

So far so good, we must all agree. Many difficulties, however, occur in the way of the realization of this new dream. It is not certain that it is any more practicable than the other. Perhaps the world has sighed with relief too soon. Also the abandon displayed by many people in enrolling themselves in this new, as it were, secret host is open to objection. Let us at all events examine this esoteric theory of life without fear and without favour.

CHAPTER III

SUPER-FREEDOM OF THE
REVOLUTIONARY RICH

THE instinct for the supreme condition of freedom which is at the bottom of every great revolutionary movement to-day could be explained, then, by some such axiom as *Emancipation and irresponsibility are commutative terms*.

But behind that are arrayed two schools of thought, or theories of happiness. One is practicable, the other is not. One will no doubt establish itself in the future into which the world is moving. The other is merely a phenomenon of transition.

When these popular movements of thought, expressing themselves as highly infectious fashions, are described as *theories*, it is not meant that they are a body of formulated social doctrine, of course, but rather an instinctive and unconscious process, which is only a theory, properly speaking, for the observer. But from the lucretian watch-tower we are possessing for the moment we are able to formulate for ourselves this pattern of instinctive behaviour observed, into an intelligible system of life.

The theory that has, of the two, been described as an ephemeral one is far too good to be true, to start with. Also it is a corruption of the old, rather than an entire convert to the new, libertarianism. This is the distinction that we have constantly to make in dealing with western society to-day. We are in a mixed society, destined eventually to separate itself out. Of this mixture many corruptions and mongrel forms spring up. Almost every variety of mixture is to be found.

In the heart of this new doctrine of freedom, then, there is a cleavage, rather like that other cleavage that produces the doctrine of *What the Public Wants* on the one hand, and revolutionary idealism on the other. One is a corruption or caricature of the other, an accommodation between the old and the new. Both types of ' freedom ' are to be found in the West, side by side and often confused,

144

and one rather compromised by the other. The disciplined *fascist* party in Italy can be taken as representing the new and healthy type of ' freedom.' Perhaps it is simpler to discriminate between them by saying that one is *political* and the other is *social.* Where the political one does not yet properly exist, a social *precursor*, cheap advance copy, social caricature of it exists.

What is happening in reality in the West is that a small privileged class is *playing* at revolution, and aping a ' proletarian' freedom that the proletariat has not yet reached the conception of. The rich are always the first ' revolutionaries.' They also mix up together the instincts, opportunities, and desires of the ruler and the ruled. They have *the apple and eat it* plan in full operation in their behaviour. It is they who have evolved the secondary, heterodox, quite impracticable notion of 'liberty' which it will be our especial task to analyse.

This type of freedom, synonymous with irresponsibility, and yet impregnated with privilege as well, is a very strange growth indeed. It will be found on examination to be the most utopian type of all.

It is only achieved sometimes by one category of creature, the human child; in a lesser degree by the young of animals. But any one *not* a child attempting by some ruse or other to secure it, seldom can succeed : for the simplest and most inexorable law of nature is there to frustrate such a plan. But it can be successful under special and very artificial conditions, in consequence of the protection and assistance of some other factor that is the equal in power of the natural principle that is challenged by it. As an instance of this, we can take the case of an old, rich, and pampered invalid lady who succeeds in attracting to herself, by means of her riches, all the advantages of childhood. She in this way may arrive at being carried about, waited on, fed, bathed, flattered, put to bed, and in the morning washed and dressed, and so steeped continually in an atmosphere of self-importance. But this is the effect of her wealth, which brings in the element of power and authority—which, though not hers, she is able to use and enjoy. So you must also add to the wealth the advantages of the ' weaker sex.' But the child is the only creature that in its own right, and under favourable conditions, can enjoy unchallenged, and without forfeiting something else that cancels the advantage, this divine irresponsibility, which is the most ideal and utopian type of *freedom*.

The other sort of freedom—or that that it is most natural to contrast with this irresponsible variety—is the responsible freedom of the individual in authority, possessing power (position, or wealth, or both). This is a precarious, imperfect, anxious, laborious freedom : but it is the only freedom within the grasp of the average man, except the great patent of ecstatic submission, the feminine type of freedom or self-expression.

The type of freedom of which the child is the perpetual emblem, irresponsible freedom, and that other of which the king or millionaire is the emblem, that reposing on authority and power, are both rigidly dependent on other people. They are both obtained at the expense of other people, and the servitude of others is their condition. The third type of freedom, the feminine type, is a parasite of power, and the first requisite for it is a master.

There is another sort of very rare freedom, that possessed by the intellect alone. It is contingent on no physical circumstance, is not obtained or held at the expense of others—indeed, is altogether independent of people ; and although it is a source of power, is an unrecognized and unofficial source, and takes with it, under favourable circumstances, some of the advantages of irresponsibility : and at the worst, and deprived of all power, still, as freedom, remains unaffected by fortune. But it is not a type with which we need concern ourselves here.

It is not as a routed army, but as a triumphant one, that the luxurious, hand-to-mouth, capitalo-revolutionary society of the interregnum has installed itself in the nursery. There a cult is being evolved by all these highly sophisticated elders, living for sensation, around the figure of a mechanical doll. But, as we have been attempting to show for many chapters now, this mechanical doll, or puppet, is the idol, or at least the symbol, of the great majority of men. It is from them that those privileged groups have stolen it. Their wild nursery devotions are conducted in its expensive shadow. There they eat bread and jam round it, dressed in short print frocks and bibs ; sit in demure and silent rows, while one dressed as a martinet scolds them, and then administers shuddering *fessées*. With costly toys, pranks, and strictly juvenile games, they conform to the object of their devotion, and do nothing inappropriate in its presence.

By this particular luxurious Western society the *artist* and the *child* are the two figures most heavily imitated and exploited to-day. So, of course, both true art and true infancy are in imminent danger of extinction or, ' worse than death, dishonour.' To these two figures should perhaps be added, as a doubtful third, *woman*.

It would be presumptuous, and indeed mad, to suppose that anything could be done, by even the most eloquent disquisition, to change this situation. If, however, *one* artist, and a *single* child, are preserved intact and unpolluted owing to my words, I should consider my pains richly rewarded. To a call to protect the children, and in a lesser degree the women—though the women and children must always go together—the English-speaking public would never fail to respond. It is less certain that they would take action if it were merely a question of saving artists and art. It is encouraging for the artist, however, to reflect that the destiny of the artist, in this instance, is bound up with that of the child. Both the Nursery and the Studio or Study are equally and simultaneously threatened, and by the same people. Both are being pillaged and overrun by a vast crowd of ' grown-ups ' who covet the irresponsibilities and unreality of those two up till now sacred retreats.

To state in its awful simplicity the true inner nature of what is happening, *every one wants to be a child*, and *every one wants to be an artist*; which is of course impossible. All the privileges of lisping innocent and petted childhood, and all the privileges of art, are coveted by the masses of the mature and the rich. The mature have developed this particular covetousness because *their* privileges, the privileges and ambitions of mature life, have been ravished from them. The rich have developed it because, as it is impossible to enjoy openly the privileges of riches in the present period of transition, to exercise power openly, and openly surround themselves with its emblems and satisfactions ; as it is necessary to pretend to be merely private

citizens when in reality they are the rulers of the world,—
so they covet the privileges of the artist, to which, and to
the privileges similarly of the child, they with some reason
consider that their *irresponsibility* affects them.   Both the
grown-up and the rich man find the natural outlet for
their ambition and vitality blocked.   Neither can expand
upwards and forwards, so they are forced back into these
roads that terminate respectively in the Nursery and in the
Studio and Study of the artist.

That is, put very briefly, but as fully as at this stage
of our argument we need, the nature of the threat to art
and to infancy.   Already a degrading effect can be regis-
tered on all hands.   It is possible to generalize in the
following way as well : that whenever men are prevented
from satisfying their ambitions in a full, active, and competitive life, they will loiter on, or, if expelled from, return
by the back door or the back window to the Nursery.
And the rich and powerful, if prevented from indulging
their natural taste for pomp and display (which in a socialist epoch is impossible)—if prevented from being artists
in action (all actions containing naturally a great æsthetic
element)—will invariably seek to be 'artists' in some
other way.

'*Action*' *to-day is starved of art.*   That is why there are
so many ' artists ' and so little good art at all.

CHAPTER IV

MILLIONAIRE SOCIETY

W E shall often have occasion to use the term ' millionaire society,' and to avoid misunderstandings some definition had better be given of what is to be meant by it. We are busy tracing the revolutionary impulse back to the head of Zeus, as it were, from which it leaps, then taking this form and that. God cannot help *thinking* of change, at all events when He thinks of us. We are all infected by His thinking, and we all interpret His thought differently. The revolutionary rich interpret it differently from the revolutionary poor. For the former it becomes *variety* or fashion, a more or less immobile thing ; or when it takes the form of movement it affects them on the *Mademoiselle Julie* pattern—they have an instinct to cast themselves down. That is the truly *aristocratic* impulse, of the satiety of power and life. But as to-day there is no aristocracy left, a different and more complex impulse manifests itself. That, in the course of this essay, I hope to throw some light on. There is at least no *humility* about the great ones of our day. There is no tendency to precipitate themselves from their fortunate eminence. And there is none of that dangerous tolerance of a true aristocracy that makes them eager to *look on at themselves* —to be their own spectators.

Marx deprecated all *valuation* of the great mass of new things dumped upon the world every day, ' until the revolution.' Till that happened it did not matter very much how things stood, so long as the radical change was effected. To that we adhere : what values are popularly attached to things is of the slenderest importance, no doubt, in such a time.

We accept the marxian formula of the usefulness of capitalism as it exists to-day, as a machine building up an immense irrefragable power, that eventually can be used by rather pleasanter people than at present have the handling of it. We match our optimism against Marx's. We are quite sure that the most glorious people will shortly appear and use all this unparalleled power, made possible by science and capitalism, more like gods than men. We admit also that it does not sound likely.

In spite of this resolve to regard giant industrialism as a great power willing night and day the evil, and destined to produce nothing but the good—and therefore forestalling somewhat this happy event, which we take on trust, treating it already as a notorious public good,—that does not enable us to live with our eyes shut.   There is really nothing very lovely about millionaire life, millionaire art, or millionaire thought.   That is why we hope that it will soon show *the good* we have been led to expect from it—that is to say, disappear or transform itself.

When, then, we use the term 'millionaire society' we refer to the capitalist world of great wealth that has been given this mandate by Marx, and which has come into its own since the War.   However few actual millionaires there may be in it, we mean all new-rich society that has the millionaire touch.   In this unavoidable poor-rich classification it is not meant that all the rich are wicked and dishonest, and all the poor honest and good, but merely that the rich *are* rich, with all that entails; and that the poor *are* poor, with what ensues from that as well.   The great millionaire in person usually has few of the faults of millionaire society. It would be an insensitive man indeed who did not feel drawn towards such a man as Henry Ford, with his splendid energy and unsocial character.   He is what Goethe would call *a nature*.   So with most millionaires proper.   But the sub-millionaire population of the world of Ritzes and Rivieras is often very ugly.

This millionaire society is replete with a barbarous optimism now.   It is no wonder that, as Benda notes (and to which observation we will return later on), there is no artist or philosopher to be found to say anything disagreeable about it—so creating a record of slavishness in literary history !   Or there may be some other reason. The artist or philosopher who refuses to identify himself with the aristocratic world may feel better able to accommodate himself to the millionaire world !   It is so democratic—that may be it : or there may be other reasons.

This optimism is not to be wondered at, for it is a *new* world ; nor, for the same reason, can its barbarity cause any surprise.   It is naturally, for itself, the best that has

ever been—it is for *it* that the earth has laboured for so
long : the least of its sons and daughters exists in a swoon
of luxury beside which the appointments of a medicean
prince or princess would appear rustic and coarse. It is
as pleased with itself as Punch, and very naturally (with
all this wealth and power and comfort) not criticism, but
pæans of exultant praise—similar to those you meet with
in the advertisement columns of its newspapers, advertising
its superlative goods—is what it expects of the writer,
philosopher, or artist, the traditional appanages of moneyed
life. And that is what ' these charming people ' get.
For itself, it appears emphatically to possess every imaginable advantage over former ages that money can buy :
for is it not more *democratic*, to start with, than any other
society comparable to it in power has ever been ? Is it
not more exquisitely ' artistic,' and above all (and that is
the thing about which there can be least question of all)
more intelligent, more on the spot, more knowing ; so that
it is almost—or is it not quite ?—intellectually ' self-
supporting,' as it were ?

Finally, under these circumstances, it is able to do what
no former society has been able to do. It is able to dispense with the disguises and graces of art and the painful
tasks of culture, its traditional shell. That remoteness
that art can throw over even the most scarified, pitted,
oozing, and shining close-up of the insolently bared human
soul is denied us.

When this society has some invention parodied or
watered down for its purposes, and a corrupt reflection of
the thought of the true revolutionary results, you will be
expected to exclaim, ' How daring ! How admirable !
How expressive of the New Age ! ' But you may know
better than that, and so find it pointless to exclaim for
ever in that way.

So it is that if you are truly irreconcilable, truly revolutionary, you will find many curious paradoxes in your
relation both with the fashionable life of the wealthy
amateur of the millionaire world, and with the revolutionary popularizer. A prophecy of a civilization that will
emerge from the present ruin will be present to you in the
work of a few inventive men of letters, science, and art.
A propagandist of the vulgarest capitalism, such as

Marinetti was or is, will in consequence not please you much. All that absurd and violent propaganda of *actuality*, stinking of the optimism of the hoardings and the smugness of the motoring millionaire, disguising the squalor of the capitalist factory beneath an epileptic rhetoric of *action*, will not stir you to sympathetic barbaric yawps. You will recognize that the Regent Street which has just disappeared had (although not much to boast of) a certain pleasant meaning that is absent from the present pretentious, stolid structures. But a deadweight of organized optimism will press on your chest. Everything will conspire to bully or hypnotize you into a *best of all possible worlds* attitude. You will have to be a very irreconcilable individual not to find yourself on this much too-obviously 'winning side.'

CHAPTER V

THE PUBLIC AND THE PRIVATE LIFE

WHAT would be the principal difference between a rigidly organized bureaucratic socialist state and a ' democratic ' state of ' get rich quick,' open competition, parliamentary government, etc. ?   The difference, where the average male citizen was concerned, would be that the same opportunities would no longer be found for his individual ' climbing ' instincts, or commercial ' push.' Fixed in the midst of a carefully regulated hierarchy, his future would be as much earmarked and evident as his past, in the sense that with the automatic graduated salary, rising a few pounds every few years, he would be able to regulate his private life on his life of work, without any likelihood either of interference or, on the other hand, of any accidental and ' lucky' element modifying his destiny spectacularly from one day to the next.

In the democratic competitive system a certain type of energy of a not very valuable sort (except to its possessor) constantly carries men up into the ruling class.   That has been happening ever since the establishment of the industrial system.   The ruling class becomes more and more a collection of personalities with no traditions, no intellectual training except such as is involved in speculation in stocks and shares or business deals, no religious beliefs usually or any attachments at all in a wider system than that of the stock market or commerce.   In a bureaucratic system, inevitably before long a different type of man to this chance jettison of the most brutal sort of success would be evolved. The *static* nature of the system would not be against it, but on the contrary for it, where the production of a valuable administrative *type* was concerned.   The breezy elasticity of competitive commerce would not be there. Life would not be a ' lottery ' any more.   There would be no golden accidents, in which success was usually secured by the least desirabe type of being.   *Sheltered* from the coarsening rough-and-tumble of commercial life, developing freely a religious consciousness of the destinies of their caste, intellectually equipped in a way that no former european rulers have ever been, you would get (to place against the certain disadvantages of a too static system) an inbred and highly organized body of rulers. Access to this caste would be by way of examination, perhaps ; at all events, by some other route than the brutal and un-satisfactory one of commercial success. They would form that necessary versatile and universal man above the specialist. That is of course at present in the nature of a myth of the future, but it is just as good a recommenda-tion to say that gods will trace their descent from us, as that we trace our descent from gods.

To return to what is happening under our eyes—and which is the first phase of a long process, differentiated from what it supersedes. The spirit of undisciplined enterprise, along freebooting commercial lines, is being crushed out of people by the great concentrations of capital which make it more impossible every day for the ' small man ' to advance. Within a few years this process must put a term to individual commercial enterprise. Already the great majority of people are salaried servants of some big trust. Their futures are as cut-and-dried and pre-dictable as the career of a post-office clerk.

Let us imagine this system somewhat more consolidated and developed than it is to-day. It would probably result in a caste system of family trades, on the pattern of India or Egypt, for instance. There would no doubt, in addition to a bureaucracy, be a priesthood : for the present irre-ligion of the Soviet, for instance, must not be taken as anything but a transitional and destructive phase. Eventu-ally it is not difficult to predict that revolutionary idealism will slip more and more into some religious mould : though it is not likely that the revolutionary handbooks of chris-tianity, with their greek idealism, will survive the opening of the millennium.

But it is the life of the human average whose destiny we are attempting to trace. The man or woman would have two lives, then as now. There would be *the serious life of work*—and professionalism, in that section of his or her life, would be as prevalent as ever, and specialization manifest itself as jealously as now. And then, work done, there would be *the life of play*.

But the first thing to notice is that, although it would

still be called play, this part of life into which all the
cultural activities would be pressed would now be the
serious part—just as the dressing and dances are the
serious part of a woman's life : the dressing the preparation of the goods for the market, and conveyed on foot,
by taxi, or bus to the dance-hall, the market-place.
Whereas now in the recreative life the majority of people
are quite content to find their pleasure in the convenient
rôle of spectator, then they would insist on a competitive
activity.   Whereas to-day (although that to-day is fast
approximating itself to the not very distant future we are
describing) the workaday business and money-making life
(in which a man is proud of being ' good at his job,' and
sets his vanity on that) is the *serious* one, then the arena
would be what is now the ' private ' life of recreation and
amusement.   Whereas now competition, at least for a man,
is confined, in a serious form, to his working business life,
then the competitive instincts would find their full expression outside in the world of play.

An *æsthetic* ideal would be substituted, in short, for a
masculine abstract one ;   a personal for an impersonal.
If you go into a smoking compartment to-day in an Underground train you find yourself surrounded by *men*, a very
different humanity (as you gaze round at their serious,
free, unselfconscious faces, ignorant of the grace that they
have never sought beneath their raw hides) to what you
would find in a compartment full of women.   This will
very rapidly change.   These *men* that you can examine
to-day on their way home in the evening have left their
best life, their life of work, behind them.   In the future
they will under such circumstances have just left a mechanical dream-life of duty, and be expanding and becoming
themselves as they approach the seat of their private and
personal life.   At least this description will apply to the
most active and ambitious.

But to-day the development of colossal industries has
already driven off the field most of the crowd of small,
ambitious men, the energetic minority of climbers and get-
rich-quicks.   All outlet to their competitive and ambitious
instincts is already occluded.   In the human machinery
of a large establishment, as in the government services,
zeal is not encouraged.   An ambitious individual, with a

devouring energy and fond of work, will hardly find an outlet for that energy in future in business.   For any display made of that energy among his fellow-workers in a large anonymous industry would cause him to be regarded with disfavour, and he would gain nothing by it at all.

There is one way open to each individual to-day—the sort who in the days before the ascendency of the cartels and trusts would unscrupulously fight his way up to the top of the tree.   This career of the business climber, where as a sort of legitimate criminal he could plunder his way up, is closed for all and sundry, or is rapidly closing. Only lawless and criminal activity, blackmail, poison, and the revolver will soon be left him.   Already to-day the difficulties put in the way of a man who yesterday, as a small business crook (of small but distinct predatory energy), would make money in ' business,' are so vexatious that he is forced to become openly a criminal.   In this way, of course, many a small-scale bird of prey is brought to light, smoked out of his business labyrinth by the advance of the anonymous power of the trust and syndicate.

The blocking up of the avenues by which the competitive instinct vented itself, and the crushing uniformity of fortune in which, in the salaried industrial armies of to-day, it has no play, is one of the circumstances that force these energies back into the non-working life ; with many of the more energetic small-scale competitive people, into crime ; and with others—less energetic—into sport and ' life ' *tout court*, the social life.

Meantime press suggestion hammers at this discomforted little man.   ' Don't worry, Mr. Everyman : never worry ! Life—so the scientists tell us—is a small mechanical affair, pleasure is the only reality.   Competition and the cares of state and success are all very well.   But for simple people like you and me a quiet, secure life is what we want, isn't it ? If your insurances are paid up, your " home " bought, an aerial installed (the hire-purchase payments kept up), a week arranged for at Worthing or Southend, or if you are near a nice city park, with sand-pits for the kids, if you have a motor-bike, etc., etc.—well, life is not so dusty !   Pleasure, or the home-life, is the thing ! '

Of course, ' art ' and ' culture' are introduced as further baits usually into these exordiums.   A *Keep off the grass* notice where the wielding of ambitions is concerned, or the great prizes of this world, that whole enclosed realm of ' power ' and government, warns Mr. Everyman of changed times. But he is recommended to approximate as nearly as possible to a ' gentleman of leisure ' and cultured tastes—reduced to earning his living from nine to six every day. Never mind ! He can be ' cultivated ' (and Mrs. Everyman can be ' refined ') for the rest of the time !

Round these abstract flames—one cold and repellent beyond description, the other gay with promises, the William Morris world, the happy valley, the eternal spring, of an electioneering poster—the multitudes of moths press and strain.

This is of course the democratic humbug of the *What the Public Wants* system. A sort of sugar-sweet mis-interpretation of the period of mediæval rebirth, when everything was happy and the workshops were full of songs, and craftsmen jostled with amateur masons, is sketched. *The World's great age begins anew, the golden years return,* is, in lyrical language, the message of this political afflatus.

It is true that *action* would still be the catchword of this new paradise. Only, the mechanical dogma of *action,* or the vitalist dogma of ' life,' would be turned back on the world of play and the private life of the individual. It would be discouraged thereby—or led gently away—from any designs it might have in the world of *business,* or what has so far been regarded as *real* activity.

Men and women would in this way both be thrown back into what is to-day still the conventional ' woman's world.' It is true that men, as well as women, dress, go to dances, and so forth. And it is true that these occupations already take on a seriousness, an *art for art's sake* air, which is novel, and very pleasantly novel. Where it is unpleasant it is owing to the inevitable cheapness injected into every-thing by *What the Public Wants.* Still, the world in which love is manufactured, and young ' homes ' built, the race perpetuated, is still conventionally regarded as the woman's province ; and the ' day's work ' as the man's.

When you are dealing with ' the world ' in the sense of the social world, it was said above, you are dealing strictly with a *woman's world*. And so in the humbler world of the great crowds, all that is not ambitious and competitive money-making and 'bread-winning' has been generally regarded as a feminine province. The wholesale invasion of that province, and the fusion of the rôles of the two regions, is what the War and its sequel has resulted in. Already the bridges are built by which the psychology of the masses (with the weakening of the deep sex distinction and sex barriers) will pass back to the conventional female pole, or transfer their energies in that direction.

The old 'man's world' of the abstract (non-personal, non-feminine) life of the earlier European is, then, to-day, rapidly becoming extinct. The power of money and the vast interlocked organization of 'big business' has gradually withdrawn all initiative from individual males. *Bourgeois* or parliamentary politics is to-day such a thin camouflage—so harassed, pointless, and discredited—the puppets have so little executive power (Lord Curzon is reported to have said shortly before he died, for example, that he had not enough 'power' to send a messenger across Whitehall), that politics no longer afford an outlet for energy comparable for a moment with the opportunities of a game of tennis or a flirtation. Hence every one, ambitious in other ways or not, is sent indiscriminately to the *salon* or the playing-field or dance-hall, and that is the only real battlefield left for masculine or feminine ambition. 'Private' life, in short, has taken the place of 'public' life.

That this is a very sad thing for many people is certain. For such a man as the Marquess Curzon to find himself starved of what he so hungered for, 'power' (over other people, to send them not only across Whitehall, but to the galleys, or anywhere else in or out of this world), is a sad disappointment. But the people who want this sort of power are not very interesting—often by no means so worthy of notice as the people over whom they exercise it. Again, it is a very sad thing that no office-boy to-day can be very sanguine about ending his life a magnate. It is no longer so easy, in fact it becomes more difficult every day, to 'get on' in this sensational way in commerce. That is very pathetic: but *quâ* office boy and *quâ* magnate people are not necessarily worthy of notice, nor as the latter does a man recommend himself more to us than as the former ; unless he showers his wealth on us, which is very unusual.

So that politics and business should have closed down on aspirants to honours and great wealth is not such a very great tragedy. But of course that is not the end of it : and all this energy bursts up in other directions. But it does not follow, because as political or commercial specialists these men were not necessarily very interesting, that as social specialists they are more so. Probably they are even better at their masculine tasks than at their feminine ones.

What has been gained is this. In the former ' democratic,' parliamentary régime, and régime of open competition, all the machinery of society worked in public. The ambitious ' public ' specialist was watched by millions, his speeches quoted with great care, his bold financial undertakings eagerly noted. Now all this will go underground. We shall never be bothered with real live politics or commerce again. At least, we shall suffer them, but have no part in them. The accounts of them in the newspapers will become more and more unreal and meaningless and difficult to follow ; and then eventually they will disappear altogether. The *results* will appear, however, in social life. Enormous pearls will collect on the necks of ladies, reaching their necks *from nowhere*—for it is unlikely that wealth will be explicit. All the ponderable forces of the world will be occult, and only flower mysteriously in social phenomena such as pearls and motorcars. As though waited on by genii, favoured persons will flourish in social life, and their ' power ' (instead of revealing its larva stages to the world, and parading its vermiform ' public ' shape in politics and industry) will appear in its final butterfly transformation as a social phenomenon.

For those who (like great artists and others) love shapes of masculine splendour and power, Belle Haulmières, prophets, visions of Infernos and so forth, and on whom the finished social article, the eternal butterfly, is likely to pall—for them also, beyond this phase, there will be others, no doubt, in which eventually, like a tremendous serpent, ' power ' once more issues from its subterranean retreat, and asserts itself again in massive magnificence. But that of course is very distant. The joys of the Leviathan are not for us. What at least will be gained for the moment is that all the decaying and unsightly publicity of *imperfect* power will disappear. And when the social world organizes itself as the only serious world, it will be very different to the place it is at present—and will remain, until the occult political machinery is consolidated.

CHAPTER VI

THE CONTEMPORARY MAN
'EXPRESSES HIS PERSONALITY'

THE 'class war' is of course a notion that extends to every possible class. And sex is of course a very important 'class' indeed, and 'sex war' a very important 'war.'

A great deal of abuse has been levelled at Marx by the opponents of marxism, as the author of this diabolical invention, the 'class struggle.' That is quite natural ; it is a tribute to Marx's sagacity, and to the effectiveness of the engine. And it is not to be disputed that Mr. Russell is right when he says that 'the intensity of organization is increased not only when a man belongs to more organ- izations, but also when the organizations to which he al- ready belongs play a larger part in his life—as, for example, the State plays a larger part in war than in peace.' The higher the state of organization, the less individual play, initiative, and ultimately power possessed by the individual so 'classified.' But although Mr. Russell regards such organization as extremely sad, I find it difficult to do so, for the reasons I have just advanced. What is of more im- portance, of course, is that the people concerned, as I have already pointed out, do not. Men and women like nothing so much as being 'classified '—not, it is true, for a ' war ' (though they do not object to that so much as is supposed : they are drugged into a state of anæsthesia by the rhythm of their 'class '), but for anything else there is no surer way to their hearts than to invent a new 'class ' for them. And sex is of course the most popular 'class ' of all.

Men have to found a class for the reception of any newly recognized idea of importance. Before it possesses this human repository it is not a fact. To be *good, a deceived husband, an artist, a one-legged man,* at once lands an individual in some aggregation or class, and adversity or good fortune both drop him in the midst of the strangest bedfellows. But, of course, first of all he has to be re- cognized as possessing the quality—the goodness, credulity, artisticness, or one-leggedness, or whatever it may be : and, sometimes luckily, it takes people a long time to arrive at the truth, except in the simplest and most conventional cases. Saints often have been known to spend their entire lives in the class of devils, and so on.

Instead, then, of the idea being left free to pass from place to place and man to man at will (which would be the dispensation most favourable to elasticity and life), it has to be penned at once—or a man representing it has to be penned—with a large collection of people, where it, or the man representing it, very likely will languish. To the herding of men nature attends : some of course can elude her rough herding, but a few sports only.

The *idées forces*, it will be recollected, result in a walking ' idea '—which is the dynamo. And it matters very little what the ' idea ' is : though we have an arbitrary class of ideas the adoption of any of which has very serious results for a man ; for example, should a man have for his motive-idea a ' potato '—should he believe himself a potato, or a piece of potato-peel, as it were—we clap him in a madhouse. But outside of this there is a wide choice.

Generally speaking, it can be said that people wish to escape from themselves (this by no means excluding the crudest selfishness). When people are encouraged, as happens in a democratic society, to believe that they wish ' to express their personality,' the question at once arises as to what their personality *is*. For the most part, if investigated, it would be rapidly found that they had none. So what would it be that they would eventually ' express ' ? And why have they been asked to ' express ' it ?

If they were subsequently watched in the act of ' expressing ' their ' personality,' it would be found that it was somebody else's personality they were expressing. If a hundred of them were observed ' expressing their personality,' all together and at the same time, it would be found that they all ' expressed ' this inalienable, mysterious, ' personality ' in the same way. In short, it would be patent at once that they only had *one* personality between them to ' express '—some ' expressing ' it with a little more virtuosity, some a little less. It would be a *group personality* that they were ' expressing '—a pattern imposed on them by means of education and the hypnotism of cinema,

wireless, and press. Each one would, however, be firmly
persuaded that it was ' his own ' personality that he was
' expressing ' : just as when he voted he would be persuaded that it was the vote of a free man that was being
cast, replete with the independence and free-will which
was the birthright of a member of a truly democratic
community.

Here, in this case, you get an individual convinced that
he is ' expressing his personality ' : that he has a thing
called a ' personality,' and that it is desirable to ' express '
it. He has been supplied with this formula, ' expressing the personality,' as a libertarian sugar-plum. He
has been taught that he is ' free,' and that it is the privilege
of the free man to ' express his personality.' Now, if you
said to this man that he *had* no personality, that he had
never been given the chance to have one, in any case, in
the standardized life into which he fitted with such religious
conformity : and secondly, that he did not *want* to have
a personality at all, really, and was quite happy as he was,—
he would reply that you might be very clever, and might
think that you were funny, but that *he* was the best judge
of whether he possessed a personality or not : that as he
' expressed ' it every Saturday afternoon and evening and
on Sundays, he probably knew more about it than you did ;
and that in consequence your gratuitous assumption that
he did not want one was absurd, as well as offensive. If
he were a savage Robot, he might confirm this statement
by directing a blow at your head.

The truth is that such an individual is induced to ' express his personality ' because it is desired absolutely to
standardize him and get him to rub off (in the process of
the ' expression ') any rough edges that may remain from
his untaught, spontaneous days. Where the avenues of
' expression ' suggested to him are more ' original ' and
sensational (as in Germany, where the *Rhythm-army of
naked male life*, the *Joy Group*, or *Naked Men's Club of Sun-
Pals* would perhaps attract him), the case is no different,
but he is of course then far more convinced, even, that his
personality is being ' expressed.' But, drawn into one orbit
or another, he must in the contemporary world submit
himself to one of several mechanical socially organized
rhythms. There is really less choice every day : the

number of group-personalities available, of course, diminishes just as the number of newspapers decreases. And it seems impossible to dispute that, as regards this side of life, and leaving aside the threat of unemployment and fresh wars, people have never been so happy. The Not-Self (and *not* the self at all) is the goal of human ambition. And not 'freedom,' or the eccentric play of the 'personality,' but submission to a group-rhythm, is what men desire.

But even if they did not desire it, it is the condition of all successful practical life, into which neither metaphysics nor personality can really enter. George Sorel's account of his manner of work emphasizes this :—

> You remember what Bergson wrote (he says) about the impersonal, the socialized, the *ready-made*, which contains a piece of advice addressed to students to whom the acquiring of knowledge that would be of use in practical life was essential. The pupil has all the more confidence in the formulas offered to him, and he retains them, in consequence, all the more easily, if he imagines that they are accepted by the majority of people. Thus his mind is relieved of any metaphysical preoccupation, and he is accustomed not to desire any personal attitude to anything. Often in the end he comes to regard as a superiority the absence of any *inventiveness*. My manner of working is the opposite of that. I submit to my readers the effort of a mind which seeks to escape from the constraint of past formulas, invented for the general use ; a mind which wishes for the personal.
>
> (*Réflexions sur la violence.*)

It is a combination of these two happy things that promises the best result for human happiness. Sorel's desire for ' the personal ' is everybody's desire, *verbally*. That is the ' ready-made ' formula, which is known to be ' accepted by the majority of people.' And the delights and proud assertions of seeking for ' the personal ' can be undertaken on one big, crowded track, laid down in any of a hundred text-books, with the certainty that every one else will be seeking it at the same time and in the same place and in identically the same manner.

CHAPTER VII

PEOPLE'S HAPPINESS FOUND IN
TYPE-LIFE

AS in another essay I have examined very thoroughly the idea of class, I will not go into it here. I need only in conclusion make a few remarks with regard to it. If from the standpoint of philosophy the sorelian science of class is negligible, and even rather childish, from a practical standpoint it is of great importance, and of the utmost potentiality. An *esprit de corps* can be worked up about anything ; the *regiment* is the unit of discipline and romance, rather than the region from which it comes. And a ' proletarian ' class obsession is essential to bind together the ' proletariat,' whatever that may be. Without some such fictitious (' artificial,' as Sorel says) bond it would fall to pieces. And even the parade of objective science and historical paraphernalia is justified if it is understood by the director of the movement which it is seeking to save.

Actually, again, the more you specialize people, the more power you can obtain over them, the more helpless and in consequence the more obedient they are. To shut people up in a water-tight, syndicalized, occupational unit is like shutting them up on an island. Further, occupation, in a world of mixed races and traditions, is the most natural classification (though it could be said from another point of view, of course, to be the most unnatural).

The ideally ' free man ' would be the man *least* specialized, the *least* stereotyped, the man approximating to the *fewest* classes, the *least* clamped into a system—in a word, the most individual. But a society of ' free men,' if such a thing could ever come about, which it certainly could not, would immediately collapse.

The chief thing to remember in such a discussion is that no one wants to be ' free ' in that sense. People ask nothing better than to be *types*—occupational types, social types, functional types of any sort. If you force them not to be, they are miserable, just as the savage grew miserable when the white man came and prevented him from living a life devoted to the forms and rituals he had made. And if so forced (by some interfering philanthropist or unintelligent reformer) to abandon some *cliché*, all men, whether white, yellow, or black, take the first opportunity to get their *cliché* back, or to find another one. For in the mass people wish to be *automata* : they wish to be *conventional* : they hate you teaching them or forcing them into ' freedom ' : they wish to be obedient, hard-working machines, as near dead as possible—as near dead (feelingless and thought-less) as they can get, without actually dying.

PART VI

SUB PERSONA INFANTIS

'*But . . . care ought to be taken that the bodies of the children may be such as will answer the expectations of the legislator.*'
Politics, XVI. Aristotle.

'*Now the iron force of adhesion to the old routine social, political, religious—has wonderfully yielded: the iron force of exclusion of all which is new has wonderfully yielded. The danger now is, not that people should obstinately refuse to allow anything but their old routine to pass for reason . . . but either that they should allow some novelty or other to pass for (that) too easily, or else that they should . . . think it enough to follow action for its own sake.*'
Culture and Anarchy. Matthew Arnold.

'*What if our urgent want now is, not to act at any price, but rather to lay in a stock of light for our difficulties?   In that case, to refuse to lend a hand to the rougher and coarser movements going on around us, to make the primary need, both for oneself and others, to consist in enlightening ourselves and qualifying ourselves to act less at random, is surely the best and in real truth the most practical line our endeavours can take.*'
Ibid.   Arnold.

CHAPTER I

THE 'TRADER' AND THE 'ARTIST'

IN the 'millionaire society' defined in Part III those fortunate enough to possess the means were shown as enjoying already the revolutionary joys of a communist millennium. They are naturally impatient of the slowness of revolution. They consequently decide to forestall the paradise to come, on a small scale, themselves. A painting, writing, acting, cultural paradise ensues, in which every one is equal (that is, equally 'a genius') and every one is free —at the expense, naturally, of the great majority, who have to *wait* for their revolutionary paradise.

The two figures most universally imitated in this happy, bohemian millionaire millennium (a small model of what is promised to all men, but which they can already examine as spectators) are *the child* and *the artist*. There are, of course, still a few artists, who are not millionaires. And it may be interesting to consider for a moment how they are affected by the turn events have taken.

That the artist could have well forgone any of the flattering advantages of the discovery just recorded— namely, that of the importance of his function, and its *life* value, vanity value, and social value—goes without saying, perhaps. Was Shakespeare much put out at ranking in the worldly scale, so far below an emperor? He was no doubt satisfied to be regarded as the humble, 'gentle' chronicler of England's stupid kings. He provided them with a 'kingliness,' and incidentally a magnificence of language, which would have made them open their eyes and prick up their ears in amazement if they could have seen it and heard it going on in a setting as 'real' as their own. There is no gain to the artist or to art, then, that this secret of his importance is out. For art will in consequence gradually acquire a destiny not unlike that of the probable monkey-gland of to-morrow : the sort of person who has the money to be an 'artist' is much the same who will have the money to pay for the monkey-gland. It is only the wealthy who will be artists, as it will only be the wealthy who will indefinitely prolong their lives.

The way in which people—those, of course, who can afford it—become 'artists' is very various. All (practically without exception) of those who formerly 'patronized' the arts of music, painting, or literature now *do it themselves instead*—which is, among other things, very much cheaper, as pictures and music were among the most costly items of the life of the primitive magnate. The 'patron' of tradition was either a pope, prince, or some other form of potentate. He was usually content with the advertisement and glamour that these appointments provided him with. To-day, people with far more wealth and power than any Medici or pope are unfortunately (owing to the democratic susceptibilities of the time, which compel them to remain hid) deprived of these robust and magnificent satisfactions. So they are inclined either to steal the thunders of the Sistine (and save themselves the painter's bill into the bargain), or else to insinuate that their own obscure and immensely lucrative occupation may not be so *pretty*, but is damned well *as good* as any bit of daubing, chipping, jingling, or strumming of noises.

This is a very strange thing at first sight : and most people would find it difficult to believe that the master of a fleet of merchant ships, or a pork king, could experience envy for Stravinsky, Bernard Shaw, or Picasso. It is indeed only repeated observation of certain facts susceptible of no other explanation that would bring you to entertain anything so absurd.

The possible existence of such sensations on the part of the pork- or rail-king is mentioned by Boswell—apparently only to be dismissed as unlikely—in his notebooks of the years 1776-1777. I quote from a *Times* review (May 6, 1925) :—

> Miss Porter told me the Birmingham people could not bear Mr. Johnson. She did not say why. I suppose from envy of his parts ; though I do not see how traders could envy such qualities.

The reviewer adds on his own account, ' I doubt if it was envy,' etc. That ' traders cannot envy such qualities ' is certainly what at first any one would be disposed to say. Perhaps the eighteenth-century Birmingham ' traders ' did not. But to-day the ' trader ' is a different sort of man.

He would envy a polecat if he thought there was any vanity value in its stink.   He *values* everything : his nose, his sense of values, is colossal.   And he resents the illusive ' value ' of art very much indeed.

If a concrete illustration of this mood were required, the late Lord Leverhulmc's vicious attack on his portrait by an eminent English painter could be instanced.   His ' vandalism ' was no doubt intended to show what he thought of the sacrosanct character of fine art !   Whether that famous ' trader ' was envious or not, he certainly advertised an insolent contempt for the products of a more aristocratic industry than soap-making.

CHAPTER II

THE DISAPPEARANCE OF THE
SPECTATOR

SHOULD there be ' players ' and ' livers,' art and life, or only one thing ? That is one way of putting the matter—not perhaps the best, but one that brings out one aspect of it.

The magnificent spirit of experiment animating the Moscow theatre is a byword, and when the usual stage performance elsewhere in Europe is recalled (except, of course, those of Germany) the intellectual deadness of the life outside these two countries must at once be apparent. But art is as yet, no doubt, too much politics in Russia. And the politics being in too elementary a stage, the art associated with it must not be taken too much *au pied de la lettre*. Russia is still in the phase, where such things as the tone of the press and so forth are concerned, of heavy court-ship and flattery. Mr. Michael Farbman writes as follows on the subject of the bolshevik ' revolutionary jargon ' :—

> It may, after all, be no paradox to say that this party, yesterday the party of most extreme revolution, is to-day becoming, in a sense, a conservative party. This statement may be difficult to believe, especially as the phraseology used by the leaders has changed very little. But words generally retain their currency longer than the ideas they stand for, and, on the other hand, the more conservative the Bolsheviks become, the readier they are to adhere to the revolutionary jargon. I personally am so convinced that there is an air of deliberate overstrain in their use of this jargon that when I read leading articles in their press proclaiming the primitive ardour of their revolutionary principles, I am sure that they are protesting too much, and that the party is probably preparing to make another step backwards. After all, this sort of duplicity is part of the stock-in-trade of the politician in every country. . . .

Bearing in mind this necessarily artificial, ' revolu-tionary,' ' proletarian ' background (this by no means involving a fundamental insincerity on the part of the group compelled, in the nature of things, for the moment, to such conventions and expedients), we shall be able to place, better than otherwise we should, the particular art manifestations that are its reflection on the russian stage, and in which the confusion of the *actor* and the *spectator* is carried deliberately to its logical conclusion. I will quote from a review (*Labour Monthly*, April 1925) on a book of Mr. Carter's on dramatic art in the Worker's Republic.

' His ' (Mierhold's) aim, we are told, is to find ' the best means of conveying the spectator into the creative author in such a way that he experiences all that the creative author has experienced.' But the link that connects this idea with Mierhold's method is missing. He seeks, we are told, to put the *spirit* of life on the stage, and the production therefore should be ' simple, highly concentrated, and abstract.' The spirit of to-day he believes to be the Machine Spirit. ' Society is a moral machine, the actor is an essential part of the machine, with movements to correspond.' But how this is expressed by ladders and levels, bare walls and spirals, actors that are disciplined and uniformed like an army, is not here explained.

The new theatre of Russia aims at emphasizing a collective personality rather than an individual one, at expressing masses not men. Tchekov's studies of introspective individuals are out of fashion. The worker, the trader, and the peasant of the new theatre do not represent any particular person whose character interested the author, but represent their class or their profession.

With this simplification goes an attempt to break down the barrier between the audience and the actor. Reinhardt had tried this, but in England the influence of the Gordon Craig school had been in the other direction. They sought to make the actor more remote, masking him, robbing him of personality, so that he should seem isolated, a creature of a different birth.

The literary theatrical tradition has for the moment partly broken down in Russia. The new school of producers will take any liberty they choose with the text, and are more concerned with the action and emotional sweep of the drama than with the dialogue. This, however, is possibly only a phase of development, at an era when plays suitable to the temper of the new audience are hard to come by, and at a time when quick methods are imperative if they are to find enough material to keep the theatres open. The lack of sympathetic plays also accounts for the growth of theatres where improvisation replaces the written word, an amusing reversion to the 'Commedia delle Arte.'

So we see the simultaneous disappearance of the *author* and of the *actor*, to all intents and purposes. The people go into the theatre as though into a large nursery, and improvise their own plays, dividing the rôles amongst themselves—or this is the tendency. The policy of such of the theatrical world as remains from the old régime is to ' break down the barrier between the audience and the actor,' to express ' masses not men,' *not* to ' represent any particular person,' but a class-type, *the trader*, *the peasant*, *the bad man*, and *the good man*.

Out of all this new, fluid material, the material of ' folk art,' poured into the theatre, new forms are certain to take shape. But at the moment it is as art a wilfully created chaos. The ἐθελονταί are in art what ' the barbarians ' are in politics. These conditions occur periodically, or are apt to : but as a dogma the theory of *the amateur* is valueless. If the *professional* is a bad professional, that means the society that has produced him is a bad society. Apart from the social snobbery which is invariably (in England and America, at all events) at the bottom of the cult of ' the amateur,' a society that begins abusing its professional artists (its Royal Academicians, etc.) is generally at fault itself. The Royal Academy in England is a perfect justification for social revolution. It is the inevitable counterpart of the nineteenth-century industrial slum.

' The amateur ' as a dogma is meaningless : as a destructive expedient it has more meaning, but only if it aims at the stage at which *everybody* is capering about, smudging pieces of paper, cutting stones and kneading clay, bellowing in every room, and scribbling couplets on every wall.

Any criticism of a genuinely imagined Utopia would no doubt be improper. But we have to-day (among the wealthy) a small-scale cultural democratic Utopia flourishing around us. It is impossible not to draw certain conclusions from having it constantly under our eyes. And they must awaken certain misgivings in the most ecstatic breast as to the possibilities of *every man his own artist* succeeding, any more than *every man his own doctor* is a great success.

The ideology of *progress*, again, so admirably exposed by George Sorel, is also in some part responsible for the cult of the amateur. Condorcet's delusion on the subject of education is dealt with in the following way by Sorel. ' Condorcet hoped,' he writes, ' that public education would result in all magical superstitions disappearing : no longer to be the dupe,' he says, ' of those popular delusions and errors which torment people with superstitious fears and chimerical hopes : to defend oneself against prejudice with the independent power of the reason : finally, to escape from the glamour of charlatanries laying their traps for our fortune, our health, our liberty of thought and conscience, under the pretext of enriching, healing, or saving us.'

These words of Condorcet's, as Sorel points out, provide themselves the evidence of a grave delusion and superstition on the part of their author : ' it is doubtful,' is Sorel's comment, ' if the sort of instruction that is given to the people is of a nature to preserve it from these follies. . . . It is impossible to foresee what a skilful vulgarization of occultism by the great press might accomplish.' ' Il n'est pas ridicule de supposer que nous approchons en ces matières de découvertes capitales.'

Popular education, at all events, has only resulted in people being infinitely more gullible. It is the most remarkable instrument of deception so far invented. The ' know-all,' the ' Je sais tout ' system is the best to keep people in complete ignorance of everything that profoundly matters to them. To-day there is *no* political, scientific, or other charlatanry that cannot be ' put across ' them. This power of imposition and suggestion, put to good uses, and in the hands of people desiring the good of the mass, would be a marvellous instrument indeed.

The cult of ' the amateur,' then, can be regarded on that side as part of the humbug of ' progress.' Yet you must guard yourself, however clearly you see the vanity or the simple trickery of that idea, from a gesture of discouragement that could affect the poor man struggling to obtain some of that culture which, owing to the circumstances of his life, has been denied him. The passion for learning that is often found in the working-man's club is a far more rare and impressive thing than what is generally the 'professional' learning of the don, or expensively trained specialist. In an adverse analysis of the cult of the amateur it is very important not to disturb some of the permanent institutions of *amateurism*, which are more valuable than most of their professional counterparts.

Any obstruction placed in the way of a poor man, longing to bathe himself in music, mesmerize himself with pictures, or drug himself with books, would be a very different thing to Prohibition. The question lies altogether in a doubt as to whether sociological thought is not apt to tread mistaken paradises : and especially whether it does not persistently tend to mistake the function of art and ' culture,' to neglect the nature of its biologic limitations, within certain rigid psychological cadres, and to overlook its dependence on certain set conditions. The catharsis effected by the greek stage is a stock picture of its satisfactory functioning.

If the actor ceased to *act*, and *lived* his acting, he would then be purging *himself*. He would soon cease, if he *acted* or *lived* at any considerable pitch of emotion, either to act or live any more. The only way in which he could perform the same tragic and purgatorial parts would be by watering down his vitality very much, and regarding his ' art ' much less *seriously*. That must inevitably be what happens when ' life ' takes over the tasks of art, and when as a form of living the many aspire to practise what can only be a ritual and artifice of a highly trained few.

So a Utopia is not necessarily an *active* Utopia. Quiescence, obedience, and receptivity are required for action, as well as the active factors, just as women and men are required to produce a child. Is not the woman usually referred to most flatteringly to-day as the ' creator,' the repository of the creative function, the really important ' partner ' in the sex arrangement; the man the ' mere executant ' ? So to be *receptive* rather than active (to just lie down and *couver* rather than execute) is by no means a humiliating rôle. And the *spectator's* godlike rôle is not a contemptible one at all. The term ' friend of man ' would not hustle him into action, or excite him to ' express his personality.' The people show that popular education has not deprived them of every vestige of common sense, in paying little attention to the incessant newspaper gibes about their going in vast crowds *to watch* (merely) football matches and other expert displays. Since they could not do it so well themselves, they much prefer to see other men, highly trained ' cracks ' and champions, doing it for them. Also they enjoy being *the spectator* and availing themselves of his privileges, detachment, and passivity ; also his greater mental satisfactions. Used not the gallery of a theatre to be referred to as ' the gods ' ? The theorist of *amateurism*, the person who wishes to compel or persuade these people no longer *to enjoy vicariously* but *to be their own* this and that, is not serving them well.

In another place I have dealt more fully with this question of the amateur, or the return of the ἐθελονταί ; and this brief summary must suffice to bring the present argument into line with the wider thesis of this essay.

CHAPTER III

'BUY ME AN AIR-BALL, *PLEASE*!'

THE sardonic genius that is putting our matrons into flesh-coloured tights and short skirts, and that will soon have our most venerable political leaders in Eton collars, and perhaps bare legs, deserves, if anything does, a memorial. I will not dishonour it with anything less compendious than it merits. Some approximation to the super-young or the naïf is a universal fashionable expedient to-day : it is the cult of *the child*, which is a far more fundamental thing than the cult of *the artist*. For this exaggeration of something common to every time a great variety of explanations is offered.

It is in freudian language, for instance, the desire of man to return into the womb from whence he came : a movement of retreat and discouragement—a part of the great strategy of defeat suggested to or evolved by our bankrupt society. Certainly there is a great deal of this discouragement and fear in it. This has been well expressed by one of the most remarkable of contemporary poets in the *Love Song of Prufrock*. After the poor tormented soul he has shown us describes his ' rather bald ' head ' being brought in on a platter,' and other blood-curdling images of what has been called the ' old man ' *complex*, the romantic magnifications of a man who allows the world to be ' too much with him ' and dominate him, he is made to conclude with quaint candour, ' And I was afraid.' At all events, at the root of the mechanical, subconscious obsession that in the fashions takes such ridiculous forms that it is impossible not to suppose that there is a mind at the back of them capable of appreciating a joke, perhaps too well (though the ' wisdom ' of this comedian can be doubted), is the reflection of political decay, the stopping-up and closing-down of the great traditional vents for ambition, and the overthrow of any ' public life ' that could claim a significance beyond the function of office-boy and valet. It is the diagnostic of a frantic longing to refresh, rejuvenate, and invigorate a life that, it is felt, has grown old and too unsimple, and lost its native direction. It is the most thoroughly organized reversal and returning on its steps of mankind that has occurred.

It is, however, a ' frantic longing ' that is very thoroughly organized indeed. All the channels of publicity foster it. It is a part of the great, and I believe fecund, solution of the problem of ' power.' For to make everybody ' like unto little children ' is not such a bad way (to start with) of disposing of them. The political power that is taking command in the world to-day seems to have said to all those immature, *inapertiva* people, who were gradually forced away from the seats of authority that they had for so long held in Europe, ' Run away and play ! ' Frightened and astonished, they ran away sure enough, and are allowed to *play* also, for a moment. But it will not be for long. That is why the fashions devised to fit this temporary situation should be disregarded when you are desirous of reaching some insight into the real tendencies of which they are only a caricatural, early phase.

The advertisement given to this phase in the newspapers is very extensive. But it is often no less sardonic than, as we have said, it is natural to suppose the Prospero of Fashion to be. Here, for instance, is an account (from the *Daily Mail*, August 1925) of the English visitors playing at children at Deauville :—

YOUNG AGAIN.

ONE JOYOUS HOUR AT DEAUVILLE.

HAPPY CHILDISH ENGLISH.

FOREIGNERS WHO DON'T UNDERSTAND.

By Our Special Correspondent.
Deauville, Aug. 20.

Watching the English playing like children is one of the regular diversions at Deauville, where there are so few real children to play.

In the quiet of the afternoons between luncheon and tea on the rare days when there is no racing, English men and women come out to play with model yachts and kites and big rubber balls, and people of other nations stand and stare at the keen zest and serious purpose of these boyish men and girlish women recapturing something of the simple joys of childhood.

A tall, blond man with the carriage of a guardsman and the limbs of a heavy-weight boxer comes striding down the shore, an old sun-hat on his head, and in his hand a toy yacht, cutter-rigged, designed and built to withstand the toy tempest.

A slender girl rushes up from the sea to meet him. She may be twenty or she may be thirty. When a woman keeps her figure she can also keep the secret of her age ; but whatever her age, she is now a little girl again walking beside a big boy, and begging prettily to be allowed to play with the beautiful boat.

And he, the proud owner of the beautiful boat, permits her to pat the hull, but she must not touch the rudder—that is the captain's privilege ; but she may swim out, and when the boat reaches her she may turn it round and send it on the other tack scudding valiantly back to the big boy.

So it is arranged, and the important game begins, all very grave and serious and young. How anxiously the two watch the launching of the boat in the water that has little more than a ripple for the fishing-boats out there, but is such a tempestuous sea to the brave little boat !

Only playful zephyrs tease the sails of the fishing-boats, but mighty winds strike the frail craft, beating it down to the gunwale, while the mad foam leaps over the bow and great seas wash the decks, and the mast bends like a whip and the spars strain, the ropes twang, as the gallant yacht lays down to her work and races through the storm. Loudly the ' skipper ' and his ' mate ' cheer her on as, reaching, beating, and scudding, she shows her paces, the crack boat of the toy regatta.

Millionaires and semi-millionaires from the Argentine, from Manhattan, from the Middle West, from Central Europe, and from the Far East, watch in wonder the childish play of the English man and the English woman, so proud of their toy, so concerned for its safety. Young Frenchmen resting from their hard-fought games on the tennis courts smile with more than a suggestion of contempt ; but the boy-man and the girl-woman heed them not at all.

Happy childhood is calling through the years, and they are content to play unashamed of their joy in the childish game, and glad to lay aside the burden of years for one fleeting hour while the sun shines and the sea sparkles and the world seems made for play.

Spurning the lazy tide, other boy-men and girl-women merrily chase a big ball as it bounces from wavelet to wavelet, and their voices, too, hold the careless rapture of childhood. ' Just for an hour,' they seem to say, ' just for an hour let us be young again. Just for an hour let nothing matter but the crazy frolics of a big, bouncing ball. Oh ! the big ball has hit Jack on the nose and knocked him floundering on his back. Look out, he is going to throw it ! Bang ! That was one for May ! Keep it going, keep it going. . . .

When a feminine figure in a costume symbolizing the tenderest years, clinging to a protecting arm, in some pastiche of an antiquated relationship, catches sight of a floating mass of air-balls, and, capering ecstatically against him, pleads with her companion, ' Oh ! pease, pease, do buy me an air-ball : that lovely gween one ! ', a situation of probably mousterian antiquity is reproduced for whoever happens to be observing the display. It is unfortunate, but there it is : people manufacture such pictures and situations out of their sexual interplay, to serve a social rather than a sexual vanity. But aside from vanity, sex will still manufacture things on the same lines. Even Jonathan Swift, at an advanced age, used ' little language,' ' oo ittle devil'd ' his Stella ; it is one of those accompaniments of human life which, when the life force is full of mettle and at its most complex and ambitious, is kept in the background. It is not so much, therefore, that there is anything intrinsically novel in the type of events described in the *Daily Mail*, as that the background has become the foreground, ' little life ' obsesses the impoverished landscape. It becomes a dogma of perfection, like Christ's ' little children.' It is a highly organized cult, associated with others of the same blood with itself. And whereas formerly it was confined to grown-up and elderly people, now real children also play at being ' children,' even outdoing their most skilful adult imitators.

CHAPTER IV

THE CHILDREN OF PETER PAN

WHEN people are told by a religious teacher that only *children* can enter the kingdom of heaven, they are glad ; for they feel as helpless and little as that, and gather gladly in vast chattering crowds beneath the fostering wings of the Church. (Christ compared himself to a hen, clucking for her chicks, and holding out her wings : but he complained that they did not come.) The *child* is, in fact, for most men, the eternal emblem of a happy irresponsibility ; of the shorn lamb for whom the wind is tempered ; of an inhabitant of fairyland where everything is rose-coloured and turns out for the best, subjected to the dream-control of the individual will : where you are shepherded and *loved*. Even the horniest old sinner will melt and ' nestle ' if invited to be a *child* once more.

There is, it has yet to be admitted, about all the repercussions from the use of this sentimental religious lever— especially in the case of the christian religion—this patent of *childhood*, in exchange for submission, an unpleasant sweetness, a self-pity, surrender of personality, that recommends it rather to one type of person than to another. The child is an equivocal figure. It is the symbol of the eleatic *Becoming*, of a malleable and impersonal thing. It is sexless, or ideally so. When invoked as a divine type it is found that, in practice, it symbolizes— of the two halves of which it is potentially composed— rather the female than the male. It is not a sexually balanced symbol, but so preponderatingly feminine as almost to merge in the mother-figure on which it is dependent, and to which it is so close. A mind abandoning itself to these emotions is betrayed into the most technical feminine rôle.

The Peter Pan psychology often conflicts more sadly with the reality (when we observe some large and mature person behaving incongruously) than does any Utopia provided with too concrete and immediate an incarnation.

Were we as self-conscious and intellectually enterprising as the Greeks, as able to give effect and a lovely concrete shape to our obsessions, we should have our towns at present full of large statues of little children. Every variety of baby boy and baby girl would ogle us from their pedestals. For that matter, if the early christian had been a plastic artist like the pagan whom he drove out, and intellectually scrupulous and imaginative at the same time, he would have filled the world with statues of little children, as the Greeks filled it with athletes.

So it is *sub persona infantis* that the strategy of to-day would present itself. The vulture and the eagle dispense with their terrifying finials and beaks, and paddle luxuriously about the advective floor like doves. The naïf psychology is *de rigueur*. If you do not ' grow up ' (with the initiative, self-reliance, and so on associated with that action) there is no need for you to have an adult psychology either. In any case the *serious* things of life are the frivolous things, are they not? So you are recommended to remain ' children '—to remain ' kids,' and not outgrow your own ' kids,' but share their nursery with them and quarrel with them over wireless sets owned in common. That is the best way. To *grow up*, to do what Peter Pan so wisely refrained from doing, is to think and struggle ; and all thinking is evil, and struggle is useless. Give up your will ; cease to think for yourself ; regard your employer as your good, kind father or uncle : leave everything in his hands.

Barrie's play, *Peter Pan*, is to our time what *Uncle Tom's Cabin* was to the Civil War period in America. It gave expression to a deep emotional current, of political origin. The *refusal to grow up* of Peter Pan was the specific found by the *narquois* mind of the Zeitgeist for the increasing difficulties connected *with* growing up. ' Don't you grow up ! Refuse ! That is what I should do ! ' through Sir James Barrie it almost gibed. ' Just go on being a kid. It's quite simple ! No one can stop you ! '

And really the Zeitgeist is kind ; and although to-day a little over-intellectual and sometimes indecorous, apt, as we have seen, to play rather humiliating tricks on those over whom he stretches his sheltering wing, he is nevertheless a true benefactor.

But people are also becoming *in reality* more childlike, and the deliberate and imitative machinery of adult life is met half way by a physical transformation. In the levelling, standardization, and pooling of the crowd-mind, as the result of a closer organization from above and greatly increased pressure on any irregularities of surface or temperamental erection, it is the masculine mind that tends to approximate to the feminine rather than the other way round. This is inevitable, seeing that the masculine is not the natural human state, but a carefully nurtured secondary development above the normal and womanly. But women have always retained much more of the childlike in their mature life than men have, otherwise they would have found it impossible to support the constant society of their children. They have been ' the children that train our children.' So it is that, as the man's mind is slowly emolliated, and his personal will called into play less and less frequently ; as he loses initiative, since he never has any opportunity of using it ; and as all the intensive machinery of education and publicity sees to it that he shall not have to think ; as he sinks to the more emotional female level,—it is natural for him also to become more truly childish. There would never have been any difficulty about persuading a woman to remain a child— for her highly important function she was forced to remain one. And now it is equally easy to effect this little conformity with the man.

So *there is no longer any* FAMILY, in one sense : there is now only a collection of children, differing in age but in nothing else. The last vestige of the *patria potestas* has been extirpated. (The *patria potestas* is now that great organizing power that is the new, pervasive, all-powerful principle of our blind and complex life.)

But in another sense the FAMILY is more obsessing with us than ever. For the reliefs to the domestic atmosphere that formerly existed are no longer so satisfactory or so numerous from the point of view of the average man. Still, this ' average man ' will soon disappear ; and children get on better with each other than women do, for instance, between themselves. There is not the same need for a complementary and contrasting nature.

PART VII

THE FAMILY AND FEMINISM

' C'est pourquoi M. de Bonald a pu dire, avec
raison, que la famille est l'embryon de l'Etat, dont
elle reproduit les catégories essentielles : le roi
dans le père, le ministre dans la mère, le sujet dans
l'enfant. C'est pour cela aussi que les socialistes
fraternitaires, qui prennent la famille pour élément
de la Société, arrivent tous à la dictature, forme la
plus exagérée du gouvernement. . . . Combien de
temps encore nous faudra-t-il pour comprendre cette
filiation d'idées ? '
> Idée générale de la révolution au xixe siècle.
> P.-J. Proudhon.

' It may be conceived, without entering into details,
how any single person, born . . . into a perfect subjection to his parents, that is, into a state of perfect
political society with respect to his parents, may
from thence pass into a perfect state of nature ; and
from thence successively into any number of different
states of political society more or less perfect, by
passing into different societies.'
> A Fragment of Government. Jeremy Bentham.

' Population, again, and bodily health and vigour,
are things which are nowhere treated in such an unintelligent, misleading, exaggerated way as in England. Both are really machinery ; yet how many
people all around us do we see rest in them and fail
to look beyond them ! Why, one has heard people,
fresh from reading certain articles of the Times on
the Registrar-General's returns of marriages and
births in this country, who would talk of our large
english families in quite a solemn strain, as if they
had something in itself beautiful, elevating, and
meritorious in them ! '
> Culture and Anarchy. Matthew Arnold.

CHAPTER I

WHY 'SOCIALISM WISHES TO ABOLISH THE FAMILY'

IT is round the question of *the family* that all the other questions of politics and social life are gathered. The break-up of the family unit to-day is the central fact of our life : it is from its central disintegration, both in fact and in our minds—the consequent readjustments of our psychology—that all the other revolutionary phases of our new society radiate. The relations of men to women, of the child to the parent, of friendship and citizenship to the new ideals of the state, are all controlled by it.

This can be easily seen by taking a few examples from the things we have just been discussing. The *child* obsession, the flight from responsibility, would naturally result from the decay of *the parent*, in the old sense of a symbol of authority. In a communist state, where children were taken from the parents at birth to a public *crèche*, the state becoming the ' breadwinner ' and the effective centre of authority or All-father, as it were, the parents would never be ' parents ' at all.

The economic incentive of the upkeep of a family circle, a wife and children, again, must affect a man's attitude to his dignity and duty in a great many ways. Relieved of that, he would care far less about his position in the world, ' getting on,' whether he remained in an irresponsible subaltern position or became a master. It would affect very deeply his attitude to women if marriage were entirely eliminated from his transactions with them. The bachelor's or the ' old maid's ' interests are very different—where interests exist—to the ' family man's ' or the ' mother of a family's.' And lastly, sex inversion is evidently not disconnected with the existence and coercive influence of the idea of the family in a man or woman's life. And to the end of their days Fortune is like a cherishing parental figure to the man or woman of fashion and fortune : however many children they have by accident, they must remain eternally the spoilt child themselves, and the family is seldom a reality for them. In that they resemble the most emancipated worker in the most complete of communist societies.

In this part the feminine, generally, is to be discussed, then, and the problems arising from family life, sex specialization, and the relations of men and women. My entrance into it is effected without the accompaniment of set teeth and battle in the eye; a few elementary precautions are observed, but none of a slighting nature. I am able to observe very little difference between men and women, and my liking and interest are equally distributed. If anything, women represent, I believe, a higher spiritual average. Even the instinct of primitive races that accorded women mystical and creative attributes denied to men seems to me very worth attention. So there where I certainly wear a uniform, it does not dispose me to militancy in a quarrel that I understand too well to become violently partisan.   Great feminists like Ibsen, for instance, have usually been followed by a great reactionary and anti-feminist like Strindberg. The headlong liberal partisanship of the first, with all it entails of stupid bitterness, raises an opposite champion, who, with excesses on the other side, soon organizes male zeal, and the sexes are on a war footing. The fit of hatred he throws himself into shows he is nearer to the feminist than he thinks—probably too near to the feminine, in the secondary sense, altogether. Feminism is a movement directed to the destruction of the family, which is a good thing. But, needless to say, the true motive is never avowed : and a quantity of fantastic doctrine is manufactured which is as seriously disputed as though some valuable discovery depended on it.

P.-J. Proudhon was not a feminist. Edouard Berth remarks on that fact as follows : ' If one wishes to estimate the depth of the *détraquement* of the contemporary world, there is no better witness of it than feminism. And that Proudhon was not a feminist is one more proof that he incarnated, in the heart of the socialist movement, the reaction of good sense and of classical reason ' (*Les*

méfaits des intellectuels).   He then proceeds to quote
Proudhon (from *Contradictions*) : I give a part of his
quotation :—

> Love and marriage, work and the family circle, property
> and *domesticity* . . . all these terms are equivalent.   On
> that point all mankind is unanimous—all except the socialists,
> who alone, in their ideologic void, protest against this unan-
> imity of the rest of mankind.   *Socialism wishes to abolish
> family life, because it costs too much.*   It wishes to abolish
> property, because it is prejudicial to the state.   Socialism
> wishes to change the rôle of the woman : from queen, as
> society has established her, it wants to make her a priestess
> of Cotytto. . . .

Proudhon, the great French revolutionary of the nineteenth century, was, however, violently assailed by the
feminists for his reactionary attitude as regards feminism.
This attitude was dictated, certainly, as Berth says, from
sheer French ' classicist ' good sense.   He was accused of
wishing to keep the woman as a family drudge, because he
wished to maintain family life.   He upheld the necessity
of this against all the shallow and fashionable insistence
of his socialist friends, who, for the most part, wanted to
destroy it.   *Socialism wishes to abolish family life, because
it costs too much*, he said, far too bluntly !   He wanted
economics to accommodate itself to the family instead of
vice versa.   In this he showed himself an imperfect
realist.

He saw the threat of a new slave-state, worse than any
former slavery.   He realized that as ' free ' creatures, in
the utopian, the european sense, the man and the woman
must remain united.   United they would stand, he considered, but forced apart by economic exigence or political
intrigue they would fall—that is, no longer be free.   So,
according to his lights, he fought very hard for the freedom
that he prized so much.   What that freedom really was,
and whether it was everybody's freedom, I have already
discussed.   Later, in connection with the general theories
of Proudhon, I shall again briefly consider it.

Proudhon was nothing if not a moralist : but in this
matter it was really not as a moralist that he was speaking,
but from the deepest sense of what he saw to be the interests
of european free institutions.   He says, for instance, in

La pornocratie (the book he wrote in reply to his feminist opponents) :—

> I have blamed, with all the energy of which I am capable, incest, abortion, rape, prostitution, all the crimes and offences against marriage and the family—I could equally say *against woman*. I have denounced them as the signs and the instruments of despotism.

But the elderly harpy of Byron's *Don Juan* putting her head out of the window in the town that is being sacked, and inquiring impatiently, ' When is the raping going to begin ? ', suggests by its truth to life that Proudhon was talking of *crimes against women* too much from the man's standpoint. Contraceptives may be inventions inimical to women in their functional capacity of mothers. But a great brood of children is not every woman's affair. There is a personality in every woman that is independent of function that has to be taken into account at least. These things that Proudhon capitulates are against the family, and against marriage certainly. But they are not for that reason *against women*, as they are represented to be by him. That is the weakness of his position. *Woman* was his Achilles' heel as a revolutionary. The utopianism of which Marx accused him is most visible in that. And he was a utopian despot.

Marriage is often *against* a woman (or a man). And the family is ' a despotism.' In many senses it could be said that the things enumerated above—as abortion or prostitution, at all events—were signs and instruments of freedom rather than despotism, exactly indeed as the conventional feminist would assert.

CHAPTER II

MR. CHESTERTON'S CONCERN FOR
THE FAMILY UNIT

BEFORE proceeding with our analysis of Proudhon's notions relative to the family and to woman, I will consider a contemporary view of the same subject, also dogmatically in favour of the family unit. It appeared in an october (1925) issue of a liberal weekly, for the direction of which Mr. G. K. Chesterton is responsible. It has the additional advantage of introducing into our debate this liberal colleague of Mr. Shaw's, who is a sort of caricature of 'a Liberal' as seen by Rowlandson.

The liberalism of Mr. Chesterton, complicated with a romantic conversion to roman catholicism, and installed in an obsessing cartoon-like John Bull physique, is very different to that of Mr. Shaw. The well-fed high spirits of the old liberal England, the strange association of humaneness with religious intolerance, a sanguine grin fiercely painted on the whole make-up, compose a sinister figure such as you would find, perhaps—exploiting its fatness, its shrewdness, its animal violence, its blustering patriotism all at once—in the centre of some nightmare Bank Holiday fair. He is all for the freedom of Old England, whose 'beer-drinking Britons can never be beat,' all for 'infallible artillery' to support the infallibility of that potentate he has heavily embraced, and to support anything else that can afford artillery to advance its peculiar claims. He cannot understand why a jolly old war (with all the usual accompaniments of poison gas and bombs, you know) cannot be arranged between Ireland and Scotland on the score of the heresy of the latter; and while this was going on he would urge the English to invade Wales, and finish off the job so half-heartedly dropped a thousand odd years ago by the ingævonic tribes. The cackling and grimacing humorousness, punctuated with flabby puns, of this strange individual, would increase immeasurably if he were able to observe the british catholics preparing to attack the british anglicans in the rear, while the latter were finishing off the last of the chapel-going Cymri.

The article is named ' The Fear of the Family,' and saw the light in consequence of a pronouncement of another liberal, of rather more mixed opinions. The writer describes the thesis of his opponent as follows. He says that, owing to ' the exhaustive and profound studies in economics ' of this erring gentleman he had reached the ' sensational ' conclusion that ' the present industrial system, founded on coal, petrol, steam, iron, railways, factories, and laboratories cannot by any conceivable means any longer support the institution known as the family, not at least in the form in which it has come down to us since the days when the first christian priests insisted that the privilege of marriage should be extended even to slaves. The continuance of marriage and the family as an institution universal throughout society is bound to land industry not merely in trade depressions, strikes, lock-outs, and extensive unemployment, but in complete stoppage and disaster.'

Under these circumstances the good economist's conclusion is that the *family must go*, of course. In this he resembles Proudhon's ' socialist.'

The writer of this article, having stated the position of his renegade, too ' economical,' opponent, explains the situation from his own pure-liberal point of view. ' The real difficulty with industry to-day is that the man who works in the mine, in the factory, or on the railway is by tradition a free man ; and he is a free man in virtue of the fact that christian civilization has made him the actual or potential head of a family, morally, socially, and legally responsible for the maintenance of that family. It is this that makes the working man of to-day so intractable. Take away from him that responsibility and that freedom, and you will make him more tractable. . . . If a man has a wife and family to support, he can always make some show at the bar of public opinion in every strike and every lock-out. If the state supports his wife and family for him, he can make no show at all. He can be told to get to work at once. And the *Daily Mail* and the people in trains and motor cars would not be slow to tell him so.'

What this says is that the workman has always been

able to hide behind his wife and children ; and the more children he had, the more sandbags he had. But has this 'responsibility' been pleasant either for him or for them ? They, the rampart for his more and more fictitious 'independence,' have received the brunt of the economic attack. As to the responsibility and the freedom with the loss of which he is threatened, he would be far happier without them. He never asked for them, and has never enjoyed them. For these two expensive words he has suffered enough hardships. It is the greatest cruelty to him to urge him to hang on to them to-day. It gives a fine sensation of heroism, no doubt, to the theorist so advising him. But for the head of the family on a low wage it is less romantic.

The romance of the *family as a unit* is a prosperous nineteenth-century english middle-class romance. To tell the impoverished english labourer to-day to keep at all costs his home-and-castle-in-one, and continue to cling to this phantom of authority, is to urge the continuance of a stupid torture.

The women and children, on their side, would be very much relieved if the state would take over their maintenance. As to the 'home-life,' the well-to-do have seldom any conception of what a mockery it is to speak in sugary or heroic terms of that to people who, like the majority, have to live in a half-savage condition of poverty.

Socrates proposed that, in his ideal state, the children should be removed from the parents. The problem of the woman, owing to the peculiarities of his greek training, he neglected. The german idea of *Gemütlichkeit* and 'home' was the last thing that would have occurred to a Greek, of course. It was rather the thing to escape from than the thing to cling to. Then his idea of 'freedom,' as well, would be different to the german, which latter would be based really on the notion of *physical* freedom, as Goethe defined it in his friend. The patriarchal is the *physical* ideal. But to be anything that can remotely be described as 'free' in industrial conditions is not to be patriarchal, or burdened with a family.

CHAPTER III

'THE WOMAN' PROUDHON'S ONLY
REVOLUTIONARY DISCOVERY

PROUDHON vaunted the latin, the roman heritage. He was very fond of returning to the law-giving and law-loving *fond* of the french nature, the roman in his inheritance. No roman father could have devised more despotic conditions than he did for the woman. He even (cf. *La pornocratie*), in the true fashion of roman antiquity, would have given the husband power of life and death over the wife. But with a slave system, and the terrible *patria potestas*, the Roman was very successful politically. It is not christian principles, which is the same as socialist principles, that make a state 'great.' And Proudhon (in the condition of complete mental confusion in which the European has remained ever since his turbulent egotism and western and northern 'push' tied itself up to its opposite, christianity) was all for a great and even warlike 'city,' on the antique, pagan, pattern.

Let us say that women are *men with a handicap*. It is a natural handicap. Proudhon was a fine example of the natural man. Nothing would have convinced him of the reasonableness of removing the handicap socially, surgically. For, being the natural man, he hated uniformity. Everything would seem for him, as for Sorel, to gain in force and power by *differentiation*. And everything about him was highly reasonable—all but his socialism, which was a madness he never completely overcame. That was the christian overlay, beneath which the pagan and roman limbs could be seen perpetually moving, evidently with iron discipline, to the most warlike and primitive airs.

So, as Proudhon regarded himself as eminently of the party of revolt (the only way in which he was not a revolutionary, he might have supposed, was in his anti-feminism), the woman was the only 'revolutionary' that he challenged. But on the principle which impelled him to challenge her, he could have challenged equally *every* item of the revolutionary programme that he so ardently supported, and so become a unique revolutionary.

The idea of government, he says, is modelled on the experience of the family; its tenacity is owing to the fact that men have always had under their eyes the small model of the state in their own family circle. The family is the embryo of the state. The father is *the king*, the mother is *the minister of state*, the child is *the subject*. Thus the fundamental age and sex categories have regulated, immemorially, the notion of government. ' That is the reason why,' he says (*Idée générale de la révolution au xixᵉ siècle*), ' the fraternist-socialists, who take the family as the model of society, all arrived at the idea of dictatorship, the most exaggerated form of government.' He finishes by asking, ' How long will it take us to understand this affiliation of ideas ? '

It is, however, an attempt to trace the affiliation, the *family* relationship, as it were, of all these revolutionary ideas, that has occupied us throughout this essay. Proudhon never understood, apparently, any affiliation except that of the man and woman. ' The woman ' was his sole *philosophic* discovery. She shook him, apparently, out of his conventional Utopia : for some reason he saw her very clearly indeed. And his attitude to *her* was in direct contradiction to all his anarchist teaching ; although very much in agreement with all his highly non-revolutionary instincts.

Above we have seen him setting out to show (in his chapter on ' The Principle of Authority ') that men have always gone wrong in their revolutionary activities because they have insisted on modelling their idea of the state on the obvious family paradigm. From the obsessing image of *the family* they have not been able to escape. So it is that, no sooner is one despotism (modelled on the traditional family) cast down, than another equally despotic is set up in its place.

Of all the great revolutionaries of the last century Proudhon dogmatized the most about the family, in the opposite sense to most of his revolutionary contemporaries. The family must at all costs be retained :

that was one of the corner-stones of his system.   Alone the family was able to guarantee freedom, and stood between 'despotism' and mankind.   And yet above we see him indicating it as the model of all governmental despotism.

CHAPTER IV

THE FAMILY AS AN OBSESSING MODEL

IF you have followed my argument and understood my meaning you will know that this essay *On the Art of being Ruled* could be described, if such a description were required, as *against the family.* On the other hand, it is not *against women.* Eventually, I believe, a considerable segregation of women and men must occur, just as segregation of those who decide for the active, the intelligent life, and those who decide (without any stigma attaching to the choice) for the ' lower ' or animal life, is likely to happen, and is very much to be desired. This, in its turn, no doubt, in the end, would lead to people being born into these respective planes of existence. Different species cut off from each other, and no longer free to choose, would be found. Interplanetary communication might settle this problem in the future. If this idea of segregation seems a disgusting one, all that can be said is that it is often suggested to us that more intelligent beings than ourselves may exist in other worlds, and may even be able to influence or control us. But we live our life just the same. It is not much to boast of ; it is a little brief thing, but we call it, at least, ' our own.'

Returning to the paradigm of the Family (at the basis, Proudhon affirms, of all ideas of government up to the present) : a gerontocracy—that the old should rule the young—would be an excellent mechanical arrangement if years brought wisdom to people ; or if the majority of people ever had, to start with, any intellectual power. But we know that that is not the case. There is very little difference between the old and the young, just as there is extremely little difference between men and women. People pretend or really believe that there is a mysterious difference; but if you go in search of it, it is hard to find. An ' old boy ' is very like a boy : in anglo-saxon countries, with the insistence on athletic sports, the whole education tending to confirm this uniformity. Its tendency is to take the spiritual quality away from youth, and to bestow a sort of degraded athletic ' youth-

fulness' on age. It deliberately stunts the spiritual
growth, so that a man remains of adolescent stature, as
far as the mind is concerned, to the end. 'Most men die
at thirty-five,' a french writer suggests. Thirty would
probably be nearer the mark : but the demise is a small
matter and is scarcely noticeable.

The family, however, perpetuates this idea of authority.
No doubt, in more primitive societies, where people have
sometimes been allowed to develop more freely, here and
there, their faculties, there may have been more reality
in this contrast : and hence the stability of such forms as
the indonesian, polynesian, or australian gerontocracies.
But to-day, in contemporary Europe, there is no such
contrast. An english cabinet minister or a great business
magnate reads the detective-story fiction of Phillips
Oppenheim ; and his son and his grandson read Phillips
Oppenheim, one in book form and the other in serial form
in the shilling magazine. The footmen and valets of these
various gentlemen also read Phillips Oppenheim, when
their masters have done with him ; they all equally live
in a Phillips Oppenheim world of 'deep diplomats,' 'keen-
eyed' men, iron-willed, hard-headed business giants,
'sporty, knowledgable girls,' 'matey' and 'clean-limbed.'
The scullery-maid reads *Peg's Paper*, and that is the same
thing, only it costs her less : and the boots reads *Sexton
Blake* or *The Magnet*, which is also the same thing. These
people are most truly *equals*—and they all equally hate the
'highbrow' with a mighty hatred—that 'highbrow' who
is another of the myths of their backstairs world.

. These people cannot be divided into age classes, or into
social classes, into classes of the educated and uneducated,
or into any class that has any reality except the class of
those who have a lot of money and those who have none.
Péguy insisted that there is a greater chasm between the
Rich and the Poor to-day than ever before. They lie
horizontally side by side, with the economic chasm separating them in between ; there is no *vertical* identity of race
or religion : as, for instance, in the case of the lowest
feudal serf and greatest feudal chatelain there would be
the mystical unity of the catholic christian world. I think
Péguy, in that description, is neglecting the fact of the
community that an *absence* of anything spiritual gives to

those merely mechanically separated worlds of Wealth and Poverty. There is greater brotherhood to-day between Dives and Lazarus than has existed probably for a long time. For both are equally *poor in spirit*, and consequently to some extent equally *blessed*. That is a great freemasonry. That could almost be called the great secret of the political world to-day : all inequality in wealth and comfort is forgiven the greatest millionaire, on account of his vulgarity, in which he is apt to far outdo his chauffeur or employee. That *little touch of nature* (or of ill-nature, as Butler would correct it), that spiritual identity, that cunning invitation to the basest form of *humility*, and the commonest form of a common humanity, is the millionaire's political secret.

But with all the resources of his fabulous wealth, the democratic magnate is able to drag the poor into depths of spiritual poverty undreamed of by any former proletariat or former ruling class. The rich have achieved this awful brotherhood with the poor by bleeding them of all character, spirituality, and mental independence. That accomplished, they join them spiritually or unspiritually in the servants' hall. All the privileges conferred by wealth are, however, still theirs. Frederick the Great, living with his *heiduques* and grooms, was better off, in the sense of enjoying greater freedom and power, than he would have been as a more conventional ruler among his courtiers. But the latter he also reduced to the level of grooms as far as possible when he went into society. If all the nobles and officials of Prussia at that time are imagined as living similarly on familiar patriarchal terms with their servants, some idea will be obtained of what the millionaire society of to-day is becoming. It is part of that wise and excellent programme of socially and politically *having the apple and eating it too*. The advantages of the poor man's child— the freedom from restraint of the animality of the life of the gutter, emancipated from *noblesse oblige* (the infantile love of dirt and garbage made such a curious use of by Fourier)—are astutely combined with all the advantages of the rich man's child—the expensive toys, servants, and so forth. A travesty of revolution is wedded to the least severe and onerous advantages of aristocracy.

A kind of gigantically luxurious patriarchate is what

202 THE FAMILY AND FEMINISM

democracy and monster industry together have invented. The analogy between a great industrial city and the desert —the emptiness and abstractness of industrial life—is patent enough. So patriarchal conditions in contemporary urban life are not so unnatural as would appear at first sight. There is no king ; but there are many mercantile despots, more or less benevolently patriarchal, indistinguishable in taste, culture, or appearance from their servants, or subjects, or 'clients.' This is how it comes that the family once more occupies the foreground of our lives. With a new *familiarity* and a flesh-creeping ' homeliness' entirely of this unreal, materialist world, where all ' sentiment ' is coarsely manufactured and advertised in colossal sickly captions, disguised for the sweet tooth of a monstrous baby called ' the Public,' the family as it is, broken up on all hands by the agency of feminist and economic propaganda, reconstitutes itself in the image of the state. The government becomes an emperor disguised as Father Christmas, an All-father, a paterfamilias with his pocket full of crystal sets, gramophones, russian boots, and flesh-coloured stockings, which he proceeds to *sell* to his ' children.'

CHAPTER V

FOURIER'S *THEORY OF GROUPS*

WE have seen—in a chapter named 'The Public and the Private Life'—how the other great factor of the barring of the roads of open competition and individual enterprise, and the consequent death of ambition, has contributed to this. In his *Theory of Groups* (ch. ii.) Fourier considers the best method by which one can establish ' le lien sociétaire.' The groups or elementary modes of social relationship, he says, are to be counted to the number of four—like the four elements, earth, air, fire, and water.

The analogical chart he draws up as follows :—

Groupes.	*Eléments.*
Majeurs.	
d'Amitié, affection unisexuelle.	*Terre.*
d'Ambition, affection corporative.	*Air.*
Mineurs.	
d'Amour, affection bissexuelle.	*Arome.*
de Famille, affection consanguine.	*Feu.*
Pivotal.	
d'Unitéisme ou fusion de liens.	*Feu.*

In examining this curious table it will be seen, if our account of the tendencies of society to-day is correct, that (1) the *unisexuelle* (friendship) affective category is being merged in the *bissexuelle* or sexual; that is to say, that friendship between man and man, or between woman and woman, tends to take with it sexual and physical implications, and the spiritual, abstract nature of this relationship becomes less clearly defined. That is to say, everywhere the non-sexual tends to become the sexual, as the family (and the normal or sexual with it) tends to disappear. This of course affects the revolutionary top layer of society first, the conservative and lower classes not yet being deeply influenced.

It will be seen that (2) the category of Ambition will shortly be obsolete, and ambition itself be extinct, for the mass of salaried slaves. In this way earth and the atmosphere disappear. Only *sexual love* and *the family* are left. We all are in the category of Minors. But *the family* to-day is also disappearing, only (in its essence) it is disappearing into government and into social life ; that is to say, that social life is being modelled more and more on a vast family pattern, with the nursery (but a universal nursery, equipped with a complete universe of toys) as its conventicle, and a state of childlike tutelage as its supreme paradigm.

But in the above chart Fourier appends a fifth category, a *pivotal* category, as he calls it, of ' unityism ' or unification. In that all the social ties are fused. Such is perhaps the position of our society : but in its case the ' unification ' is all impregnated with the neighbouring family metaphysics. It is further reinforced and furnished with the bankrupt stocks of the other categories.

In social life, as in the government, the family image obsesses people. Even in an ectogenetically produced society, where the family would have ceased to exist, it is quite possible that the family paradigm, the phantom of the superseded family organization, would still exist, in its full conventionality. So I agree with Proudhon that the obsession of the family should be overcome except for the purposes of the narrow family circle—so long as that exists : that its reflection, in the life of government or in the life of society, should be abolished. But I do not agree with Proudhon that the family in itself should at all costs be retained. For, if you object to its shadow so much, and call that shadow ' despotic,' why should you be so eager to embrace and cherish its substance ?

CHAPTER VI

THE WAR OF 'ONE HALF AGAINST
THE OTHER'

Wealth is the only thing to-day that confers power or ' class ' on an individual. Wealth is an abstract thing independent of social organization, or of national organization, or of a secular ' stake in the country.' When it pretends to delegate power to other categories of things or of people, the democracy or what not, it is merely acting through them, they are its helpless and hypnotized instruments. And naturally it chooses for its instruments the most helpless and ill-equipped classes of the community. It is thus that a hundred things are done to-day in the divine name of Youth, that if they showed their true colours would be seen by rights to belong rather to old age. Things are done, likewise, in the name of Liberty, that are, in truth, the promptings of oppression. As Proudhon truly says, ' Grâce au prestige de ce mot *liberté*, si étrangement prostitué, on a rendu les travailleurs eux-mêmes complices de leur propre infortune ' (' Thanks to the prestige of this word *liberty*, so strangely prostituted, the workers have been made the accomplices of their own misfortune ') (*La capacité politique, etc.*). All the rashness, ignorance, and weakness of women are similarly exploited. Things are undertaken in their name, or in that of their supposed cause, *feminism*, that have nothing at all to do with them. The following speech from Renan's remarkable continuation of the *Tempest* of Shakespeare puts the matter in its true light, for every epoch, for ever and ever without end—unless the capitalistic unification of the world works the miracle that it may, and the cannon-fodder is turned into a more productive, humane article :—

Orlando. . . . A clear, reflecting, self-loving consciousness would say to itself that the essential thing in a battle is not to be killed. It is, therefore, necessary to maintain a vast reserve of ignorance and stupidity, a mass of people so simple that they can be taught to believe that if they are killed they will either go to heaven or that their lot is to be envied by the living. They make their armies of such creatures as those and not out of the intelligent classes; for if all were people of sense, nobody would be sacrificed, as each would say, ' My life is worth more to me than anything else.'   As a rule, all heroism is due to a lack of reflection, and thus it is necessary to maintain a mass of imbeciles.   If they once understand themselves the ruling men will be lost.   A man rules by employing one half of these animals to conquer the other half.   In the same way the art of politics lies in dividing the people and controlling each section by means of the other.   To do that one of these halves must be brutalized, so that the rest may be more easily separated from them ; for if the armed and unarmed once realize their position, the very structure of society will be wrecked.

RUGIERO. That is truly spoken.   There is one thing which always fills me with uncontrollable laughter, and that is when Turks and Christians go to war.   Each fights without nourishment or pay, and each buoys up his heart with the assurance that if the fortune of battle decrees his death he will go forthwith to paradise.   Now, either the Turk or the Christian must be deceived, for if the Christian's heaven exists it precludes that of the Turk, on the ground of total unlikeness. . . . It is impossible that both of the enraged combatants can be right at the same time . . . etc.

(*Caliban, Act II. Scene i.   Renan.*)

If you do not regard feminism with an uplifting sense of the gloriousness of woman's industrial destiny, or in the way, in short, that it is prescribed, by the rules of the political publicist, that you should, that will be interpreted by your opponents as an attack on *woman*.   But it is not necessarily that, of course.   It might even be a chivalrous *defence* instead of an attack.   I lay no claim here to any chivalrous intention ; but it is certainly not as an anti-feminist that I am writing.

Traditionally women and children are the most helpless and ill-equipped categories of mankind.   Up to the present, equality of opportunity has not been achieved, and they are still the most credulous and influenceable of us.   It is natural, therefore, that a great political power, interested only in domination and in nothing else, would seize on them as its most readily manipulated tools.   By flattery and coercion it would discipline their ignorance and weakness into an organized instrument of social and political

domination. As an alternative to the system suggested
in the speech quoted above, by which one half of the mass
of ' those animals ' or ' imbeciles ' is used against the other
half, there is that by which the mass of the ill equipped,
easily influenced, and credulous can be used to destroy the
minority that knows a little more than it is proper that it
should know, that is not so easy to fool, therefore, and is
not so helpless. The ' war ' of the lowbrow against the
highbrow is a conflict fomented on the same principle.

We live beset with civil wars, in the envenomed and
bitterly organized world. Almost any generalization must
range against you the legions of this or that zealous social
host, daily subjected to press discipline, breathing defiance, whether really affected by your statement or not.
I am about to examine very briefly a prediction of
Mr. Haldane's. In doing so I shall occasionally refer to
' woman.' Before permitting myself that dangerous licence
I must define what I mean. A very great superficial
difference still exists between women and men. As you
see women walking about the streets they are (as far as
possible) luxuriously and exquisitely dressed, very neat,
as far as possible ' chaque cheveu à sa place ' ; their
clothes are chosen as far as possible of flimsy and seductive
material : they are still, in short, more ornamental, silken,
frail, treated with cosmetics, and sedulously trimmed than
are men. The sex specialization is with them in the nature
of an obsession, therefore, to that extent, in the sense that
they still think of themselves more as ' women ' than men
think first and foremost of themselves as ' men.' They
get themselves up so that they shall be graceful and seductive. But the mind of the woman, stripped of this secondary
equipment of grace and feminineness, is not, almost every
one will admit, very different to that of the man.

When speaking of ' women,' then, as we must sometimes
do, it is naturally of this artificial, secondary creature—
not of a platonic androgyne, of a naked soul, or of the
violent or gentle, charming or offensive creature that you
know Rose or Mary to be at the heart of her specialization.
Every specialization or ' shop,' when earnestly attended
to for a long time, is apt to take on an obsessional tinge.
The woman's ' shop ' no doubt is no exception to this rule.
The ' woman '—the delicate, perfumed, carefully arranged,

stilted, painted, and coloured feminine shell is a thing that
a training as a painter can only help you to appreciate.
I do not believe that any painter would be inconsolable at
the thought that he lived in this backward world of sex
differentiation.   In the present essay the ' manly ' male
is written about with sufficient boldness for us to be permitted perhaps a brief though penetrating glance at the
complementary figure of the woman : though if attacked
in consequence of this latter licence, I am well aware that
it would be a more serious affair than would be the resentment of the poor, bloated cave-man.

CHAPTER VII

SCIENCE AND THE FEMININE

IN *Dædalus*, recently published, Mr. Haldane has briefly prophesied the triumph of ectogenesis, placing its experimental realization in the year 1951. In spite of the fact that he asserts that opposition to these innovations will come from the feeling of the conservative majority that such innovations have an air ' of presumption and indecency ' (p. 53), it is not really the majority that is in question ; and, of course, what is intended in any case is to stress the essential ' indecency ' of the present arrangement, and the great decency of the proposed ectogenetic realization of life. All of which confirms us in the conviction of the essential puritanism and squeamishness of the scientific outlook—the outlook, that is, of the average man of science. The ' substitution of the doctor for the priest ' is not really, as it would seem to be, in the interest of carnal joys. Science, as a *religion*, would be a very austere affair indeed, outdoing all, it is most likely, in its cheerless intolerance. Let us consider, for instance, with Mr. Haldane, the simple act of milking a cow :—

> Consider so simple and time-honoured a process as the milking of a cow. The milk, which should have been an intimate and almost sacramental bond between mother and child, is elicited by the deft fingers of a milkmaid, and drunk, cooked, or even allowed to rot into cheese. We have only to imagine ourselves as drinking any of its other secretions, in order to realize the radical indecency of our relation to the cow.

This is in order to show how, if it were proposed to milk a cow electrically, and we protested that that was ' indecent,' we could be convicted of an agelong indecency in milking it with our hands. But biological inventions are abhorrent to humanity, and they call them ' indecent,' Mr. Haldane thinks. Yet such inventions, beginning as a perversion and monstrosity, end as a ritual. ' Even now surgical cleanliness is developing its rites and its dogmas, which, it may be remarked, are accepted most religiously by women ' (p. 50).

It is precisely the clinical rites of cleanliness and the growth of a whole network of ordinances, whose administration might be at first in the hands of women, that will probably produce the most intensive ceremonial that has ever been elaborated. When the clinic becomes the temple, and the white-coated surgeon the officiating priest, men will surpass themselves in cleanliness, spending the day in lustrations.

The puritanic potentialities of science have never been forecast. If it evolves a body of organized rites, and is established as a religion, hierarchically organized, things more than anything else will be done in the name of ' decency.' The coarse fumes of tobacco and liquors, the consequent tainting of the breath and staining of white fingers and teeth, which is so offensive to many women, will be the first things attended to. A scantling of the immaculate, non-carnal world of the future can be examined on all sides to-day.

Two ideas of freedom are involved in these opposite principles of the mechanical disposal of the detritus of life and the natural disposal of the same. *A philosophy of dirt* (which is a tract which should be added to Messrs. Kegan Paul's series) would oppose nature to art, the ancient or animal world to the non-animal world of science. What we still call ' art ' is the science of the ancient world —that of nature. Michelangelo, aside from his primitive titanism, would be a suitable hero for such a philosophy, which would dwell on the admirable picture of this ancient master engaging in his yearly change of boots and nether garments, which never quitted his body except to make way for a new outfit. We are told that when he pulled them off, the skin used to come away with them. His colossal prophetic images, and scenes of the first creation, and his rough personal habits, would provide the requisite background for that thought that gave its preference to the natural. It would be contrasted with the world of the microscope, and the minutiæ and tidiness that have been a preserve conventionally of the feminine. That squeamishness (suggesting, physiologically, a bad conscience) of the woman, always heading to some ascetic ritual of orderly automatism, would be there opposing the animal *sans-gêne* of the workman of the early world.

' Surgical cleanliness . . . developing its rites ' is ' most religiously accepted by women.'   The liaison between the woman and applied science is as evident as the ascetic tendencies of science, and the puritanic standards that must ensue as its organization grows.   It is science that will lay by the heels the last descendants of the ' colossal, impetuous, adventurous wanderer ' of the early world, as well as the *animally-working* pre-industrial man, substituting the machine, of far greater power than any animal or ' titan,' controlled by some creature, ectogenetically produced, with a small beardless shaven head, very fussy about specks of dust and dirt, very partial to ' cosmic ' studies, bitterly resenting anything indecorous, with most of the beliefs and innocence of the nursery, a highly organized, shrewd, androgynous Peter Pan.   That is the logical forecast from the tendency of the moment.   But, of course, so many things may interfere with this that there is as much chance of its not reaching its goal as of its doing so.   Indeed, what is suggested here, with every possible apology for its flagrant optimism, is that it will probably not happen.   That is not the sort of world that will necessarily ensue.   It is the nightmare, nothing more, that the present tendencies would predict if literally worked out.   Their realization would imply, however, that people had ceased to be conscious personalities.   The world would in that case have melted into inanity.

It is only a question of being pessimistic enough, or irreconcilable and thorough enough in your revolutionary zeal, and you find yourself quite naturally emerging into the region of healthy optimism prescribed here as a change from the unwholesome reality of the moment.

CHAPTER VIII

POSSIBILITIES OF BIOLOGIC TRANS-
FORMATION : AND LOCKE'S HUMANISM

WHAT is responsible for that nightmare is the
dogma of *Science for Science' sake*, which, like
Art for Art's sake, or, as Proudhon said, Liberty
for the sake of Liberty, or any of the other *closed* formulas,
is an absurdity. The mephistophelean picture with which
Mr. Haldane ends his book—' Black is his robe from top
to toe,' etc.—is not only a ridiculous and sentimental,
an unscientific, one, but one that human beings of any sort
at all, highbrow or lowbrow, do not want. The human-
ization of science could only strengthen it, just as it must
strengthen art. The war on ' the human '—which is
simply a war on all life, ' human ' being not merely anything particular, feeble, and peculiar to us, but something
common to all forms of life, a mountain even being ' human'
in so far as it is *alive*,—that war will cause men soon to
revolt against not science, but Science-for-Science'-sake.
That is a sort of *revolutionary* for whom our time cries out.

As to the possibilities of biologic transformation, the
following remarks may prevent misunderstandings. The
human body appears very ridiculous, feeble, and even
grotesque, no doubt. This impression loses all solid
support when the mind has its proper ascendency. Regarded as an entelechy (this term not involving here any
especial theory of substance, but only standing for any
non-mechanical animating principle), space and dimension
become insignificant. For him a cabbage the size of three
universes would still be a cabbage. Explanations of the
mystery of life by the tape measure become meaningless.

It is found by creative artists that all the resources of
the palette—the accumulation of every possible colour
and technical device—or the most elaborate orchestra,
containing every imaginable instrument, is not at all a
guarantee of successful expression. *One* instrument, *one*
colour, and the discipline imposed by the simplest and
most restricted means, is often the most satisfactory. So

the conservatism imposed on us by the peculiar and not very striking vessel through which we exist is not necessarily a misfortune. Pineal eyes, great stature, a formidable carapace, would not necessarily help us. The greater our spiritual power and development, the less such considerations would occupy us : transformation, if it came, would come necessarily in the incandescence of some endeavour.

That question—of biologic transformation—is significant in some ways, for the essence of the futurist form of thought is an accumulation on the *individual* of all the instruments and physiological extensions or ' interpenetrations ' of which life is susceptible. But if we *control* a thing, it is *us*. And the physical joining-up, as it were, of the futurist (which is also the bergsonian) sensibility, seems beside the point. It produces a monster, a hydra, a leviathan, and is a megalomaniac creation. The latter tendency seems to be the expression of the ' scientific ' in the vulgar and shallow sense—the last stage of the mechanical, material fancy, the bankruptcy of the imagination.

A few of the questions that scientific advances present have been dealt with in the course of this essay. That the era of vulgarization and popular discussion of *everything* is drawing to a close, I signalled as something to be thankful for. Locke, a long time before the spectacular development of natural science, stated this problem very well. Here is his estimate of what human life (always from the point of view of the human conservative average which is the object of all orthodox revolutionary solicitude) can hope to benefit from natural science :—

Could we discover the minute particles of bodies, and the constitution on which their sensible qualities depend, they would produce very different ideas in us. Microscopes discover to us, that what to our naked eye produces a certain colour, is quite a different thing. So sand or pounded glass, which is white to the naked eye, is pellucid in a microscope. Blood to the naked eye is red, but a microscope shows only some few globules of red swimming in a pellucid liquor.

Our wise Creator has fitted our senses and faculties for the convenience of life, and the business we have to do here : we are able to examine and distinguish things so as to apply them to our use ; but God, it appears, intended not that we should have a perfect and adequate knowledge of them . . .

were our senses made much more acute, things would have quite another face to us, and it would be inconsistent with our wellbeing. If our sense of hearing were but 1000 times quicker, a perpetual noise would distract us ; were the sense of seeing in any man 100 or 100,000 times more acute than it now is by the best microscope, he would come nearer to the discovery of the texture and motion of the animate parts of corporeal things, but he would be in a quite different world from other people. Such a quickness and tenderness of sight would not endure open daylight. He that was sharp-sighted enough to see the configuration of the minute particles of the spring of a clock, and observe on what its elasticity depends, would discover something very admirable ; but if eyes so framed could not at a distance see what o'clock it was, their owner would not be benefited by their acuteness. (Locke, *Essay on Human Understanding*, II. xxiii.)

The vulgarization of science accounts for many of the most threatening aspects of modern life. The selling of science to the rich—that sort of rich man, that is to say, who is at about the neanderthal stage of existence—is perhaps the greatest crime of any. If what Le Bon calls the *élite* could only combine against this outrageous sub-man, instead of selling him deadly gases and weapons and inventing things for him to destroy everybody with—if, IF !—what a syndic that would be !   But it is unfair even to mention such an absurd dream. It is much better to say : Since you *must*, arm him to the teeth ! He may destroy *himself*.

CHAPTER IX

THE MEANING OF THE 'SEX WAR'

THE sex war, which we will now study a little more closely, is destined to free not only women, but men. But it led off, naturally, as a war to free the woman. The woman was the chattel or slave of this terrible little despot, the father of the family. There were millions of such despicable little despots. Their power must be broken. The ' despot' smiled indulgently ; he knew he was not much of a despot, he didn't know what all the fuss was about, but concluded that ' those women ' had become possessed of some obstinate piece of illogic that they had better be allowed to ' get on with.'

' Socialism wishes to abolish family life, because it costs too much,' was Proudhon's explanation of feminism. And that in one sense must be accepted as the true one, on the economic side. Feminism in that sense was simply the conscription, under a revolutionary egalitarian banner, of an army of women, for the purpose of the attack on and destruction of the home and the family. There is much more in the war in the family than the economic factor. But it is certainly the economic factor that persuades capitalism to favour the feminist movement and urge the conventional socialist to this form of ' war.'

Men as a ' class,' the masculine class, have recently had to support a great number of wars all at the same time : the ' Great War,' which was of a traditional type, and yet very novel in its barbarity ; the ' class war,' of course ; and then a war that was regarded originally as a joke, the ' sex war.' All these wars are wars of freedom : but their ultimate objects are generally misunderstood.

When *feminism* first assumed the proportions of a universal movement it was popularly regarded as a movement directed to the righting of a little series of political wrongs. Woman had been unjustly treated, had been a chattel to be bought and sold and disposed of : men were *free*, women in chains—chained to the hearthstone in the home, which was also referred to as the *castle* of the male gaoler. A thousand chivalrous gentlemen leapt to arms and rushed to the assistance of this matron in distress. With great gestures of christian magnanimity they divested themselves of all traditional masculine authority or masculine advantage of any sort. Tearfully they laid them all at the feet of the dishonoured matron, who dried her burning tears, and with a dark glance of withering indignation picked them up and hurried away. The general herd of men smiled with indulgent superiority. So that was all settled ; it was a bloodless revolution.

Feminism was recognized by the average man as a conflict in which it was impossible for a man, as a chivalrous *gentleman*, as a respecter of the rights of little nations (like little Belgium), as a highly evolved citizen of a highly civilized community, to refuse the claim of this better-half to self-determination. There were spectacular ' wrongs ' that had, ' in all decency,' to be righted. The issue was put to him, of course, in a one-sided way. He accepted it as a one-sided thing. Ever since it has continued one-sided, in the sense that, although the ' wrong ' has been ' righted,' the man is still in the ashamed position of the brutal usurper and tyrant. He finds his rôle in the ' sex war ' something in the nature of the immense conventional figure of the ' boss ' in the neighbouring ' class war ' : although there in the ' class war ' his own rôle is probably a very humble and far less imposing one.

How the sex war links up with the class war, the age war, and the war of the high and the low-brow, is as follows. ' The prevalent dominance of men ' is a phrase used commonly. Man in himself is a symbol of authority. *Masculinity* (in a state describable as above) is in itself authoritative and hence arbitrary. The most miserable and feeble specimen of the male ' class ' is in that paradoxical position of representing the most devilish despotism and symbolizing brute force. He suffers from the accident that he symbolizes ' authority ' in an era of change and militant revolutionary revaluation.

So, in the sex department (conterminous with that of administrative political power, or of the master-man relationship in industry or in domestic life, and with the family relation of parent and child), the revolutionary attack would, in its most generalized form, have the character of an attack on *man* and on masculinity. For, apart from *man as father*, or *man as husband*, or *man as leader* (in tribe or state), there is an even more irreducible way in which man is a symbol of power and domination. *Man as man tout court* is an anachronism, is ' unscientific.'

When Christ said to the Rich Man, ' Give all to the poor and come along with me, barefoot, and I will show you the road to heaven,' the Rich Man usually laughed and went his way. Man, or his political representatives, when recommended to give up all his privileges enjoyed at the expense of ' woman,' did not show this cynical front at all, except a few contumacious figures here and there. He immediately disgorged *everything*, in a true christian and chivalrous spirit. He considered himself most amply rewarded with the nice kiss that his generous action earned him. Had some one asked the same man to give all he had to the poor, or to hand over a thousand pounds of his capital to a distressed friend, he would, like the Rich Man in the Gospels, have laughed. Yet effectively he was doing the same thing in his sentimental capitulation to the feminist propaganda. This is merely noted as a matter of historical interest. Had men resisted, the struggle would have been more bitter, but would have had the same result. It was very lucky in this particular case that the usual veil of stupidity let down over their eyes obscured the issue : and any one looking back on these events when the movement is complete, at some future day, will agree that the feminine combatant was even blinder. In the long run both will be the gainers, in being relieved of too much of each other's company, and all the domestic burdens and responsibilities imposed by the family. The nightmare, ' sex,' will not force people into each other's society for life, when a half an hour would answer the purpose. But from the conventional point of view of the moment, certainly the women were the least wise : for according to those standards, they had most to lose.

So man gave up his privileges ' like a lamb,' but, needless to say, it is not the Rich Man, either of the Bible story or of any other story, who is the loser in these or any similar transactions. He gives nothing up—quite as in the days of Christ. But Man also in this will in the end be a little better off. Prohibition is another case of the same sort.

The Rich Man wishes it, of course, in order to get more work out of the Poor Man : he does not propose, himself, to knock off drink for the moment—only to make it so expensive that the workman cannot get it. But also, whatever you may think of this one-sided law, the workman will be better without drink. It is true that the Rich Man immediately sells his workman a crystal set and a cheap motor-car, and (so the Tester assures us) gets forty per cent. more work out of him. But the workman enjoys using the crystal set as much as the Rich Man enjoys selling it to him.

The object of the capitalo-socialist promoters of the sex war was dual. One object was the quite temporary one of discrediting authority, and reducing this smallest and feeblest of kings, the little father of the family squatting rather miserably in his shabby, uncomfortable little castle, like a ' king ' of *Alice in Wonderland*. But the break-up of this expensive and useless unit, the family, and the releasing of the hordes of idle women, waiting on little 'kings,' for industrial purposes, was the principal object. Ten housewives daily performed in the way of washing, cooking, and so forth, what two could perform under a communal system of the Fourier type, or that being introduced in communist Russia. The remaining eight would then be available for other forms of work. That is the economic object of the destruction of the idea of the family and the home. Incidentally, it will break up and root out all those little congeries of often ill-assorted beings ; and terminate that terrible, agelong *tête-à-tête* of the husband and wife, chained to each other for life for the practical purpose of perpetuating the species, which could now be effected more successfully *without* this often unhappy union.

In the mind of the most villainous and black-hearted of ' capitalists,' no doubt, it presented itself solely as a problem to get hold of cheap female labour. The hordes of unmarried women would be formed into a *third sex* like the sterile female workers of the beehive. This could not be done without the displacement of an equal quantity of men. So a ' sex war ' would be a good thing. Funds were forthcoming for feminist equipment. Such an attitude did no doubt exist, and does, among a certain type of men. But that does not affect the ultimate utility of the movement ; nor is it any reflection on the motives of such a man as Fourier, who recommended a social reorganization on these lines a century ago in his phalansterian system.

If, every time a great man of science, like Faraday, was about to engage on some research, he reflected what terrible uses it might be put to : if, every time an inventive artist was about to engage in some kind of experiment in literature, painting, or music, he grew disgusted at the thought of all the travesties and vulgarizations that must ensue, degrading and caricaturing his invention : or if the social reformer like Fourier were overcome with the thought of what quantities of evil people would exploit and corrupt his dreams of human regeneration : then perhaps all these men would never create. So we should not benefit by that. Whenever we get a good thing, its shadow comes with it, its *ape* and familiar. It is in order to disentangle these things, principally, that this essay has been written. The extreme complexity and inter-mixture of the good and the bad, in the sense of what is good for people in general and what is bad for them, makes this task a very difficult one. It is the supreme task for the sociologist or philosopher to-day. But almost anything that can be praised or advocated has been put to some disgusting use. There is no principle, however immaculate, that has not its compromising manipulator. All that must be borne in mind, and the shadow and the reality, the ' real thing ' and the imitation, brought forward to some extent together.

At all times there have been a host of men who performed a simple work which a woman, or a child for that matter, could undertake equally well. On account of the sex prerogative, and sex privilege, they claimed a wage superior to what a woman would claim for a similar employment. It was for this reason that *male privilege* had to be broken. ' Woman's rights ' was, from the point of view of many of the most influential of its supporters, simply an expedient to reverse this position. The pretentious claims of the white male had to be broken.

Now, the sequel of the ' sex war ' is in many ways very unpleasant. It must be remembered, however, that the

change round is only very partial as yet, and the period of
conflict and friction has not ended.   Also it must be
remembered that in western society the destinies of this
war are still in the hands of people likely to exploit it for
the most evil motives.   Let us consider it from this point
of view for a moment, as a struggle carried on in the midst
of a system bound to exploit it and turn it to its own
detestable uses.

We observe to-day that technically women ' have won
their war.'   Yet, so far, the ' peace ' after the ' sex war '
is of the same dubious character as the peace after the
Great War.   Even the ' victors ' are a little laughed at
by the less delicate of the agents of the great system on
which their success reposes.   The soldiers, in the same
way, were laughed at when, their Great War over, they
came and showed their mutilated limbs, lost jobs, and
broken health to their masters.   This cannot be better
illustrated than by an article entitled ' Is there really a
Sex-war ? ' in a great sunday newspaper, which devotes
a good deal of space to chattily instructing its readers
(the soft *drilling* of the great and docile public which is
the great function of publicity) as to how they should go,
and what attitude they should take on great domestic
and international questions.

The writer of this particular article starts by mocking
the ' feminist ' and partisan of the sex war as an ' unsexed,' rawboned, unattractive tribe of ' female ' cranks.
No wonder, he says, there is a ' sex war ' for them !   But
does any pretty girl think there is such a thing as a sex
war ?

> The result (of the fact that ' the female constitution is of
> sterner stuff ' than the male) is the well-known surplus of
> women, roughly 2,000,000, in this country.
> There is nothing more curious than the way life adjusts
> itself to local conditions.   Since a large number of women
> are plainly condemned to sterility by the fact of the surplus,
> a percentage of the female population automatically and
> instinctively makes a type that can be seen in large numbers
> at any university, and with all the plausibility it can command
> it preaches a career and celibacy for woman, and hatred of man.
> . . . The ' sex war ' of the feminists is a thing of which
> no woman of average good looks and pleasant temper is ever
> conscious.   No pretty woman every complained of the hos-

tility of men as a sex. No normal man ever complained of the ' sex war ' waged against him by woman.

Never was a war so peculiarly carried on as that alleged by the feminists to be incessant between man and woman. These mortal antagonists apparently cannot exist apart. Take any thoroughfare at random. The immensely preponderant proportion of the passers-by are two-and-two in the smiling company of a person of the other sex. The unhappy-looking ones are those who are without the company of members of the opposite sex.

There the poor disappointed ' feminist ' type, claiming her ' rights,' which she had secured in her ' war,' gets it ' straight and strong.' The industrial boss—in the person of his journalistic employee—laughs at her, of course. ' You poor, hard-featured, unsexed drone, that no man would have—who goes *alone* down the street, envying all the pretty girls hanging smiling on the arms of their beaux —or, if in company, in the company of another female much like yourself—so *you want more money*, do you ? Well, you won't get it. You have slightly misunderstood the significance of your " famous victoree." It was a victory for *me*, not for you ! '

Woman frequently gets the job because, not having another woman and several children to support, she can afford to accept a lower salary than a man. And then, resenting this lower salary, she sometimes talks bitterly about *sex discrimination* and the *sex war*. The agitation of the female school teachers for salaries on the male scale, though not quite on the same plane, is a cognate case.

The ' feminists,' having obtained practically all they had ever clamoured for, now unanimously chorus the slogan, *Equal pay for equal work*—whether performed by man or woman. They are pathetically unconscious of the fact that, apart from the teaching profession, were this principle to be enforced, a great percentage of employed women would immediately lose their jobs to men.

Since the principle of equal pay is not in force, they raise the old cry of the ' sex war ' and point once again to the brutal domination of the unscrupulous male.

The harsh fact, however, is that the ' sex war ' as between man and woman is a myth. It does not exist. There is, indeed, a ' sex war ' always in full swing—a war in which no quarter is given on either side—and that is the ' sex war ' between woman and woman.

One ' war,' you notice, is guffawed away, and another little one started, or an old one restarted.

' There *is* a war,' he says in effect, ' but it is a war between woman and woman.'   And he recommends them more or less to go and pull each other's hair out, and to forget the ' sex war.'   *That* is over, that has served its purpose.

The readers of such an article grin : and, insinuating itself beneath the veil of ' kindly humour ' and gossip, the sense slips into their minds and installs itself there.   They notice that the writer is ' a man '—if he is impolite about the opposite sex, they giggle and express the opinion that he has probably been ' jilted.'   In any case they regard him as a harmless gossiping personality, supposing him to have the same prejudices and preoccupations as themselves, since it takes a great deal to show to people that others are not invariably just like themselves.   A little ' sex war ' talk springs up, perhaps between Mummy and Daddy ; to which the children (part of quite another category or ' class ') disdainfully listen, or else attend to something else.

CHAPTER X

THE MATRIARCHATE AND FEMININE ASCENDENCY

ALL orthodox opinion—that is, to-day, 'revolutionary' opinion either of the pure or the impure variety—is *anti-man*. Its terms are those of a war or insurrection still, although theoretically the war is over and the position gained. But subtly and in the nature of things, it is no longer a question of adjusting an inequality, but of advancing (as of a *superior* nature) the qualities of the 'down-trodden,' of the 'weaker' sex. On the scientific, or the pseudo-scientific, front of the world-movement of sex reversal, it issues in the form of a great deal of insistence on the phenomenon of the Matriarchate. The Matriarchate tends to be represented as a more absolute thing than it ever was, and as in a sense the *natural*, the *primitive* social organization. Such a war as the 'sex war,' as was to be expected, does not end in a stabilization in which the man and the woman exist on *equal* terms. It necessarily ends in a situation in which feminine values are predominant.

That the 'sex war' is not at the finish (whatever it may have been at the start) an egalitarian movement is certain. It is not an insurrection with an egalitarian watchword any longer, but a 'war' for domination, not 'equal rights.' The nietzschean notions that converted in the vague general mind the darwinian formula of *a struggle for existence* into that of *a struggle for power* operates here as elsewhere. In innumerable books and articles on the subject this tendency can be traced. A highly characteristic one is *The Dominant Sex*, by Matilda and Mathias Vaerting. (Whether the order in which their names are printed is a survival of the days of chivalry, or is a token of the surrender of Mathias, we are not told.)

Abusing and over-using the slender evidence of the Matriarchate, these writers' theory is that sometimes men have ruled the world and sometimes women : that the pendulum swings backwards and forwards : but that *equal rights*, or a rule shared equally by both, is only a transitional state, and is not the characteristic one. That one or other should be the *top dog* is the natural condition.

> There is, indeed, a tendency towards fixity in the relationship of power between the sexes, whatever that relationship may be.   But there is a still stronger countervailing tendency towards change, towards progressive modification.   The relationship of power is subject to the laws of motion.   The present authors' researches seem to justify the contention that the movement of the relationship of power between the sexes is undulatory, or that it resembles the swing of a pendulum.   Automatically, masculine dominance is replaced by feminine, and feminine by masculine.   In the swing from the prevalence of one form of sexual dominance to the other, the pendulum necessarily traverses the stage in which there is a balance of power between the sexes : this is the phase of equal rights.
> This movement, however, does not seem to be a simple oscillation.   We do not find that the power of one of the sexes continuously diminishes, while that of the other continuously increases.   The subordinate sex experiences from time to time reverses in its march to power, these reverses being followed by fresh advances. . . . The dominant sex, on the other hand, the one whose power is declining, will win occasional victories even during that decline. . . . The highest point of the movement of the pendulum is that at which the reversal of the movement begins.   After the dominance of one of the sexes has been pushed to the pitch of absolutism, and when the power has reached a climax, the descent into the valley of equal rights begins.

These writers excuse themselves presumably for the unsatisfactory nature of the evidence on which they have to rely for this mechanical and well-ordered picture by inventing something like Freud's *Censor*.   They imagine a despotic and marvellously thorough sex soul, carefully erasing all traces of the rule of the sex recently dispossessed.

It will be seen that the Vaertings deal in a type of historic psychology like the fatalism of the *decline and fall* of all empires ; although for the foundations of their statements they have to get into the vague, ' vast,' convenient region of proto-history and unlimited pre-history.

But as to any movement on the part of these two minds to question the desirability of ' empire ' and *domination* at all, you would look in vain for it.

If this mechanical oscillatory movement were, for the history of which we have any reliable record, correct, then would it not be strange to find these ' rebel minds,' because a certain mechanical movement has always taken place, accepting it for all time ? Should not the ' progressive ' ticket oblige its holder to something different to that ? Is not, in fact, the historic attitude the very negation of ' progress '—if ' progress ' is to break the spell (for is it not that ?) of mechanical necessity ? So the historic conservatism of such mechanistic writers throws them into the sort of strange opposition with their ' revolutionary ' label that we have noticed occurring elsewhere. Their evidence is collected on the same principle as that directing the inquisitorial procedure in which the functions of judge, attorney, jury, etc., were vested in one person : their evidence of the order and value of that extracted by torture and hypnotic suggestion.

To wish back the patriarchal family (with the *patria potestas* of the roman domestic despot at the end of the reactionary road, or the slave-wife) because feminism seems to be rapidly becoming affected to a vast scheme of political exploitation ; or because men, not yet free of women, have not the necessary initiative to institute a secondary war, to hasten the dissolution that has begun. and which, as things stand at present, falls most heavily on them,—is the natural reactionary gesture. Men do not do anything, but they are dissatisfied. They feel too guilty in their capacity of hereditary ' tyrant ' or ' sultan ' to say much openly. And ' chivalry ' is a great obstacle to declaring war.

The recommendation of Christ to the Rich Man has already been mentioned in connection with the Man as an emblem of sex-authority. The surrender of the Plain Man to the feminizing woman was a piece of chivalrous nonsense, if it was not coercion. So christianity is responsible for it, since chivalry dictated it ; unless force covers the whole transaction. But if the Rich Man, when he had given up his possessions, should howl like Timon because he was not then of so much importance, he would be a poor christian. It is against christianity that man should turn, the source of all his sexual woes. These two actions—that of surrendering any wealth you may have accumulated or inherited, and that of surrendering the privileges acquired and inherited by the caste or sex to which you belong—are highly to be commended, in my opinion. But what is not usually recognized is that they are of exactly the same order : just as a magnanimous christian self-sacrifice in sex is the same as it would be in race. According to any worldly standard they are both excessively stupid.

The ' right ' of the child to freedom from family control is of a piece with the ' right ' of the woman to an ' independent ' existence. They and the rest of the sex innovations and theories of the family are in the nature of factory regulations, nothing more. The multitudinous mollusc in the body of which these changes occur has to be found a soft or a sentimental reason for everything that happens in such a tender and respectable place. But the real reason, although matter-of-fact enough, is not from the public point of view threatening or alarming. The truth *always* has to be hidden, whether it is good or bad. In itself it causes alarm : *any* truth is impossible to utter.

Sorel writes : ' Marx, as is known, proposed this law, that " every class which, successively, has seized power has sought to safeguard its newly acquired position of mastery by imposing on society conditions calculated to ensure it (the conquering class) its own revenue." Several times the same principle is employed by him in attempting to predict what would happen to the world as a result of a proletarian revolution. It is in this way that he comes to announce the disappearance of the *bourgeois* family, because the proletarians will not find themselves in conditions likely to permit them to practise this type of sexual union.'

Since the great masses of the people are not likely to be in a position to prolong the family arrangement based on an individual ' home ' (marriage, and the family circle to which the European is accustomed), it will be abolished. That is the economic fact at the bottom of ' feminism.' Given industrial conditions, the Plain Man and the Plain

Woman will be better off if the unit of the family is abandoned. But that consideration would perhaps not have been sufficient to bring this revolution about. It is an economic adjustment primarily : after that a great deal of relief from responsibility, and from a too constant conjugal *tête-à-tête*, is to be laid to its credit.

CHAPTER XI

THE PIECEMEALING OF THE PERSONALITY

RACE is the queen of the ' classes ' : but in Europe to-day its power is very slight—for one reason, because it lacks all organization or even reality. But there are less fundamental ones, but usually far more present to our consciousness in everyday life, needing the greatest attention, and involving a variety of ritual. The other ' classes,' it is true, have never been recognized as of the same standing as *race*. As a *casus belli* they have been inferior to it. None of these other differences, or the membership of any of the other classes, was recognized as a pretext for taking life. Race or nationality, on the other hand, has, in the modern world, been recognized as a sanction for murder by every State. But this sanction usually had only ' nationality ' to repose on, which was a very different thing to race. Marx, with his ' class war,' indirectly demonstrated the absurdity of these privileges of race—especially when it was not *race* at all. The success of his system has shown how easy it is to substitute, in a disorganized, non-racially founded society, any ' class ' for the classical ' racial ' unit of the State.

Once ' war ' between classes started spreading, from the teaching of Marx, it did not stop at social ' class,' naturally. Schopenhauer, for instance, early in the last century, called women the ' short-legged race.' So women were thenceforth one *race* and men another *race*. The idea of race substituted itself for that of sex. But where there are *races* there are *wars*. The ' sex war ' was soon in full swing. Schopenhauer himself, it is interesting to recall, was one of the first in the field. He early in life flung himself on a strange woman whom he found conversing on the staircase of the house where he lived, and threw her downstairs. For this pioneer engagement, however, he was forced for the rest of his life to pay a crushing pension to this crippled member of the enemy ' race.'

Women are notoriously unamenable to strictly *racial*

mysteries. The classical example of this is that of the Sabine women deciding, as it is supposed, to remain the property of the Sabine ravishers rather than return to the defeated men of their own race.

The child is the 'class' that is most nearly associated with the sex-classification : or rather, the age-difference it represents. 'The child is father to the man' : and the child is, as primitive societies saw, actually a different being, in spite of physiological continuity, to the grown man into which he develops. It is the case of the worm and the butterfly—only in inverse order, the butterfly coming first. So Master Smith and Mister Smith are as different almost (when they are the same person at different ages of Smith's career) as though they were offspring and parent.

But the difference diminishes when you are dealing with *Isaac Newton*, or even with Clara Vere de Vere, in place of poor ' Smith.' The more highly developed an individual is, or the more civilized a race, this *discontinuity* tends to disappear. The ' personality ' is born. Continuity, in the individual as in the race, is the diagnostic of a civilized condition. If you can break this personal continuity in an individual, you can break *him*. For *he* is that continuity. It is against these *joints* and sutures of the personality that an able attack will always be directed. You can divide a person against himself, unless he is very well organized : as the two halves of a severed earwig become estranged and fight with each other when they meet.

A good demonstration of the rationale of this piece-mealing of the personality for attack was given the other day by a caricaturist. He divided his celebrated victims into their Young and Old Selves : in this way he had them in half, like hydras, and made the angry tail discourse with the fiery head. But you can effect far more than this. You can with luck cut men up so thoroughly that they become almost ' six-months men,' as they might be called, rather than men of one continuous personal life—than ' life men.' It is only necessary to mention the central subject of the very effective and fashionable plays of Pirandello, to show how, systematically presented in a dramatic form, this segregation of the ' selves ' of which the personality is composed can affect the public mind.

But there is no way in which people differ, however minutely, that does not supply material for a ' war.' And the general contention throughout this essay is that they cannot have too much of ' class ' : that people's passion for ' class ' and for reposing their personality in a network of conventional ' classification,' is not often realized. Where war is concerned you must, of course, disregard entirely the humanitarian standpoint. *Passively* men may even enjoy war, as the bird enjoys being drawn irresistibly to the fang of the snake. The blowing off of heads and arms is a very secondary matter with the majority of people. But that does not justify you as a responsible ruler in abusing this insensitiveness.

When really well mixed into a good, strong group, men are so many automata : they hardly notice any disturbance, like a war. But that the conscious self (in so far as it remains) of the average human being is terribly bloodthirsty and combative, much as I should like to, I find it difficult to credit. *By themselves* people are, every one admits, averse to fighting : it demands too much energy. Perhaps a really *perfect* group, or class, to prevent itself from dying of inanition, would favour war, as a stimulant. But I think the more the question is examined, the more certain it is that people *for themselves* (not for others—they enjoy seeing other people fighting, and dying, naturally), and *in the mass*, prefer eating, sleeping, fornicating, and playing games of skill to killing each other. And even if *the happiness of the greatest number* is not so individual a matter as Bentham supposed—even if the happiness of dying, let alone living, with a huge crowd of people must have a serious claim on our attention —nevertheless the individual, betrayed momentarily by some collapse or etiolation of the communistic medium, does object very strongly to dying. As *an individual* he is all for not dying or being crippled—that *is* the law of nature. And the ruler who bases his action on the stability of this Artificial Man of communism constantly risks sinning against God.

PART VIII

THE 'VICIOUS' CIRCLE

' The dog-headed monkey finds its mate in the female gibbon ; the elk and the axis deer cohabit ; and the eel enjoys itself with other fishes. Mâo Tzhiang and Li Ki were accounted by men to be most beautiful, but when fishes saw them they dived deep in the water from them ; when birds, they flew from them aloft ; and when deer saw them, they separated and fled away. But did any of these four know which in the world is the right female attraction ? . . . the paths of approval and disapproval are inextricably mixed and confused together. . . .'

Khi Wú Lun.   Kwang-tze.

' Toute forme, toute idée classique est ici un contre-sens. Un pareil marécage est un lieu d'exil pour les arts antiques. . . . Waterloo Bridge . . . les petits bateaux à vapeur qui courent sur le fleuve . . . à voir leurs passagers qui embarquent et débarquent, un Grec eût pensé au Styx. Il aurait trouvé que vivre ici, ce n'est pas vivre ; en effet, on vit ici autrement que chez lui ; l'idéal a changé avec le climat.'   Notes sur l'Angleterre.   H. Taine.

CHAPTER I

THE PHYSIOLOGICAL NORM AND
THE ' VICIOUS '

OF all the tokens of the flight of the contemporary european personality from the old arduous and responsible position in whose rigours it delighted, now made too hot for it, there is none so significant as the sex-transformation that is such a feature of post-war life. A few years ago this topic would have been exceedingly difficult to deal with in a book destined for public sale. Even to-day it is not an easy one, but for rather different reasons.

On what tone are we to address ourselves to the consideration of this inverted fashion, abstracting ourselves, of necessity, from any prejudices we may feel for the purpose ? Dr. Matignon (*Archives d'anthropologic criminelle*), the great authority on China, said that he had never heard a Chinese express any disapproval of sexual inversion except that it was universally agreed to be bad for the eyes. Until quite recently european society took a very severe view of it ; which dislike was apparently a sort of tradition in any case among the germanic peoples. Genuine, fully developed physical inversion in men is probably quite rare : in a time unfavourable to its practice it makes a sort of martyr of the individual born with it— a martyr to his glands, like ' the painter called Sandys ' in the limerick, or in the sense that we say ' a martyr to the gout.' People regard it askance as a kind of possession ; and in many rough communities every misfortune would befall these delinquents of natural processes, whose quite simple and harmless topsy-turvydom was associated with witchcraft and treated on that basis. Even so late as the famous 'nineties the english courts made a martyr of that description of Oscar Wilde. He became almost a political martyr, other countries using his well-advertised agony to point to the philistinism of England. A very amiable and charming person, he awakened the chivalrous instincts everywhere, like a very attractive maiden in distress. And as he possessed to the full the proselytizing zeal that usually goes with sex inversion (as with any other intensification of sex), he prepared the ground with his martyrdom, ecstatic recantations, eloquent and tearful confessions, and the great prestige of his wit, for the complete reversal of the erotic machinery that has ensued or is ensuing.

An admission of complete *moral* blindness and indifference, although it might be damaging under certain circumstances, will not be misplaced in handling this subject. But there is another aspect of the matter that also claims attention. There are many people, perhaps, who would be lacking, as I am, in *moral* sensitiveness, and who would yet be in some way physically offended by practices ' against nature.' This would be extremely unreasonable, as I have already suggested ; for to an impartial taste, divinely exempt from participation in either normal or ' abnormal ' joys, as we call them, their ' normality ' would be just as offensive. They might very well offend the most fastidious god more than the object of *their* disgust ; for their ' norm ' would be merely the dislike or revolt of the senses against something *different*, not part of their personal norm or system. It would, in short, be the animal self-complacency and self-love that thinks itself ' natural ' and engaging, and everything else ' unnatural ' and disengaging.

The physical is the only aspect that interests the majority of people, however : which makes the non-physical impracticable as a basis of discussion, or at least very difficult. That there is any other side to a fundamental thing of common experience—about *themselves*, in short—they require much persuading. Nevertheless, the attempt has to be made, since the subject is important.

There is still, of course, one thing, but that a physical and exterior one, that plays an important part with many people in any such question as this. A drunkard soon develops a red nose and a generally inflamed, bloated, and dissipated appearance. Red noses are for some reason universally disliked by both men and women. So in the case of the drunkard, although no one would be likely to raise any objection to or experience any disgust at the physical act of pouring into the mouth a probably attractively coloured liquid, the result of this action in the long run is the red nose by which people are generally repelled for some reason. The 'Nancyism' of the joy-boy or joy-man—the over-mannered personality, the queer insistence on 'delicate nurture,' that air of assuring those met that he is a 'real lady,' like the traditional music-hall 'tart' who is always a 'clergyman's daughter,' the grating or falsetto lisp, or the rather cross hauteur of the democratic teashop waitress—are to some human norm almost as central as that which resents the red nose, or the big paunch, offensive.

But the drunkard is at peace with his red nose, probably, and left to himself can live on terms of mutual respect with his paunch, no doubt. Some human norm—the same one, perhaps, that is outraged by the red nose—hates the rat and the beetle. But its idea of the rat is not at all that which the rat has of itself; it loves its swift, clammy sausage of a body as much as the human being does his hairless, erect machine. That erect, conceited human norm may yet have to bend to the will of the rat or the serpent, and go about on its belly near the ground. And then it will be just as pleased with itself as at present : and indeed be happier relieved of the white man's burden *cum* the human burden *cum* its amazing moral rectitude.

I suggest that it is only the over-instinctive person, the slave of the human-all-too-human norm, who would be such a stickler for the 'natural' as the reactions sketched above imply. It is this unfortunate conservative human-all-too-human norm that we are incessantly combating. It is even that Old Adam in the 'Nancy' that makes him so satisfied with his humble eccentricity, and insignificant loudly-advertised change of gear—like the exultant cackling of a hen who had laid an egg of an, for it, unwonted calibre.

It is not, alas! by victories of such modest proportions over our too rigid physiologic norm that we can hope to break it down, if that is our intention. We merely flatter and preserve it by such indirect attentions.

But in order to advance a little farther into the physical problems involved in such a scrutiny, let us take the objections of the conventional bridegroom on his marriage night to evidences of unchastity in his bride. Marrying, the man of the approved masculine type is distressed and disillusioned if he find that some one has forestalled him in the tasting of this fruit.   The gilt is off the gingerbread. This painful situation we usually take at its *face* value. We think we know what we mean by the gingerbread, and where it is situated.   It is on the *physical* plane, in short, that we believe this deception to have occurred.   In this, I think, we are wrong.

Suppose, for instance, that the disappointed bridegroom learns that, instead of being deflowered in the course of a love intrigue, his bride has been deflowered against her will on a lonely road by a tramp.   Then the situation changes for him at once.   There is a flood of bitter tears on the part of the bride ; he folds her in his arms and all is well.   *For it is not the physical fact that has disturbed his repose of mind.*   It is the person, *she*, gazing at him out of her lovely, *personal* eyes, that it has caused him such a disagreeable shock to find he was not the first with. The act of deflowering, it is true, occurred, technically, on the physical plane.   But that—were there no *person* attached to it—would be of no more importance than something happening to an automaton : no more than the daily dirtying of the hands, which are washed and then they are clean again : no more than the figure in the Bois, in Mallarmé's prose poem, observed embracing mother earth.   For it is a person, a mind, that he has married ; incarnated and expressed, it is true, by a certain body. But that body is, in a sense (in the things that happen to it, if that is possible, independently of the mind), as unimportant by itself as the materials by which it is surrounded—its clothes, the tables and chairs, dust on the road, or bricks of the house.   Disconnect it from the *person*, if that may be, and it is *dead*.   In short, the body outraged by the tramp would be a *corpse* only.   The body enjoyed by an earlier lover would be *alive*.   In the latter case it would be *she*—Daphne, Joan, or Elizabeth.   It is the personality he is in touch with when he looks into her eyes (and not a bit of flesh—that is, as flesh, of the same impersonal order as a bit of cloth, a lump of clay, a sponge, a vegetable) that all the trouble is about.

This illustration will, I hope, suffice to suggest to us that in all such things the physical event is of very little im-

portance by itself. In the case of sex, more than anything
else, the fuss is supposed to be about that, and localized
to physical experience. In reality we are always dealing
with something else. It is in this misunderstanding that
morals thrive. The shallow disgust or indignation of the
moralist is installed in an elementary materialism that
appeals directly to the animal machinery of combat or
rut. Its pompous censure is able to surround, as though
with an aureole of intelligence and martyrdom, something
that is—what ? If we paused to think what it is we should
no doubt laugh at the conjuring trick : the piece of
sardonic illusionism to which we all surrender. But when
that comic screen had been removed, at the heart of the
tissue would be found the same entelechical reality which
gives significance to all the material life we know.

But that physical delusion, with all its mocking symbolism, that has roused us to protest or repulsion—clasping
to our hearts, with no repulsion, an almost identical object
ourselves !—is of the very essence also of the practice
responsible for it. The moral indignation, or loudly
expressed disgust, of the Plain Man or the Plain Woman
is the twin and complement of that self-satisfaction and
sense of outrageous discovery that is the incentive on the
other (' unnatural ') side of this sexual pale.

The sex revolution of the invert is a *bourgeois* revolution,
in other words. The *petit bourgeois* type predominates :
a red tie, or its equivalent in the approved badges of
sexual revolt, tells its theatrical tale. The puritan conscience, in anglo-saxon countries, provides the basis of
the condiment, and gives sex inversion there its particular
material physiognomy of *protest* and over-importance.
How moral, essentially, the anti-moral stimulus must be
is not difficult to grasp, when you are privileged to witness
its operation in the English or American. And so the
' vicious ' circle is described.

CHAPTER II

THE INTOLERANT TRADITION OF
THE ANGLO-SAXON

T HESE disparaging remarks (for in employing the epithet *petit bourgeois* I have gone as far as human vituperation will go) do not, of course, apply to those people whom a displacement of the sex psychology marks out for physical paradox. The most agreeable inverts to be met—and every one, in post-war society, meets a great number of every sort—are the true-blue inverts : those who, whatever the orthodoxy of the moment, would certainly be unaffected by it, and would be there busy with all the rather complicated arrangements incident to their favourite pursuit. This male-pole type of invert is often entirely free from that feminine bias, resulting in caricature so often, of the female of the genus; or that of the convert to inversion, the most fanatical of all. What this male invert thinks of his female it is impossible to say without being one yourself. But certainly he gives the impression of being much more *male* in the traditional and doctrinaire sense than any other male. His pride is often enormous in his maleness. If perhaps a little over-fine and even mad, he can meet on equal terms the male of any other species—either the lion, the male of the farmyard-fowl, the Samurai, the powdered male gallant of the Stuart stage. The frantic and monstrous cock, that notorious nobleman, *Monsieur le comte de Six Fois*, of the Casanova dispensation, he would easily put to flight.

Just as there are a few born revolutionaries, but in great numbers people who are ' revolutionary ' because other people are : so in the ranks of each respective legion of revolt to-day there is the small nucleus of ' pukka ' material, the ' regulars,' and the sheeplike indoctrinated majority. So it is that the neglected, despised, and rejected adept of Sodom, so well described in his formerly outlawed state by Proust, suddenly finds himself, owing to one of those freaks peculiar to political life, the leader of a highly disciplined host. It must be an Arabian Nights entertainment for some of the more hardened old perverts. All their life they have been chivied from pillar to post, till very recently living in the shadow of the Oscar Wilde case, the British equivalent of the *affaire Dreyfus*. Then all at once, as though by magic, they find themselves Princes of Sodom : every university in Christendom is pouring out, as thick as herrings, shoals of their natural prey, duly indoctrinated and suitably polished. They must rub their old heavily painted eyes and pinch their corseted ribs to ascertain if they are dreaming or not.

If the physiology of abnormal love as of normal love does not seem to you a matter of great importance ; if you have not the puritan itch or the spur of an over-sharp vanity to make such things important and, indirectly, mentally exciting; if ' righteousness ' as Arnold would say, or sanctimoniousness as Butler corrected him, is not your strong point,—there, you would think, must be an end of the matter as far as you are concerned. But you would find very soon that you had reckoned without your host. First of all you would discover that other people were not so accommodating as yourself. Indeed, a violent and jealous intolerance, you would begin to notice, accompanied most people's devotion to a sex fashion, as indeed to any other fashion. You would find, if you began to examine the machinery of fashion, that all fashions to-day tend to be organized on religious lines ; and that, where sex especially is concerned, the same puritan spirit, in the anglo-saxon countries, that made people in the anglo-saxon past such intolerant maniacs where ' immorality ' and all sexual ' enormities ' were concerned, makes them also, when they are recruited to an *opposite* fashion, just as snobbishly intolerant on behalf of the ' immorality ' to which they have gleefully, and with a sense of diabolical naughtiness, surrendered. You will perhaps recall the traditional *laissez vivre* of the French, and the wide measure of liberty left to personal taste—so that in the streets of Paris (the home of fashion) it has always seemed impossible to astonish or attract the attention of the passer-by, by even the most revolutionary costume : whereas any departure from fashionable convention has been met, always, with fierce resentment or fierce ridicule in England. Oscar Wilde invariably referred, I have been

told, to ' Get your hair cut ! ' as the english national
anthem.

Far more important, you would find that this prairie-
fire of sex revolution (of feminism and then of inversion)
altered fundamentally the status of ideas socially. As the
psychic element existing in even the simplest sexual operation escapes people, so the percurrent nature of a great
sex fashion is either not understood or not admitted.
Certain people, highly educated and belonging to millionaire circles, indulge in an ancient, universally prevalent,
' vice ' or pleasure, of a privileged and exceptional kind,
which, because it seems to contradict nature's arrangements, we call ' unnatural.' And there, for most people,
is the end of it. It is on the pleasure or distraction basis
alone that discussion of it is relevant.

That attitude resembles another obtuseness that sees
in the newspaper, cinema, or wireless only one of the
innocent, non-political distractions of mankind : or that
attributes ' serious ' political significance solely to the
Parliament and Crown. ' Mr. Gossip ' in the newspaper is
a harmless, idle, ' gossipy ' fellow. The novel, again, is as
little of a ' political force ' as little Jackie's new rag doll or
scooter. Those weighty columns that occupy the centre
of the *Times*, dealing with matters of patent consequence ;
or (to contrast with the mere novel) a political history of
England, for instance—they are the only things worthy
to rank as ' politics.' It is the mistake illustrated elsewhere by a cutting from the *Sporting Times*.

The social value of ideas, you would find altered, then,
by this revolution in a novel sense. Not only was it a
case of one set of ideas being exchanged for another set,
as usually happens. But in place of anything in the shape
of an *idea*, a *sensation* had been installed, you would discover. The very organ responsible for the making of
an idea would be looked at askance. The sex revolution
started as sex, but had ended as something else, rather in
the way that religious ecstasy may begin as religion and
end as sex. The various forms it had taken since the war
did not, as they became more ' social ' and less ' political,'
become less militant. So this revolution had often little
to do with sex ultimately. And then, of course—at last—
it might enter your head that *in the first place*, too—not

only in its result, but in its first motive—it was not sexual either. ' The socialists wish to abolish the family, *because it costs too much !* ' we have heard Proudhon saying. (It is strange that the ' socialists ' so early in the day should have been preoccupied to that extent with ways and means and displayed such an anxious foresight !) May it not be, too, that all the phases of the sex revolt—from the suffragette to the joy-boy—are equally *political* at the start—as they certainly become at the finish ? Is it not the same old hag that in a ' morality ' would be labelled Power, and for whom pleasure, in the simplest sense, means very little, who has pupped this batch of related fashions ?

CHAPTER III

THE RÔLE OF INVERSION IN THE WAR ON THE INTELLECT

A SORT of war of revenge on the intellect is what, for some reason, thrives in the contemporary social atmosphere. This has for effect a substitution of animal 'creation' for intellectual 'creation.' It is as though a war broke out between the picture or poem and the proud and jealous beauty that it represented : a war between the Vouzie and its waters. 'Creative' becomes a term of abuse in consequence : and elegant sterility, or cautious and critical eking out of a little jet of *naïveté* left over on purpose, is the idea, instead.

These readjustments are undertaken with a view to meeting the democratic requirements of 'the greatest vanity of the greatest number.' That vanity must be sheltered from painful comparisons and revenged for humiliations in the past. So a revolution in favour of standards unfriendly to the intellect, and friendly to all that had been formerly subordinated to it, is the first and most evident result of sex-transformation. The 'passions,' 'intuitions,' all the features of the emotive life—with which women were formerly exclusively accommodated—are enthroned on all hands, in any place reached by social life ; which is increasingly (in the decay of visible, public life) everywhere.

In this admirably organized sensationalist philosophy resulting from the common objects of these movements, life would seem to end where the baby was produced. The creative act of producing the baby is the first and last 'creative' act understood or allowed by it. The human being is only legitimately creative on one occasion, namely, in the production of *another* human being. And not only is the baby the supreme 'creation,' but babyhood, in one form or another, is the supreme condition of perfection.

We will follow for a moment the probable stages of this revolution as manifested in the life of ' society.'

First, the *salon* (the home of the *précieuses ridicules*) will

254

be pitched next door to the nursery ; then gradually the connecting door will become a large folding-door ; and then at length all septum of any sort will disappear. The *pré-cieuses ridicules*, dressed in baby frocks, will be on the floor with their dolls, or riding rocking-horses in Greek draperies.

The next stage in this human dissolution will almost certainly be spared the future generations. For the house is to be rebuilt ; and it will be rebuilt, without any doubt at all, on a more admirable pattern than ever before. But at the moment at which the last scrap of wall between the *salon* and the nursery disappears, you may find it difficult to summon your optimism to this prophetic reconstruction. These pages are written principally in order to enable you to grasp the method of that especial social *ritournelle*, and play your part without *gaucherie*. Once you have the key to the transaction, you may find it diverting up to a point.

The part that male inversion, the latest child of feminism, plays in these neighbouring battlefields of the high and the low-brow, or the specifically feminist battle of feminine ecstasy and ' intuition ' against the male ' intellect,' is of the highest utility. It, too, is in arms against the family, with all its ' natural ' machinery—namely, of human affection and man-and-woman sexual love. With that insurgent and militant instinct of an oppressed brotherhood defined so accurately by Proust, it helps its brother or sister insurgents in their attack on science, the fine arts, established, and usually desiccated, culture.

It is the ' refaynment ' that goes with male inversion (the *obligation* of culture, of a ' refayned ' speech, and the unreality of millionaire luxury as a necessary background)— that is where it comes in touch and into conflict with the more generalized life. (The mannishness of the woman invert—so different from and so inferior to the manliness of the male of the masculine side of inversion—is the counterpart of this ' refaynment.' The deep, throaty voice, the rather rough gestures, of the woman invert contrast again with that shrinking modesty—the ' shyness ' of the transformed *shaman*, the ' well-behaved ' child, in whose mouth butter would not melt, who will never, never, never speak-until-he-is-spoken-to—of the female of the masculine species.)

CHAPTER IV

THE 'HOMO' THE CHILD OF THE 'SUFFRAGETTE'

TO come, then, to the heart of the reason why it is worth while to spend so much time in analysing this fashion : it is because in the contemporary world it is a part of the feminist revolution. It is as an integral part of feminism proper that it should be considered, a gigantic phase of the sex war. The 'homo' is the legitimate child of the ' suffragette.'

The reason, again, why an analysis is so difficult is this. The majority of people live in the ordinary way, at any period, principally through *sensation*. The atmosphere of ideas or ' the intellect' is not congenial to them. Their reactions to their environment seldom rise into the region of ' clear ideas,' or indeed of any detached definition at all of what happens to them. It would be a hypocrisy to pretend that it matters very much how, under such circumstances, they spend their time.

The difficulty to-day is that, owing to the high state of organization of the different democratic communities, and the insane requirements to which liberalist doctrine has led, sensation is drilled to masquerade as intelligence. Multitudes of people who under a more reasonable system would be living, without self-consciousness or ' the pale cast of thought ' at all, animal lives of plain, unvarnished *sensation*, are now compelled to adopt a hundred pretentious disguises. Each little sensation has to be decked out as though it were a ' big idea.' Again, simple sensation has become ashamed of itself. It is persuaded to complicate itself, to *invert* itself with a movement of mechanical paradox. So, in reality, sensation pure and simple is disappearing, and a sort of spurious *idea* is everywhere taking its place.

But side by side with this disintegration of sensation, a very learned, intricate, and ingenious *philosophy of sensation* is built up. The result is that the more sensation *borrows* from the intellect, the more it abuses it and points

244

to *sensation* (which it no longer is in the purest sense) as the aim and end of life. Similarly, the more self-conscious it becomes, the more it repudiates consciousness and also (for another reason) ' self.' The more ' conscious ' it grows, in a limited and ineffective way, the more it talks about the ' unconscious.' It is as though it were breaking into a dithyramb about what it *just* no longer was.

The difficulty lies, then, in (1) the propaganda *for* sensation ; (2) the propaganda *against* the intellect ; (8) the imitation of the intellect, and of the things of the intellect, by all that is most deeply committed to pure sensation ; and (4) the movement to merge cleverly these opposites and pretend that they are one, forcing what has outstripped the human sensational average to return on its steps and put itself at the service of what it had laboured to transcend.

The strangest contradiction of all is that every movement *away* from the intelligence (and how can the term intelligence be dissociated from intellect ?) is encouraged in the name of *intelligence*. That is the secret of the difficulties that most people experience in analysing this order of things.

The male-invert fashion is not by any means favourable to the woman, of course, although it is *feminist*. But, on the other hand, it is hostile to many things to which the average woman is hostile. Through it the stupider, more excitable and aggressive kind of woman will revenge herself on those things towards which she has always been in a position of veiled hostility ; or on people she has come to regard as responsible for her misfortunes. It is often said that the male invert shelters himself behind— uses and acts through—women. But it would be equally true to put it the other way round.

There are two snobberies that exercise a very great leverage in all sex fashion. ' Intellectual snobbery ' is very powerful, as has just been pointed out ; it is on the score of ' intelligence ' that extreme sex revolution is effected. Social snobbery also plays a great part. To boldly concentrate on a less humdrum practice where your pleasures are concerned has always been, you are reminded, the habit of the privileged few. Membership of the highest or richest organized society—reflecting the egalitarian revolutionary glare from the masses beneath, while floating like a sumptuous emanation at a safe distance above them —is essential.

To be ' revolutionary,' yet a social snob : to be an ' intelligence ' snob, and yet to run *sensation* against *intellect*, to sniff and curl the lip at the advantages of the intellect—such are the contradictory habits that go hand in hand.

' We speak sometimes in these pages,' says Benda in his *Belphégor*, ' of the bad taste of our " democratic " society. We mean to say that society of which the tastes have become those of the people, at least those that one expects of the people (namely, indifference to intellectual values—religion of emotion). We do not intend either to abuse or to flatter any especial political régime. Further, we would say willingly with an eighteenth-century woman : " I call ' people ' all those who think vulgarly and basely : the court is full of them." '

Actually the vulgarest people of all, it has only recently been recognized, thanks to the fashionableness of revolutionary doctrines, have always been, necessarily, in the court or among the rich. For what has a so-called upper class been but a set of people furnished with the means to gratify the most ordinary tastes ? Or what is the use of riches except to enable some unpleasant fool to be vulgarer than it would otherwise be possible for him or her to be ?

A road to a new conception of *class*, in which the intelligence in reality, and not as a make-believe, took its place, would be *via* such analyses as these, with all their implications thoroughly apprehended.

CHAPTER V

GENIUS IN THE RÔLE OF CALIBAN

NO one has explored the regions of post-war decay so brilliantly, if superficially, as Julien Benda. And the pages in his *Belphégor*, where he describes the organized hatred of the intellect existing everywhere to-day in our society, are so just that I cannot do better than quote from them :—

> One of the most curious traits of this society (is) its hatred of the intelligence. Elsewhere we have specified the numerous forms by means of which it expresses this hatred : its wish to confuse intelligence with reasoning of a dry and uninventive sort, in order to thoroughly misrepresent it ; to believe that the great discoveries are due to a function (the ' intuition ') which ' transcends intelligence ' . . . its delight at witnessing what it believes to be the set-backs, the ' failures,' of science (instead of regarding them as misfortunes). . . . This violent dislike, conscious and organized, of the intelligence—' intellectual ' has become almost a term of contempt in our *salons*—constitutes something entirely new in French society. . . . This dislike will be the mark of our time in the history of French civilization.

Admirable as it is to be able to see that situation as Benda has (being almost alone in that, and with the surplus of courage to give expression to it), he does not go in search, very seriously, of the reasons for what he has described. People are—french people—for some reason, he says, the enemies of that culture of which they used to be the friends : french culture and european culture in general. And that state of affairs is apparently regarded by Benda as natural, although very unfortunate. What he means by *french society*, and how far what he so describes could in the nature of things be expected to carry on the traditions of feudal and monarchical France, he does not specify.

For him Taine, Renan, and Anatole France (I believe) are the last great representatives, in all probability, of french culture. There will be no more figures of that sort : of that stature, of that integrity, of that aloofness.

But that does not mean the French State will not be wealthy and powerful. The Roman Empire got on very well as a state with a frantically materialized society in which the light of learning and the intelligence was extinct, as with us. Such conditions do not prevent people from making money. It rather enables them to do that better than ever before. Greek speculative intelligence is not good for war or commerce.

In spite of the fact that Benda describes this ' hatred of the intellect ' as ' something entirely new,' and in a sense peculiar to contemporary society, he does not wish to go into the reasons for it. He rests within conventional historical parallels. Having first said it is a novelty, he then says it is common to many societies. So he forgoes the merit of having grasped the relative novelty of this fact. For example, he says (and very well and very truly) :

> At the bottom of this taste of our contemporaries for the writer without clear and distinct ideas, let us learn to recognize something profounder still, and common, it seems, to every fashionable gathering or circle : namely, the preference for the *feeble* intelligence, the aversion to the powerful one. Let the reader recall, going back a little way into history, the gallery of talents—poets, thinkers, journalists, talkers—especially favoured by society. How many minds described as ' fins,' ' délicats,' ' aimable,' ' plein de grâce.' he will find : how few minds to which ' vigoureux ' would be applied ! How many Meleagers, Pliny the Youngers, de la Fares, Abbé de Choisys, Jules Janius, de Caros, Bergsons, there are : how few de la Rochefoucaulds or Montesquieus ! How many feminine natures : how few men ! '

That is of course a matter of common observation. It is evident that the hero of the intellect, no more than the hero of war or finance, is a suitable inmate for the world of the *salon*. The Bachs and Handels, David Humes and Schopenhauers of this life have always been somewhat uncouth. Such names evoke such familiar pictures as that of the Princess of Wales saying, ' Hush, hush : Handel is angry ! ' when the courtiers preferred talking to listening to the great abstract orator : or of David Hume, like a burly carving in red brick, in the front of the box at the Paris theatre, hung with a festoon of several ladies of the court. In such instances the intellect, or its possessor, is treated like some strange—it is true—but very sacred animal. The most spoilt of societies in the past have not repudiated their intellectual obligation—while making full use of it, as we do. Where we differ so much is in our repudiation of the debt. We compose ourselves into a militant league of hatred against the ' creative ' monster, the inventive brute. Genius has become for us Caliban : what *we* have become, to make this possible, we do not care to consider.

CHAPTER VI

THE TABOO ON GENERIC TERMS, AND THE ABSTRACT CREATURE OF DEMOCRACY

AS the result of the feminist revolution, ' feminine ' becomes an abusive epithet. When you say that the *salon* world, society, is essentially a *feminine world,* you encounter that difficulty for which provision has already been made. The number of generic terms that you may not use increases daily. This is natural in a period of radical upheaval. Classifications which people wish to transcend are indicated by them : so when you say ' feminine ' it is as though you said ' women before the revolution.' Any term of differentiation is taboo. The recognition of the human standard of industrial standard-ization, the abstract ' man ' without narrowing specifica-tions, is *de rigueur* in forms of address. That is the ultimate stage of the *democratic* system. It is not, I need not point out, what we regard as the goal of revolutionary thought. For us, as for Sorel, it is the last decadence of that false-revolutionary movement that began with the great monarchies in Europe in the sixteenth century. It is of the essence of democracy, not of radical social revolution and non-democratic revaluation.

The central question, then, is still (and in this part of our discussion as much as elsewhere) that of differentiation or non-differentiation. Some things, which from every human standpoint we should regard as bad, feeble, corrupt, or even imbecile, we should nevertheless regard as good and profitable in their destructive capacity. But their essential degeneracy remains. They are, like the mercenaries, to be got rid of as soon as possible.

So, with these things in mind, we can go on with our questions. Whether it would be better, as it appears to you, if the world were peopled by and society composed of persons differing from each other in certain well-marked ways (not necessarily the ways in which they have so far differed, perhaps very different ones or modifications of them)? or would it amuse you more if they were all on one pattern?

Sex is one of the capital respects in which people differ from each other. And as far as sex is concerned, one of four things can happen. People can either be divided (1) into men and women as we know them—into people, roughly, like President Roosevelt, Nurmi, Dempsey, or Bernard Shaw, to take at random some notorious *men*, on the one hand ; and Signora Dusé, Lady Diana Manners, Jane Austen, and Mary Queen of Scots on the other, to take some celebrated *women* : or (2) they can resolve their secondary sex characteristics and become either *all feminine* or (3) *all masculine* (approximating to one or other of the poles illustrated above) ; or (4) evolve some one undifferentiated human type, at least as far as sex went, unlike either of the two that we know.

At present a fusion is taking place : carried to its logical conclusion, it would result in a standardization on the feminine side of the secondary sex-barrier. This appears to me a less promising adjustment than that which No. 4 of my table would produce. No animosity to women, but rather a feeling of the psychic lopsidedness that would result, accounts for this preference.

Perhaps the exact half and half would be a solution— not so good, I believe, however, as No. 4. The latter would involve a new creative element. It would not always be reminding people what a close shave it was that they had not divaricated to one side or the other.

As I am not occupied with prophecy, but with things as they present themselves to-day, it is with the second eventuality that we are confronted—that is, with an increasingly feminine world. This, under correction, would be more puritanic and fastidious, more excessive and emotional, than a masculine one. No make-weight of typical masculine phlegmatism would *deaden* it. More uniquely alive to the things of the moment ; more docile and mercurial ; more burdened with and swayed by the tidal movements of the unconscious—finally, more *un-conscious*, less 'intellectual' : that is what, for convenience, I call ' feminine.'

Once more, perhaps, it will be better to insist that it is not meant that (1) ' all women ' are more ' emotional ' than any man; (2) that some cannot be as indifferent to hamperingly polite rules as the standard man ; (3) that women cannot be as ' phlegmatic ' or as highly ' intellectual ' as that same not very inspiring standard.

A miner or drayman gets from his occupation a certain body and habits, and the majority of women get certain well-defined characteristics from theirs ; both inherit others.   So we can forbear from argument as to whether the drayman could not be made into a picture-postcard beauty, or the woman made to support the heaviest drudgery.   We know that the women of Dahomi are reported (or were by Burton) to be hardier and more masculine than the men, and to do the heavier field-work ; and that if the drayman makes his fortune, his grandson, who goes to Eton, is not so big and rough and may become very small and smooth.   We are obviously talking of realities as we find them, and not as some interested propagandist would arrange them.

The european ideal of force—even when it has the majesty that was given it in renaissance art—is not so much favoured in the scheme outlined here as forms slightly less monotonously martial and heroic.   Especially I think the present moment is inappropriate for insisting on this masculinity.   Its *weakness* we must, as Europeans, have found out recently, unless very blind indeed.   So far from wishing to engage in propaganda for the physical standards of the policeman, I would rather see these monuments to the vanity of physical force abolished and have nothing but policewomen.   Also, those battleships that to-day can keep no enemy that matters out of a country get up the nose of any patriot.   The really powerful modern enemy contents himself with buying a rail and ship ticket, and is propelled or dragged comfortably into your fatherland, while the battleships, flashing their bull's-eyes over the waves, go rolling majestically round the coasts.   When you behold these traditional symbols, therefore, can they appear anything but animated satires on the poor European's obsession of the efficacy of the physical ? It is even astonishing that that bubble, which is a Beadle or a John Bull, was not pricked by some little Charlie Chaplin-like pin long ago.   So alas for our helpless, childish, masculine idols of force, then !

CHAPTER VII

SAMUEL BUTLER'S 'LOVE,' AND THE *ROMANCE OF DESTRUCTION* OF THE MAN OF SCIENCE

BEFORE closing this section of my argument I will make a few more general observations which may help to clarify it further. Samuel Butler, in his *Note-Books*, describes all human love as eating and swallowing. Here are his words (' Who would kiss an oyster ? ') :—

Loving and Hating.

I have often said that there is no true love short of eating and consequent assimilation ; the embryonic processes are but one long course of eating and assimilation—the sperm and germ cells, or the two elements that go to form the new animal, whatever they should be called, eat one another up, and then the mother assimilates them, more or less, through mutual inter-feeding and inter-breeding between her and them. . . . We think we dote upon our horses and dogs : but we do not really love them (because we do not eat them).

What, on the other hand, can awaken less consciousness of warm affection than an oyster ? Who would press an oyster to his heart, or pat it and want to kiss it ? Yet nothing short of its complete absorption into our own being can in the least satisfy us. No merely superficial, temporary contact of exterior form to exterior form will serve us. The embrace must be consummate, not achieved by a mocking environ-ment of draped and muffled arms that leaves no lasting trace on organization or consciousness, but by an enfolding within the bare and warm bosom of an open mouth—a grinding out of all differences of opinion by the sweet persuasion of the jaws, and the eloquence of a tongue that now convinces all the more powerfully because it is inarticulate and deals but with the one universal language of agglutination. Then we become made one with what we love—not heart to heart, but protoplasm to protoplasm, and this is far more to the purpose.

This is the darwinian nightmare of the struggle for existence, operating on a sensitive mind, converted into a spectacular paradox. ' I could *eat* you ! ' one lover says to another at the paroxysm of their lubricity. And indeed, if one were considerably smaller than the other, as in the case of the male of the epira, that no doubt would happen very often. But if the supreme caress is to *swallow* the person you love, either at a mouthful or in pieces, then it seems reasonable to say that there is little difference between sexual love and swallowing a half-dozen oysters. ' All men kill the thing they love,' Oscar Wilde says (in his *Reading Gaol*). ' All men eat the thing they love,' Butler says in his *Note-Books*.

In the above quotation our affection for a dog is con-trasted with our lack of affection for an oyster. Yet we do not love dogs, or we would *eat* them, it says. I believe a definition of beauty is to be found by following out the dog and oyster parallel. It is only when something is independent of us, a non-assimilable universe of its own, that we ' love ' it, as we call it. Most men dislike the look of an oyster, as they dislike the appearance of the under-neath of their tongue (' love is the *pearl* of the oyster ' in Sappho, not the oyster), but they find it ' lovely ' to *eat*. Two creatures of opposite sex ' love ' each other : they do not eat each other usually, or *come together* in that way. As Butler says, they ' pet ' and ' kiss ' each other. There is a ' superficial temporary contact of exterior form ' only. It is in the creation of a third, and again separate, being that they *mingle* completely.

This act of *creation*, of a something more, is an act of love. The eating of the oyster is an act of destruction, however it may, indirectly, make tissue.

The ' superficial contact of exterior form ' which char-acterizes the ' love ' of the more complex animals is essential to the existence of ' love ' or ' affection ' ; that is an emotion for something different to the self, that cannot be absorbed into the self, in the sense of be eaten. That *detachment, distance*, and, as it were, chastity, and intense *personal* sensation on our side, is at the bottom of all our *spiritual* values, as we name what about us is independent of feeding and renewing our machine.

Butler's sentiments for the oyster would literally have to become *platonic* (on the principle of Gilbert's ' affection à la Plato, for a bashful young potato, or a not too *french*

french bean') for him to be justified in giving the same name to it as to what he would feel for Mary or Kate.

The platonic condition (always in the gilbertian sense) is essential, then, also to the existence of *beauty*. The ideas of beauty, of a god, or of love, depend severally on separation and differentiation. The savage ate his god to procure divinity for himself, so showing his foolishness ; for his act was like attempting to devour the *beauty* of a mountain or a river, or to convert his *love* for another person into the tissue of his own body, or like buying or selling a dream. Freud's obsession of incest is in the same order of things.

Bergson has a lot of one side of Butler in him (perhaps he consumed a good deal of him at one time of his life) : his *creative evolution*, like Nietzsche's *will to power* and glorification of carnage and the sentiment aroused by acts of destruction, is of course (like Butler) under the shadow of Darwin. Mr. Shaw's version of *creative evolution* (cf. *Methuselah*, preface) relates Bergson and Butler further.

I have devoted so much space to this definition of love because it has a great deal of bearing on what presently I shall have to say on the subject of bergsonism. Bergson's doctrinaire immersion in the waves of the vital flux is the same thing—only, in that case it would be the 'love' of the eater as he englobed what was plunged into him, the 'love' of the blood-stream for the juices that reach it.

Returning again to Butler's amusing 'note,' in the ordinary way we take these desperate statements with a grain of appropriate salt, as a philosopher's jest or a poet's madness. We know that all the married couples in a London suburb do not, in fact, *eat* each other, except figuratively. Nor do they make meals off their children, nor *vice versa*. At such extravagances we consider we can afford to smile with civilized superiority : yet we register the truth they symbolically contain.

As we have erected, developed, and organized ourselves in a variety of ways, become 'human,' and deliberately and by a great effort of consciousness marked ourselves off from 'animals' (when we say we are 'humane' we mean precisely that we do not *destroy* and subsequently *eat* one another, or eat one another alive), then it is certain that biology or science generally is not helping us in our

ambitious make-believe by referring us back gleefully to
the oyster, the male of the epira, the ichneumon fly, etc.
Science, or the man of science—of the Butler type, or like
Mr. Haldane—are romantically destructive. The *romance
of destruction* is as natural to them, and they can resist it
as little, as can a child. And it is both possible and useful
to associate this *romance of destruction* of the man of science
with the *romance of destruction* illustrated by the nihilist—
by Herzen or Bakunin.

This *romance* can become a *rage*. Both with the man of
science, drunken with the notion of the power he is handling,
of the vastness of the forces he is tapping, of the smallness
of the individual human destiny, of the puniness of the
human will, briefness of life, meanness of human knowledge,
etc., and with the nihilist, from delight in frightening other
children, the warm egotistic glow, this *romance of destruction* can easily pass over into sadism and homicide.

With what Dostoievsky described as the *possessed*, with
people at all events *obsessed* by some such thing as this
romance of destruction, as I have called it, the step from a
beneficent activity to a malevolent one is imperceptible.
All love, in that connection, could be said to turn into
hate. The ' love ' of the fanatic—like the brotherly ' love '
of the primitive christian—always takes the form of
destruction.

> Je t'ai aimé trop ; voilà pourquoi
> Je t'ai dit : Sors de cette vie !

The christian notion of the destruction of the world,
other-worldliness altogether, was an expression of the
fanatical love—hate, *romance of destruction*—of the religious
variety. Scientific thought (or rather the *feeling* produced
in men of science by scientific thought) is full of such
material as that. Mr. Haldane ends his little book,
Dædalus, on a note of that sort : he says :—

> The scientific worker of the future will more and more
> resemble the lonely figure of Dædalus as he becomes con-
> scious of his ghastly mission and proud of it.

> Black is his robe from top to toe.

> All through his silent veins flow free
> Hunger and thirst and venery.

The verse ends in a description of the diabolical figure riding along ' singing a song of deicides.'   So Mr. Haldane's ideal man of science is a *god-killer* like Kant in Heine's romantic picture ; that in which the author of the *Kritik* is compared to Robespierre, only more formidable than the latter, because the philosopher's natural prey is a god instead of a mere king.   Mr. Haldane's scientist is riding along on an apocalyptic charger (suspect), trampling with the plunging movement of a ship, in the waves of a thick blood-red cloud.   It is very likely, indeed, that *The Three Horsemen of the Apocalypse* suggested this pretty emotional ending to Mr. Haldane.   For it is a matter of common knowledge that most biologists and physicists spend their spare time in the cinema, especially favouring the apocalyptic or sensationally historical type of film.   After inventing a new poison-gas, for instance, Professor X will drop into the nearest super-house if a good war-film is being shown there at the moment (to get people into the mood for the next war), and to the intoxicating thumping and throbbing of the large orchestra will, in fancy, launch his latest discovery on a choking mass of the less scientific of his kind.

I will quote from another man of science, certainly with more justification in useful works than Mr. Haldane (from an essay appearing in another series produced by Messrs. Kegan Paul) :—

> But, let the consequences of such a belief be as dire as they may, one thing is certain : that the state of the facts, whatever it may be, will surely get found out, and no human prudence can long arrest the triumphal car of truth— no, not if the discovery were such as to drive every individual of our race to suicide ! (*Chance and Logic.   C. S. Peirce.*)

I should not dwell at such length on this subject if it were not of such obvious importance to us, who are not men of science, to understand the personal and private dispositions of those who are.   Science is often referred to as *the religion of the present day*, just as socialism is. Like the socialist, the man of science is apt to be of a religious and fanatical temper.   (He may even be a socialist as well.)   This involves a lack of ' human feeling ' as a principle.   No scotch pastor, genevan mystic, parson from the world of the ' Way of All Flesh,' not St. Augustine himself, could be more callous, intolerant, militant, and resolved to make ' existence ' a very bitter ' struggle ' indeed for the survival of the holiest, fittest, humblest, strongest, and best in the imperium of a bitter and jealous god, than the average man of science for whom Mr. Haldane is the spokesman.   We are told that ' there can be no truce between science and religion,' that ' we must learn not to take traditional morals too seriously.'   What painful verbiage that must sound to any one not a sectary of science or its enemy religion !   For, whoever ' we ' are likely to be, shall we be able to dispense so gaily with traditional morals? The large lay audience of such a book as *Dædalus* is left with nothing more useful than the conviction that it will shortly be finished off in a most ingenious manner, and so all its trouble brought to a timely conclusion.

You cannot insist enough, it seems to me, on the human factor in the man of science.   Scientific discovery or the teaching of science is one thing, and the man of science as private man, reflecting on his functions and applying his discoveries or selling them to other people, is another : the layman wants often reminding of this to counteract his romantic tendencies.   An engineer may build a remarkably fine bridge to enable people to cross a wide and powerful river ; but if he sits down to write a little book about his engineer's function, it may become apparent, after you have read a few pages, that he is really explaining to people what an excellent jumping-off board his bridge is for those tired of life and desiring to get right into the middle of the river without trouble.   The *romance of destruction* could be regarded as a sort of vertigo that haunts the minds of those handling the forces of nature, in touch, at least, with almost magical powers.

CHAPTER VIII

WHAT THE ANONYMITY OF
SCIENCE COVERS

AND here it is perhaps apropos to point out once more how criminal the egalitarian position is in its logical results. We depend entirely, for our relatively enviable position above the animal flux and chaos, on a very few men. To reduce men to an abstract average of ' phantom men ' of the type envisaged by the Enlightenment, is to repudiate our sense of those discrepancies the maintenance of which is so important to our welfare. To pretend (for some motive of egalitarian vanity) that most men are not like the mad and brutalized crowds, charged with a sadism that identifies love with murder, at a bull-fight, is criminal for this reason : it delivers *us all* over into the hands of *anybody*. *The anonymity of science covers that howling, foaming mob.* Why should we expect the average man of science—a man of very average intelligence, trained as a physicist or a chemist by some chance, instead of as an accountant, an acrobat, or a solicitor—not to behave, if he gets the chance, like the average of the mob at the Plaza de Toros or in the roman amphitheatre ? Why should we expect him to resist the thrilling spectacle of our agony and blood ? Have we any reason to expect him not to make a ' penny shocker ' *out of us* if he can : since we know that his natural mental food is *Sexton Blake, The Magnet*, Phillips Oppenheim, and the films ?

With the artist, alone, are we safe in that respect. He has no need, we know, of our *real and living blood* and *real tears*. But most men of science are not artists. They *do* need these realities to play with. From this it will be seen how we prepare our own destruction when we lose our sense for people, or deliberately destroy it, in the interests of an abstraction—the one and only, equal and undivided, human average. Why, as Peirce says, the very word *average* is a journalistic absurdity in its origin.

That these things *on the surface* are different to what

they are in the depths or the interior, and that we are *surface creatures*, is the truth that Nietzsche insisted on so wisely. All the meaning of life is of a superficial sort, of course : there is no meaning except on the surface. It is physiologically the latest, the ectodermic, and most *exterior* material of our body that is responsible for our intellectual life : it is on a faculty for exteriorization that our life depends.

Butler's *swallowing of the oyster*, to return to that, shows us very well the nature of our problem. It is the separation of one organization from another, this merely *exterior* cuddling of which he speaks with irony, that constitutes our human nature. Love, as we discursively understand it, can only exist on the surface. An inch beneath, and it is no longer love, but the abstract rage of hunger and reproduction of which the swallowing of the oyster, or the swallowing of the male by the female epira, is an illustration. And it is the spirit of the artist that maintains this superficiality, differentiation of existence, for us : our personal, our detached life, in short, in distinction to our crowd-life.

Where Julien Benda is discussing the *emotional*—and hence decadent, imperfect, romantic—character of most art to-day, he writes : ' Note, also, *a strong emotion*, caused at the sight of this innate conjunction procured between the soul of the artist and that of the object, such as the sight of two people intimately embracing would awaken. Let us learn to recognize, also, in their will *to instal themselves inside* things, a kind of thirst to sexually invade everything— to violate any intimity. and mix themselves in the most intimate recesses of the being of everything met ' (*Belphégor*). That describes admirably the spirit in which Butler's *note* on love and the oyster was written.

Science (on its human, non-technical, philosophic side) tends to the reverse, then, of what is ideally the function of art—a function which, as Benda says, it has forgotten. Science is the science of the *inside* of things : art is the science of their *outside*. Art is the differentiator: science is the identifier. Science would merge us into a mutually devouring mass. That is the ultimate tendency of religion too, with its Ends of the World and Apocalypses. The *pagan* and the *artist* sensibility is on the side of life, and is superficial, in the sense indicated above. Religion and the philosophy (or religion) of science are on the side of death, and are impregnated with the *romance of destruction*. The primitive christian, the nihilist like Herzen, and the man of science of the type we have been discussing, are all *destructive* first and foremost. They recommend, or prophesy, each in his own way, the suicide of our race.

CHAPTER IX

THE PROS AND CONS OF DOMINY-ATION

SUPPOSE that (*one*) you were a ruler : that (*two*) you
lived in an educationalist era, that your rule, like the
jesuit rule in their paraguayan *reductions*, necessarily took the form of pedagogy, that you ruled by means
of popular instruction and *suggestion*, rather than of armed
force—as is the case in a modern democracy : what type
of person would you favour ? You would yourself be a
typical dominy. And ideally the Infants' Class would be
what you would choose to take.

The reason for your choosing the Infants' Class, or for
your being a dominy at all, would be an innate desire to
boss others, and be a little providence or all-knowing god
to a little world lying in the palm of your hand. And these
characteristics would be found in all of your kind. But
also the drastic, top-to-bottom, changes that had to be
effected in the generations you had come suddenly to
control—in order to change them quickly from their
agelong habits to other very different habits more in
conformity with your own taste—would necessitate this.
The 'Give us a child up to six, and do what you like with
him afterwards' of the jesuits would also apply to your
task. It took the jesuits in their *reductions* three generations to transform the Indians into civilized people. This
meant a three-generation-long concentration on the child-
population. That too would be your task. Both from
your pedagogic disposition and the political requirements
of the case, the child would be your natural quarry. Or
a race of Neuters would be preferred by you to anything
galvanized into independent life by sex. (Fourier very
justly called children, before the age of puberty, the
neuter sex—rather on the principle of Schopenhauer's
famous description of woman as 'the short-legged race.')

When the children grow up a little, sex descends on
them ; at puberty this threatens to 'make men of them,'
or 'women,' as the case may be. They are inclined to be
no longer so tractable. They think for themselves, they
begin to ask awkward questions. In short, they are no

longer helpless, suggestionable, credulous children. Your interest in them is at an end.

Now *sex*, when it means marriage and for a man the responsibility of a family, destroys the ' child ' at once. This descent of sex at the age of puberty, turning the child's thought to images of love and courtship, is a social, and so a political as much as a physiological, event. *Sex* always has for the popular mind a physiological—*pleasure* —connotation. But this *simpliste* manner of regarding it obscures many things about it which have nothing to do with pleasure, as we have already attempted to show. The uniquely sensual interpretation of it enables many a three-card trick to be played in its shadow. The isolation, for political purposes, of the *pleasure* principle in sex is a tried and ancient expedient that seldom fails the person who has learnt its use. In the result it leads to an attitude towards sex as false as, and very similar to, the popular and contemporary way of regarding the fine arts. In both cases *the isolation of the pleasure principle*, and the interpretation of their function only in terms of pleasure, result in a distorted and untrue idea of them.

That pleasure is the incentive to both—to both *sex* and *art*—is certain. But what pleasure enables you to reach is something different to itself, or, if you like, different sorts of pleasure : for all life must in some way be pleasure— even, as we discussed earlier, the horror of destruction or the ' narrow escape' from it—namely, the pleasures of the battlefield, or of any ' moving accidents,' political or domestic.

In a society the political and social machinery of which could be logically reduced, for the purposes of grasping it in its simplest, most radical workings, to such a figure as the above, what type of being would be pointed to as the ideal of human perfection ? Obviously a child of some sort—of the same race of ' little children ' as that of which Christ proposed to build his heaven. But Christ's charm would be absent. The grace and gentleness of his evangel would not come to mind on reading the harsh and fussy text-books of this political faith, prepared for the mechanization and fixing of the new child-type. It would inevitably be some sort of neuter and sexless creature that would be pointed out to us as a model for

all citizens of that New Jerusalem. When the citizen
was no longer physiologically a child or a neuter, he would
be recommended to remain a child or a neuter or both,
in every way except in age. Especially would the necessity of remaining in tutelage, in helplessness, in neutrality,
in childishness, *mentally*, be insisted on. The image of the
famous child of Kensington Gardens ' who never grew up '
would be constantly held up before him as a cherished ideal.

As to sex and the family, the same line would be taken
in suggestion and argument. Sex—the crude cutting up
into ' men ' and ' women '—destroys that divine neutrality
of the tender, tractable first years. This would involve
something else. It would be preferable that only the
pleasure principle should remain in sex : and so far as
possible it should be isolated in a neuter organism.

But what sort of person would be held up for the scorn
and hatred of all, the great model of all that human beings
should *avoid* ? ' P.J.,' or professional jealousy, on the part
of the dominy would come into that. And sure enough,
what would be regarded as another potential dominy would
be the target chosen. ' Intellectualness ' would be the
thing to which, above all others, no one must ever aspire.
Intellectual matters must be the dominy's prerogative—
but he would not put it that way to his little charges.
He would say, ' An " intellectual " is a supercilious dog,
mark you : have nothing ever to do—ever—with an
" intellectual " ! He is known to corrupt little children—
he has been known to kidnap them. So beware of him !
Spit—and make the *mano fica*, as I have taught you to—
at the mere name of " intellect " : for *that* is the disgusting
thing that the wicked " intellectual " uses to corrupt little
children with. Amen.'

In the contemporary world the intellectual will slowly
get a position similar to that of a witch or practitioner of
the black arts in the Middle Ages. Men will yet be burnt
because they have been discovered reading a forbidden
scientific treatise. But when that time comes it will
certainly testify to a contumacious, evasive, and dangerous
disposition for a man to have done such a thing. We are
talking of the present, of course.

So with this know-all, knowing dominy in charge, with
a ' jealous ' eye on the fruits of the tree of knowledge, any

one who knows anything will not be liked. So you must know as little as possible to be popular. But there is nothing very unusual in that: for we all know that an at all active or ambitious man or woman—such as might become a dominy or a master or mistress—is only interested, naturally, being a *dominy*, in people he or she can *dominate*. People who desire power experience interest in, not to say love for, only those inferior to themselves in knowledge or capacity. *Their world is a world of inferiors*. It is for that reason that they desire and attempt to bring about *an inferior world*! Therefore, if you wish to recommend yourself to such a man or woman, it is only as an ignorant, helpless, eternally subaltern individual that you can do so. And this is always true of the sort of man or woman with a taste for domination.

There is one further thing to be added to this picture (which will relate it to the contemporary picture already drawn): that is, that all the behaviour to which the children are urged will invariably be in the name of *intelligence* and culture. It is more *intelligent* to model yourself on the fashionable social diagram of this highly political schoolroom, and to become what the dominy wishes you to become, etc. How this can be reconciled with the hymn of hate against the ' intellect,' there is no necessity to go into, for every one can discover that by means of a slight effort of observation.

When all this has been said—in order that a few of us should understand exactly what our position must be in the modern world, and the exact nature of the forces at work, and all the significance of the social fashions by means of which they operate—it is necessary to add at once that this is by no means a tragedy for the majority of people. The standardized type evolved will be well enough off for a short time. The reason for this I have given at considerable length in the discussions on the question of responsibility and irresponsibility in Part III. It is not by any means the worst fate for a man or woman to be fooled, or led by the nose as asses are. *Where ignorance is bliss* is the proverb—but ignorance is bliss everywhere. Sex—all except the pleasure principle—is, like art, an almost intolerable burden. The family is a curse. And this, in some ways, unpleasant picture is merely an intellectual organization, on ' rigid scientific lines,' of what has virtually been the structure of society at all times. The attitude towards the ' intellectual ' means only that the era of vulgarization, of ' free speech,' is drawing to a close : not that the intellect is bankrupt or can be dispensed with.   It can be dispensed with in its travestied form of absurd *enlightenment* on the popular plane, that is all. And that is the last thing to be regretted.   It will only be the private and unauthorized study of science that will be black magic.   Only, during the revolutionary violence of this change of standpoint, the intellect has to be shielded.

PART IX

MAN AND SHAMAN

'*A man that is commanded as a soldier to fight against the enemy . . . may nevertheless in many cases refuse, without injustice. . . . And there is allowance to be made for natural timorousness, not only to women (of whom no such dangerous duty is expected) but also to men of feminine courage.*'
Leviathan, Part II. chap. xxi. Hobbes.

'*Still the deterioration and decay continued till the lords of Thang and Yü began to administer the world. These introduced the method of governing by transformation, resorting to the stream (instead of to the spring), thus . . . destroying the simplicity of nature. . . . After this they forsook their nature and followed (the promptings of) their minds. . . . Then they added . . . external and elegant forms, and went on to make these more and more numerous. The forms extinguished the first simplicity, till the mind was drowned in their multiplicity. After this the people began to be perplexed and disordered, and had no way by which they might return to their true nature. . . .*' *Shan Hsing. Kwang-tze.*

CHAPTER I

THE FEMININE CONCEPTION
OF FREEDOM

THE foregoing analysis will have defined the way in which this subject is approached in this essay, and the reasons that have necessitated its discussion. It is impossible to-day to discuss feminism intelligently without discussing sex inversion. Similarly (1) *the disintegration of the family unit*, (2) *the cult of the child*, (3) *doctrinaire dilettantism*, (4) *the war on the intellect*— all these subjects are intimately connected with it; if you discuss one with any thoroughness, you are compelled to discuss the others.

That the present widespread invert fashion is not an Oscar-Wildeism, or the excrescence of a dilettante sex-snobbery only, is certain—although such elements are to be found in it and are part of its conspicuous advertisement. It is much more an instinctive capitulation of the will on the part of the ruling male sex. It is much more a political phenomenon than anything else, too : its sensual character, although it is from that angle that it is popularly viewed, of course, is insignificant. Shamanization, and the affecting of inversion by a great number of people not physiologically abnormal, is a social device to gain freedom, that new type of freedom which at the opening of our argument an attempt was made to define. It is as much one of the classes of the complex phenomenon of revolution as is feminism or a wage-conflict. It might properly be allocated under the heading Minors, or the still wider heading Education, though in practice it stretches into the ripest manhood, or deepest old age.

The commutative nature of *freedom* and *irresponsibility* in what I have called the feminine conception of freedom— which is the type of freedom which is gradually substituting itself to-day with the European for the masculine, which circumstances have almost compelled him to discard— that is the true key to this great movement throughout Europe. And it is a law that, if left alone, or sufficiently supported by the intricacies of civilization, an individual invariably tends to evade any position of burdensome trust, or indeed any *position* at all. A receipt for such evasion can be the most popular of social specifics. Sex inversion for the male is such a receipt.

All normal human effort or competitive ambition has for its end to place you in a position of power or prestige. If you succeed, you consequently find yourself in a position of *responsibility*. You are also in the male category of initiative at once.

But all popular social revolution must be against a *superior* in power or fortune, and it is even directly aimed at terminating the control exercised over the life and action of the insurrected. If you trace the operations of authority and control you will find that wherever these exist at the present time, the social organism is agitated at that point. The *father* is the emblem of authority : the idea of the family is universally attacked. Control is exercised in the family over the women, children, and dependants : all these functionaries have their banner and class in social revolution. Then the man on the score of his sex had certain privileges. Chivalry outweighed these in some cases. But there was the material for an insurrection. The warder and prison governor is in authority over the convict, and the schoolmaster or the nurse over the child. So every imaginable form of authority is ferreted out.

Separated from its physical peculiarities, disincarnate, and in its form of social impulse, if we can imagine it so, before it had been furnished with the particular body it at present has, male sex-inversion can be regarded, I believe, as the prognostication of a deep revolution in the european character. The bold, adventurous, ' independent,' but uncreative European of the past, dies with this fashion, perhaps ; and may, it is to be hoped, be reborn after it as another creature : in short, more what the Asiatic is. This burst of *childhood* also (the child-cult which is associated in our time with these fashions) may be the last senile burst of the *old* european spirit, the immature, over-physical European who carried on the Roman Empire.

Taken purely as a phenomenon of ' revolutionary ' *anti-authority*, it is most obviously linked to the obsession of *childhood,* which stretches right through it and into every department of life.

The two chief orders of authority are the principles of *natural* superiority specified above, on the one hand (of a natural gift of strength, intelligence, daring, or what not), and the organized power of numbers, or any authority established in defiance of and not in complicity with natural laws, on the other. All anti-authority is of this second order. It is this that more and more has reigned, until the point of chaos has been reached. It is this that (through the vehicle of all this group of subversive fashions) is breaking itself. And it is breaking itself in the belief that it is breaking the other order of authority. There is no fashion which bears in itself the seeds of a new dispensation in which the true and natural order of power will be revived and reinstated as the ' unnatural ' fashion we have just been discussing.

The educational and press encouragement for the mood favourable to the development of such fashions is very striking. And indeed there is little trouble in showing even the obtusest person how his happiness may really lie in the last quarter in which he would expect to discover it. It is easy to show him how extremely disagreeable it is to be in a position of authority, how very foolish it is to desire authority, how authority, responsibility, is in every form to be shunned : how it is *much pleasanter in everything to be the under dog.* The wild bull or the wild boar—who can envy his lot ? Even the *male*—that queer expression of the masculine pride of the race : is it worth being *him* ? It is not difficult to show that *he,* if he is poor, is no great shakes, is poor white trash, and any woman, let alone a child, is better off than he is. (The child, not yet a part of ' real life,' still in a sheltered tutelage, is the ideal, of course.)

To be a sweetmeat-sucking, joke-cracking, indolently thumbs-up or thumbs-down member of the *audience,* is surely better than being a gladiator—that should be evident enough. For ' who would bear the whips and scorns of time,' and so on, who could, *without dying,* avoid it, and instead luxuriously watch other people sweating and dying ? No one but would assent to that. Then, says the patentee of the means of evasion, *I will show you how you can just step aside* and avoid all further labour or

anxiety. You will neither be rich, nor ' great,' nor beautiful, nor anything troublesome of that sort.   Who wants all
that ?   You can, if you want to, be eternally in the position
of a little silent, giggling, crafty child, watching and
exploding with pretty tinkling mirth ; or of an imbecile
that no one takes seriously, and of whom *nothing is expected*,
and in whom there is no ambitious vanity that can be
wounded, of whom no martial virtue is expected, nor
lover's absurd devotion—with the extravagant claims of
the over-indulged woman, overestimating her sex-leverage.
Nothing of all that ! Would you like to be *a woman* ?
It sounds a come-down ; but why ? She has the best of
it ! There is always some fool to look after her : she has
no harassing anxieties, unless she is a fool herself. She
is outside the life of bustle, boring business, mechanical
work done to get *money* (to keep *her*)—war, politics, and
all the rest of the solemn rigmarole—almost as much as
the child is.

    That is the gist of the insidious and disgraceful proposal
made to man, when in the war of the sexes, turned into a
class war, he has been defeated. For the smooth working
of the industrial machine some degree of castration of
the pugnacious, smally and uselessly, wastefully competitive, european male is necessary. He has been
hypnotized (by snobbery—one of his weak points) into
carrying out this operation himself. Objectionable as this
is to be present at, a sense of the great benefits that must
result from it should make it easier to support. If it is
best to turn the ' surplus women ' into a *neuter* sex, it is
also best to turn all ' surplus ' mankind, all the ' unprogressive mass,' into something *neuter* too, the modern ruler
seems to have said. There is nothing to be gained by its
being either too ' masculine ' or too ' feminine.' As an
active competitive mass it can only lead to chaos and
annihilation. And the pugnacious ' free,' democratic
European through two millenniums of unproductive
violence (which culturally and in every important way has
actually been a retrogression from the human standards
of antiquity, for who would to-day pretend that London
or Berlin compares favourably with periclean Athens ?)
has proved it beyond all possible dispute.

    That the male invert, being more ' womanly ' than any

woman, *plus royaliste que le roi*, is an unconscious propagandist of feminism is obvious. The modes and incentives of his obsessional life supply the propaganda-picture of a feminized universe.

Just as the backbone of the Dahomi army consisted of a corps of amazons, so the backbone of the *feminist* army in the sex war consists of a corps of *exoleti*, of active and passive epicenes.

Whether or not you regard the sex inversion of man as an act of instinctive revenge on the part of the defeated sex, it is certain that it is to that phenomenon that you have to look for the curious contrast between the technically improved conditions of women, their brilliant display of luxury and taste, in the interests of which armies of people are occupied, and their admitted dissatisfaction with life and disappointment with the results of all this fastidious effort. Millions of women are equipped and appointed, in the matter of toilette and artifices for preserving youth, improving looks, and so forth, in a way that none of the queens of the pre-industrial age can have been. And yet they are not queens, their social influence is less even than that possessed by their grandmothers ; and the most seductives toilettes do not, if we are to believe them, madden, as would be expected, the strange male. ' Why so great cost, having so short a lease ! '—and, it would have in their circumstances to be added, registering such relatively meagre returns.

In this situation the *exoletos* plays his part—a very important social one. His adaptation, and if anything overdone advertisement, of the feminine mind and habits is in a sense the wrong sort of advertisement. In a curious way it is a fashion that originates in a sexlessness, or sex-weariness, and at the same time an over-sexing of the organism. And although all the standards of *pæderastia* are feminine standards, women are merely surrounded by so many more women, which is a thing no woman would feel pleased about in the abstract. Contempt for the thing imitated is further a dogma of the male recruits to the female side of the world : and this undercurrent of contempt or hostility—like that of one woman for another— does not help the woman's cause.

For evidence of this, contemporary fiction and newspaper

articles provide all that is required. I will quote some
passages in an article entitled ' The Neglected Girl of the
Period,' from the *Sunday Express*, written by a lady whose
articles are often worth reading on other grounds than that
of finding in them an unconscious revelation of the mind
of the time :—

The Girl of the Period probably appears at her window in
striped pyjamas, and drops down into the garden to smoke a
cigarette or feed her ferret before dressing; but then, poor
Cinderella, where is her Meredith ?   The Girl of the Period
is no less neglected by the painters.

Dramatists show the same meanness to girls, the same lack
of interest in them, so that across the stage goes a bleak
procession of colourless young creatures with no apparent
hearts and souls, no sentiment, no ambition. . . . The
seriousness of this neglect or degradation of the girl in art
depends on whether you regard poetry, painting, and the
theatre as moulding life or merely reflecting it.   Personally
I believe that nature copies art. . . .

Perhaps girls are having to pay too big a price for their
physical prowess, and especially for the infantile freedom of
their clothes.   The girl of to-day is so sensibly dressed that
she looks like an overgrown child until she is well into her
teens, and the Muses will have none of her.   At the same
age, her mother dressed in such a way that she was clearly
immature woman, and, as such, had an appealing charm.

Girls to-day look jolly.   They have what they call good
times.   But when you hear anybody say that they are
pampered and spoiled, don't believe it.   As a matter of fact,
the Girl of the Period is neglected and dethroned.

CHAPTER II

THE PROPAGANDIST INDICTMENT
OF THE FEMININE

BOTH sides in the sex war are provided with arguments by sex inversion, both the man and woman.
There is ' defeatism,' but also a deep racial tendency
of withdrawal from the absurd position of heroism that
could only end in the extermination of the white race.
There is a great deal of the intellectual snob about the
invert : but since he converts what he borrows from the
intellect to the purposes of *sex*, he is a great enemy of the
intellect. As a feminine facsimile, further, he takes over
the traditional idiosyncrasies of the feminine rôle ; and
certainly one of them has always been to be the ' enemy
of the Absolute.' The natural feminine hostility to the
intellect, and a desire to belittle the purely masculine and
abstract type of success, he takes over.

This type of success and the satisfactions to be obtained
from it have always deeply offended the feminine nature.
For the stronghold of the male (inaccessible to sexual
attack, pure of all that rich and turbulent romance of
sexual passion and the utilitarian claims of ' reproducing
the species '), has not that always been the abstract region
of his ' work,' of the productions of his intelligence and
specialized energy ? This ' other world ' of endeavour
into which men have always been able to retire has been
deeply offensive to women. Although that Bastille technically has fallen, yet, in the abstract, ' the intellect,' and
especially a certain sort of intellect, remains. And of this
there is no bitterer enemy than the turncoat, or ' turn-
sex,' male, feminizing invert. Proust himself is an arch
sex-mixer, a great democrat, a great enemy of the intellect.
For he desires in the deepest way to see everything converted into terms of sex, to have everything and everybody
on that violent, scented, cloying, and unreal plane, where
there is nothing that cannot be handled, the very substance
of illusion sniffed at and tasted by everybody, and put to
the uses of sensation. In that world most of the values

of the intellect are reversed. 'Imperial Cæsar, dead and turned to clay' was used to 'stop a hole to keep the wind away': 'turned to clay' in the other sense, without becoming a corpse, his fate would be a similar one. No man is a hero to his valet: and it is to a world of highly energized, orthodoxly perverted valets, with a great many scores to pay off, that Proust invites society. In this sense he is a great revolutionary figure. But it is one of the more distasteful, treacherous tasks of revolution that can be well left to the Prousts of this world. Nevertheless, his usefulness is undeniable: 'il travail le bien celui-là!' His hands are apt at unpicking, if only because they are small, agile, and feminine ones.

But, effective as male sex-inversion is against the masculine intellect, it is very effective, too, to some extent, against the privileges of women. A man transforming himself into a woman enters into rivalry with women. He affects, naturally, to be a *superior* sort of woman. And a great deal of the nineteenth-century criticism of woman with which the 'sex war' opened, or which was used to stir it up, is employed by him.

The arguments used against the normal procedures of sex by invert or misogynist are somewhat as follows. Sex as arranged by nature is vulgarly advertised, at bottom utilitarian, and the protagonists, the male and the female, are mortal enemies and temperamental opposites. The woman with her haunches and breasts is like an advertisement for some food 'to build bonnie babies.' At the best, the over-suave, vulgarly inviting lines of her body—a chocolate-cream trap to catch a rustic fool—are not æsthetically of the same value as the lean, flat 'idealism' of the male adolescent. The woman—the abstract woman against whom this propaganda is directed—is a sex specialist, always thinking about her personal appearance and incapable of any less *personal* sensations. With her little, earnest, permanently juvenile mask peering at a hat in a shop window; solemn, secretive, and self-conscious, pat-patting like a fantastically decorated automaton up the street; always *pretending*—never *herself* or able to forget the world around her; by turns maudlin and vicious, cruel like a child; inconsiderate, with no disciplined sense of 'fairness,' living on her mimetic sense solely, so that no idea or mannerism is her own, but only a reflection of some other personality or of fashion : that is a specimen inventory of the conventional male indictment.

Sex, as arranged by nature, it is said, is for nature's famous ' ends,' not ours, and there necessarily is a catch in it. At all costs the bagman, nature, with his (or her) bag, must be circumvented. Sex brings into play our spot qualities, and our most elaborately developed sensibilities are immediately invoked (and cheapened) at the touch of its ' potato-fingers.' Some think that *all* our trumps are involved in its displays, or that all our displays involve it. Is sex a worthy object for the lavishing of all this treasure ? Or could not the human symbol, the typical ' eternal feminine,' be improved on ? As regards the physique of this symbol, that has been dealt with above. For the rest, her narrow specialist intelligence, her inaptitude for great intellectual adventure, the sterility of her mind, like the potential fecundity of her body, all indispose her for the position that chivalrous poetry allotted her in the teeth of ancient and more brutal usage and good sense. Then she is not only a shallow, but a peculiarly ' false ' enemy. Or when the enemy is not being ' false ' (the rhetorical shakespearean epithet) she is being detestably ' true ' in the *Gretchen* sense. Her mind (as it appears in the schopen-hauerian colouring) is full of bibs, bread-and-butter-and-jam, beef-tea, rocking-horses, and school bills : or (in the laforguesque sense) smells of iodoform, the nurse's self-sacrificing plain costume, doctor's visits, vases of flowers, and darkened rooms. That was the position of the average enlightened european male contemporary to Schopenhauer, Laforgue, Weiniger, or Wilde.

Try as women will to *engarçonner* themselves, to ' reduce ' and ' reduce ' till they can pass as a diminutive male adolescent, they cannot entirely banish the reflection, in those for whom they perform these feats, that they are nature's agents, imitating their betters by a sleight of hand.

Against the woman, as here represented, there is always the classical remedy. And to-day that panacea (of non-sex or of perverted sex) has been almost universally adopted.

That this male indictment of the other sex, on the lips of a male invert, is somewhat inconsistent, is evident.

For all his care is directed to imitating this compound of contemptible defects. But still these charges are not forgotten and are often used : for of course it is no valid objection against the use of some slighting epithet that it exactly describes yourself—rather the contrary. It is perhaps no wonder, all things considered, that women are more cowed by ' the new man ' than they were by the old. The shamanizing contemporary male (who has changed his sex without the assistance of ' arctic hysteria ') is now their silken, attentive, caressing friend, and at the same time redoubtable adversary. The rôles are reversed and the tables turned. But the non-transformed male is if anything worse off than the woman. It is thus in every sense a drawn battle as between the traditional sex-principles opposed in this particular revolution. A pyrrhic victory is intended, and is achieved.

CHAPTER III

'CALL YOURSELF A MAN!'

AND it is in the experiences of war time that we must seek not only the impulsion, but in some sense the justification, of male sex-inversion, apart from its rôle in relation to the disintegration of the family unit. As a war-time birth it can be regarded as a reply to the implications of *responsibility* of those times : nature's *never again* in the overstrained male organism.

After the war it was reported that french mothers (who had lost masses of expensive children at the moment when their long task of nurture was about to be rewarded) were vociferating, as they probably did, that they would bring no more children into the world to be brought up and then killed. But more than the mothers, during the war no doubt men too were saying to themselves subconsciously that at last, beyond any doubt, the game was not worth the candle : that the Heroic Age was nothing to this : that the ' kiss ' they would receive ' when they came back again,' if they ever did, did not make them look any less foolish as ' heroes,' but more so ; and that the institution of manhood had in some way overreached itself or got into the caricatural stage.

Men were only made into ' men ' with great difficulty even in primitive society : the male is not naturally ' a man ' any more than the woman. He has to be propped up into that position with some ingenuity, and is always likely to collapse.

We have defined with some care what was intended by the term ' woman,' and we can now do the same for the term ' man.' The term MAN implies a variety of indispensable but not necessarily pleasant things, quite independently of the specific sex characters, although it can only be attached to an individual falling within the subdivision of the adult male. The identification by means of sex-character on the part of adult males has always been a source of mortification to women and children : and at the present juncture some more neutral term should be substituted for it if we are to divert female energy into a less competitive and imitative channel. There is no visible alternative to this except that of abandoning entirely to women the attributes associated with this term. Either the *word*, or the attributes for which it stands, would have to be given up. Otherwise women must still insist on being ' men ' ; and war to the knife over that ridiculous name, and the ghastly privileges that accompany it, must result.

A man, then, is made, not born : and he is made, of course, with very great difficulty. From the time he yells and kicks in his cradle, to the time he receives his last kick at school, he is recalcitrant. And it is not until he is about thirty years old that the present European becomes resigned to an erect position.

There are very many male Europeans to-day who never become reconciled to the idea of being ' men ' (leaving out of count those who are congenitally unadapted for the rigours of manhood). At thirty-five, forty-five, fifty-five. *und so weiter*, you find them still luxuriously and rebelliously prostrate ; still pouting, lisping, and sobbing, spread-eagled on their backs, helpless and inviting caresses, like a bald-stomached dog.

With infinite difficulty ' a man ' is, in the first place as a baby, put upon his feet, and invited to toddle. A period elapses which is the equivalent of the life of many a large-sized animal before he can walk on his hind legs at all respectably : and few men ever become entirely at ease in the erect position. So that eventually he should be able to get about without danger to himself and other people—cross the road, mount a bus, and so forth—infinite pains are expended on him. He is taught during ten years a host of symbols to prepare him for the subsequent feats of independence expected of him : and at every moment of his tutelage he is resentful and rebellious. *He does not want, if he can possibly help it, to be a man,* not at least if it is so *difficult*.

And to the end of his life he is not persuaded of the point of it all ; and when he reflects about it, regards all this preparation and fuss (for *nothing*, or so little—for what is the famous adult life for which all preparation is made ?— that it is hardly worth mentioning) as a meaningless evolution.

So ' a man ' is an entirely artificial thing, like everything else that is the object of our grudging ' admiration.' Or if there is an exception to this rule, it is the abnormal or exceptional man, whom we worship as a ' hero,' and whose unnatural *erectness* arouses almost more hatred than surprise. Prostration is our natural position. A worm-like movement from a spot of sunlight to a spot of shade, and back, is the type of movement that is natural to men. As active, erect, and humane creatures they are in a constantly false position, and behaving in an abnormal way. They have to be pushed up into it, and held there, till it has become a habit only to lie down at night ; and at the first real opportunity they collapse and are full length once more.

The snarling objurgations of the poor man's life, such as ' *Be* a MAN!' (banteringly and coaxingly) or 'CALL YOURSELF A MAN!' (with threatening contempt), arouse ' the man ' in the male still : but we can confidently look forward to the time, now, when this feminine taunt will be without effect.

A sense of DUTY is what we call the system of psychological injunctions (painfully learnt and easily discarded) by which all the useful actions of social life are effected. But that sense, in its turn, depends on the vanity : and the vanity requires its regulation food, which gets scarcer every day. Although all people depend for this staff of life, like a populous island for its nourishment, on other people : since few are such monsters as to grow it themselves.

But the vanity even is not such a primary thing as is usually supposed. CALL YOURSELF A *MAN*! at once puts it in motion. But it depends on the concept MAN for its effectiveness. And that is a belief, like a belief in God. Reduce a man's vanity below a certain point, or destroy his capacity for belief, and he subsides into his natural and primitive conditions.

The *instinct of self-preservation* would be dragged in as a hypothetic support of the man attacked with the remark, CALL YOURSELF A *MAN*! But the instinct of self-preservation is artificial too. It is the result of training and experience. Before a child has burnt its finger or is sufficiently documented about what will ensue if it puts its finger in the fire, it is not afraid of fire. What it is painfully acquiring during the years of its gradual propping up and training in erectness, is a *personality*. Without a *personality* there is no instinct of preservation : or rather, the less personality there is, the less horror is there at the idea of losing it. Many animals whose lot it is to be eaten are probably *willingly* eaten, as has been already suggested. When the male of the epira is devoured by its mate in the midst of its tumescence, that is part of the fun.

The average civilized man is so precariously erect that it is almost laughable to watch him at times : on those occasions, for instance, when from vanity or a sense of duty he is addressing himself to a distasteful and difficult task—like looking at pictures in a gallery, reading *Das Kapital*, or watching a good play. The grinding boredom you realize that he must be experiencing makes a mechanical hero of him—as a very heavy machine that lifts itself into the air, and flies like an eagle, could be termed *a hero* in the way of a machine. The gravitational pull from the prostrate depths of the abyss which he had to sustain should earn him, on these occasions, any title he might covet.

It is not more natural for one sex than for the other to be heroic or to be responsible, then.

The position of the male to-day, and the symbolism of the word MAN, are purely artificial : no more for one sex than for the other are the heroic ardours, ' intellectuality,' *responsibility*, and so forth, that we associate with the male, *natural*. Men had grown to regard them as natural, because in the first place they had seemed profitable. But now the rewards associated with the exercise of these manly duties are a little flat and stale. The depreciation in the value of the psychological side has brought down with it in some obscure way the physical or sensual side. (The psychological element in the *reward* for ' the man ' was, of course, the vanity element in the notion of power.)

The industry, courage, and responsibility of the male are artificial, and have only been sustained and kept in place by a system of rewards, like everything else in this world : reward that has sometimes been of the nature of loot, and sometimes of a juridical nexum. (We will examine in a moment the nature of these rewards.) The male has been persuaded to assume a certain onerous and disagreeable rôle with the promise of rewards—material and psychological. Women may in the first place even have put it into his head. BE A MAN! may have been, metaphorically, what Eve uttered at the critical moment in the garden of Eden.

The large, bloated, and sinewy appearance of the male, again, is partly the result of manual work or physical exercise, but is the result as well of thousands of years of ACTING THE MAN. The more muscular frame of the male, and his greater hardihood, are illusions, like everything else about him, provisionally and precariously realized, but no more stable than the muscular development produced by some intensive course of physical exercise, resulting in the inflation of this system of muscles or that. He is blown out by vanity into a *bigger* and *bonier* creature than his consort, like Shakespeare's Ajax. *He is in reality just the same size, and of just the same sort.*

The male is by nature (uninflated by vanity and physical exercise) as muscleless, slight, and as we say 'feminine,' both physically and mentally, as the female. There is no mysterious *difference* between the nature of the sexes, except the secondary differences we have been considering. If you persist in referring to 'the woman' not only as 'the woman' but as 'the sphinx' (as a certain contemporary intellectual *énergumène* does), what word would you have left for yourself?

Remove the arbitrary psychological machinery that in this way constitutes the mere male 'a man,' or tamper with it too much, or overtax it, and he collapses and becomes to all intents and purposes a woman. The functional difference, then, alone separates them. It is only functional differences that separate any one thing from another. If the duration of this collapse were at all considerable, even a functional readjustment would probably occur. The extreme rapidity with which these collapses occur (both in the specifically adipose bulk of the female, and the secondary muscular 'manliness' of the male) has been witnessed since the war.

In more primitive times than ours the exaggerated dimensions of the northern male—who vaingloriously blew himself out, and tiptoed himself up, till he was over six feet high, and weighed fifteen stone—has probably been the cause of our northern stock sticking culturally as it has done. The little mediterranean man would not have understood these ' manly ' monstrosities : nor could he have done what he did if he had allowed himself any such functional specialization. For this *size* actually suggested to our ancestors perhaps the idea of an independent *function* (like the female's procreative one)—the function, namely, of the ' fighting machine.' Northern neighbours, or neighbouring northern tribes, would flash their eyes at each other, and blow themselves out till they hardly had room for any more spectacular sinew, and then fling themselves on each other in mortal combat. Their ' manliness ' became a mania.

CHAPTER IV

THE POSITION OF THE CULT OF *THE CHILD* IN THE PRESENT SYSTEM

I WILL interpolate here a brief account of how *the child* cult should be placed politically in relation to the attack on the family unit and the sex war. If you explained it entirely on the score of a defeated vitality, or of political eclipse, you would be mistaken, I think.

The contributory causes of the cult of *the child*—in relation to the questions we have just been discussing—could be capitulated as follows :—

(1) Its usefulness as a kind of defeatist paradise for most of those accepting it : (2) its rôle as a factor in the ' sex war ' : and (3) its usefulness to those responsible for it and to some extent imposing it. It is obvious how closely it is related in that case with the wave of masculine inversion.

With No. 1 we have already dealt. The second aspect of it, namely, how some of its power is derived from the forces set in motion by the sex war, is not very difficult to trace. A woman's relation with the other sex is in two compartments. There is her relation to her husband and her relation to her son. In the manufacture of the family brood, in the traditional type of family, the husband and wife are rather like two workmen engaged on the same job. He is her *mate*, and she is his, their relation is a business one. When you hear a working man addressing his wife as ' mother ' (the mother of their children), his attitude to her is very like that subsisting between his ' mates ' and himself. It is a ' job ' he takes on in his spare time.

The woman's attitude to the son is a different one : he is her friend, for whom she keeps her best affection, in contrast to the businesslike ' comradeship ' felt for her ' mate.' Also her traditional occupation is that of a specialist in children of all sorts. These two contemporaries, of opposite sex, engaged in the maintenance of a small child-farm, have never known anything in the shape of *esprit de corps*, in reality, on the basis of two adults engaged together on the same task, over against creatures of another size and almost kind, at all events of another generation, to whom they sacrifice a great part of their life. This common task does sometimes endear them to each other, and affection no doubt often results from these associations ; but that is not, it is unnecessary to say, always the case, or at all necessarily so. There are elements of rivalry and technical friction that make it often difficult for such sentiments to be entertained. That, I suppose it will be agreed, is the situation in the unmodified family—that unit that is in process of breaking up at present.

The child as a symbol and object of worship, with exclusive claims, is a woman-value, then. That it should at once develop an antagonism for the adult, or ' the man,' is natural enough, seeing that at the time of its birth, as a fashion, the woman was engaged in a ' war ' of freedom with ' the man.' It is perhaps as well to add that all the freudian œdipus-complex propaganda has greatly assisted this situation.

The uses of *the child* as a piece of political machinery are, again, quite obvious. When *education* and the drilling into people of new ideas becomes an urgent problem and so an obsession, the child (as the jesuits saw in their famous remark, already quoted, ' Give us a child up to the age of six,' etc.) is the object of principal political solicitude ; just as during an election certain classes assume a sudden significance. In the present intensive revolutionary epoch, for the great masses of people in the West, there is little hope that any adults will be able to discard the democratic traditions in which they have been brought up. (The tiny minority able to think for themselves, and not fixed into unalterable moulds, do not come into calculations of this type : it is a rough-and-ready calculation, in the gross.) The ' jeunesse communiste ' and ' jeunesse patriote,' the sovietic boy-scout movement, child associations of every description, are an intensive reinforcement of the school, which is itself also a political and religious drilling.

The extreme reformer to-day—he whose ideas are a good many steps ' in advance of his time '—can only work to stable success through children and very young persons.

So it is upon *the child* that he bends his pedagogic eye. Also the teacher and propagandist is naturally the rival (in his designs on the child's mind) of the child's grown-up relations and friends. Hence one source of the ' age war.' For he has to stir up the *immature class*, as it could be called, whose adherence and affection he wishes to gain, against the adult generations, no longer intellectually sensitive. But this same figure—the highly educatable, sensitive child—has already been stirred up against papa by his feminist mamma, and is pondering already, if he is a reader of Freud, if he shall slay and eat him. So the arrival of the jesuit with further designs on his little mind confirms the work of mamma, and between them he is flung into a militant attitude towards all other sexes, classes, ages (which machinery of classification reverberates in his head), but those to which his mentor and his mamma both seek to confine him. So the class-conscious, age-conscious, sex-conscious child advances, frenzied by the announcement of a whole series of holy wars, towards the citadel of tradition, which it is his traditional task to assail.

We have already seen how important it is, for the purposes of political domination, to *separate* people as *rigidly* as possible. The *more* classes, associations, syndics—occupational, sex, age, cultural categories—into which you can cut them up and pen them, the more manageable (for the more divided and helpless) they are. Now what really is happening to-day (and this will continue until the full circle of social revolution has been described) is that the *opposite* of the initiatory ceremonies of puberty, universal amongst primitive people, are performed. The puberty ceremony of primitive life was directed to separating the adolescent male from the women and children (with whom up to then he had lived) for ever. Simultaneously he became a ' tribesman,' and was initiated into the ceremonies over which the male leaders of the tribe presided. To-day at the age of puberty, or indeed long before, the child receives, and is destined more and more to receive, an intensive ritualistic teaching opposite in its aim : namely, away from the traditions of the tribe and its traditional rulers. *He*, he is told, is henceforth the ruler. (This in effect would be the rule not by childhood, of course, but by the mentor or teacher, the dominy, and by the queen-mother, sitting upon an ideologic matriarchal throne.) That is, of course, the political point of *the child*. It is the same impulse that makes a dictatorial and ambitious personality prefer stupid and ignorant people to intelligent and instructed ones. From the former his ' power ' is to be derived.

CHAPTER V

UNIVERSAL CHARACTER OF INVERSION

IN conclusion I will assemble a few facts that will serve as a superficial historical background of the practice we are discussing.

The analysis of sexual inversion is of course to-day a thriving study : and yet it has so far not been vulgarized as it deserves. A great deal of the literature of sexual inversion is too technical to allow of its being used in public discussion. But it is not at all necessary to enter the laboratory or the clinic to-day: it is in its effects on society, and as it can be observed without specialist investigation and in the ordinary course of life, that it is probably most interesting, except of course for the person attracted to this study for other reasons.

At the outset I had better add, for the sake of those who may be disappointed at not finding a display of erudition in the matter of sex literature, with perhaps some new tit-bits, that I have avoided drawing on anything that would confer on my argument an interest of that kind.

In his *History of Moral Ideas* Dr. Westermarck devotes a chapter to the history of sex inversion. He shows the very wide diffusion of invert practices, of their status among different peoples, along with a few curious facts.

Throughout the entire history of the subject, homosexuality and male transformation of sex have been more or less associated in men's minds with magic and witchcraft. From that point of view sexual inversion (so baffling and in some cases disturbing a thing to the normal eye) is in the same category as epilepsy. Both are associated in some way with divinity. But whereas the one—epilepsy— is the object of a tender veneration, inversion of sex has usually elicited less sympathy from barbarous peoples. Both agree, however, in awakening fear and the awe of the unknown. Their practitioners or victims have been in a class apart, regarded as strange creatures not like other men.

In this connection we are told by Dr. Westermarck that

the ancient Scandinavians associated pederasty with witchcraft, and consequently punished it by burial alive in a morass. It was in their capacity of wizards that people convicted of homosexual practices were treated as moral delinquents.

As a curious confirmation of the way in which sex inversion has been bracketed by people with magical or religious phenomena, the colloquial english word for a congenital invert signifies in its origin *heretic*. The french word *bougre* (from the Latin *Bulgarus*, Bulgarian) was first applied to an eleventh-century heretical sect hailing from Bulgaria—and hence the least elegant english expression set aside for the sectaries of Sodom. Among the ancient Hebrews, and so through christianized or judaized Europe, sexual inversion was identified with heresy. With the Hebrews themselves it had the special character of an unpatriotic act. To be convicted of homosexual practices was to be stigmatized as *unpatriotic*. For the Hebrews identified it with foreign, and therefore idolatrous, cults. It was a political rather than a moral misdemeanour. The Cities of the Plain would thus have been thought of, by a patriotic Hebrew of antiquity, as having been overwhelmed on account of their adoption of *foreign* habits, rather than of *bad* habits.

To give some idea of the universality and general character of sex inversion, I will quote a few passages from Dr. Westermarck's chapter, ' Homosexual Love ' :—

In his description of the Koriaks, Krashenninikoff makes mention of the *ke'kcuc*, as he calls them—that is, men transformed into women. Every *koe'kcuc*, he says, is regarded as a magician and interpreter of dreams, but from his confused description Mr. Jockelson thinks it may be inferred that the most important feature of the institution of the *koe'kcuc* lay, not in their shamanistic power, but in their position with regard to the satisfaction of the unnatural inclinations of the Kamchadales. The *koe'kcuc* wore women's clothes, did women's work, and were in the position of women concubines.

It (homosexuality) is widely spread among the Bataks of Sumatra. In Bali it is practised openly, and there are persons who make it a profession. The *basir* of the Dyaks are men who make their living by witchcraft and debauchery. They ' are dressed as women, they are made use of at idolatrous feasts and for sodomitic abominations, and many of them are formally married to other men.'

So the same state of affairs obtains in the **Malay Archipelago**, the inversion being associated with magic, as in the sub-arctic region (in which shamanism occurs).
As to the Pacific Islanders :—

Homosexual love is reported as common among the Marshall Islanders and in Hawaii. From Tahiti we hear of a set of men called by the natives *mahoos*, who ' assume the dress, attitude, and manners of women, and affect all the fantastic oddities and coquetries of the vainest of females. They mostly associate with the women, who court their acquaintance. With the manners of the women, they adopt their peculiar employments. The encouragement of this abomination is almost wholly confined to the chiefs.'
(Turnbull, *Voyage round the World*.)

Of the New Caledonians M. Foley writes :—

La plus grande fraternité n'est pas chez eux la fraternité utérine, mais la fraternité des armes. Il en est ainsi surtout au village de Poeps. Il est vrai que cette fraternité des armes est compliquée de péderastie.

As to the *shaman*, the most characteristic figure in this strange, primitive half-world of sex inversion, with him the transformation is associated with the idea, very common amongst primitive people, of the superior power in ' mystery ' of the average woman compared with the average man.

In the case of the *shamans*, the change of sex may also result from the belief that such transformed *shamans*, like their female colleagues, are particularly powerful.
(Westermarck.)

Therefore it is natural that men should have come to think that one of the first steps towards a career as a magician was to change their sex. In that way they would be able to steal the thunders, perhaps, allotted to the opposite sex, and yet benefit by their own various male advantages. It is the example of a far-sighted calculation or strategy : one of the maddest flights of primitive human cunning attempting to harness supernatural energy by a *feigning*, for the easily deceived powers of the natural world, of femininity. It is in this way associated with all those other subterfuges of primitive life, legal fictions, and naïf deceits, such as the world-wide rites of adoption, which sought to circumvent nature, and escape by artifice from the iron rule of physical laws.

That in these regions of northern Asia sex inversion is a habit of old standing is shown by the following note of Döllinger—though I do not know how far the Chukchee are supposed to have derived their characteristic invert practices from these more central regions of historic conquest: ' The descendants of those hordes who conquered central and northern Asia under Ganghis Khan and Timour. the Usbeck Khans, had plunged so deep in it (pederasty) as to consider it a bad sign and a weakness for one to keep himself free from this universal habit.'

But since the Chukchee are found on both sides of the Behring Sea, and since what is true of the asiatic side is equally true of the american side, it is not necessary to look elsewhere for the stimulus to these habits. The anthropology of the american continent provides an un-interrupted chain of evidence of their universal character. Dr. Westermarck furnishes us with the following information on that head :—

> In America homosexual customs have been observed among a great number of the native tribes. In nearly every part of the continent there seem to have been, since ancient times. men dressing in the clothes and performing the functions of women, and living with other men as their concubines or wives. Moreover, between young men who are comrades in arms there are *liaisons d'amitié* which, according to Lafitan, ' ne laissent aucun soupçon de vice apparent quoiqu'il y puisse avoir beaucoup de vice réel.'

Homosexual practices are, or have been, very prominent among the peoples in the neighbourhood of Behring Sea. In Kadiak it was the custom for parents who had a girl-like son to dress and rear him as a girl, teaching him only domestic duties, keeping him at women's work, and letting him associate only with women and girls. Arriving at the age of ten or fifteen years, he was married to some wealthy man, and was then called a *schnuchik* or *shoopan*. Dr.

Bogoraz gives the following account of a similar practice prevalent among the Chukchee :—

> It happens frequently that, under the supernatural influence of one of the *shamans,* or priests, a Chukchee lad of sixteen years of age will suddenly relinquish his sex, and let his hair grow, and devote himself altogether to female occupations. Furthermore, the disowner of his sex takes a husband into the *yurt* and does all the work which is usually incumbent on the wife, in most unnatural and voluntary subjection. Thus it frequently happens in a *yurt* that the husband is a woman while the wife is a man! These abnormal changes of sex appear to be strongly encouraged by the *shamans,* who interpret such cases as an injunction of their individuality. The change of sex was usually accompanied by future shamanship; indeed, nearly all the *shamans* were former delinquents of their sex.

Dr. Westermarck cites as authorities, in addition to Bogoraz, a great number of accounts of these practices all over the american continent : such as von Spix and von Martius (*Travels in Brazil*), Cuja de Leon (*Peruvian Indians at time of Conquest*), Bancroft (*Native Races of the Pacific States*), Bossu (*Travels through Louisiana*), M'Coy (*History of Baptist Indian Missions*), Heriot (*Travels through the Canadas*), Catkin (*North American Indians*), Dall (*Alaska*), Waitz (*Anthropologie der Naturvolker*), and a host of others.

CHAPTER VI

THE TRANSFORMED SHAMAN

IN pursuance of a plan to approach *via* Siberia the particular variety of demasculinization developing like a prairie fire in what Mr. Thomas Eliot describes as those ' heads of straw ' in the great european centres, we will now turn to the *shaman*. This shy, nervous, romantic voluptuary of the tundras and steppes will be our chief illustration. The luxurious stuffiness in which M. Charlus and his engaging little victim are immersed will thus be blown aside for us by the icy winds that are the accompaniment of more primitive Chukchee inversion. The remarkable accounts given by Bogoraz in his book on the Chukchee will throughout be used. In this peculiar arctic flower of sensuality and religion, whose manifestations come under the heading of what has been called ' arctic hysteria,' the real character of this tendency will also be seen with more salience than is possible in the mess of scientific catchwords, millionaire luxury, roman brutality, literature, and senile ecstasy in which Proust can show it us.

The Chukchees are a powerful sub-arctic tribe inhabiting the peninsula which forms the farthest north-eastern extremity of Asia. But they are also settled, as indicated above, on the farther side of the Behring Sea. By race they are related to the numerous tribes stretching across Siberia and northern America : living as reindeer herdsmen and fishermen. They are apparently related both to the Esquimaux and the Aryan, varying considerably in their racial character : the women usually exhibiting more than the men the Esquimaux characteristics. With bodies varying from an aryan white to swarthy brown, a bright blood-red complexion is that most valued by them : the most beautiful people in their poems always possess it. They lead a very hard life, and are great hero-worshippers, feats of strength being very much prized by them. As an example of how much physical strength counts among these tribes, the case of marriage by seizure practised among the Kamshadal (their neighbours) can be instanced. It is an account given by Miss Czaplicka in her book dealing with the anthropology of all that russian sub-arctic region :—

> Having obtained permission to take his bride, he (the suitor) is still obliged to capture her.   She is dressed up in a great many heavy layers of clothes ; these he has to tear off until she is naked, and he then places his hand on her organ of sex : which is in fact the whole of the marriage ceremony. Once he has done that he can take her home.   But besides being permanently entrenched in half a dozen dresses worn one on top of the other, she is protected by a bodyguard of girl friends, who attack the bridegroom the moment he appears, and are very active in their defence of her. . . . There is a case on record of a man who for ten years had been trying to obtain his wife, and his head and body were much disfigured by his struggles.

When, however, he has touched the sexual organ, he then withdraws hurriedly, and the girl is supposed to call after him in a caressing voice, ' Mi ! Mi ! Mi ! Mi ! '   That night they sleep together (all this taking place in her native village, of course), and next day he takes her home.

Among the Chukchee rapid eating is one of the things to which they attach most importance.   The man who can swallow his food most rapidly is an object of the greatest admiration : ' Look at that *wolf* ! ' they will say, drawing the stranger's attention to one of their champion eaters engaged in breaking a quick-lunch record.

In spite of their hardiness, they are, however, subject to annihilating collapses of vitality of which the phenomenon of ' arctic hysteria ' is a celebrated symptom.   But another symptom is equally striking.   Prolonged slumber, lasting many weeks, is common with them—a suddenly occurring hibernation or estivation.   A man will collapse, feeling unwell, and go to bed and to sleep, and so remain until he either dies or recovers.   So the rigour of the climate, claiming of them unnatural hardihood and powers of resistance, overwhelms them in this way once it passes their guard.   After the subjection of the neighbouring tribes by the Cossacks some fifty years ago, it is said that the whole population suddenly collapsed : they lost all interest and zest in life, neglected their usual occupations, sank into a listless poverty, and became almost a burden and menace to their conquerors.   These facts are interesting as showing the precarious nature of this sublime hardiness and male virtue that we associate with many northern races : how, a spring of activity and the sense of freedom once touched roughly, the whole structure of what we connect with manhood can crash, in the way that the personality of a shell-shocked man disintegrates in a moment.

There is no need for our present purpose to go into the specific functions of the *shaman*. He is the tribal or family priest or magician : and he claims (by the observation of the strictest rules of life, and the help of ecstatic states and hypnotic trances) very wide powers over the crowds of entelechial presences with which nature, by these people, is supposed to be informed. To give a glimpse of their customary activities, I will quote the following passage from Teit, on the *shamans* of the Allocet Indians :—

> *Shamans* would bewitch parties of hunters so that they could neither shoot nor snare game. The *shaman* summoned a ghost to accompany the hunters, or to stand near their snares, and to frighten away the game. If there were no *shaman* in the party, one of the hunters who was powerful in ' mystery,' or who had a strong protection and great power over certain animals, sang a magic lay at night in the hunting-lodge. Soon the people would hear the noise of animals passing, or their cries at the back of the lodge. Then the singer would say, ' Lo ! the souls of deer and of other animals are going past. These are the ones that will be caught in our snares and shot by us to-morrow.' Then the people lighted torches and, going outside, counted the tracks of the different animals, and thus knew what success they would have on the morrow.

To appreciate what I am about to quote from Bogoraz relating to the phenomenon of shamanistic transformation, the above brief account of the people among whom it occurs and of the rôle of their *shamans* will, I think, suffice.

It is in order, as I have said, to relate these phenomena to those nearer at hand, and because it is more convenient always to take a distant case and use it paradigmatically for comparison, that I have chosen the Chukchee *shaman*. No one can get passionate about the untaught behaviour of a poor oriental savage. But actually these accounts of the Chukchee, for their own sake, are so curious, that they would be worth reading even if we had no special motive for doing so.

One peculiarity of the transformed *shaman* that is emphasized over and over again is his BASHFULNESS or SHYNESS. This traditional, though now quickly disappearing, characteristic of feminine psychology is taken over and exaggerated (as everything else thus borrowed is exaggerated) by the Chukchee when he gets the shamanistic call and determines to transform himself radically. A disposition to silence and reserve (the phenomenon, only exaggerated, of the ' shy boy,' or the ' nice boy,' so reserved and modest) is so frequent among shamanized individuals met frequently to-day in Europe, that in reading the passages referring to this trait among the Chukchee *shamans* the reader will have no difficulty in establishing the necessary link to make these pictures of a strange life apposite and illuminating :—

> It is certainly a fact that the expression of a *shaman* is peculiar, a combination of cunning and shyness; and by this it is often possible to pick him out from among many others.
>
> The Chukchee are well aware of the extreme nervousness of their *shamans*, and express it by the word *nini'rkilgin* (' he is bashful '). By this word they mean to convey the idea that the *shaman* is highly sensitive even to the slightest changes of the psychic atmosphere surrounding him during his exercises. . . . He (the *shaman*) is shy of strange people, of a house to which he is unaccustomed. . . .
>
> In his performance the slightest tendency to express scepticism or laugh at him results in his abandoning the performance and retiring.

The shamanistic ' spirits' are likewise described as ' fleeting ' (*nire'nagcm*), meaning that they want to fly at the sound of a voice or on noticing a face to which they are not accustomed. Among the visitors to a shamanistic performance it is important not to have too many strangers, or the spirits will be shy of appearing. Even when they do come under such circumstances, they are all the time anxious to slip away. Bogoraz says that on one occasion, when he prevailed on a *shaman* to practise at his house, his ' spirits ' (of a ventriloquial variety) refused for a long time to put in an appearance. When at last they came, they were heard walking about outside the house and tapping on its walls, apparently undecided whether to go in or not. And even when they came inside they kept in the corners, avoiding contact with those present.

' *Ke'let* belong to the wilderness,' say the *shamans*, ' just as much as any wild animal. . . .' The animal *ke'let* display this shyness to an extreme degree.

The Chukchee even attribute shyness to certain diseases (which they personify or entelechize), especially such as cannot harm man much—for instance, a cold in the head. In one of their tales, on this principle, a cold in the head, desirous of entering a house, lacks courage to do so. It makes several attempts, but each time retreats, vanquished by its shyness.

> It seems to me that Mr. Jockelson has in mind the same high degree of susceptibility when he calls attention to the fact that the young men of the Yukaghir were said in ancient times to be exceedingly bashful, so much so that they would die when a sudden affront was given them, even by their own relatives. The *shamans* possess this nervous sensitiveness in a still higher degree than other people. This finds expression in the proverb that *shamans* are even more ' soft to die ' than ordinary people. (Bogoraz.)

The emotional ' despised and rejected ' part in shamanism is very strong. It is the unfortunate or a person overtaken by some calamity who calls up the supernatural world to his aid, and so becomes a *shaman*. Many Chukchee tales tell how young orphans, despised and ill-treated by all their neighbours, call to the ' spirits ' and with their supernatural assistance turn the tables, becoming powerful *shamans*.

This is the description giving the phases in detail of a shamanistic transformation :—

> A young man who is undergoing it leaves off all pursuits and customs of his sex, and takes up those of a woman. He throws away the rifle and lance, the lasso of the reindeer herdsman, and the harpoon of the seal-hunter, and takes to the needle and the skin-scraper. He learns the use of these quickly, because the ' spirits ' are helping him all the time. Even his pronunciation changes from the male to the female mode. At the same time his body alters, if not in its outward appearance, at least in its faculties and forces. He loses

masculine strength, fleetness of foot in the race, endurance in wrestling, and acquires instead the helplessness of a woman. Even his physical character changes, the transformed person loses his brute courage and fighting spirit, and becomes shy of strangers, even fond of small talk and of nursing small children. Generally speaking, he becomes a woman with the appearance of a man.

Of course, it is difficult to find out how far auto-suggestion is responsible for the change in a person transformed in such a manner. . . .

The most important part of the transformations is, however, the change of sex. The 'soft man' begins to feel like a woman. He seeks to win the good graces of men, and succeeds easily with the aid of 'spirits.' Thus he has all the young men he would wish for striving to obtain his favour. From them he chooses his lover, and after a time takes a husband. The marriage is performed with the usual rites, and I must say that it forms a quite solid union which often lasts till the death of one of the parties. The couple live in much the same way as do other people. The man tends his herd and goes hunting and fishing, while the 'wife' takes care of the house, performing all domestic pursuits and work. They cohabit in a perverse way, *modo Socratis*, in which the transformed wife always plays the passive rôle. In this, again, some of the 'soft men' are said to lose altogether the man's desire and in the end to even acquire the organs of a woman. . . .

The state of a transformed man is so peculiar that it attracts much gossip and jests on the part of the neighbours. Such jests are of course interchanged in whispers, because the people are extremely afraid of the transformed, much more so than of ordinary *shamans*.

The 'soft man,' or transformed *shaman*, is supposed, in addition to his terrestrial mate, to have a spirit as well at his disposal, a supernatural protector, who is at the same time a more ethereal sort of husband. This is called the *ke'le* husband of the transformed one. The slightest insult to his 'wife' is very much resented by this *ke'le* husband, for he knows how very bashful the 'soft man' is.

The 'soft man' is supposed, of course, to excel in all the arts of the *shaman*, ventriloquism being one of the more important accomplishments. Owing to the fact that each 'soft man' is believed to possess a personal supernatural protector, they are very much dreaded. Even non-transformed *shamans* share this dread with the general run of people. Everybody, in short, avoids all contact with them, especially with young ones. For the younger they are, the more 'bashful': the very young ones being self-effacing and un-hardy to a painful degree. They give in to the pretensions of anybody at all, standing 'bashfully' aside, or taking to flight. But it is then that the *ke'le* husband puts in an appearance, and the younger and consequently more 'bash-ful' the 'soft man' who has been 'put upon,' the more angry he is, and the more violently he is apt to retaliate on the offender.

Here is a very vivid description of a 'transformed *shaman*' named Tilu'wgi :—

Tilu'wgi was young, and looked about thirty-five years of age. He was tall and well developed. His large rough hands especially exhibited no trace of womanhood.

I stayed for two days in his tent, and slept in his small inner room, which was hardly large enough to accommodate four sleepers. Thus I had a chance to observe quite closely the details of his physique, which, of course, were all masculine. He refused obstinately, however, to permit himself to be fully inspected. His husband, Ya'tirgin, tempted by the offered price, tried to persuade him, but, after some useless attempts, was at last silenced by one scowling look from his peculiar 'wife.' He felt sorry, however, that I had been baffled in justifying my curiosity, and therefore offered me, to use his own words, his eyes in place of my own.

He described the physique of Tilu'wgi as wholly masculine, and well developed besides. He confessed that he was sorry for it, but he hoped that in time, with the aid of his *ke'let*, Tilu'wgi would be able to change the organs of his sex alto-gether, which would be much more convenient than the present state. Notwithstanding all this, and even the brownish down which covered his upper lip, Tilu'wgi's face, encircled with braids of thick hair arranged after the manner of Chukchee women, looked very different from masculine faces. It was something like a female tragic mask fitted to a body of a giantess of a race different from our own. All the ways of this strange creature were decidedly feminine. He was so 'bashful,' that whenever I asked a question of somewhat indiscreet character, you could see, under the layer of its usual dirt, a blush spread over his face, and he would cover his eyes with his sleeve, like a young beauty of sixteen. I heard him gossip with the female neighbours in a most feminine way, and even saw him hug small children with evident envy for the joys of motherhood ; but this even the *ke'le* husband could not place within the limits of the trans-formation. . . .

I heard . . . from the neighbours a curious story, that one time when Ya'tirgin was angry at something and wanted to chastise his giant wife, the latter suddenly gave him so powerful a kick that it sent him head foremost from their common sleeping-room.   This proves that the femininity of Tilu'wgi was more apparent than real.

A few more ' soft men ' are described by **Bogoraz** : he does not appear to have succeeded in finding many :—

Another *shaman* of transformed sex was W'chuk, whom I met at the Ani Fair.   He was a person of about forty, tall and strong, of rather indecent behaviour, and strongly peppered talk.   He boasted even that he had been able to bear two sons from his own body, through the assistance of his *ke'le* protector.

Koe'ulim, of the village of A'con, was an old man of sixty, a widower, whose wife had borne him several children.   At the same time the people asserted that he had a male lover with whom he had lived for more than twenty years.   Now his male lover was also dead, so he was doubly widowed. He wore female dress, but his face was covered with stubs of grey beard, and his head was too bald to have enough hair to be arranged in braids.   He was quite poor, and even his shamanistic power had gone from him to a considerable degree.   He was said, however, to have a new lover—another old man, who lived in the same house with him.

Two other cases that I met personally were very young men living with their parents.   One was a nimble young fellow and a very able herdsman, but the people accused him of perverting all his young companions, who beset him with their courtship.   The other one was a sickly fellow, who, however, was told to look seriously for a husband. Both were so ' bashful ' that they carefully avoided giving me time or opportunity for any annoying questions.

I heard also of another ' soft man ' who was womanlike in face, talked in a thin, piping voice, and had very long hair.   He changed his sex completely from the very beginning of his shamanistic call.

How the ' call ' actually comes to a *shaman* can be best seen by considering the events that accompany the period of puberty.   This crisis in primitive life is almost invariably accompanied by rites of rebirth and initiation, by means of which the postulant, if a male, is introduced to the male mysteries of his tribe, received among the male tribesmen, and finally, and in some cases for ever, severs his connection

with the women and children.   In certain african tribes
the first action of a boy after the initiation rite is to go to
the women's quarters and abuse and probably beat his
mother.   These ceremonies everywhere, in any case, have
the character of a death and reincarnation.   Up to puberty
the male child has remained with the women and other
children, and shared their more or less inferior state,
excluded from all manly mysteries and honours.   The
becoming ' a man ' involves a more or less violent and
dramatic repudiation of the immature associations.

It is natural that at this juncture, faced with the often
very unnerving and disagreeable tests which accompany
initiation, a certain percentage of boys should shrink
from crossing this bridge to *responsibility* and *manhood*.
The ' spoilt child ' would no doubt much rather stop with
its mother.   Also the initiatory ceremonies are, or used
to be, in many parts of the world, surrounded by a great
deal of mystery, and made very terrifying, for the benefit
of the women and children.   Often it was even given out
by the officials that the initiate was actually killed in the
initiatory hut or in the woods, and revived with a new
soul, different from his old one.   The point and beauty of
these outlandish ardours would escape a certain type of
male child.   The ' girlish ' boy is an evident case of the
type who would remain among the women if that could
be arranged.   And something of this sort seems to have
happened among most of these sub-arctic tribes and in
other parts of the world.

Teit's account of the Lilloets, a north american tribe
closely akin to the Chukchee, contains a good description
of these events :—

> Among the Lilloets, on the attainment of puberty (indicated
> to him by dreams, among the Shuswap, of women, arrows,
> and canoes) a boy would tie his hair in a knot behind his
> head.   For the first four days he painted his face red, after
> that yellow.   His neck, chest, arms, and legs he also painted
> yellow.   Repairing to the mountains, he built himself a
> sweat-house, where he sweated, fasted, and prayed. . . .
> On each of the four nights he had to build a large fire on a
> mountain-top, and by its light he shot at small figures of
> deer made of bark or grass, praying that he might become
> an expert archer.   If he made many hits, he would become
> a successful hunter.   (Teit.)

A strange parallel to this is met among the Masai, the great warlike semitic tribe of North-West Africa. The Masai boys, after the ceremony of circumcision, dress like the women, paint their faces, and shoot at diminutive birds with little bows and arrows (cf. Merker, *Der Masai*).

It is easy to see how this part of the ceremony might be made to go wrong under certain conditions, and how the boy might *remain* with his face painted, and in women's clothes, and rejoin the women. This in any case is what happens with the Chukchee and other siberian and american tribes ; only, the initiation *manquée* is accompanied usually by the adoption of the priestly calling.

As to the *bashfulness*—especially that traditional girlish shrinking where any allusion to sex is concerned—we have many primitive extra-shamanistic parallels for that. Indeed, sexual modesty and extreme sensitiveness to any reference to such matters seems to characterize primitive people rather than not. In this way a man or woman with nothing but the scantiest strip of material covering their organs of sex, and otherwise quite naked, will display the most exaggerated punctilio about reference to this point, to which you would suppose them past care, as its concealment was so little attended to.

On the score of their sexual hyper-sensitiveness we are told, for example, that ' in the district of Lair in New Ireland, men and women, boys and girls, sometimes commit suicide when an indecent word is shouted to them as an insult.'

In the south-eastern parts of British New Guinea visited by Dr. Seligmann, in spite of the great freedom granted to the unmarried of both sexes, the people ' were absolutely modest in their behaviour, and nowhere was an indecent gesture seen.' In some other parts of the same island the notions of decency require that a married man shall never be seen publicly in the company of his wife, nor take the slightest notice of her in the presence of others. In various islands belonging to the Malay Archipelago sexual inter-course takes place in the forest, not in the house. Tessman says that if you discuss anything sexual with a West African Pangwe negro, you will hear him repeatedly utter the word *oson*, which means ' shame.' Of the negroes of Accra, Mourad wrote that they, in spite of their licentious and obscene dances, otherwise observe in their relations to the fair sex a decency which is often lacking among civilized Europeans. . . . Among various peoples it is considered indecent, it is even prohibited, to have sexual intercourse in the daytime. (E. Westermarck, *The Origin of Sexual Modesty*.)

These extracts tend to show that the *sex*-shyness at least of the transformed *shaman* is not necessarily due altogether to their equivocal position. But the general account of their *bashfulness* tallies so well with the manners observed in their contemporary european sex-correlates, that it is natural to conclude that a general shyness and bashfulness of manner, and shrinking and childlike air, is inseparable from the shamanized personality of the male, whether occurring in Asia or Europe.

There is much evidence of various types of abnormal and usually mystical sex-eccentricity among the sub-arctic people. Czaplicka quotes the following instance :—

Krashenninikoff mentions another ' marriage relation ' which can be called abnormal or mystical. The Maritime Koryak have at times ordinary stones instead of wives. A man will put clothes on such a stone, put it in his bed, and sometimes caress it as if it were living. Two such stones were given to Krashenninikoff by a man called Pkerach from Ukinsh. One of them he called his wife and the other his son.

The epileptic naïf and mystical element in nearly all nineteenth-century russian literature has no doubt some relation to this extreme inconstancy and collapsibility of the siberian peoples ; though how it is that it comes to pervade the whole slav world it is difficult to say. The actual appearance of a transformed *shaman* is not that of the ' mongolian ' imbecile of our clinics, but is a mask of fixed wild pathos, rather less mongolian than the normal mask. Bogoraz describes it exactly when he says it is a female mask of tragedy.

The calling of the priest in every nationality offers a convenient refuge from the stress of life to the defeated or quietist vitality. And in some cases the priesthood is in this way a social expedient of great use, extracting from life the practically unfit, and so offering a suitable occupation to people who would otherwise be a drag on the active community.   At present the prevalent shamanistic fashion serves a similar purpose. It withdraws from life and to some extent segregates into a community of elegant drones, with a high *esprit de corps*, a number of people not necessarily sexual inverts, but possessed of a *defeatist* vitality and unadapted for the rigours of less specialized life.   The idleness, the life of insipid amenities and gossip, that goes with it (the monastic life, as it were, and that of a highly fashionable girls' school both imitated) would be found intolerable by the more active.

It throws thousands of fresh old maids—or people who will in due course become old maids—on the community every year.   It has many things that do not recommend it.   But it is impossible not to agree that, placed as Europe is at present, it is a useful institution.

CHAPTER VII

THE ROMAN *EXOLETOS*

ALTHOUGH more distant from us in time, a glance at the nature of sexual inversion in the greek and roman worlds—the latter especially too near us in many ways—will advance our understanding of its natural place and uses in society. I will take the roman first, and quote from Professor Döllinger's excellent book, *Gentile and Jew in the Courts of the Temple of Christ.* Writing in 1860 or thereabouts, for Döllinger ' paiderastia ' was an abominable vice, and his attitude one of purely orthodox reprobation. That does not make his account any the less useful in its enlarging of certain lively details, and it gives it a distinct advantage for my purposes. He claims for it a ' share in the cumulative destruction of (roman) society,' for instance. With all his knowledge and insight into the history of those periods, it is permissible to doubt if Döllinger realized all the implications of this inversion of normal life.

In the earlier centuries of the Republic Döllinger says that cases of paiderastia were infrequent. From the fifth century onwards, however, in spite of the heavy penalty imposed for prostituting a freeman, instances of male prostitution became more frequent. By the end of the sixteenth century Polybius describes this habit as grown general, and mentions a talent as what a roman was prepared to pay to satisfy this taste. The abuse of man slaves was a recognized licence ; and Caius Gracchus boasted publicly of his roman self-restraint in never having coveted the slave of a neighbour in that way. The Scantinian Law (imposing a pecuniary mulct for this offence) fell into disuse. At least it was dormant throughout the Empire, only Domitian enforcing it. There was no roman emperor—this including the ' best of them,' such as Antonius and Trajan—who did not indulge this taste. Cæsar's infatuation for the Bithynian king, Nicomedes (Suetonius, *Cæs.*, 49), whom he had captured, was the subject of satirical songs among his soldiery during his gallic triumph.

306

During the last days of the Republic the handsome sons of senatorial fathers in difficulties served to soften the hearts of such roman judges as were not accessible to other bribes. All the poets of the augustan age except Ovid have left the record of their homosexual predilections : and Ovid's reasons for ' contenting himself with women, are,' says Döllinger, ' worthy of the man and the age.'

With the Romans homosexuality took a grosser form, as was to be expected, than among the Greeks. The latter poetized it very much more, making it an institution more reminiscent of chivalry than anything. All the unfortunate heats and appetites inseparable from the human state were, as later with chivalrous european love, disguised (in the way that a ham is dressed ·in paper frills and powdered with toasted crumbs) on an elaborate system of make-believe adapted to the physiological facts of the case. But with the Romans these accessories and more indirect features were dispensed with. With that teutonic grossness and taste for raw meat that produced the mortuary games and the gladiatorial contests, they went to this innovation baited by a bald and staring flesh rather than melting insinuation of delectable limbs in the softened light of the more measured greek imagination.

Again, in place of the romantic male friendships intruding everywhere in the platonic dialogues of Socrates, the Romans were more businesslike. The wealthy Roman would have a harem of male slaves, which he called facetiously a ' paidagogia.' The boys chosen for this harem were called *exoleti*. The first step was to castrate them, as this ' exposed them to abuse the longer ' (' Exoletos suos, ut ad longiorem patientiam impudicitiae idonei sint, amputant,' Seneca, *Controv.*, exc., x. 4). Some considerable trouble was also taken with their education ; a certain literary polish was insisted on, to render them more complicated objects of desire, on the same principle that young ladies are taught to sing and paint, the mind thereby playing its part in the long civilized preparation for mating. If a closer contemporary parallel were desired, no doubt it could be found in that peculiar cultural furnishing, rather dainty, sickly, and smart, that an expensive modern university provides, along with aristocratic manners ; and an inquiry as to how subsequently it was spent would usually elicit the fact that it served the same purpose as the matrimonial accomplishments of the middle-class girl—only, not so much in aiding simple Nature as in frustrating her.

With the roman *exoleti* ' all artifices were resorted to to delay the development of the child into the youth, and the youth into the man.' ' Decked out like a woman,' as Seneca says of one of these, ' he wrestles and fights with his years. He must not pass beyond his age of boyhood. He is kept back perforce, and, though robust as a soldier, he retains his smooth chin ; his hair is all shaved off, and removed by the roots ' (*Epist.*, 47). These epicenes were sometimes classed together by nations and colour, so that all were equally smooth and their hair all of one tint. That they might keep a fresh complexion longer, they were obliged, when on a journey with their master, to cover their face with a mask. It was thus that Clodius on his travels took his *exoleti* about with him as well as his women of pleasure. Tiberius, at Caprea, and even Trajan, kept such boys in droves, and in those days formal marriages between man and man were introduced, with all the solemnities of ordinary nuptials (Juvenal, ii. 117 sqq. ; Martial, xii. 42). On one of these occasions Nero made the Romans exhibit the tokens of a public rejoicing and treat his elect, Sporus, with all the honours of an empress (Döllinger, *Gentile and Jew in the Courts of the Temple of Christ*).

There again, in Seneca's account of the roman *exoletos*, who ' wrestles and fights with his years ' because ' he must not pass beyond the age of boyhood,' we see the reflection of our own time. The crowds of mild and veiled *exoleti* produce the impression of people ' playing children '— a childhood that is indefinitely prolonged, for none ' must pass beyond the age of boyhood.' The aged mind (with its devitalization, anxieties, and yearning for youth and its abundant freshness) is thus reproduced in the processes of this super-sexual obsession. It is thus that male sex-inversion contributes its share to the cult of *the child*.

What becomes of the epicene of the feminine kind ? Is a horde of new old maids produced in this way ? We know, however, that if he has some personality and intelligence he survives, battered but still mincing ; and again there are some big rough men, known to most of us, tweed- or corduroy-suited, pipe-smoking *and* inverted, not unlike the vigorous transformed *shamans* described by Bogoraz. But they are the exceptions; most are small, mild, correct, discreetly solicitous, and both the chukchee ' bashfulness ' and the cultural accessories of the roman *exoleti* can be recognized in their invariable mannerisms. There was a greek proverb to the effect that *it was easier to hide five elephants under one's arm than one pathic.* The elaborate display of ' bashfulness ' and ' correctness ' is perhaps the surest advertisement of the presence of a pathic.

CHAPTER VIII

PAIDERASTIA IN THE GREEK WORLD

DÖLLINGER complains that in Greece ' the strictest moralists,' even, were very indulgent where inversion was concerned ; ' nay, worse than merely indulgent,' he exclaims : ' for they actually treated it with ridicule.' Ridicule is not a thing on which fashions in vice, any more than other fashions, ultimately thrive. So perhaps Döllinger was here a little beside the mark in his censure of the greek attitude. The sternest moralists could not devise a better system for dealing with inversion than treating it on equal terms with other forms of sex emotion. Its prestige relies entirely on the assumption that it is a non-sexual, or super-sexual, cult, which of course it is not. At its most natural (in the case of the congenital invert) it is always a passion, colouring everything about the life of the individual marked down as its prey; but, this intensity apart, it has a right to rank without comment alongside other forms of sex liveliness. When acquired or affected as a social asset it is a snobbery rather than a vice, and often involves other sorts of snobbery as well. The spanish ambassador (who took the place of a defective one) in the *Memoirs* of Saint-Simon, and who exclaimed ecstatically, peeping sideways, as Monsieur rose to receive him, ' Oh ! quel joli cul ! ', could provide one of the links between this snobbery and that of the social snob.

Paiderastia, love of boys, was organized politically in Greece, whereas in the countries of the Ancient East, though naturally flourishing, it had not this utilitarian character. It was left to the Greek to discover the educational possibilities of pederasty. In the doric states. Crete and Sparta, it was of course equally recognized as part of the educational machinery. Xenophon claimed an equal purity for the spartan love of the adult man for the boy as for the love of the parent for the child. However, a great deal of etiquette existed in connection with these habits. Not only was the utilitarian side of the question not neglected, but chivalry was foreshadowed by the Greeks in their ideal manipulation of this ruling passion. A glimpse of a beautiful boy half-naked causes the really sensitive person to swoon : when the youthful Megabetis offers to kiss Agesilaus, and he, calling up the self-mastery of which only a Spartan would be capable, refuses, Maximus of Tyre considers that he is a hero of the same order as Leonidas, and that his refraining from this simple operation was a feat comparable to Thermopylæ.

' In the whole literature of the pre-christian period there is hardly a writer to be met with who has expressed himself in decidedly hostile terms of homosexuality,' says Döllinger. Both eminent men of all sorts and the gods were employed to advertise it and so subjugate the social snob and the superstitious. The legislation of Solon, preventing slaves from indulging this form of love, was designed to reserve it for free persons only, and so still further excite the snobbery of the time in surrounding it with the glamour of privilege. The philosopher, who was of course an important person, further advertised it : ' The marriage bond was made for all other men, but the philosopher might be indulged in his passion for boys.' In this way the support of intellectual snobbery was secured.

The athenian legislation against habits of sex inversion amongst slaves was very analogous to the Prohibition laws in the United States—suppression directed only at one class of society. Beautiful male slaves, however, were forced into public brothels appropriated to male traffic only. In this way it was said that Phædo, the founder of the Socratic-elean school, started life. Agathocles, the tyrant of Syracuse, made his *début* in a similar establishment. Male prostitution was, however, taxed, and so became a source of revenue.

As to the chivalrous observances and claims to purity of the man-obsession in Greece, it is easy to believe that it may have been, on the whole, slightly more ' platonic ' than woman-man relationship would be. But ' the two wild horses ' must have ' met together ' fairly often in an aristocratic society devoted to good living and a studied idleness. Schools, gymnasia, and palastræ were supposed not to be entered by adults, but this law fell into disuse, and many of the hours the athenian citizen had daily on his hands were spent there. In many gymnasia and palastræ altars to Eros were erected. This was 'the ordinary resort of the paiderasts,' says Döllinger. There ' his wings grew so large,' according to Plutarch, ' that there was no containing him.'

However, it was the status of women that determined the flourishing of this other form of sex. The displacement of the relative positions of the sexes, ' the degradation of the woman, and the exclusion of the uninitiated part of them from men's society,' was the cause, as well as the sign, of the rival attachment. The social contempt for women played a capital part, and social snobbery transferred the attentions of the indifferent average in the direction of the more philosophic and peculiar principle of love. For a free citizen or a man of education, love for a woman was regarded as a dishonourable and vulgar passion. Women suffered in every way from its prevalence. And it is at this point that it is easy to see how very greatly greek homosexual chivalry and idealism must have differed from the same movement in our time. For the position of women and the status of the slave at the time of the prevalence of such a fashion must both affect its form very much.

Plato says that ' it is not naturally, but only by the compulsion of the law, that a man whose inclinations have been to the love of boys enters into the bonds of matrimony.' The free Hellene appears to have regarded matrimony as a great burden. But to remain celibate was regarded as disgraceful, for one of the only forms of work that was expected of a free Hellene was once or twice in a lifetime the reproducing of his kind. But this patriotism made obligatory. With the dissolution of the greek republics and the consequent removal of the laws of compulsion, the marriage duty appears to have been universally neglected, and depopulation ensued.

With this attitude towards women the form pederasty would take would be different to that found in the midst of a society more and more dominated by women, as is the case to-day. When the Hellene, experiencing a contempt and distaste for creatures that he considered as of an inferior kind or class, withdrew as far as possible from their society, he would not be so likely to admire specifically feminine qualities in the new male object of his interest. The specifically *feminine*—though certainly it is impossible to imagine pederasty without to some extent a conversion of the male into a female—would be less prized, and theoretically (since it was that from which men were attempting to escape) some masculine version of the sexual charm would be *de rigueur*.

PART X

SOCIALIST THEORY

' *Nous sommes en outre . . . des révoltés de toutes les heures, hommes vraiment sans dieu, sans maître et sans patrie, les ennemis irréconciliables de tout despotisme, moral ou collectif, c'est-à-dire des lois et des dictatures (y compris celle du prolétariat) et les amants passionnés de la culture de soi-même.*'

Fernand Pelloutier.

' *The nation did not need to be protected against its own will. There was no fear of its tyrannizing over itself. . . . In time, however . . . it was . . . perceived that such phrases as " self-government " and " the power of the people over themselves " do not express the true state of the case. The " people " who exercise the power are not always the same people with those over whom it is exercised ; and the " self-government " spoken of is not the government of each by himself, but of each by all the rest.*'

On Liberty. J. S. Mill.

' *The border between the Few and the Many, and again between the varieties of the Many, is necessarily indeterminate ; but Democracy not the less remains a mere form of government ; and . . . is most accurately described as inverted Monarchy.*'

Popular Government. H. S. Maine.

' *Let them study those arts whereby the opinions of a minority may be made to seem those of a majority.*'

Material for Erewhon Revisited. Samuel Butler.

' *The centrality of the presiding person's situation will have its use at all events ; for the purpose of direction and order at least, if for no other. The concealment of his person will be of use. . . .*'

Panopticon. Jeremy Bentham.

CHAPTER I

WHAT GENERAL TERM ARE WE TO USE IN DISCUSSING SOCIALIST THEORY?

THE contradictions I have already indicated in the heart of the doctrine of Proudhon will seem so gross to you, perhaps, if you are not familiar with the details of socialist teaching, that you may lose patience. Socialism makes no claim to ' truth ' or exactitude ; and no more than in the dogma of a religion should any consistency be expected in its teaching.   It teems with every description of heresy, and has not even the steadying symbolism of a god, to keep it a little to one track.   Further, its prophets by no means yield in rancour and fury to the followers of a great religion.   If they do not fall to among themselves, tooth and claw, and thoroughly discredit their doctrine in everybody's eyes, it is not their fault.   It is the fault of other people's eyes, its enemies could say : or we should say, owing to an act of especial grace.   Primitive christianity, with the same difficulties to contend with, was nevertheless highly successful, as it was very similar in its appeal.

It will be better, perhaps, to go the whole way in the statement of these violent discrepancies :   showing as briefly as possible, at once and without concealment, *the worst.*   No one should attempt to defend socialism on the score of consistency or clearness.   It is a living thing, a natural science, and not a philosophy.   Regarded as anything else it makes nonsense.   It is mixed up with a thousand warring racial needs and prejudices, and every sort of person for a century and a half has pulled its theory this way and that to suit his fancy.   As a theory it is a rag-doll at the best, or, if you like, a gutta-percha baby. You cannot extract from the reading of the great revolutionary theorists any unanimity or agreement.   They only have one thing in common, the religious fervour animating most of them.   Their hearts agree, but all their minds agree to differ.   And they have gradually come, in consequence, to regard their minds, and still more other people's, with dislike.

But what first are we to call the subject of our discussion ? Is socialist the best generic term : or should we choose some other ? Proudhon disliked above all men what he called ' socialists.' To begin with he called himself an ' anarchist ' to distinguish himself from the hated socialist. But eventually he became what he called a ' federalist.' His own original label, ' anarchist,' nevertheless, he would hurl abusively at the head of the capitalist exploiter. He had no more devastating word in his armoury, none so weighted with disgust, indignation, and hatred, as *anarchist* (when applied to a trust magnate). Yet he took this word confidingly to his heart when he was looking for a name for his own creed.

Collectivist, again, is a term of violent abuse—if used by a *syndicalist*. And yet all—anarchists, state-socialists, syndicalists, reformists, collectivists—are most conveniently grouped, and they consent to that grouping, under the term socialist. This initial difficulty overcome, and admitting that we are on very shifting ground indeed, we can proceed to ask what socialism is.

Socialism (embracing a great variety of sects) is simply the religion that has superseded christianity, built largely on it. It is the religion of modern christian Europe, specially prepared from evangelical doctrines. The great revolutionary is simply its priest or fakir. Gustave Le Bon says of the revolutionary personality in general : ' Many revolutionaries are only, in reality, true believers who have changed the name of their god. Socialists. freemasons, communists, worshippers of fetishes or of formulas destined to regenerate mankind, owe the intensity of their fanaticism to the exaggerated development of this mystical state of mind, always found in the apostle of a new faith.' (*Le déséquilibre du monde.*)

In the introduction to one of the volumes of Péguy's *Complete Works*, André Suarès describes Péguy as follows:—

Péguy is to start with political and moralistic. True politics, for him, is the morals of the nation. But this predicant brother, this little capucin . . . had no need of a pulpit in a cathedral. . . . He is a man of conscience, before everything. . . . He has a great deal of Proudhon about him. . . . He has powerful dislikes, which comes from powerful principles. No one has ever been so little of a *doubter*, even in doubting himself. . . . He was born to be the conscience of the Republic.

Péguy is as good an illustration as could be desired of what I have said. His magnificent declamation (an example of which I have used as an epigraph to Part xiii.) is in the accent of edification. He is as hortative and apocalyptic as any preacher who has ever drawn weeping crowds in a time of disillusion and misery. Proudhon, Bakunin, Pelloutier, Sorel are, in one degree or another, just the same. It is also their *moral* teaching on which they insist ; it is their *moral* force that makes them interesting. Their function is declamatory, hortative, and prophetic. And what great prophets some of them have been, and what magnificent lightnings of truth, as well, have been struck accidentally from them, is hardly realized yet by people who go to them for things not to be found in the nature of things in such activities.

They are all, without exception, and very strictly (whatever may be said about them), *utopian* and *other-worldly*. When Marx accuses Proudhon of being ' utopian,' he is of course *utopian* himself, though not so much. They would arrange a life for man—without exception—on a plan as indifferent to the average plain man's conception of happiness or a ' good time ' as it is possible to imagine. No religious teacher promising paradise could be harsher in his disciplinary proposals than Sorel. They are indifferent to the ' happiness ' of others not because they are heartless, but because they are fanatical, and because they believe that their proposals are *ad majorem dei gloriam*. They would willingly throw people to the alligators for saying the world is flat, if socialism at the moment requires it to be round. They are always mentally intoxicated ; and an ' eternity of intoxication,' in Plato's phrase, of the same sort as their own, is what they promise to the faithful.

But, as the writer I quoted above said of Péguy, they are also *politicians*. In them politics are once more married to theology or to the theologic mind—on the eastern as opposed to the western pattern. Likewise they are usually violent and militant, not to say military. In this they are also carrying out the religious analogy ; since the first thing a new religion does is to proceed to cut every non-orthodox throat within sight—' or what's a Heaven for ? '

CHAPTER II

THE CITY-STATE OF ANTIQUITY: WAR-LIKE IDEALS OF FRENCH SOCIALISM

M AN *is a fighting animal*, Hobbes unwisely remarked ; and Proudhon is pleased to have him to quote from. Proudhon, quite as much as the author of *Les réflexions sur la violence*, was an advocate of violence, though, curiously enough, not of revolutionary violence : and as he had not Nietzsche's writings to inflame him, as Sorel had, he was perhaps even more naturally bellicose. It is true that he insisted always that he was 'not a man of action,' and he was not a catastrophist where the social revolution was concerned. But that has nothing to do with the question of the *bloodshed*. (He had quite different motives for that strange forbearance.) It was an epic and antique nationalist violence that he favoured.

Like Machiavelli, both Sorel and Proudhon were always looking *back* to antiquity. It is thus that the latter can say :—

> The man of the antique city thought quite differently. War, with its blood-stained weapons and heaps of corpses, seems to us, from every point of view, an atrocity. Is that a proof of our *progress* ? (*La guerre et la paix*, Book III. chap. i.)

'But do your clients, the People, wish to be warriors, Monsieur Proudhon?' you could, in quite good taste, inquire. Do most people wish to be 'heroes' to please M. Sorel, or to show M. Proudhon how much antique *virtù* they possess ? *Would they not be just as well off with the capitalists as with the authors of 'Réflexions sur la violence' or of 'La guerre et la paix' ?* It is impossible for a fairly reflective reader of socialist literature not to ask himself such painful questions. The position taken in this essay I will briefly recapitulate.

Just as you probably cannot be a good artist and a good moralist at the same time, so righteousness or mysticism and the speculative reason do not mix well. Proudhon was an excellent moralist, but not a very good philosopher. It is strange, but in practice the ' detached ' intelligence is more ' moral,' in the sense that it is more humane, than is morality or righteousness.

The moralist does not necessarily love men at all. Indeed, feeling as he does about things, it must be rather difficult for him to do anything but hate them. We observe the hebrew prophets full of dislike for other human beings. How could they have been so conscious of their extreme ' wickedness' and not have detested them ? A ' good lover,' we say, is a ' good hater ' : love and hate are near together. But ' love ' is a term, probably, that should only be applied to the experiences of quiet or gentle creatures. With the religious teacher of the active and fanatical type to which we are most accustomed, there is usually not much except the good (but the *very good*) ' hater ' left. Homicide, or suicide, or a suicide pact is a characteristic solution above a certain temperature. The early christian insisted on *the destruction of the world*. Nothing short of that would satisfy him. He wanted *to wipe out entirely* everything that existed, in order to instal his Kingdom of Heaven. Absolute denial of life is the logical solution of the thought of the religious fanatic : and whenever you follow him for long, you will find him leading you to destruction, so far as this life is concerned. Péguy, Proudhon, Sorel, Bakunin, Herzen, etc., all desired the End of the World as thoroughly as any primitive christian awaiting with pious satisfaction that much-canvassed event. Since they were the professionals of other people's misfortunes and had systematically exposed their consciousness to the sense of universal injustice, it could not be otherwise. *Hatred of the oppressor is a more chronic and lasting sentiment than love of the oppressed.*

The miniature End of the World advertised by all the great revolutionaries of the last century is there plainly enough for us who are not religious fanatics. The destructive and religious visionary says that he is delighted at the spectacle of the Apocalypse because ' destruction is creation,' and is the only way to come at paradise. But it is difficult to believe him : his paradise has an evangelical impossibility about it. And its adept usually has such a thin imagination that he would, you feel, be compelled to resort to the destruction of human life as we know it, in sheer impotence.   But even apart from that, to reach his rigid doctrinaire ideal he must, logically, first kill all the human beings in the world.   The *real,* unreligious paradise of chinese art was reached by more perfect organisms.

An extreme view of this situation would be the statement that we are situated between two sets of men, one which wishes to destroy us for our own good, and another which wishes to destroy us for their own gain and the fun of doing it.   Would not a Seventh Day Adventist, if he were suddenly provided with the means of blowing up the earth, probably do so, and regard it as a virtuous action ? —a chastisement administered to the human race for their want of faith in the End of the World !

In his *Ruine du monde antique,* Sorel quotes a letter by Proudhon which it may be instructive to quote.   I will give the few lines with which Sorel introduces it :—

From now on everything is given over to disorder ; nothing is *of necessity* any more, no foresight is possible.   I think that it is not unprofitable to put before my readers an important passage from a letter which Proudhon wrote on the 29th of October 1860 to a doctor and fellow-countryman :—

' Under Louis-Philippe the disintegration of society had already begun, and philosophic intelligences could not doubt that an immense revolution had started. . . . To-day civilization is undoubtedly at a crisis for which one finds one analogy only in history.   That is the crisis that marked the advent of christianity.   All traditions are worn out, all beliefs abolished.   In return, the new programme is not *made*: I mean that it has not entered into the consciousness of the masses.   Hence what I call the *disintegration.*   This is the most frightful moment in the existence of societies.   Everything contributes to the despair of men of goodwill : prostitution of conscience, triumph of mediocrity, confusion of the true and the false, oppression of truth, reward of the liar, the courtier, the charlatan, and the vicious. . . . I have few illusions, and I do not expect, to-morrow, to see the rebirth in our land, as by a stroke of a magic wand, of liberty, respect of right, public honesty, freedom of opinion, good faith in the press, morality in the government, reason with the *bourgeois,* and common-sense with the people.   No, no ;

decadence is our lot, and that for a period to which I can assign no term, and which will not be less than one or two generations. I shall see nothing but evil, I shall die in deepest darkness, branded by my antecedents with the seal of reprobation in a rotten society.'

The situation is still graver than in 1860 because we are issuing from a war which is mother of endless ruin. Imagining that Napoleon iii could indeed once more hurl France into adventures, Proudhon said on the 27th of October at Chaudry :—

My profound conviction is that we are entering more and more on an era of dissolution and of trouble. . . . Butcheries will come, and the prostration which will follow these baths of blood will be terrible. We shall not see the work of the new age ; we shall fight in the night : we must contrive to support this life without too much sadness by doing our duty. Let us help one another ; let us call to one another in the shadows ; and every time that the occasion presents itself, let us do justice.

The words of Péguy that I use later as an epigraph are a lamentation of the same description. ' *Tout le monde est malheureux dans le monde moderne*,' the climax of his despairing rhetoric, has the true hebraic note of boundless pessimism. And all these ardent, intoxicated, eloquent men desire the destruction of the world, in a sort of restless, but virtuous, impotence.

CHAPTER III

THE WHOLE WORLD NOW FILLED WITH THE GLOOM OF THE PURITAN SOUL

THAT the religious temperament tends always to hatred, intolerance, and egotism has often been observed. The man consumed with the fire of *righteousness* must be a humbug, and is a violent and dangerous one usually. The Englishman of the New Model, the puritan of the New World, must have been first-rate haters rather than anything else—they left it to Jesus in the jewish backgrounds, quite properly, to do all the *loving*, showing the infallibility of their own personal corner in salvation by means of ' infallible artillery ' and ' pike and gun.' They were very gloomy souls indeed ; they filled, they have filled, the whole world with the gloom of their souls. But the more you examine the works of Sorel, Proudhon, Pelloutier, the more you will feel the injustice of Taine's remark that France was very lucky to have the pontine moat between herself and the Old Testament, puritan Englishman. Ferocious as the Old Testament is, it is not more so than the Saint-Barthélemy or the French Revolution. Bakunin in his pre-revolutionary days expresses disgust with the French on the score of their insane turbulence and taste for carnage ; the history of Russia would provide the material for a complete *tu quoque* ; and that is the situation of every country.

While all the dogmatic religions (says Fouillée) commit the two capital sins, *par excellence*, of pride and hatred, the philosopher knows that he knows nothing, or very little ; he enjoys being contradicted, for contradiction reveals to him an aspect of the truth different to his own idea of it. His adversaries seem, at bottom, his best friends. He has no desire to massacre and to burn. (*Humanitaires et libertaires.*)

However utopian this picture of Fouillée's ' philosopher ' may be, I would rather meet a philosopher with whom I disagreed, in a lonely spot on a dark night, than a very religious man to whose dogma I could not subscribe.

324

Religion was defined by Schopenhauer as philosophy for the crowd : people who had not the time, training, or intelligence to have a philosophy, he thought, had a religion provided for them.   Socialism, in so far as it is not a pervasive, fanatical dogma, could be described as a little honour, a little unselfishness, a hint of the humane and just, a pinch of compassion, provided for people who would otherwise be without these things, both proletarians and capitalists.

CHAPTER IV

THE IDEA THAT HAUNTS ALL
SOCIALIST THEORY

THE socialist impulse is omniform; there are as
many systems of collectivism, reformism, syndicalism, communism, anarchism, etc., as there are days
in the year. They have, however, one thing in common.
Each and all they are haunted by the belief that neighbouring socialist systems conceal *a despot.* Everywhere
a tyranny is scented. Every socialist theorist spends a
good part of his time prowling round his neighbour's
Utopia in the hope of surprising the terrible tyrant that he
is certain is in hiding there, sumptuously entertained by
his treacherous rival. The adept of any of the famous
systems, in speaking of any one of his neighbours, will
invariably whisper in your ear, ' Have nothing to do with
him : he is a wolf in sheep's clothing. As a matter of
fact, he is in reality *a born tyrant and despot,* disguised as
a socialist. He's out for what he can get. He would
set up the most monstrous tyranny if he could. You
take my tip and have nothing to do with him.' And his
neighbour, if you found yourself with him, would say the
same thing.

These people usually do each other a grave injustice :
for most of the famous socialist theorists have been excellent men. But it must be admitted that often the
theories are less perfect than their makers : some of them
do seem peculiarly adapted for the reception of the most
absolute tyrant.

The fall of the ancient (european) world was decided by
the question of social injustice, said Lange, which would
also be the cause of our modern european disintegration.
But when he described the core of the problem as ' the
struggle against the struggle for existence,' he was nearer
the mark than perhaps he knew. To *struggle* eternally
against a struggle is a circular operation. The theories of
that struggle (the more organized, on both sides, they
become) are bound to begin fatally to resemble each other.

326

All warriors equipped by the same civilization and engaged eternally in a civil war, or revolution, would have a family likeness at last.   The *struggle against a struggle* has the uncomforting sound of *a war to end war.*

To *lessen the effort and struggle for existence* was, thought Lange, who was a great socialist, the aim of socialism. Sorel, who was a great socialist, ' the greatest socialist since Marx,' thought it was *the struggle alone* that made existence worth while.   The business of socialism was to make the struggle far more severe.   It must screw it up to epic proportions.   That was a radical difference in point of view, we must admit.   It can be taken as the characteristic fissure to be discovered across all socialist theory.   Is the aim of the revolution that people should become a dense mass of *messieurs*, a dense mass of ' gentlemen,' living in godlike ease and plenty—nature, with its horrible struggle-for-existence, left far behind ?   If not that, what is its objective ?   Is it not rather that of a titanic but magnificent discomfort, all pleasure repudiated ?

One seems to be the optative dream of a small mammal, liable to be rudely awakened by an earthquake or the appulsion of a star, or any of those monsters in the way of forces-of-nature, over which he has been unable to extend his sway.   The other gets body, at least, and physical importance, by merging him in the mass of his kind.   He becomes generic, a ' class ' (even if only a downtrodden one) ;   and his dreams (entirely owing to the factor of *scale*) have a prouder air.   They puff themselves out—or are invited to by Sorel—at the thought of their irresistible size and physical importance.   Sorel is indeed a sort of splenetic Ariel flying above an ocean and exhorting it to do something *spectacular* and *napoleonic*, as an ocean should.   It is never the debatable Everything of pyrrhonic idealism that he addresses, but a local, put-upon, poor, relative vastness.

CHAPTER V

THE ' NAPOLEONISM ' OF FOURIER, SAINT-SIMON, SOREL, ETC.

LET us take Berth and illustrate by him what I mean. He makes the following assertions, for instance, of the socialist systems that followed, in France, the revolution and Empire :—

'Your saint-simonist socialism, *soi-disant*, democratic, and egalitarian, would be exploitation carried to its farthest limit, since the State would be master of everything, and the State would be *you.*' Berth (talking for a third party, the dim syndicalist mass of his possible readers) thus addresses his fellow-socialist, of the saint-simonist variety. The saint - simonist system, he says elsewhere, is ' from top to bottom *autoritaire* and hierarchical.' It was the fillip given to the idea of authority by the napoleonic régime, with its satisfying epic heroism, that enabled saint-simonism and fourierism to flourish—both, according to him, napoleonic types of Utopias. Of Fourier's system he says : ' The whole of his system presupposes, for its proper working, the ubiquitous presence (invisible but none the less real and quite indispensable) *of Fourier himself* : alone able to get, in truly napoleonic style, the most out of human passions and to harmonize them. . . .' (*Méfaits des intellectuels.*)

Fourier and Saint-Simon are both accounted for by Sorel in the same way, by their position in the shadow of the French Revolution and the napoleonic wars. Of Fourier he says : ' People have regarded him as a libertarian : but from many passages it is clear that the support of Authority would not have displeased him.' We know, besides, that in all sentimental organization an iron discipline is automatically established : monastic bodies, savage bands, etc., supply the proof of that.

These wars (the napoleonic) had a great influence on the propagation of the ideas of the saint-simonians. France had been like a vast besieged city, and all her economic resources had been conscripted in order to secure the life of the civil population. The state had been com-

pelled, sometimes, to take over almost completely the control
of production. Under Napoleon the military administration had carried through operations beside which all that
industry had up till then been capable of was a small
matter. Why not apply this ‘direction unitaire’ of military
control to the arts of peace ? people asked themselves.

People go where they are pushed, then, according to
Sorel, and their ideas follow suit ; wars *occur*, and people
have certain ideas after them (like Sorel’s, of martial glory ;
or Saint-Simon’s, of authority, discipline, control). The
iron disciplines of wars are applied to peace, so that peace
is not very different from war. When an inter-tribal war
is not in progress, a civil war should be used to fill the gap.
But war we must have, for did not Darwin describe the
obstinate struggle for survival in the animal world ?
And are we not satisfied that we shall never be anything
but animals ? It is true that the Egyptians seemed to
get along very well without wars—better, some people
believe, than any other race. But there must be exceptions
to every rule. We *must* have wars, to remind us that we
are descended from Vikings—not to say apelike ancestors.

So Sorel and his disciple Berth both criticize their great
predecessors, Fourier and Saint-Simon, on the ground of
their *despotic*, napoleonic dispositions and intentions.
And in this way they are only following Proudhon, who
smelt *despotism* in all those post-napoleonic systems of
reform, as indeed in almost every system except his own.

But in his *Réflexions sur la violence*, Sorel reveals himself as
a full-blooded *napoleonist* himself—interpreted, as it were,
by Nietzsche. All his exhortation to the workers is to con-
ceive their class-struggle *epically*. The napoleonic epic is
incessantly invoked. It is the great example to all Frenchmen of discipline, militant energy, and, in a word, of honour
and glory of the first order. Helvetius said of the ‘ rigorism ’
of Dunoyer : ‘ On veut que les malheureux soient parfaits.’
Sorel similarly wanted every workman to be a perfect hero.

Workmen, of course, very unfortunately, have other
ideas about their destiny. They do not want to be heroes
of the sort that interested Sorel or Napoleon. ‘ One night
of Paris will repair all this,’ said Napoleon at Eylau, as
he surveyed the heaps of corpses, with his unforgettable
cæsarian smile. But the workman does not think on those

lines : unless he is allowed to be Napoleon, which of course would put another complexion on the matter.

But Pelloutier, so much admired by Sorel, says: ' We are the irreconcilable enemies of all despotism, moral or collective—that is to say, of laws, and of dictatorships (of the proletariat as much as of the rest)—and the fervent supporters of the culture of self.' Or again he says that a man's ' little finger . . . appears of more consequence than the conquest of an empire.' That is not the spirit of the napoleonic armies, nor of any epical transaction. Such a spirit of militant individualism would certainly be destructive of all discipline, military, monastic, or industrial. And *discipline* (with that of the napoleonic armies as a model) is the thing on which above all others Sorel insists. In the essentials, in the very heart of their doctrine of emancipation, all the great theorists profoundly disagree : but they usually agree in sketching a life for the workman emancipated from capitalism of such a spartan description that, should the workman ever take it into his head to read their works attentively, he would undoubtedly recoil with horror and consign them to the dustbin with full force of the popular vocabulary salvoing behind them.

But every one knows, who understands anything about it at all, where Berth says above that the saint-simonist state would be Saint-Simon himself, or that of the most powerful of his followers, and nobody else's state except those few people's who invented it and set it up, that that must apply to *every* form of state—as much one set up by Berth or Sorel as by Saint-Simon. A master you *must* have and *will* have. It is your prospective masters who are squabbling amongst themselves over you. All you can do is to pray that ' the best man may win,' or the best woman : and if possible, intervene at what you judge a critical moment in his (or her) favour. A marketing or hawking of myths proceeds briskly : those who exclaim most scornfully about other people's Utopias are all the time, naturally, trying to sell us a Utopia of their own. But that they are not consistent, and do not appeal by way of the reason but by way of emotion, is not their fault. The multitude, ' which does nothing by Reason,' as La Rochefoucauld says, exacts these methods to a great extent. It wants a fine myth for its money or its life : · and it is not critical of the technique that produced it.

PART XI

PROUDHON AND ROUSSEAU

' *If there was a city of good men, the contest would be* not *to be in the government, as at present it is to govern.*'   *Plato's Republic, Book I.*

E debbesi pigliari questo per una regola generale che non mai, o di rado occorre che alcuna repubblica o regno sia da principio ordinato bene, o al tutto di nuovo fuori degli ordini vecchi riformato, se non è ordinato da uno ; anzi è necessario che uno solo sia quello che dia il nodo, e dalla cui mente dipenda qualunque simile ordinazione.
      Discorsi, Book I. chap. ix.   *Machiavelli.*

' *When society is itself the tyrant—society collectively over the separate individuals who compose it—its means of tyrannizing are not restricted to the acts which it may do by the hands of its political function-aries. Society can and does execute its own mandates ; and if it issues wrong mandates instead of right, or any mandates at all in things with which it ought not to meddle, it practises a social tyranny more formidable than many kinds of political oppression, since, though not usually upheld by such extreme penalties, it leaves fewer means of escape, penetrating much more deeply into the details of life, and enslaving the soul itself. Protection, therefore, against the tyranny of the magistrate is not enough; there needs protection also against the tyranny of the prevailing opinion and feeling ; against the tendency of society to impose, by other means than civil penalties, its own ideas and practices as rules of conduct . . . to fetter the development, and, if possible, prevent the forma-tion, of any individuality not in harmony with its ways, and compel all characters to fashion themselves upon the model of its own.*'
      On Liberty.   *J. S. Mill.*

CHAPTER I

THE ANTAGONISM OF PROUDHON
AND MARX

THE problem of the domestic needle is at the basis of all controversy between the communist and the collectivist, and that object has proved an insurmountable obstacle. If everything is to belong to the community and to be held in common, are you to stop anywhere (at the domestic needle, for instance) in your repartition of goods ? That is one of the natural landmarks by which the jealously guarded frontiers of these two regions of socialism can be recognized. But in many ways the frontiers are extremely indistinct. For example, Pelloutier is a doctrinaire anti-clerical ; whereas his great admirer, Sorel, is for the Roman Church, as is also Péguy. Sorel claims Proudhon as his principal master (and all syndicalist doctrine derives from Proudhon). But he also believes very much in Marx. But Marx and Proudhon, on the other hand, are at daggers drawn. Marx, in his *Miseries of Philosophy*, attacks Proudhon with the greatest vehemence, even referring to him repeatedly as a *bourgeois*. He also applies to Proudhon the same epithet that Proudhon applies to Rousseau : he calls him a blackguard or *scélérat*. He refers to the ' child's pedestal on which this intellectual champion of the French *bourgeoisie* is stuck.'

Marx's real quarrel with Proudhon was that the latter stood for the independence of the small farmer and artisan, the ' small man ' generally. Proudhon was against a centralized control on the capitalist model : whereas Marx was, of course, in favour of a great bureaucratic hegemony, which would result in a world-state on capitalist lines, but theoretically purged of capitalist oppression. This was such a radical difference that it made their doctrines mortally inimical. What, however, Marx, in his reply to Proudhon's *Philosophie de la misère*, accuses Proudhon of is political compromise of the basest description ; which, he adds, is only what you would expect of such a doctrine as Proudhon's. Here are Marx's words :—

What, however, can no longer be considered merely incapacity, but plain treachery—which, however, is in perfect keeping with the character of the small shopkeeper—is the book on the Coup d'Etat, in which he (Proudhon) coquets with L. Bonaparte, and attempts to reconcile the French working class with the latter ; or that (book) against Poland, which country, in honour of the Czar, he treats with the cynicism of a *crétin*.

Proudhon has often been compared with J.-J. Rousseau, etc.

Scientific charlatanism and political compromise are inseparable from such a standpoint (as Proudhon's). Only one motive then remains, personal *vanity*; and, as is the way with all vain people, the only thing that matters is the momentary effect to be produced, the success of a day.

In this manner the simple moral tact that preserved a Rousseau, for example, from any compromise, even apparent, with the powers that be, necessarily vanishes.

Perhaps posterity will say, to describe this most recent phase of French history, that Louis Bonaparte was its Napoleon, and Proudhon its Rousseau-Voltaire.

So in Marx's description we find Proudhon first of all as the ' little grocer.' (All great socialists, if their parents were middle-class rather than working people—like Sorel, Marx, or Mr. Shaw,—speak of the ' lower classes ' and their shortcomings very loftily indeed. To this, in reading socialist theory, you will soon grow accustomed.) But Proudhon also is even figuring, if not as a Napoleon, at least as the servant of a Napoleon ; so he becomes at least closely related to Sorel's or to Berth's idea of Saint-Simon or of Fourier. He also is made into a sort of Rousseau, only a Rousseau without the (in Marx's opinion) integrity of the latter. This is especially curious in view of Proudhon's attitude to Rousseau, in which he describes Rousseau very much as he himself is described by Marx.

CHAPTER II

THE WAR BETWEEN THE DIFFERENT
SOCIALISMS

BUT Marx, on his side, has nothing to complain about on the score of the bouquets he receives from his fellow-revolutionaries. And in conjunction with the above attack on Proudhon the following remarks by Bakunin are interesting (I take them from a little account of Bakunin appearing in the ' Spur ' Glasgow Library : *Michael Bakunin, Communist*, 6d.) :—

> I respected him (Marx) much for his learning and serious devotion—always mixed, however, with personal vanity— to the cause of the proletariat. I sought eagerly his conversation, which was always instructive and clever, when it was not inspired by a petty hate, which, alas ! happened only too often. . . . He called me a sentimental idealist, and he was right. I called him a vain man, perfidious, and crafty. And I, also, was right.

' Personal vanity,' Marx says in the passage quoted on the opposite page, was the cause of Proudhon's short-comings. Bakunin evidently considered that this was the characteristic failing of Marx.

Again, Marx, in the same paper, attacks Proudhon as an amateur, as it were, in the theories they both were so famous for. He writes :—

> Proudhon, on the other hand, says of Rousseau, in attacking his *Social Contract* : ' Not a word has he to say either about work, about property, or about the forces of industry. Rousseau does not even know what economy is. His programme pays attention exclusively to *political* rights : *economic* rights are not recognized by him.'

But Mr. Shaw, in his telling way, refers as follows to Marx in his *Methuselah* preface :—

> Marx was by no means infallible : his economics, half borrowed and half home-made by a literary amateur, were not, when strictly followed up, even favourable to socialism. His theory of civilization had been promulgated already in

335

Buckle's *History of Civilization*. . . . There was nothing about socialism in the widely read first volume of *Das Kapital*: every reference it made to workers and capitalists showed that Marx had never breathed industrial air, and had dug his case out of bluebooks in the British Museum. Compared to Darwin, he seemed to have no power of observation : there was not a fact in *Das Kapital* that had not been taken out of a book, nor a discussion that had not been opened by somebody else's pamphlet. Marx possessed, however, luckily for his success, terrible powers of hatred, invective, irony, and all the bitter qualities bred, first in the oppression of a rather pampered young genius (Marx was the spoilt child of a well-to-do family) by a social system utterly uncongenial to him, and later on by exile and poverty.

From the point of view of the militant socialist, the immense glass-house of prosperity and success in which Mr. Shaw so genially dwells would not have been a difficult mark for the ' invective and irony ' of the ' pampered ' genius thus demolished. To imagine Marx's rejoinder is not very difficult. We can, without unduly stretching the imagination, assume, therefore, that Mr. Shaw is lying in the dust beside Proudhon, Marx, and the rest.

To me, by far the most interesting of these sectarian battles is the well-known attack on J.-J. Rousseau in the *Idée générale de la révolution*. It seems to me of such great importance in the region of ideas of which the present essay treats, that I will give an outline of it (quoting a few of the most important passages).

CHAPTER III

PROUDHON'S ATTACK ON ROUSSEAU

THE pages in which Proudhon expresses himself so forcibly on the subject of J.-J. Rousseau occur in his *Idée générale de la révolution au xixe siècle*, in the *quatrième étude*, in which the *Principle of Authority* is analysed at length.

Proudhon begins by confuting the fashionable doctrine of *direct government* or *simplified government*: *Législation directe* of Rittinghausen and Considérant, *Abolition de l'autorité par la simplification du gouvernement* of de Girondin. He shows that if you abolish authority you must simultaneously and by the same gesture abolish government. For government and authority are one. He then shows how organized human society has so far turned in a circle—Monarchy, Aristocracy, Democracy being the names of the principal segments. As soon as the last death-rattle of the last revolutionary fanatic at the last and most desperate barricade has ceased, the fanfare is sounded, and the dictator or emperor steps on to the scene once more, with the clockwork aplomb of the figures of a musical-box. This is owing, he thinks, to the *préjugé gouvernemental*, the fixed idea of the necessity for a government of some sort (which, in an earlier part of this essay, we saw him tracing to the obsessing paradigm of the family). So it is that the people, in their revolutions, have always, ' instead of a protector, provided themselves with a tyrant.'

Here you have, for thousands of years, says Proudhon, this same old theory of *direct government*, which has always given every tribune and agitator what he required. It has been the theory-up-the-sleeve of every revolutionary demagogue. *Direct government (gouvernement directe)* does not date from Rousseau. It dates from the foundation of human society. Here is how the old reasoning has always gone :—

No more hereditary royalty !
No more presidency !
No more representation !

No more delegation !
No more alienation of power !
Direct government ! THE PEOPLE ! in the permanent
exercise of its sovereignty !

That is the order of ideas or emotions invariably followed.
Dictatorship of the proletariat is the formula to-day ; the
russian revolution would have fully confirmed Proudhon's
forecast for all revolutions that retain the sentiment or
idea for authority, that allow the notion of *power* of any
sort to enter into their schemes.

' What is there,' he asks, ' at the bottom of this *ritournelle* that people have just taken up again as a " new "
and " revolutionary " thesis—what is there in it unknown
to Athenians, Beotians, Lacedæmonians, Romans ? '
Nothing, he concludes. *Direct government* will be the
prelude, in modern Europe, to cæsarism. ' An empire,
with or without a Napoleon,' is what is in store.

So against this menacing political sophistry, as he considers it, of *direct government* he sets up his notion of a
pact or of the *social contract*. The contrast between *pact*
or *contract* and *power, government, imperium,* ἀρχή, cannot
be missed. And so he arrives at Rousseau.

What is the social contract ? he asks. ' The social
contract is an agreement concluded between man and
man, agreement from which results what we call
society.'

J.-J. Rousseau, he then affirms, understood nothing at
all about the social contract. It was a closed book to him,
and his ' social contract ' was a malignant farce. The idea
of *contract* precludes that of government. If into the idea
of *contract* any ' leonine conditions ' were allowed to insinuate themselves ; if a portion of the community, by
reason of such a *contract*, found themselves in a subaltern
position, exploited by another portion—then this *contract*
would be nothing but ' a conspiracy against the liberty
and the well-being of the most ignorant, the weakest, and
the most numerous.' Rousseau's ' contract ' is a contract
of *that* nature, he asserts. And he warns his readers
dramatically against this treacherous impostor :—

Méfiez-vous de cette philosophie, de cette politique, de ce
socialisme à la Rousseau. Sa philosophie est toute en

phrases, et ne couvre que le vide ; sa politique est pleine de domination.   Quant à ses idées sur la société, elles déguisent à peine leur profonde hypocrisie.

(Beware of this philosophy, of these politics, of this socialism *à la Rousseau*.   His philosophy is phrases only, masking a void ; his politics are full of domination.   As to his ideas on social questions, they scarcely disguise his profound hypocrisy.)

P.-J. Proudhon's indignation with J.-J. Rousseau knows no bounds.   He says that the remains of the master who ' in the frenzy of his lubricity sent his bastards to the Foundling Hospital ' (for the famous bastards come into it) ' should be dragged by the outraged people from their dignified burial-place in the catacombs of the Pantheon, where they repose glorious and venerated.   If the people understood the meaning of the words Liberty, Justice, Morality, Reason, Society, Order, this is what they would do.   They would carry the tomb of Rousseau by assault and drag his execrable remains, with cries of righteous indignation, to Montfaucon.

' The vogue of Rousseau has cost France more gold, more blood, more shame, than the hated reign of the three famous harlots, Cotillon 1er, Cotillon II, Cotillon III.'

As to the *Contrat Social* itself, it is a ' pact of hatred,' only equalled by Rousseau's depraved and disgusting notions on the subject of education.   ' It is this same pact of hatred,' he exclaims, ' this monument of incurable misanthropy, it is this coalition of the property barons, of those of commerce and of industry, against the dis-inherited of the proletariat, this oath of civil war, in short, that Rousseau, with an audacity that I should qualify as blackguardly (*scélérate*) if I believed in the genius of this man, calls *social contract* !

' But had the virtuous and sensitive Jean-Jacques aimed at perpetuating discord among men, could he have gone about it a better way than by offering them, as a contract of union, this charter of their eternal antagonism ?   Watch him at work !   You will find in his theory of government the same spirit that animated his theory of education.   As he is as a schoolmaster, so is he as a statesman.   The pedagogue preached isolation : the publicist sows division.'

CHAPTER IV

THE CHIEF REASON FOR THE HOSTILITY OF PROUDHON TO ROUSSEAU

THERE we arrive, of course, at the sensitive centre of Proudhon's objection to Rousseau—to the thing that would in any case have marked these two individuals out as cat and dog, so that, wherever they had met, they would have fought : or rather, Proudhon would have chased Rousseau—*not* into the catacombs, as I was almost saying, for it was *out* of them that he would have driven him—but into the nearest cellar, as the outraged hussar or dragoon does in his *Confessions*. It is because Rousseau had a taste for isolation, and because, when he came to teach, he ' preached isolation,' that Proudhon principally objected to him. Proudhon was an excessively sociable creature, enjoying and believing implicitly in the benefits of company ; believing in its possibilities of organization on highly socialized, ' free,' utopian lines. All his doctrine was of a highly associational type, consequently. Rousseau was the opposite.

Voltaire acknowledged a book of Rousseau's with the words, ' Thank you for sending me your latest book against the human race ! ' It was evidently this angle of Rousseau that Proudhon caught as well, different as he was to Voltaire.

As this outburst of Proudhon against the rival socialism of Rousseau is the last one I shall quote, it will be as well, before proceeding to a brief analysis of the two standpoints involved in that outburst, to finish with the question of the occurrence of these tempests at all. That no harmony is educed from the stormy material of destructive revolutionary thought is not surprising, however. It would be ridiculous to expect socialists to agree as to whether everything should be destroyed at once, or only the *worst* portions of the present system should be destroyed—either (1) *gradually*, or (2) *at once*. Beyond that, still more difficult must it be for two men to have identical ideas of what should be built in place of the present proscribed structure.

One man's dream is a multitude of little rural federal townships (a ' socialism for peasants ' as Marx put it, referring to Proudhon's views); another's is that of a great industrial hive. One wants privacy, another wants the bed of Ware. And the violence and intolerance that has everywhere marked the teaching of the christian religion, naturally has also marked the socialist doctrine of brotherhood, to some extent its child.

Socialism is first and foremost a european thing, like christianity. The European's blood is still ' full of domination,' as Proudhon would call it. His idea of ' brotherly love ' is of a very hearty and alarming description, in the nature of things : it is necessarily a case of ' *my* love or your life ' ; *meum* and *tuum* is the opposite of commutative in the materialism of western life.

But if you repudiate socialism, however vague a thing that may be, dragged this way and that by the war of sects, then what is your position ? There is the enormous grimacing fact expressed by Proudhon as follows :—

> Il est de nécessité économique . . . que le pauvre, en travaillant davantage, soit toujours plus pauvre, et le riche, sans travailler, toujours plus riche. . . .

The european poor become poorer every day : whatever the reason may be for this, you cannot, unless you are a heartless fool, do nothing. And there is an immense instrument to your hand (in socialism), especially organized for the correcting of this terrible situation. As regards socialism, whatever brand you affect, yours is Hobson's choice : to-day you are compelled to be a socialist, at all events in anglo-saxon countries. In Italy fascismo provides you with a creditable alternative. The words I have just quoted of Proudhon are from a chapter headed, ' Is a revolution necessary in the nineteenth century ? ', and he ends it by the simple affirmation, ' There is sufficient reason for a revolution in the nineteenth century.' The answer must be the same to-day.

Now I will return to the place where, for a moment, I left Rousseau overwhelmed by the denunciation of Proudhon.

CHAPTER V

THE SOCIABLE AND THE UNSOCIABLE MAN

THE radical contrast between Rousseau and Proudhon was, as I have said, between an unsociable man and a sociable one. And the theories of both of them were antagonistic necessarily, as were the minds of those responsible for them. And to say that a man is ' unsociable ' would seem, at first sight, to convict him, and consequently his doctrine, of misanthropy. But that is not such a safe conclusion, I think, as it looks. It is in Rousseau's case particularly unsound.

A few remarks about the progress of Proudhon's revolutionary thought at this point are required. All the best french revolutionary thought is nearer to Proudhon than to anybody else. It is antagonistic by nature to Marx. and it has not the nihilistic and metaphysical character of the russian. Syndicalism, which as a doctrine has probably failed, along with its pet conception of the ' general strike ' and the ' gymnastic ' of mass-movement, is still the most well-marked and powerful endeavour of a constructive sort that the french revolutionary mind has made since Proudhon. And it owes its origin integrally to the teaching of Proudhon. Proudhon is one of the two great socialists of the last century, Marx being the other. And it could be said that he stands, philosophically, for the *small man*—the hero of Part II of the present essay : whereas Marx stands for the great urban state machine, and is against the *small man*.

But syndicalism has, as well as its central *federative* notion—of which the *bourses de travail* are the constructive expression—several of the ideas of Marx, with which Proudhon would certainly not have agreed. This cannot be better illustrated than in the following passage from George Sorel's introduction to the *Bourses de travail*. In it you get the complete marxian attitude towards capitalism—regarded by him as a sort of *spirit which wills the evil and does the good*, or, better perhaps, which *wills nothing at all*, but into which the will of the proletariat can be put.

Capitalism creates the heritage which socialism will receive. . . . Capitalism begets new ways of working. . . . After having solved the great problem of the organization of labour, to effect which utopians have brought forward so many naïve or stupid hypotheses, capitalism provokes the birth of the cause which will overthrow it, and thus renders useless everything that utopians have written to induce enlightened people to make reforms : and it gradually ruins the traditional order. . . . It might therefore be said that capitalism plays a part analogous to that attributed by Hartmann to the Unconscious in nature . . . without any ideal of a future world, it is the cause of an inevitable revolution . . . it performs in an almost mechanical manner all that is necessary, in order that a new order may appear, and that this new era may break every link with the idealism of the present times, while preserving the acquisitions of the capitalistic economic system.

Socialists' . . . sole function is that of explaining to the proletariat the greatness of the revolutionary part they are called upon to play.

In 1851 Proudhon described himself as ' a theorist of anarchy.' In 1862 he became what he described as a ' federalist.' That is to say, he abandoned his position of *intransigeance* with regard to authority. Anarchy is *the affirmation of liberty and the negation of authority*, he would tell us ; whereas federation was the balancing of the two.

In his book *Du principe fédératif*, Proudhon affirms that a government of *absolute liberty*, and likewise a government of *absolute authority*, are both dreams, both *a priori* and over-theoretical. And so he arrives at his compromise of *federation*. What might Proudhon not have reached had he had another century or so of life, as Mr. Shaw imagines people having ?

His idea for the working of federalism in France was that the country should be cut up into thirty-six small sovereign states of one million inhabitants each, and of 6000 square kilometres. He was still ardently against any form of centralization. It was indeed really in order to avoid the danger of centralization that he was inspired to create his federalist theory. That is still his greatest bugbear. Had he lived to be a thousand he would probably only have gone on inventing escapes for humanity from this monstrous political dragon, this withering abstraction. ' Political centralization has for principal corollary . . . commercial anarchy—that is to say, the negation of all economic right, of all social guarantee.' The bitterest opponent of state-socialism could not state the case against it more forcibly than Proudhon.

PAUL LEROY-BEAULIEU'S FORECAST OF A COLLECTIVIST STATE, AND A *PONS ASINORUM* OF SOCIALIST THEORY

A T this point I will quote at length a passage from the excellent treatise of Paul Leroy-Beaulieu (*Le collectivisme*) combating in great detail this same system of centralized administration which was the bugbear of Proudhon, but which was the foundation of the doctrine of Marx. It is no exaggeration to say that the polemic of this hostile professor of political economy corresponds exactly to Proudhon's objections to 'the socialist' as the arch enemy (' Only the *socialist*, of all human beings, would, etc.') : in that passage he was envisaging the socialist in exactly the same way as Leroy-Beaulieu does in the book from which I am about to quote.

Leroy-Beaulieu, beginning with definitions of the various sorts of socialism, proceeds to show how the collectivism of Marx *cum* Collins would result in a new feudal system far more rigorous than that of feudal Europe. The fundamental question of the division of labour, that division dominating all contemporary production, is carefully examined. But this division results, as he shows, in the direction and administration of our enterprises falling to an administrative class. That this must ultimately be in the nature of a caste, and that in a collectivist state it would inevitably assume the form of an hereditary caste, is again inevitable. For administration requires different faculties to manual work, and the habit of administrative command, the technique of the functionary, cannot be learnt too young. ' Supposing the intellectual and moral qualities to be exactly the same, the son of the head of a business will be much more likely to become a good business man than the son of a workman.' He instances the marvellous business aptitude of the Jews to support this. So ' the separation of these two categories of functions, the one intellectual and administrative, the other specifically manual and subordinate, would not disappear, because this separation is of the essence of great-scale industry. . . .'

In a collectivist State a workman could come to be a mental worker and be promoted to be an administrative official, it is true, as happens at present. But compared to the great mass of workers, the director and the administrators would always necessarily be few in number. ' Elected or appointed, the members of the administrative committees would form naturally a concentrated authority . . . and the generality of the workers would be as they are to-day, or more so—subordinate. So when manual workers are promised under a collectivist régime the direction of their respective industries, they are being deceived. . . .' It is the same with the promise of the ownership of tools. The tools would belong to ' the collectivity.' But what would this abstraction, ' the collectivity,' really signify ? It would mean, of course, a functionary who kept and distributed the tools. ' Just as to-day (the workman) addresses himself to his master to have the use (of his " moyens de travail "), he would then be obliged to address himself to " the collectivity." ' But who is ' the collectivity ' ? It is a reasoning being who, in effect, would take the form of this or that functionary. He would be obliged to solicit of this functionary the use of his tools : in other words, he would be absolutely at the discretion of his (new) masters. Imagine, for instance, the mayor of a commune having in his hands the direction and distribution of all the work done in his commune—not only the municipal work on the roads, schools, and other public institutions, but all the domestic or private work, the tillage, pasturage, the building or repairing of private houses, the trade of the locksmith, carpentry, weaving, tailoring, everything down to the most insignificant occupations. It would be this functionary, the mayor or his deputy or some person of that kind, that every workman would have to go to each month, or week, or every morning, to ask for his tools (which belonged to ' the collectivity '), and for the material or land which had to be worked, and also the remuneration for his work. To-day, if he is sent about his business by a ' capitalist ' master, the workman can go and look for another master ; if the trade he has chosen becomes too unprofitable, he can, if the worst comes to the worst, abandon it and choose another. If where he lives he is not popular and no one will employ him, he is free to go somewhere else, to a neighbouring or a more distant township or commune.

In the collectivist system, the workman would have to deal with nothing but officials ; these would have in their possession all the tools and all the material, all the various branches of human production, and all the remuneration. These functionaries, to use a happy word of Fourier's, would be veritable *omniarchs*—that is to say, despots to a degree and on a scale of which humanity has up till now had no experience. They would not have the right, you will say, to refuse work and remuneration to anybody placed under their jurisdiction. That may be true ; but what conditions might not be imposed relative to this work, as payment for this remuneration ? with what insults might it not be accompanied ? There will be, you may reply, higher authorities to whom appeal could be made. Imagine as you will adjustments without number, and of the most ingenious description, you will never get anything but *a man who has to borrow from 'the community'*— that is to say, from officials—his tools to work with ; a man who will not have choice of several masters ; a man unable to change his trade, or his place of residence, without a permit. And you cannot alter the fact that this man will be infinitely more of a slave and more dependent than the serf of the Middle Ages ! The latter at least possessed, on terms fixed by inviolable habit, the instrument of his labour, namely the earth.

As to the position of the workman in society, collectivism would not make the workman independent or autonomous —the rejection by the adepts of collectivism of the periodic sharing-out precludes that. No more than to-day would the workman own his tools ; no more than to-day would he direct the business for which he worked. As to the election to the committees of management, again it would be the same thing. Most collectivists do not seem to like very much the idea of representative government. ' Once the change to socialism has been effected,' says Schaeffle. ' universal suffrage is not at all necessary. No doubt, during the period of transition, while the battle with liberalism is in progress, socialism will not drop universal suffrage.' Again Schaeffle speaks (not in a very cheering way for the poor ' unemancipated ' wage-slave) of the future of individual liberty, the free choice of domicile, industrial liberty, *perhaps* ' being retained.' More decided than this on the subject of the retention of all these liberal and democratic ' liberties,' Schaeffle, this great collectivist authority, cannot be. *Perhaps* it might be possible to preserve a *little* liberty in the new collectivist system, but not much.

But Schaeffle's politeness where these ancient ' liberties ' are concerned is a matter of form only ; for they are all ' absolutely contrary to the working of the system that he is advocating.'

So, ' from the point of view of liberty and independence, the workman has nothing to gain from collectivism : it is, indeed, exactly the contrary.' Collectivism would generalize, or rather universalize, what we are agreed on as constituting an evil—namely, the separation of man from the tools and material which are necessary to his existence. Yet how bitter is the criticism that collectivism brings to bear on the existing ' capitalist ' society, which it is yet so powerless to improve on ! One contrasts *collectivism* with *capitalism*, collectivist society with capitalist society ! This, Professor Leroy-Beaulieu says, is absurd, for they are in fact almost one and the same thing. And this is the general form that the contention of the opponents of revolution takes. And yet this description of Leroy-Beaulieu's is almost exactly what Proudhon would think of the matter, as I said to start with, either as anarchist or federalist.

If you have absorbed the criticism of Leroy-Beaulieu contained in *Le collectivisme* and that of Proudhon scattered all over his works, but found at its best in *La capacité politique des classes ouvrières*, and if you are still unconvinced, then nothing can shake you. You can then consider yourself as possessing the equivalent of a diploma as a *centralist* or *étatiste*. You will then be definitely on the marxian side of the fence. To be at all an intelligent socialist that problem is the first and most fundamental one. It is elementary, a *pons asinorum* of socialist theory. But it is often not properly mastered. If you are a little marxian, you must meet the dragon called Proudhon (or, if you like, Leroy-Beaulieu) and withstand successfully their full assault, following all their objections out to the fullest extent and most ' despotic ' consequences. And if you are a little proudhonian, you must dispose of that ' pampered ' monster, that colossal bulk of venom and vanity, Marx.

CHAPTER VII

THE FEDERATIVE *PEASANT-SOCIALISM*
OF PROUDHON

THE federative commune, then, was Proudhon's way out of his characteristic difficulty, which is also to some extent the difficulty of every ' free-born,' white, european man. And, as we have seen, as regards his own country he contemplated cutting it up into thirty-six small sovereign states of a million inhabitants each. Speaking of his federative commune, he says :—

> The commune is in its essence (like man, like the family, like every *individual* thing or intelligent collectivity) moral and free, a sovereign being. By reason of that the commune has the right to govern itself : to proceed to its own administration, to decide what taxes it shall have, to appoint teachers to them, to arrange for its own police, to have its *gendarmerie* and its civic guard, to appoint its own judges, to have its newspapers, its assemblies, its associations, its customs, its bank, etc.—what would prevent it from going as far as making its own laws ? (*La capacité politique des classes ouvrières.*)

It will be seen that the autonomy of his federative commune would be absolute. Among those million souls (composing the small sovereign states, of which France would possess, according to his arrangement, thirty-six) those fortunate enough to get themselves into a position of control would have very great power. Or *public opinion* (if things worked out as Proudhon hoped) would be a very powerful and concentrated thing indeed. The greek or roman city state was of course what he was aiming at. But the difference would be that there would be no slave labour, no fundamental class distinction. The very great difference that this introduces into the structure of such a small state really makes all such classical parallels as those indulged in by Proudhon futile.

I suggest that the fallacy in this scheme of Proudhon's is indeed the one on which Marx put his finger : that it is a world for peasants only. Industry is the obstacle that

Proudhon never faced ; all his ' thoughts ' were ' agricultural.'

On the score of ' freedom ' his mistake was much of a kind with Rousseau's on that head. Rousseau dreamt of a ' free,' natural, savage state. Proudhon talks as though a small land-owning peasant or artisan, in a village or small town, is ' freer ' than an individual worker. But the conditions of village life, like those of the family (though it is true people are not, as Rousseau would dramatically put it, ' in chains '), are the opposite of ' free.' In a village ruled by public opinion or by gossip, which is the expression of public opinion, you get a complete natural *socialization*, far superior to any socialization of the factory. But there is little freedom of action or opinion—both are curtailed and held down by public opinion, more effectively than any police force could do it. Freedom only exists in the heart of the anonymous crowd. Probably there has never been so much personal freedom as there is to-day where it *does* exist—for it cannot exist everywhere, and the habits of the village are reproduced throughout urban life wherever that is possible.

To look round at the large, *empty* landscape, and to watch the birds flying ' freely ' about in the air, you would say—many people have said—in the country, ' this is the place to be *free* in ! ' That is what Rousseau said : and the more savage the landscape became, the more ' free ' it seemed to him. He forgot, of course, that his artificial freedom was contingent on the civilization that he had momentarily left. Had he really been translated into the wild past, behind village life, all the villagers would have become cave-men, or wolves and bears, and he would be far too busy circumventing their destructive intentions to be able to indulge in ' freedom.'

The more, however, you examine the life of the primitive tribe, the more it is seen to reproduce the tyrannous socialization of village life : and the more you know of village life (in spite of the moss-grown thatched cottages, and the roses round the door), the more you recognize in it the signs of the most suffocating oppression of all, that of a small congery of highly standardized human beings, manufacturing daily *public opinion* like a lethal gas. And you know that the strongest, that is, by nature the ' freest,' suffer most. Renan describes this unequal *partage* when he writes : ' One catches the spirit of the multitude as one catches a fever. The exhausted systems will go safe through the greatest ills, owing to the debility of their constitution, just the same as enfeebled people resist a poisonous atmosphere better than more robust ones, from having already accustomed themselves to a partial respiration.' The ' multitude ' referred to is not necessarily a vast gathering in a city square : it is any collection of people, and a fair-sized village provides all the necessary elements for such an infection.

We can now turn once more to a few of the most significant details of Proudhon's adverse analysis of the *Contrat social* of Rousseau, with a better chance of understanding the principles involved.

CHAPTER VIII

'ONLY THE INDIVIDUAL IS GOOD'

IN his demagogic 'programme' Rousseau starts from 'the lying, spoliative, homicidal supposition that *only the individual is good*, that society corrupts him : that, consequently, it is better for man, as far as possible, to abstain from all relations with his fellows ' : that, Proudhon says, is the criminal, foul, anti-social, disgusting foundation on which the despicable, hypocritical demagogue, Jean-Jacques Rousseau, has the effrontery to build.

Having advanced this insidious and lying principle, the rest of the system outlined in the *Contrat social* follows in the nature of things. All that it remains to men to do in this wicked world, regulating their proceedings on this programme of systematic isolation, is to establish between each other a mutual assurance for the protection of their person and their property. That is the social contract of Rousseau in all its naked horror.

> In a word, the social contract, as conceived by Rousseau, is nothing but the offensive and defensive alliance of those who own something, against those who own nothing : and the share of each citizen is the police duties incumbent on him under this contract, his functions assessed *pro rata*, and according to the risks he runs at the hands of pauperism.

Proudhon then proceeds to stress the exclusively *political* nature of Rousseau's creed. All the right allowed to a man is the right to vote for a political representative. The *abstract* collectivity thus formed (the political power), in short, can be made to serve the ends of oppression as well as could the feudal or slave system of antiquity. Rousseau teaches that the people is a collective being, an *abstract* person. By itself this *abstract* personality is unable to think or act at all. From this ensues that ' the general (collective) reason is in no way distinguished from the individual reason : and consequently the former (the collective reason) is mostly represented by that man in whom the second (namely, the individual) reason is most developed.' Arrived at this conclusion, Proudhon cries with exultant indignation : ' A false theorem, and one which leads straight to despotism ! '

Rousseau places the individual above the crowd : Proudhon places the crowd above the individual. As *individuals* we should feel pleased with Rousseau, as a member of a crowd we should applaud Proudhon. But, of course, what really happens is this : if we feel that *in the class of individuals*, as it were, we have a more important and privileged place than in the class of *crowd-individualities*, then Rousseau would be likely to appeal to us : if the reverse, Proudhon. But most of us do not fancy ourselves much as individuals. We feel safer and stronger —indeed, *only* safe and strong—when associated with some great class, or crowd. It is very few of us who care for the responsibilities devolving on the *individual*. Hence it is that, when properly understood, Proudhon's must be by far the more popular doctrine. But it is unlikely that it will ever be understood. And it is likely that Rousseau will be on the winning side in the contest of which this is an incident.

Yet, of course, although the majority of us do not fancy our luck so much as *individuals* as in protective herd-association with other people, nevertheless *if we could* we would all be individuals. It is as individuals that we experience our keenest satisfactions. It is our successes as individuals that count most with us. We are, in short, first and foremost, where our instincts are concerned, individuals. So it is no wonder that Rousseau's doctrine should have had such a great appeal. To the unreflective man it would always have one. It has in every way a more seductive sound. And people prefer, very naturally, to be seduced rather than to be drilled for their own ultimate good. Rousseau was the true anarchist ; and Proudhon was never an anarchist at all. Emotionally the anarchist reaches us more surely and quickly than the socialist, with the schoolroom implications of his doctrine. Rousseau would have turned children wild in the country to bird's-nest, whereas Proudhon would have set them down at desks and taught them economics. There is no need to say who would have been the more popular with the children.

So there is a conflict between our interests (which are

associational) and our pleasures, with the risks they entail, which are many of them individual and anarchic. That is why we all have such a very marked tendency to be socialists in theory and anarchists in practice, as far as ever our associates will let us—the difficulty, of course, of this excellent plan being that our associates are busy doing the same thing.

CHAPTER IX

PROUDHON'S TABULATION OF THE SOCIAL CONTRACT

SOME of the aphorisms ·by which Rousseau taught his ' liberticide theory ' are then capitulated by Proudhon. His list is as follows :—

That popular *direct* government results essentially from the alienation of his liberty that each man makes in favour of all.

That *the separation of authority is the first condition of a free government* (i.e. *separation of legislative and executive powers, for instance : note of Editor*).

That in a well-constituted republic no association or private assembly of citizens could be tolerated, since that would be a state within the State. . . .

That the sovereign is one thing, the prince another.

That the first does not exclude the second, so that the most direct of governments may very well be an hereditary monarchy. . . .

That the sovereign—that is to say, the People,—fictitious being, ethical personage, pure intellectual concept, has for natural and visible representative the prince, who is all the better the more he is truly a ruler.

That government is not one with society, but is *exterior* to it.

After all these considerations, which follow each other in Rousseau-like geometric theorems :

That no true democracy ever has existed, or ever will exist : seeing that in a democracy it is the majority who vote the law and exercise the power ; while it is in fact contrary to nature that the majority should govern the minority.

That direct government is especially impracticable in a country like France : because before anything else you would have to equalize private fortunes, and equality of fortune is impossible.

That, for the rest, and just because of the impossibility of establishing equality of fortune, a direct government is of all the most unstable, the most dangerous, the most productive of catastrophe and civil wars.

That the democracies of antiquity, in spite of their small-ness and the powerful support of the slave system, were unable to maintain themselves ; and it would be in vain for us to attempt to establish that form of government.

That it is made for gods, not for men.

After having gone on in this way for a long time at the expense of his readers, after having formulated, under the deceptive title of *Social Contract*, this code of capitalist and mercantile tyranny, the Genevan charlatan concludes to the effect that a proletariat is unavoidable—concludes in favour of the subalternization of the worker, of dictatorship, and of inquisition.

And Proudhon then begins his grand attack on Rousseau as a man :—

Never has man combined to such a degree intellectual pride, aridity of soul, baseness of instincts, depravity of life, ingratitude : never has passionate eloquence, sentimental ostentation, paradoxical effrontery, produced such an overwhelming effect on the public.

That is Proudhon's indictment, and it is an honest and simple one—much more genuine than Marx's of him. But I believe it is the inevitable shock of two natures who could never have understood each other ; and is, without Proudhon at all knowing it, very unjust to Rousseau.   I have already indicated the nature of my objections to this attack : and it remains for me briefly to assemble them.

CHAPTER X

ROUSSEAU'S MYSTERIOUS POWER OF AWAKENING HOSTILITY

IT is characteristic of the destiny of Rousseau that, long dead and buried, men should still, at the contact of his mind, wish to rush to his grave and drag him out. Proudhon behaves almost as though his enemy were alive. The evocation of a living person, which is one of the great attributes of Rousseau's writings, worked on him to the full. And it is no wonder that this quality of *life*, when Rousseau was *actually* alive and in the flesh, should have caused the hostile ebullience that it did.

But it is not only the quality of *life* that makes Rousseau remarkable. In reading any of the *dossier* of his violent misunderstandings with his contemporaries, you recognize some force at work of such a peculiar, or at all events alien, nature that immediately it produces a violent ferment wherever he moves. The contemporary intellectual world of Paris, the society of the ' philosophic ' eighteenth century, presents a strange spectacle as it is traversed by this disturbing genius, admittedly so much more powerful and original than anything else that it met. Rousseau, the great traditional landmark of revolutionary France, the traditional inspirer of the Revolution, was yet the opposite of all his ' revolutionary ' contemporaries : so strangely opposed to them in temper and intelligence, indeed, that however much they might vary among themselves, beside him they all draw together, and all you see is this isolated, foreign intelligence, like a messenger from another universe, and all the others grouped as one man against him.

And still, nearly a century afterwards, the scandal, the shock, had not subsided. Another typical Frenchman, who would have been thoroughly at home in pre-revolutionary french ' philosophe ' society, Proudhon, is still quivering with rage as he reads Rousseau's book, and contemplates in horror the bold delinquencies of this personality.

Rousseau, it is true, was a Swiss ; but that will not account for the extent and depth of this fissure that divided him from all that typical, discursive, sociable french society in the midst of which he burst his anti-social code, so that he remains the loneliest figure in the intellectual history of any european country. As you watch with astonishment in the dark backward and abysm of history all those people separating themselves from this famous figure with a chemical and mathematical precision, you feel that some force is at work similar to the extremest racial disparity. The few that adhere to him are not the most characteristic of their time and country.

So where Rousseau was concerned Proudhon was being, as in everything else, traditional. He is, of course, nothing if not conventional—the conventional french ' revolutionary ' man of the people. He possesses hardly any originality at all—even his famous saying, ' La propriété c'est un vol,' is a theft, is somebody else's. All his force is in his race and class—in the long *organization* that he has behind him, and of which he is an obedient, hypnotized product.

But there was truly a principle of disintegration, a nihilism, in Rousseau that accounted for all the instinctive hatred of him. Any little organization that Europe has ever had has been centred in France, and symbolized by her classicist culture. And it was a true instinct on the part of the contemporaries of both Proudhon and Rousseau that made them, as Frenchmen, bristle at the contact of this un-european mind, of this powerful mystical intelligence who had strayed amongst them. Of all the roman provincials the French have been the ones who inherited most of that marvellous organizing capacity of the Romans. Had the whole of Western Europe had this racial, organizing instinct of the French, Europe might have met Asia on more equal terms when the conflict came, as it has come to-day. It was the french culture of the english ruling caste that made England's power possible. And it was this highly organized french social instinct that absorbed with so much disgust the revolutionary doctrine of Rousseau.

Rousseau was as truly a revolutionary as Bakunin. Proudhon was as little a revolutionary as Bouvard or

Pécuchet. Proudhon, as an anti-revolutionary, anti-religious mind, can be regarded as one of the last bulwarks of the roman world. There is nothing so *french* in France to-day as Proudhon. The *roman* becomes more and more eroded and emolliated.

On the other hand, Rousseau is the great landmark of the new world of revolutionary modern Europe. This has nothing to do with whether or to what extent he was responsible for the French Revolution. He stands just behind it, as a great symbol of disintegration, of the final abdication of the roman, pagan, legal intelligence to the forces of a nature ' stronger in mystery,' of an intenser life and deeper intelligence than itself. It is as though the militant East had entered into Europe with Rousseau. He seems like a messenger sent to the gossiping, agnostic, mechanical eighteenth-century philosophic *salon*, to announce a god's displeasure ; or to throw it, with his eloquence, into a preliminary disarray.

CHAPTER XI

ROUSSEAU'S THEORY OF THE ABDICATION OF LIBERTY

SO in a general sense the full-blown zeal of Proudhon can be accounted for : his prudential, roman mind scented something like the airy tread of its traditional enemy. But the details of Rousseau's political theory, with their affinities to other centralizing doctrines, were also particularly shocking to him. The simultaneous abdication of liberty, in obedience to one purely political abstract authority which Rousseau advocated, was the identical contrary of his own plan. The aphoristic table given above might have been drawn up by somebody merely by contradicting all Proudhon's most cherished theories.

For Proudhon the individual hardly exists. As Dr. Estey says (*Revolutionary Syndicalism*), Proudhon's anarchism was one of *groups*, not of *individuals*. Proudhon never thought of the individual at all. All his work is a panegyric of *association*. Spontaneous dispersed exercise of power was of the essence of his teaching—in place of the dead docility of Rousseau's system,—but the spontaneity was the sociable spontaneity of groups. For him the individual had no rights whatever.

As this associational instinct or *organizing* instinct is the first essential of political success of any sort, it was as a politician, really, that he was always thinking. And all essentially political thought is non-individualistic. Rousseau, on the other hand—who for him never touches anything but political considerations—disposed of politics once and for all by handing them over to a central, professedly political, power. Proudhon wished to retain *politics* in everything; down to the smallest domestic detail they must enter into everything. Man is a *political animal* for him more than for anybody. His relations with his baker and bootmaker would be *political*. When Proudhon says ' economics ' he again means ' politics.' For politics would be diffused everywhere, and would equally share the marriage bed with the man and wife, and direct the game of bowls in the inn garden.

To say that ' man is a political animal ' is to envisage him as an integrant of a group, to consider him as a being the realest thing about whom is his *group*. He lives entirely through, in, and with others. The individual, for such a person, is an insurgent, a breaker-up of homes, an indelicate interloper, a walking lie, a disturbing absurdity. If there were such things, such monsters, as *individuals*, then of course a central specialized political authority to look after them all would certainly be necessary, Proudhon might have said. But as there are no such things as individuals in reality, but only groups, they can look after themselves very well without the assistance of *outside* authority. They are *their own* politicians.

The individualism of Rousseau relegated the political part of the animal, man, to a political machine, in order to free him for *personal* satisfactions. From his point of view it would be a far worse slavery to belong to an active political organism, involved in all the legalities and endless civic activities of its life, never for a moment to be *abstract* —to abstract your personality from the machine, that is to say—than to be despotically governed by some one power, in whose hands every one agrees to leave the outward political direction of their existence. He would have said that if you were going to run yourself, politically, you would never have time for anything else. Politics, the duties of a highly responsible citizen, if he takes them seriously, occupy all his time and energy. His attitude would have been more like that of the people of India, who have seen so many conquerors establish themselves in overlordship of their soil, and who have indifferently accepted them, always hoping for the best. It is to that, at least, that his attitude would lead.

The mysticism of Rousseau was un-european, or not characteristic of Western thought, for that reason. It implied a disbelief in the efficiency of the roman standards of material power and of universal political initiative. What is the use of *pretending* that you are ' free ' and self-governing peoples, it would contend, when a little reflection would tell you that you can never be that ? The real executive must always elude you : there will always be some cleverer or better-placed fellow than yourself who will slip in between yourself and the working out of your enactments. Why not, at almost any price, hand over all that barren executive function to some one with a taste for it ?

But he had also an active anti-social propaganda ; and that was the supreme offence. Man in society, civilized man, became more and more corrupt and disgusting. A man by himself might be a charming fellow : put him with half a dozen other people, and all his disagreeable qualities punctually transpire—his vanity, falsity, ill-nature, and so forth. By himself he is a gentle, reflective, industrious, engaging creature : as one of a crowd he becomes a soulless monster, as though some mystery of scale, or some trick of duplication, then got to work on him.

This is, however, the reverse of misanthropy. All the *intense* emotions are experienced by us as individuals, and experienced *for* individuals. You can hardly say that you ' love ' the golf club or slate club (meaning the entire body of its members), or any associational unit, in the way that you may ' love ' a person. To wish to get down to the individual and encourage personality—to attempt to persuade the individual against losing himself in the social round, when the world will be ' too much with him '—does not suggest hatred of man, but the reverse. All it can be said truly to imply is a dislike—either with or without foundation—for groups or crowds of people, and the impoverishment of the personal life.

Such a doctrine is, however, admittedly anarchic. Associational or group life does not furnish the *intensest* life, but it arbitrarily mobilizes certain faculties of each of the members of the group—those they possess *in common* —and enables them to employ this massed, organized, facultative personality effectively. *Politically* the group is stronger than the individual. In every other way the individual is stronger than the group ; but usually in ways that do not count on the prudential plane.

' Direct government is for gods not men ' is not flattering, perhaps. But where would the flatterer lead men to, in making them believe they were gods ? Or the liberal charlatan, in making them believe that they were ' free ' ? Usually to worse despotisms than any concealed by the Social Contract of Rousseau.

Where the syndicalists, or proudhonists, ' desire,' in Dr. Estey's words, ' to impose upon society a system of federalism, wherein autonomy is respected, and voluntary agreements take the place of the compulsion of the law,' it is a strange sort of ' freedom,' is it not, on the face of it ? Take the words, only, in which we find Dr. Estey describing their aim—not chosen with any especial care, I expect, but more valuable, perhaps, for that reason. The syndicalists desire to *impose*, he says, upon society, ' voluntary agreements ' ! What sort of ' voluntary agreements ' can these be that are thus *imposed* ? Would even the ' compulsion of the law ' be less absolute, I wonder, or in many cases onerous, than this ' voluntary ' form of law thus *imposed* ?

' The association of men must be achieved by purely voluntary bonds, free from every element of compulsion.' But is the gendarme's or the policeman's the *worst* and most ' despotic ' compulsion ? Is not the persecution, ostracism, and all the social machinery of *society* (free association) of which any country village supplies an excellent scantling, far worse, far crueller, and more un- reasoning ? Is it not just the *personal* touch that makes the difference ? Is not the *impersonality* of the machinery of the law better than that ?

Rousseau was perhaps more man's friend, after all, with his *abstract political* machinery, than Proudhon with his *personal* machinery of public opinion of the small ' federal- ist ' town, governed by a ' bureau de travail,' and regu- lated by functionaries who were at the same time ' friends ' and ' neighbours,' with all the licence of familiarity, and backed by all the power of public opinion. Unless it were to be regarded as extremely ' misanthropic ' to say that all friends are not necessarily ' friends indeed,' and that all men are not seen at their best in the capacity of ' friends ' and ' neighbours,' then it certainly looks as though there were something to be said for Rousseau's side of the ques- tion. He has not that mechanical, shallow, emphatic optimism about human nature, of the more *associational* type of man. But he is not, for that reason, such a treacherous villain as Proudhon would have him.

Because people do not value the products of the prudential mind, and are not in love with duty, the eloquent, irresponsible teaching of an intellectual anarchist like Rousseau will always appeal to them more. On the other hand, in practice, *intense* pleasures, and the ardour of personal highly conscious life, are not their affair either. The more relaxed, lazier, less intense group or team-pleasures that Proudhon's system would encourage would, in practice, please them better. Every man's ego or personality is his wicked double, as it were : he likes reading about him, but would not really enjoy living with him. With him life would be too exciting. Rousseau's picture was *exciting*, coloured, and romantic, hence its success. But when the dream comes true it is another matter.

The syndicalist ideal could be illustrated very well in a curious unit found among the maritime Chukchee. It is called ' a boatful ' (*attwat-yirim*), and consists of eight oarsmen and one helmsman. The latter, called ' boat-master,' (*attw-ermecin*), owns, and used to build, the boat. The crew is composed of his nearest relatives. This little water-tight, compact group-unit, working as one man, must provide for its members many of the elements of ordinary happiness. It is easier to be nine men than one. All the ' politics ' of their life would be in that boat. But one of the difficulties of syndicalism is that, short of imagining sweeping and radical changes in the distribution of the population, and a deliberate return to simpler conditions, it is not easy to find anything satisfying the group instinct, and placing it in a position where it can really exercise any political power in any likely modern world. A good deal even of syndicalist theory refers to things as remote from reality as the chukchee ' boatful,' or the minds of the galilean fishermen.

So we have caught a glimpse of Proudhon momentarily in the rôle of the homicidal puppet in Petrouchka, ferociously pointing to the Pantheon, and making the unbecoming suggestion we have read. Like the Hussar in the ballet, or the one who pursued the young Rousseau with drawn sabre—like, in short, the eternal policeman of the world,—the great french philosopher of federalism has

appeared for a moment.   And to conclude, it is probably
Proudhon who is the ' despot ' where these two are concerned, rather than the ' virtuous and sensitive ' Jean-
Jacques.   It was no doubt against the Proudhons of this
world (more or less) that Jean-Jacques was anxious to
come to some arrangement with his less arbitrary fellows,
against whom he may have felt that a little governmental protection would not be a bad thing.   At least
it would insure him against disturbance in the vaults
of the Pantheon.

CHAPTER XII

FASCISM AS AN ALTERNATIVE

I WILL now return to, and bring to a conclusion, the general question of the contrasting ideals of the federalist or syndicalist on the one hand, and the collectivist or marxian socialist on the other. The objection to a centralized control is that you are being controlled by somebody you have never seen, with whom you are not in personal touch, and who does not therefore personally sympathize with your conditions. But the vanity of that *Ah! si le roi savait!*—Ah ! if the king only knew !—has been exposed too often to require restating. The rich person intimately acquainted with the conditions of your misery is not usually more kind — that is the universal experience of the poor—than the stranger. Indeed, the reverse is the case. A stranger does not at least *personally* dislike you, and you benefit to that extent from being unacquainted with your tyrant. An officially appointed *podesta* is not likely to be a kindly old gentleman or Father Christmas. But at least, on the whole, he would be pleasanter to deal with than a successful and overweening member of your own parish and street. The *abstractness* that is so much shied at is really in the position of the ' winter wind ' of Shakespeare's song : it is better than a *person*. However ' unkind ' it is, you can be philosophic about it, for it is ' only the wind.' That is why Rousseau or Marx appear to me more humane, even, in the end, than is the pervasive, familiar, parish-pump sociability of Proudhon, which is extremely *human*, but might not, for that reason, be very humane.

Finally, I will take the other objection, namely, that of the ' genius of a people ' or the ' genius of a countryside,' which is supposed to be outraged by the principle of centralization if carried as far as is proposed by the italian fascist government. Renan, in discussing the characteristic beliefs of Israel, insists that you can only judge a people by its aristocracy. The rest of a ' people ' is a falling-away from this intense, conscious, more highly evolved, and sharply defined centre of life. Thus, in the case that he

was considering, it was with great difficulty that the
theocratic rulers of Israel succeeded in imposing on
their subjects the monotheism that we associate with the
jewish race; and especially the northern tribes remained
obstinately idolatrous.

But supposing that view of the matter to be correct,
what ensues ? First, the ruling caste in a country has
usually been of a different race from the subject population.
Class starts by being merely *race*, as the result of some form
of conquest. If, owing to the firmness and energy of this
ruling caste, the ' nation ' so formed becomes a powerful
one, what, applying Renan's rule, *is* the nation, with all
its characteristic institutions ? It is a system of foreign
values imposed on an already mixed bed of earlier stocks.
But the dominant ideology is that of the rulers, invariably.
The ideas of a people are always the ideas of the class in
power. On the top of that you have to erect the equally
important fact that the individual, more or less educated
and informed, of whatever race, thinks and feels differently,
desiderates a different set of things, from serf or subject.
The ruling caste is *less* national, therefore, in one sense,
although *more* so in another. An english, french, or
italian noble of the seventeenth century was evidently far
more international than a small shopkeeper or farmer of
the nation to which he belonged. Yet the governmental
ideology, the *governmental metaphysic*, which is imposed
on the people and the world without as the characteristic
product of such and such a ' nation,' is not at all identical
with the temper of the majority, although it is no doubt
influenced by it. We are able to-day in Europe to observe
the release, with the breakdown of authority, of the true
nationalism so long held down under this system or that.
The English, for instance, are, I believe, appearing in their
true colours, relieved of the overlordship of their french
or celtic masters. Just for a moment, in such times as
these, before a new harness is assumed, we catch a glimpse
of the true animal, so difficult to destroy, underneath.
I once heard of a mad doctor in Hereford who had a pony
which he used to paint different colours ; except on rainy
days, he was able in this way to defeat nature's pigmentary
provisions according to his fancy. That is what happens
to the subject bulk of a population.

Certainly every settled population—as every place—
has a 'genius' of its own. And certainly it will affect
whoever rules it, as well as be affected itself in return.
But the 'genius' can look after itself. It is a vast vege-
tative thing of a certain colour and shape. It is perhaps
a pity that the lily must be painted—Rousseau is best
known for his advocacy of its being left alone, with its
'natural' colours. But that side of Rousseau's teaching is universally admitted to be 'utopian' and quite
impossible.

If to-day you must be a socialist of some sort, what order
of socialist are you going to be? For, evidently, you will
say, 'socialist' means very different and indeed opposite
things. I have already said that in the abstract I believe
the sovietic system to be the best. It has spectacularly
broken with all the past of Europe : it looks to the East,
which is spiritually so much greater and intellectually so
much finer than Europe, for inspiration. It springs
ostensibly from a desire to alleviate the lot of the poor and
outcast, and not merely to set up a cast-iron, militarist-
looking state. And yet for anglo-saxon countries as they
are constituted to-day some modified form of fascism
would probably be the best. The United States is, of
course, in a unique position : and for the moment it is
the only country in the world of which you can say it
would not benefit by a revolution. And eventually, with
its great potentialities, it may be able to evolve some
novel form of government of its own.

The only socialism that differs very much in principle
from *fascismo* is reformist socialism, or the early nineteenth-
century utopias, or, to a somewhat less extent, Proudhon.
All marxian doctrine, all *étatisme* or collectivism, conforms
very nearly in practice to the fascist ideal. *Fascismo* is
merely a spectacular marinettian flourish put on to the
tail, or, if you like, the head, of marxism : that is, of course,
fascism as interpreted by its founder, Mussolini. And that
is the sort of socialism that this essay would indicate as
the most suitable for anglo-saxon countries or colonies,
with as much of sovietic proletarian sentiment as could be
got into it without impairing its discipline, and as little
coercion as is compatible with good sense. In short, to
get some sort of peace to enable us to work, we should

naturally seek the most powerful and stable authority that can be devised.

Mussolini is considered by many people as an unfortunately theatrical, grimacing personage, and is perhaps a little prejudicial to the régime of which he is the official figure-head. The power that he represents has, in its choice of a figure-head, showed, perhaps, bad taste. But in everything except taste it cannot be denied that it has chosen well. What has been effected through him is, in any case, in another category altogether from taste. His government is doing for Italy—starting ostensibly from the other end—what the soviet has done for Russia. The more militant liberalist elements are being heavily discouraged in a very systematic way. They are not being physically wiped out, as happened in Russia, but they are being eliminated quite satisfactorily without recourse to murder on a large scale. What will shortly be reached will be a great socialist state such as Marx intended, rigidly centralized, working from top to bottom with the regularity and smoothness of a machine. The *case di lavoro* are occupied by the governmental labour organizations : *podestas* are appointed to every township and commune, everything is centralized to the smallest detail. Complete political standardization, with the suppression of the last vestiges of the party system, will rescue masses of energy otherwise wasted in politics for more productive ends. All the humbug of a democratic suffrage, all the imbecility that is so wastefully manufactured, will henceforth be spared this happy people. There will not be an extremely efficient ruling caste, pretending to possess a ' liberal ' section, or soft place in its heart for the struggling people, on the traditional english model, but the opposite to that. There will be instead an organization that proclaims its intention to rule without interminable palaver, without a ' talking house ' to humbug its servants in, sweating them but enabling them to call themselves ' free.' In short, all the clumsy and gigantic characteristic shams of anglo-saxon life will have no parallel in such a régime. Such humbug as still remains will no doubt slowly vanish.

In ten years a state will have been built in which at last no trace of european ' liberalism,' or its accompanying democratic ' liberty,' exists. This will have been the

creation of a tyrant or dictator, with virtual powers of life
and death : for with his highly disciplined, implicitly
obedient, fascist bands, no person anywhere will be able
to escape assassination if he causes trouble to the central
government, or holds, too loudly, opinions that displease
it. As the press will be—is already—under the direct
control of the central government, and its editors and
responsible staffs appointed by it, death, imprisonment, or
banishment can be inflicted on anybody, anywhere, without ruffling the surface of opinion—indeed, can occur, if
required, without its being reported. In such a state it is
difficult to see how ' politics ' could exist. ' Economics '
will similarly disappear. All the boring and wasteful
sham-sciences that have sprung up in support of the
great pretences of democracy, and in deference to notions
of democratic freedom, will die from one day to the next :
for they are the most barren of luxuries, and no one would
be interested to keep them alive for their own sakes (in the
way that arts are sometimes kept alive) for an hour.

That the greater number of socialists, especially of the
reformist type, still live in a quite unreal world of liberal
idealism is an absurdity that cannot be imputed to any
neglect on the part of fate in supplying them with portents.
Darker portents, from their point of view, could hardly
have been devised for them. Nor can leaders of revolutionary opinion, like Sorel, be accused of leaving them
unenlightened as to what a dark and desperate world
they have chosen to dream their dreams in. But if they
were all awaiting execution the next morning (on the
capital offence of stupidity, for instance), they would still
believe that it was some kindly if tactless joke, between
friends, on the part of those terrible fellows their brother-
socialists of a somewhat more realistic temper. The
intelligence of the white races has been softened by success,
they have been used for so long to easy and unchallenged
power where other races were concerned ; they suc-
cumb at once to a little intelligence. That is the weapon
they have scorned and neglected, alas for them : and a
litany of such scorn they are being to-day carefully taught,
to the tune of ' You may have those highbrow airs.'

CHAPTER XIII

DEMOCRATIC FREEDOM AND THE CASTE COMMUNITY

I AM very aware that what we regard as the ancient and valuable ' liberties ' of Europe are not lightly to be put aside. But it is as well to examine of what exactly they have consisted, and to whom they have belonged in the past. They would be found in most cases to be the lumber and old rubbish accumulated by the sham fight of the conservative-liberal party system. They are largely the dummy artillery employed by the staffs manning the liberal opera-bouffe parliamentary barricades. While such ' revolutionary ' aristocrats as Byron or Shelley were writing melodious verses about liberty on the Riviera, millions of people were plunged in misery everywhere—especially in France, as a result of its great Revolution, which was the principal source of poetic inspiration for wealthy Englishmen for the first half of the nineteenth century.

A slave is apt to be better kept than a penniless ' freeman,' with no political right except to read, for a penny, the stirring speeches of gilded demagogues of luxurious habits, engaged in verbal sparring with another team got up in the tory colours. The sickening thud of their words is the only distraction that such a person has, very often ; and the chance of a free ride on election day. Liberty is manufactured with words, all our struggles are about words ; for no one would fight for reality, since without a name they would not be able to recognize it. *Freedom* was the name of a square in Aristotle's ideal city. In that square it was intended that the select band of ruling elders and the magistrates should exercise themselves daily in suitable gymnastics. Here is how this square is referred to (*Politics*, XII.) :—

> Adjoining this there ought to be a great square, like that which in Thessaly they call the square of freedom . . . into which no low mechanic or husbandman or any such person should be permitted to enter.

There are many places to-day that no ' low mechanic ' is encouraged to enter; only, they are not called squares of freedom with the same insolent frankness, nor is a necessitous mechanic called a slave. He is called Mr. Everyman, and his rulers try and sell him a toothbrush or a bassinette. When he is compelled to kill other mechanics of neighbouring states for certain well-defined purposes, of which he is completely, indeed blissfully, ignorant, with bombs and shells, he is described as a volunteer. That part of the earth on which he has had the misfortune to be born is called ' *his* country,' which is as though you called the Ritz *his* hotel. And now that at last there is a *real* antagonism and cleavage between groups of his rulers, socialism takes the place of the milder liberalism : that, too, is *his*. All is done for *him*. These are the commonplaces of democratic rule. Can this poor man be the loser —has he *anything* to lose ?—by his rulers shedding the pickwickian masks, the socialist noses, the kindly liberal twinkles of the european egalitarian masquerade, and appearing as men and women very like himself, only luckier; resolved, just as he would be in their shoes, to keep him firmly in the gutter, and treat him, as he knows he would treat them, like a dog ? Only, without exaggeration at all, understanding indeed the case, as a *dog* he will be better treated than as that troublesome and embarrassing thing, a *man*. So why not waive the little word and accept the status of a dog, or of a slave, since there are such heavy penalties attached to being called ' a man ' ? Even a dog may sometimes bite the hand that feeds it *too* kindly : and the lethal chamber at the vet.'s is more humane than the shell-shock sanatorium. And whether you call it ' war,' with Napoleon, or ' revolution,' with Sorel, the penalty is too heavy now for the use of that word, *man*.

Words, however, certainly make people happy, it could be objected. And there is no limit to the disparity that is allowed between a word and a fact—the fact may quite well be on another world : that is the secret of the success of the *other-worldliness* of the original christian heaven. This is a considerable objection to an open, highly organized, state despotism. But the very absolute nature of their material loss, once the despotism had been imposed on them, would persuade people to cease from seeking always outside themselves objects of happiness. They would be thrown back on ' their own resources,' and discover, it is to be hoped, their own reality. The truly childish objects of the contemporary European's desires, all the toys provided for the spoilt, softened, democratic mind, could not fail to give place to truer satisfactions. Even the fact that eventually the political order indicated above must lead to the establishment of a caste system does not seem a misfortune, once the caste system is there. Most people not only must be, but enjoy being, the proverbial fishes, fowls, or herrings : and to-day they are suspended in the void, as some sort of democratic abstraction, the history of which Sorel has sketched in such a masterly fashion. They have no real taste for abstraction at all, and hence none for democracy. For there is nothing wrong with democracy except the people who compose it.

How would the caste system be built up ?   It would no doubt ensue from the more and more rigid establishment of vocational tests on the american pattern, which are already being introduced into Europe.   This will probably develop into an examination system on chinese lines. This caste system would then be entirely built on faculties or gifts, not on what we roughly call ' character ' ; and certainly animal physique would become negligible. That small fact alone—and it is an important one—would modify an entire set of things that still have some influence to-day.

But we have reached the point at which two types of life are strikingly contrasted :   the traditional european life, large, rough-and-ready, free-and-easy, haphazard, violent, and wasteful : and another in which personal bluff and bluster—often attractive and with a good if frantically wasteful thing to its credit—will count far less. *Luck* is the enemy of the new system. In a rigid caste system there is a minimum of luck, of the events dear to the heart of the gambler, of fluke and fortune. Its object, ideally, is to eliminate this element of luck—so kind to one person, the ' lucky dog,' and so oppressive to the rest. How many people to-day, not because they are in any way remarkable, or indeed of the faintest interest to any one except themselves—who are often the least gifted, meanest, and most ridiculous of their kind—simply because they are *lucky*, possess wealth and consequently social satisfactions of all sorts! It is that meaningless inequality, so offensive to any intelligent person, that would be done away with by such a system as is in view to-day.

We have also to some extent reached a point at which we can see all the possibilities of human life, so far as it is to be physically constant and intellectually constant. That should enable us to interrupt the old *ritournelle* described by Proudhon, to overcome the charm of the circle. If only we arrive at describing the fashionable circle quickly enough, we should virtually possess all its successive phases simultaneously. That point we have almost if not quite reached. Out of the integral impression we should construct our new political equilibrium.

PART XII

THE 'INTELLECTUAL'

' Barbares, honteux de leur barbarie!'
Belphégor. J. Benda.

*' If the hook and line were destroyed, the compass
and the square thrown away, and the fingers of men
like the artful Khui smashed, all men would begin
to possess and employ their natural skill: as it is
said, " the greatest art is like stupidity." '*
Khü Khieh. Kwang-tze.

*' Faith in machinery is our besetting danger : . . .
always in machinery, as if it had a value in itself.
. . . Our coal, thousands of people were saying
(during the late discussions as to the possible failure
of coal), is the real basis of our national greatness. . . .
But what is greatness ?—culture makes us ask.
Greatness is a spiritual condition worthy to excite
love, interest and admiration. . . . If England were
swallowed up by the sea to-morrow, which of the two,
a hundred years hence, would most excite the love,
interest and admiration of mankind—would most,
therefore, show the evidences of having possessed greatness—the England of the last twenty years, or the
England of Elizabeth, of a time of splendid spiritual
effort, but when our coal, and our industrial operations depending on coal, were very little developed ? . . .*
*' The commonest of commonplaces tells us how
men are always apt to regard wealth as a precious
end in itself ; and certainly they have never been so
apt thus to regard it as they are in England at the
present time . . . the use of culture is that it helps
us, by means of our spiritual standard of perfection,
to regard wealth as but machinery. . . . Culture
says : " Consider these people (whom we call
Philistines) . . . look at them attentively ; observe*

*the literature they read, the things which give them
pleasure, the words which come forth out of their
minds ; would any amount of wealth be worth having
with the condition that one was to become just like
these people by having it ? " '*

      Culture and Anarchy. Matthew Arnold.

CHAPTER I

THE HYPNOTISM OF THE ANTI-INTELLECTUAL FASHION

WHEN Péguy says, ' Je ne suis pas un intellectuel, qui descend et condescend quand il parle au peuple,' you know what he means : the noble sincerity that marked all he said and did is our guarantee. He is not a great personage, a *bourgeois*, condescending when he speaks to the plain man. If it were almost anybody else saying that, it would be necessary to see whether this were not the usual publicist's or demagogue's manœuvre to prejudice the ' people,' their lucrative clients, against another leader, whom that seemed the best way of attacking. He would probably be saying : ' He (the rival) is a " highbrow "—he comes to you from *l'école normale,* or Oxford or Harvard. He does not speak your language. His voice is that of the hated aristocrat in reality. Do not listen to him : he will betray you, or at the best condescend to you. Listen to me : I am one of you. I have worked in a mine (or driven a train, or canned meat).'

But Péguy himself was by no means secure. His *Cahiers* were attacked repeatedly on the ground of their *dilettantism* (as can be seen, for instance, in the piece entitled ' Pour moi' : *Œuvres complètes,* vol. ii.). He was dealing in literature and forgetting the social revolution. He was a normalien, an amuser, a dilettante, and so on. Yet he was of the most irreproachable peasant stock, and by nature ideally aggressive. He was installed in the midst of a mass of quarrels. The hatred he provoked on all sides was the result of his aggressively simple sincerity—that is quite easy to appreciate at this distance. His stiffness and straightness caused endless dislocation in the smooth (that is, the crooked) running of life. So a hubbub arose wherever he appeared. There was something Rousseau-like in his situation, one in which he had the entire world against him—though of course on a different scale. But I think also that the reasons for it cannot be sought in any particular similarity between Jean-Jacques and himself.

But although by no means immune from criticism on the score of his academic accomplishments and love for letters, Péguy shared his adversaries' (or colleagues', as they of course also were) dislike of the ' intellectual.' In *La chanson du roi Dagobert* he gives an eloquent expression to this :—

> Eloi, j'ai connu des hommes qui ne te ressemblent pas. Heureusement qu'il y a deux races d'hommes. Et j'ai connu la deuxième race des hommes. J'ai connu des hommes qui ne connaissent pas par les livres. J'ai connu les hommes qui connaissent les réalités.
>
> (Eloi, I have known men who do not resemble thee. Happily there are two races of men. And I have known the second race of men. I have known men who did not know things through books. I have known men who knew realities.)

Like another very learned man, Descartes, he recommended and praised the *tabula rasa*. Even Montaigne was on the side of the ignorant : ' Que c'est un mol chevet, pour une tête bien faite, que l'ignorance et l'incuriosité.' But of course all learned men prefer ignorant people, but scarcely for the flattering reasons that they pretend.

But to know the stream of Vouzie, rather than the bulging, buzzing name Vouzie, was a capital part of Péguy's philosophy, which took its colour, as did that of Sorel, from bergsonism and its vital flux. And perhaps, without knowing it, they were fouling their own nest to order. The orders perhaps came through channels they had not charted, from the very sources against which their revolutionary rage was directed. This question— that of the credentials of ' the intelligence,' of ' the intellectual '—is such an important one that I will devote a few more pages to elucidating it. Such ' intellectuals ' as Sorel, Péguy, or Berth, to take no others, were hypnotized to strike at themselves ; their clamour against the mind, of which they possessed a fair share, was the result, I think, of an enchantment.

The ' war ' of the highbrow and the lowbrow, with which we have already dealt at some length, is a very important class-war indeed for the world at large. In killing the intellect, or its trained servants, men would certainly be killing the goose that lays the golden eggs : not the eggs of Mammon, which are devoured only at the tables of the millionaire world, but the more universally valuable eggs of intelligent endeavour. It is worth pausing to think whether this war is a very sensible one. Bergson was one of the principal administrative figures in its earlier stages. Poor Péguy was, I am afraid, a hallucinated victim, rather.

CHAPTER II

FOURIER'S 'INTELLECTUAL' CON-TRASTED WITH SOREL'S

I WILL get at the question by way of Fourier. I hope that the rather extensive quotation with which I shall begin will not be found fatiguing. He is one of the thinkers most in vogue at present with the russian communist party. He is one of the great figures of nineteenth-century revolutionary thought. No *résumé* of a doctrine can be so effective as is even a short extract, with the actual words of the person who held it with such authority as did Fourier :—

> The philosophers, accustomed to reverence everything which comes in the name and under the sanction of commerce, will . . . consecrate their servile powers to celebrating its (the new order's) praises. . . . Its result will be an Industrial Inquisition ; subordinating the whole people to the affiliated monopolists. Such are the melancholy results of our confidence in social guides who have no other object than to raise themselves by political intrigue to position and fortune. Philosophy needed some new subject to replace the old theological controversies . . . it was therefore to the Golden Calf, to Commerce, that it turned its eyes. . . .
>
> It is no longer to the Muses nor to their votaries, but to Traffic and its heroes, that Fame now consecrates her hundred voices. . . . The true grandeur of a nation, its only glory, according to the economists, is to sell to neighbouring nations more clothes and calicoes than we purchase of them. . . . The savants of the nineteenth century are those who explain to us the mysteries of the stock market. Poesy and the fine arts are disdained, and the Temple of Fame is open no longer except to those who tell us why sugars are 'feeble,' why soap is 'firm.' Since Philosophy has conceived a passion for Commerce, Polyhymnia decks the new science with flowers. The tenderest expressions have replaced the old language of the merchants, and it is now said, in elegant phrase, that 'sugars are languid '—that is, are falling ; that 'soaps are looking up '—that is, have advanced. Formerly . . . manœuvres of monopoly . . . excited the indignation of writers : but now these

schemes are a title to distinction ; and fame announces them in a pindaric strain, saying : ' A rapid and unexpected movement has suddenly taken place in soaps '—at which words we seem to see bars of soap leap from their boxes and wing their way to the clouds, while the speculators in soap hear their names resound through the whole land. . . . All those flowers of rhetoric contribute, doubtless, to the success of Industry, which has found in the support of the philosophers the same kind of assistance they have extended to the people—namely, fine phrases, but no results.

That would seem at first sight to be the attitude of the social revolutionary towards the ' philosopher ' or the ' intellectual ' with which we are now familiar. It is an archaic example of the policy that is illustrated in the title of Berth's sorelian treatise, *Les méfaits des intellectuels*. But it differs very much in reality from a great deal of anti-highbrow socialist doctrine.

In the first place, it shares with the later syndicalists their bitter hostility (so well exemplified in Sorel) to the ' affiliated monopolists.' A *centralized* power was as much the bugbear of Fourier as it is of the syndicalist. The *syndicat* and the *phalanstère* are both little, dispersionist, idyllic forts against Monopoly. Sorel's syndics, or autonomous occupational communities, are both sentimental, or poetical, in origin. Both bear the stigmata of the democratic régime. But—strangely enough—they both serve in their way the power of Monopoly and centralized administration.

Considérant—Fourier's great disciple—emphasizes the non-communistic nature of his master's system. And Sorel was rigidly non-communistic. There would be a scale of remuneration corresponding to merit. How elastic in practice this condition can be is witnessed in Russia, where, as Mr. Farbman shows us, communism is no more than a name. But as a theorist Fourier would have been horror-struck at the centralized dictatorship of soviet Russia and its marxian perpetuation of capitalist conditions. Sorel admires it very much—and has abandoned syndicalism ! Fourier would probably have admired it very much too—and have abandoned fourierism !

But Fourier differs principally in the nature of his attack on ' the philosophers ' by his attitude to ' Poesy and the

fine arts ' on the one hand, and to ' commerce,' industrialism, and the ' new science ' of economy on the other.
' Since philosophy has conceived a passion for commerce '
(which would have described for him, no doubt, the case
of Marx), the Muses are employed to embellish its products,
to wreathe its soaps, cold-creams, boot-polishes, and
tooth-pastes in flowers of rhetoric.   In short, it was the
opening of the epoch of great advertisement and big
business that he was hailing with disgust.

With centralization and universal control, however—
which Fourier disliked—the sickly rage of advertisement
would also pass.   When there was only *one* state brand
of soap that every one would have to buy or take because
there was no other, the need to tell them in gigantic letters
on every hoarding that they would ' keep their schoolgirl
complexions ' if they used it, would be no longer necessary.
And their complexions, in the sequel, would be neither
less nor more school-girlish than before.   The ridiculous
announcement, merely, would have disappeared.

The difference, then, between Fourier's objection to
' the philosopher,' and Péguy's to ' the intellectual,' is
that the former objects to him on diametrically opposite
grounds.   Whereas Fourier objects to him because he is
the advocate of ' sordid industrialism,' ' economics,' and
the practical side of life, Péguy's or Sorel's objection is that
he is too poetical, unpractical, too much a word-man—
the man of the *word*, Vouzie, and not of the stream known
by that name.

So there was a complete reversal of attitude between
the time of Fourier and that of Péguy and Sorel.

Listen to Fourier, for instance, on the subject of France's
great shopkeeping neighbour and political rival, England :

> Because an insular nation, favoured by the commercial
> indolence of France, has enriched itself by monopoly and
> maritime spoliation, behold all the old doctrines of philosophy
> disdained, Commerce extolled as the only road to truth, to
> wisdom, and to happiness, and the merchants become the
> pillars of the state. . . . One is ready to believe in magic
> on seeing kings and empires thus circumvented by a few
> commercial sophisms, and the race of monopolists, stock-
> jobbers, *agioteurs* exalted to the skies . . . who employ their
> influence in concentrating masses of capital, in producing

fluctuations in the price of products—ruining alternately all branches of industry. . . .

That is the french agriculturist mind speaking, associated, of course, with traditional political antagonism. It is what has been the distinguishing attitude of the Frenchman until recently. Now, of course, that is changing. The anglo-saxon idea, the commercial idea, has gained the day, and Europe is standardizing itself on anglo-saxon lines. It will soon be, perhaps, the british chestertonian small-holders of the future who will be cursing their rich neighbours across the Channel for their soulless industrialism. But, however that may be, it is evident that this attitude towards a great and successful industrial nation (with exactly a thirty years' start of Europe, as Marx estimated it) is not at all the approved attitude of the moment. It would not conform to the most widely held contemporary doctrine of the revolutionary state. So we have to pick our way. *The 'intellectual' of Fourier's day was in the opposite camp, and an opposite person, to the 'intellectual' of to-day.* I hold that the 'intellectuals' or 'philosophers' of Fourier's denunciations were darker villains than those of a later dispensation, facing in the opposite direction.

Actually, I believe that Péguy and Sorel were without knowing it *invectivating themselves*; both were nearer to Fourier than they were to those philosophers he so much disliked. Both were more enamoured, no doubt, of 'poesy and the fine arts' than their socialist ticket would have allowed them to confess. They were too glad to avoid discussing economics, which is no less repellent a subject for being got up to look like a philosophy. Indeed, the first thing to strike you in the theory of revolutionary syndicalism is the entire absence of economics. History, luckily, takes the place of economics, and the *coup de poigne* and the *coup d'état* take the place of ridiculous visionary economics for futures that are extremely unlikely ever to be heard of again, once the *coups de poigne* have done their work.

But how was it that such strong-minded, clear-headed people as Péguy and Sorel came to attack and abuse themselves and their intellects so heartily ? Why did they so vociferously declaim against what was the most remarkable thing about them, without knowing apparently that they were addressing these hard words to themselves all the time ? Bergson, as has already been said, was a good deal responsible for that. So we must turn to him for an explanation of it. He has been the great organizer of disintegration in the modern world : it is he who has found all the *reasons* (eloquently dressed in a ' style that bribes one in advance,' as William James says of it) for the destruction of the things of the intellect, and the handing over to sensation of the privileges and heirlooms of the mind, and the enslaving of the intelligent to the affective nature. His philosophy of *movement* and *change* makes him the best spokesman of the life lived by the typical american business man. The vulgar frenzy of Nietzsche, and Bergson's gospel of fluidity and illiquation, form in about equal measure the philosophic basis of futurism and similar movements. Further, as Benda shows with such admirable force, it is the implications of bergsonism that provide the best system of defence or aggression for the *mondain* enemy of the mind and lover of sensation. His is the doctrine of *sensation for sensation's sake*, a worthy fellow of *art for art's sake*. His is the ideal apology for the worst and ugliest *salon* of the worst of all possible millionaire worlds.

Julien Benda has not left much in Bergson worth destroying in his *Le bergsonisme, ou une philosophie de la mobilité*, and other books. But I will very briefly examine bergsonism here, especially as it applies to the material and objects of the present essay. The causes of bergsonism, again, are not dealt with by Benda, except by implication.

CHAPTER III

THE GREAT GOD FLUX

WE have had since the publication of Bergson's *Données immédiates de la conscience* a series of movements, given the widest publicity, and affecting every branch of educational activity, which might have originated in a single brain, which all bear the same stamp. As an example of this, Bergson has announced that he is in such agreement with Einstein that he will devote the rest of his life to adjusting his philosophy to the Relativity theory. Whence comes this unusual unanimity ? Is it because at length the intellectual leaders are at one ? Are the less unfortunate results of it due to the popularisers only ? Or are we witnessing the sudden flowering of a certain human type, which the political atmosphere especially favours ? The latter is, I believe, the case. Its supreme expansion is all round us, a display probably never to be repeated.

Sorel says : ' We must not judge a century by the famous people whose works come down to us from it ' (*Illusions du progrès*). They contradict it rather than express it, he says. Faguet said likewise that good writers, far from embodying, as was generally supposed, the prejudices of their time, did the exact contrary—namely, they opposed them. But Benda says, writing in 1918, that Faguet's remark is no longer true. Writers now, he says, *never* contradict the prejudices and ideas accepted and favoured by their epoch. They are its careful flunkeys. This significant emendment of Benda's should be given especial attention. How true it is, you only have to pass in review a few of the most eminent figures to convince yourself of. The causes of this new conformity are analysed throughout this book. What I have just said above about the flowering of a unique type to the practical exclusion of any other is another way of putting it. The over-political nature and great fundamental uniformity of all contemporary thought, is another. It is in the very sullage or backwash of revolution that these unanimous organisms thrive. There is hardly a mind that could be

properly described as ' revolutionary ' among them ; there
are none that are original, for the plain reason that they
are all on the side of the big battalions.   They are all the
reliable servants of a rigid programme.

Their great political services should be evident to anybody.   But if pure science and the free speculative mind
are to survive, they must evidently at this point divorce
themselves from politics.   It is in order to escape from
politics that it is necessary to analyse this situation so
radically.

The Relativity theory, the copernican upheaval, or any
great scientific convulsion, leaves a new landscape.   There
is a period of stunned dreariness ;   then people begin,
antlike, the building of a new human world.   They soon
forget the last disturbance.   But from these shocks they
derive a slightly augmented vocabulary, a new blind spot
in their vision, a few new blepharospasms or tics, and
perhaps a revised method of computing time.   Time,
especially, has received a very severe shaking from
Einstein :   although it is not by any means a new experience for that ancient abstraction, nor will it be the last.

The immediate effect of the latest upset can be traced
everywhere in the press and writing generally by a universal
squint at anything in the shape of a VALUE.   This squint,
usually circumspectly hidden, has never been more open
and malignant.

The born crook, gulping down his first thrill of alarm,
welcomes almost any period of disorder, certain that he
can turn it to good account.   A tramp in an earthquake,
riding hardily on the naked billows of the field where he
has been sleeping, must watch the cloud-capped towers
of the lords of the earth crumbling with satisfaction.   The
Man in the Street, from the street, will cock an exultant
eye at the collapse of some expensive monument to which
he has always had to pay lip-service, as well as money for
upkeep, but which he has liked as little as he has understood it.   What have these humble figures to do, you
may ask, with copernican upheavals or Einstein's theories ?
Einstein, for instance, can never be of any importance to
the world at large.

But the plain man, the intellectual crook, and the society
hostess are the only people, for all practical purposes,

with whom we have to deal. And they are affected by, and use for their own peculiar ends, any scientific disturbance. Benda, I think, is wrong, therefore, in supposing that Einstein has not done his bit in the *salon* and the street.

It is true that what a great discovery means to most people is something big, picturesque, and utilizable. Darwin penetrated everywhere, in the form of '*a great scientist who has said that men were descended from monkeys.*' Einstein has penetrated everywhere as '*a great scientist who has said that everything was relative*': or (as Pirandello popularizes it for the stage), If you *think* it is so, then it *is* so. How true or false an interpretation this may be of Einstein I am not discussing.

The popular upshot of the Relativity theory, then, is to shake people's confidence everywhere in their own opinion, but it enables them to circumvent other people's. So, *popularly*, Relativity is another agent of emancipation from the fixed to the super-fluid. And this *fluidity* is the life-blood of the philosophy of Bergson.

Briefly, the root impulse in Bergson's philosophy was a rendering back to LIFE, magiscular abstraction of a feverish chaos, all that the mind had taken from her to build into forms and concepts.

Perhaps by quoting a few passages from Bergson's *Introduction to Metaphysics*, contact can be established at once with his mind.

' Philosophy,' he says, ' can only be an effort to transcend the human condition.' But the ' thought of man as far as it is simply human ' he has just described as consisting in the erection of stations in the wilderness, points along the line of the flight of Zeno's celebrated arrow, concepts like towers above Heraclitus' famous flux. To replunge entirely into this flux, to *become* the flux and taste it, to be the ' intuitive knowledge which instals itself in that which is moving and adopts the very life of things,' in his words, will be to ' attain the absolute.'

In this way the Man in the Street is provided with an ' absolute.' He did not ask for one ; it is what might be termed A Philosopher's Present. But the philosopher, bending his courtly eye on him, may think ' he 'd rather have that funny present than *nothing*.'

How could they (the masters of modern philosophy) have
abstained from placing themselves in what we call concrete
duration ? They have done so to a greater extent than they
were aware ; above all, much more than they said. If we
endeavour to link together, by a continuous connection,
the intuitions about which systems have become organized,
we find, together with other convergent and divergent lines,
one very determinate direction of thought and feeling.
What is this latent thought ? How shall we express the
feeling ? To borrow once more the language of the platonists, we will say—depriving the words of their psychological
sense, and giving the name of IDEA to a certain settling down
into an easy intelligibility, and that of SOUL to a certain
longing after the restlessness of life—that an inevitable
current causes modern philosophy to place the Soul above
the Idea. It thus tends, like modern science, and even more
so than modern science, to advance in an opposite direction
to ancient thought.

Before this he has summarized : ' To philosophize,
therefore, is to invert the habitual direction of thought.'
And that inversion consists in ' placing the intelligence
within the mobile reality ' and ' reversing the direction
of the operation by which it habitually thinks.'
Again :—

The kantian criticism is valid . . . especially against
a science and a metaphysic presenting themselves with the
architectural simplicity of the platonic theory of ideas or
of a greek temple.
The dream of a universal mathematic is itself but a survival of platonism. Universal mathematic is what the world
of ideas becomes when we suppose that the Idea consists in a
relation or in a law, and no longer in a thing.

The ' THING ' is the heart of the popularized version of
the Einstein theory. The ' invisible ' current that causes
modern philosophy to place the Soul above the IDEA, and
which gives it a ' certain longing for the restlessness of
life,' is the current that I have been talking about above.
It is the plunge into the stream of life, smashing the watch-
towers, Baudelaires, ' light-houses ' (as the futurists recommended), identifying yourself with the fluid and the
natural, becoming ' capable of following reality in all its
sinuosities,' that produces the typical conventional *modern-*

ist, false-revolutionary tendency ; and the support for the organized hatred of the intellect spoken of by Benda.

Bergson is throughout recommending capitulation to the material *in struggle against which* the greatest things in the world have been constructed.   This fashionable, unskeletal, feminine philosopher of the flux wished (with more chance of succeeding than the merely very noisy Marinetti) to deliver all this up to the river-god, to the god Flux, once more.

I am an artist, and, through my eye, must confess to a tremendous bias.   In my purely literary voyages my eye is always my compass.   ' The architectural simplicity '— whether of a platonic idea or a greek temple—I far prefer to no *idea* at all, or no *temple* at all, or, for instance, to most of the complicated and too tropical structures of India. Nothing could ever convince my EYE—even if my intelligence were otherwise overcome—that anything that did not possess this simplicity, conceptual quality, hard exact outline, grand architectural proportion, was the greatest art.   Bergson is indeed the arch enemy of every impulse having its seat in the apparatus of vision, and requiring a concrete world.   Bergson is the enemy of the Eye, from the start ; though he might arrive at some emotional compromise with the Ear.   But I can hardly imagine any way in which he is not against every form of intelligent life.

CHAPTER IV

HATRED OF LANGUAGE AND THE
BEHAVIORIST 'WORD-HABIT'

HATRED of *the word* goes hand in hand with hatred of the intellect, for *the word* is, of course, its sign. Language is one of the things to be broken up—a stammer, a hiatus, an ellipsis, a syncope, a hiccup, is installed in the midst of the verb, and the mind attacked through its instrument. A great deal of very good work (politically) has been done in that direction.

Aside from politics, language has been jolted into life in some cases where it was in decay. But the word has also been set up against its master, the intellect, and a ' war ' been invented for language. The intellect has in every case lost ground. Where its instrument, *the word*, has been made to repudiate and attack it, it has lost ground to its own instrument, and surrendered this and that to language. Language has had unusual power for a moment, thanks to this transaction. But very quickly it has lost caste in its mindless state : and without the control of the intellect, words have tended to go over into music and be broken up.

' What ? Does the father of the gods wish to take away from men the arts that he gave them in their youth ? Is it his intention to deprive them, along with *language*, of the *reason* that guides them ? ' These words of Sulpicia convey the sense in which the war against words should be taken—what it is sought to attack *behind* the word.

Behind the *word* is the *mind* or *reason*, which is the metaphysical enemy. In the schools of american psychology, deriving from William James, you find this war of words, or against words, being waged more epically and with more concentration than elsewhere. In examining the *tester*, or *behaviorist-tester*, at work for a moment, we shall be transporting ourselves to the so-called ' laboratory ' where *the word* is actually being annihilated, or where the ' mind,' the ' intellect,' is being drilled out of it. And Professor Watson is the greatest exponent of behaviorism, and the king of *testers*.

Professor Watson is himself a very ' clear-cut ' and perfect type of american agent-heroism, or of the typical american gospel of *action*. He is the most perfect logical product of that process by which in the american world (initiated by the practical, ' matter-of-fact ' anglo-saxon puritan stock) the human civilized notions (which up till the beginning of the nineteenth century Europe retained —its græco-roman heritage) have been transformed into an unwieldy and breathless mechanism; from which, quite apart from any ' theories,' behaviorist or other, on the subject, ' mind ' is gradually crushed out.

There are for Watson two main points of behaviour, and two only. And into these two physiologically controllable forms the whole of the human personality is contained. There is no metaphysical or non-metaphysical element of personality.

These two forms of behaviour are the big and the little ; or, as he puts it, those affecting the large musculature of the animal, and those affecting the small. The former, the big, he calls *explicit* behaviour. The lesser, the small, he calls *implicit* behaviour. Stowed away in this second category, hidden in the almost imperceptible muscular movements of the language machinery, are all the mysteries and metaphysics of life. ' The larynx and tongue, we believe, are the *loci* of most of the phenomena (*i.e.* of implicit behaviour).' For the observation of this there exists no method at present.

A man hits you on the head. Either (1) you respond by striking him back : in which you are giving an example of *explicit behaviour*; or (2) you go away and think it over, and perhaps ten years after you approach him again, and return the blow. His blow is *a stimulus* whose response, your blow, will then be ten years overdue.

Where explicit behaviour is delayed (*i.e.* where deliberation ensues) the intervening time between stimulus and response is given over to implicit behaviour (to ' thought processes '). That is, in the example chosen by me, you would have been engaged for ten years in implicit behaviour: or in other words you would have been ' thinking.' Thereby you would have been causing the behaviorist a great deal of trouble: for, pencil in hand, he would have to have waited ten years for your explicit

response. (For ' there ought to exist a method' for observing such behaviour. But, ' there is none at present.')

Now it is this type of implicit behaviour that the intro-
spectist claims as his own and denies to us because its neural
seat is cortical, and because it goes on without adequate
bodily portrayal. Why in psychology the stage for the
neural drama was ever transferred from periphery to cortex
must remain somewhat of a mystery. The old idea of strict
localization of brain function is in part responsible. Religious
convictions are even more largely responsible for it. . . .
When the psychologist threw away the soul he compromised
with his conscience by setting up a ' mind ' which was to
remain always hidden and difficult of access.

' Word habits ' make up the bulk of the *implicit* forms of
behaviour. Now it is admitted by all of us that words
spoken or faintly articulated belong really in the realm of
behaviour, as do movements of the arms and legs. If implicit behaviour can be shown to consist of nothing but word
movements (or expressive movements of the word-type)
the behaviour of the human being as a whole is as open to
objective control as the behaviour of the lowest organism.

Of all the enemies of behaviour (and the behaviorist
is not slow to see it) WORDS and SPEECH (next to consciousness) are the greatest. It is in the forest or undergrowth
of words that the behaviorist tiger of clear-cut stimulus-
response, or his ' futurist ' maker, can become entangled.

The environment in the widest sense forces the formation
of habits. These are exhibited first in the organs which are
most mobile : the arms, hands, fingers, legs, etc. By this
we do not mean to imply that there is any fixed order in
their formation. After such general bodily habits are well
under way, speech habits begin. All of the recent work
shows that these reach enormous complexity in a comparatively short time. Furthermore, as language habits
become more and more complex, behaviour takes a refine-
ment : short cuts are formed, and finally words come to be,
on occasion, substituted for acts. That is, a stimulus which,
in early stages, would produce an act (and which will always
do so under appropriate conditions), now produces merely
a spoken word or a mere movement of the larynx (or of
some other expressive organ).

In the *mere* spoken word—which might have been a
fine blow in the solar plexus, or a grand sprint for a bus—

so many good *actions* are, alas ! lost to this world for ever. When you think of all the fine actions that have been lost in this way, it makes you feel *mad* !

We live largely, then, in an indirect world of *symbols*. ' Thought ' having been substituted for action, the word for the deed, we live in an unreal word-world, a sort of voluminous maze or stronghold built against *behaviour*, out of which we only occasionally issue into *action* when the cruder necessities of life compel us to.   Some of us live in this world more than others, of course.   Some of us actually *like* it.   And (a democratic note) *what* sort of person do you suppose enjoys living in this word-world ? Words are symbols of ideas, as the old psychology would put it—some people ' have ideas,' are ' theorists,' ' high- brows,' and so forth : and SOME (like YOU and ME) are just plain people who prefer *deeds to words* ! (That 's US— that 's our way !)   What 's the use of a word-world to *us* ? We 're not brilliant conversationalists, or anything of that sort !   Speech is of silver, silence is of gold.   And this is the age of *iron*, the age of *action*.   We may not have much to *say* for ourselves, but we can hit a ball or turn a screw with the best.   To hell with mere words !   Up behaviour !   And the devil take the hindmost !

Once upon a time our world was nothing but *action* : it was entirely a stimulus-and-response world of ' uncon- scious ' behaviour.   The behaviorist, as observer of *action*, is frequently baffled in the maze, and even indefinitely held up.   This must unfortunately be *admitted*.

So, insensibly, the behaviorist (on account of the in- adequacy of his method where the word-world is concerned) is driven into an utopian attitude.   Like all other animals, the behaviorist animal dreams of a *perfect* world (for behaviorists) where everything would occur ' in terms of stimulus and response ' (immediate, evident, unequivocal, objectively ascertainable, response), and ' in terms of habit formation.'   And insensibly he is driven into a dogma of *action* and into a more or less disguised attitude of im- patience with human beings who ' delay ' or hold up their natural responses an undue length of time, or who convert them into *words*.   *Words* are the arch enemies of any behaviorist, comparative psychologist, physiologist, vital- ist, or actionist of any sort.

CHAPTER V

FOUR PHASES IN ART AND SCIENCE
OF THE WAR ON THE INTELLECT

BUT with the alienation of *the word* from its meaning, on the one hand, and the carrying of it over into the region of music : or, on the other, the campaign against language and the articulate altogether, on account of its eternally compromising association with the intellect ;— with these transactions comes in, as well, a doctrine of *mobility* where any meaning at all is concerned. The traditional ' divine illogic ' of the woman is preferred to supposed masculine rigour and method. The ' woman's right to change her mind ' is installed in the heart of philosophy. *The philosopher, in short, is taking a leaf out of the woman's book, as we have seen other men doing.* Why should not he, poor devil, the philosopher seems to say, benefit by the general immunity from exactitude ? What *is true* is what *succeeds* ! The *pragmatic* for ever ! Why should the woman have all the privileges where the ' changing of the mind ' is concerned ? And—as everybody else is doing it—why should not he ' become like unto a little child ' too ? So all the jolly old peter-pannish professors slip their legs over the sash of the window and land in the flower-bed : and off they scamper to join *l'école buisson-nière* in the enchanted forests of childhood ; ogling duch-esses on the way and supplying them with little philosophic dispensations from the ardours of the intelligence ; giving them a hundred neat proofs that the ways of the duchess are ' intuitively ' in a higher category than the ways of the stupid and pernicious ' intellectual.'

Thus it is that, as Benda says, ' writers who give them-selves out to be thinkers are prized for the " mobility " ... the " fluidity " of their doctrine.' He cites R. Rolland, G. Sorel, and William James as examples of these new ' fluid ' thinkers. ' Cursed be the day,' cries one of our æsthetes, *à propos* of one of his idols, ' *cursed be the day when this mind becomes fixed!* ' Philosophy ought to consist in an ' unseizable ' affirmation (because it must at all cost

imitate life) ; the philosopher should proceed in everything
' as an artist.'

We know in social life what depths of vulgarity that
word *artist* is used to cover.   And in philosophy and science
it serves a similar purpose.   To be *an artist* excuses every
imbecility ; for is not the ' man of genius ' an imbecile,
or at the best a child ?   The myth of the imbecile, the
childish artist, has been one of the most destructive engines
in the war against the conceptual stronghold of the
intellect.

It may be useful to draw up a short table of the principal
forms this anti-intellect campaign has taken.   I should
group its manifestations as follows :—

1. The Child.
2. The Amateur.
3. The Demented.
4. The Pragmatic.

1. Under the heading of *the Child* we can group the
child-draughtsman, juvenile geniuses of all sorts, adults
who adopt the child-mind, such books as *The Little Visitors*,
Charlie Chaplin's art (he is always the small put-upon
little Neuter, the little David confronting the giant world);
Klee (to some extent), Matisse, etc.

2. Under the heading of *the Amateur* you get the many
wealthy people who, in the general *déménagement* of
Mayfair into ' bohemian ' quarters, have adopted art either
as a disguise or as a desultorily followed highbrow game.

3. Under the heading of *the Demented* you get Miss
Gertrude Stein and the various stammering, squinting,
punning group who follow her.

4. Under the heading of *the Pragmatic* come, of course,
the american pragmatists, and all those people in France,
such as Sorel, influenced by Bergson.

Within the dominions, generally speaking, of the Great
God Flux, are to be found (distributed amongst all or any
of these four groupings) the psycho-analysts, futurists,
dadas, proustites, etc.

We are all the patients of a great cult.   The ' maladie
du siècle ' becomes, with Péguy, the ' mal moderne.'
From it *everybody* suffers, he says.   A sort of clinical
religion is being built up to accommodate us, the priesthood

of which is recruited principally from the ranks of the alienists. In every case it is our weakness, our smallness, our ignorance, or our dementia that is catered for.

Buddha found the same type of man dispersed among all the classes and social ranks of a people who were good and kind (and above all inoffensive) owing to indolence, and who, likewise owing to indolence, lived abstemiously, almost without requirements. He understood that such a type of man, with all its *vis inertiæ*, has inevitably to glide into a religious belief which offers the promise of avoidance of a return of earthly ill (that is to say, labour and activity generally). This ' understanding ' was his genius. The founder of a religion possesses psychological infallibility in the knowledge of a definite average type of souls, who have not yet *recognized* themselves as akin.

Thus Nietzsche (in the *Joyful Wisdom*) describes the nature of Buddha's psychological genius. A similar movement has perhaps started to-day in Europe and the West generally. But the curious difference in the situation is that the patients are first systematically *sickened*, as you *fatten* a pig, and then supplied with a nurse and a prescription. Or at all events things are inclined to follow that course.

How simple it would be if we could leave it at that, as most people who grasp a little this situation do ! But the docility and tutelage, the disgust with or carelessness of life, that supplied Buddha with his clientèle is not a thing to be despised. European energy (of which american energy is such a remarkable caricature) is as dismal as the *vis inertiæ* of the Hindu. And it is not kind to allow the European to aim at the upkeep of this european energy now that Europe is no longer politically able to afford it.

Further, a great deal of the art and thought produced in conjunction with this great movement of corruption and overthrow is actually better, I believe, as a standard at all events, than former european art. Europeans are exchanging political success for spiritual advantages. A higher sensitiveness and intelligence are apparent, as must be expected.

But there is a further complexity, and that is what I have been attempting to define for you. The destroyer cannot be at the same time the creator. The political impulses at work constantly distort the issue. The artist or the thinker is apt to find himself making something, but ending it with dynamite, as it were. The political necessities underneath the surface are perpetually interfering, magnetically or otherwise, with artistic creation or scientific research. The result is that almost all contemporary thought, science, or art is spoilt, and its speculative integrity, its detachment, sacrificed. It all seems to acquire a mad, evil, or hysterical twist. But also it frequently reaches a beauty that is new in Europe. That, I think, is our problem : and it is not easy to see an issue just yet.

CHAPTER VI

MR. JINGLE AND MR. BLOOM

T HE *Lunatic*, or the *Demented*, and the *Child* are linked together by psycho-analysis, the link being its dogma of the Unconscious. The *Amateur* is closely connected with the socialist religion of Demos and the dithyrambic action of the crowd. The *willed* sickness of the modern man is connected also with the atmosphere of revolution and threatening chaos—it could even be taken as a measure of precaution against the crowd-atmosphere. Renan puts into the mouth of one of his characters in *Caliban* : ' One catches the spirit of the multitude as one catches a fever. Exhausted systems will go safe through the greatest ills, owing to the debility of their constitution, just as enfeebled people resist a poisonous atmosphere better than more robust ones, from having already accustomed themselves to a partial respiration.' Make yourself *weak*, make yourself *ill*, in order to survive, whispers the knowing Spirit of the Species ; just as it would recommend the male spiders of certain species to make themselves *small* for the same reason.

Even make yourself *mad*, it might advise the Hamlets of the present time.

Miss Gertrude Stein is the best-known exponent of a literary system that consists in a sort of gargantuan mental stutter. What she is exploiting in her method is the processes of the demented. For any one less strong-minded than Miss Stein this might prove a dangerous occupation : just as you often hear it said that Pirandello's game is a ' dangerous ' one. Her art is composed, first, of repetition, which lyricizes her utterances on the same principle as that of the hebrew poetry. But the repetition is also in the nature of a photograph of the unorganized word-dreaming of the mind when not concentrated for some logical functional purpose. Mr. Joyce employed this method with success (not so radically and rather differently) in *Ulysses*. The thought-stream or word-stream of his hero's mind was supposed to be photographed. The effect was not unlike the conversation of Mr. Jingle in *Pickwick*.

The reason why you get this Mr. Jingle effect is that, in *Ulysses*, a considerable degree of naturalism being aimed at, Mr. Joyce had not the freedom of movement possessed by the more ostensibly personal, semi-lyrical, utterances of Miss Stein. He had to pretend that we were really surprising the private thought of a real and average human creature, Mr. Bloom. But the fact is that Mr. Bloom was abnormally *wordy*. He *thought in words*, not images, for our benefit, in a fashion as unreal, from the point of view of the strictest naturalist dogma, as a Hamlet soliloquy. And yet the *pretence* of naturalism involved Mr. Joyce in something less satisfying than Miss Stein's more direct and arbitrary arrangements.

Both Miss Stein and Mr. Joyce—who has followed her in that—achieve a *comic* effect very often, and it is principally on this ground that their method could recommend itself.

There is a well-known fidgety obsession of the insane which compels them, when they have left a table, for instance, to return to it and adjust something on it, or rearrange the chair they have left. They will return again and again, and often it is impossible to drag them away from it. No sooner have they left it than they must go back and at least touch it again. Miss Stein's method resembles this : she goes on fumbling with the same words, repeating them again and again, turning them different ways.

The exploitation of madness, of ticks, blephorospasms, and eccentricities of the mechanism of the brain, is a thing of a similar order in language to the exploitation of the physical aspect of imbecility in contemporary painting. The acromegalic monsters of Picasso, which gaze at you with the impenetrable dullness of the idiot, are an example of this. Matisse provides, throughout his work, an excellent illustration of the fascination felt for not only disease and deformity, but imbecility.

If you contrast for a moment any collection of photographs of pictures by renaissance masters, you will be struck by the absence of any horror in the descriptive detail of scenes of carnage or martyrdom, the absence of any diseased, squinting, or humanly repellent organisms. In short, the physical health of the italian renaissance artists, as I have remarked on another occasion, is what is borne in on you still more if you compare their work with such examples of contemporary work as I have cited.

To give an example of the success on the comic side of Miss Stein's writing : the following few lines will convey what I mean :—

> If you hear her snore
> It is not before you love her
> You love her so that to be her beau is very lovely
> She is sweetly there and her curly hair is very lovely
> She is my tender sweet and her little feet are stretched out
>   well which is a treat and very lovely.

For Mr. Joyce's use of Miss Stein's method the following passage will suffice (it is of the more genial, Mr. Jingle, order) :—

> Provost's house. The reverend Dr. Salmon : tinned salmon. Well tinned in there. Wouldn't live in it if they paid me. Hope they have liver and bacon to-day. Nature abhors a vacuum. There he is : the brother. Image of him. Haunting face. Now that's a coincidence. Course hundreds of times you think of a person : etc.
>
> Feel better. Burgundy. Good pick-me-up. Who distilled first. Some chap in the blues. Dutch courage. That *Kilkenny People* in the national library now I must.

Here is Mr. Jingle, from *Pickwick* :—

> Rather short in the waist, ain't it ?—Like a general postman's coat—queer coats those—made by contract—no measuring—mysterious dispensations of Providence—all the short men get the long coats—all the long men short ones.
>
> Come—stopping at Crown—Crown at Muggleton—met a party—flannel jackets—white trousers—anchovy sandwiches —devilled kidneys—splendid fellows—glorious.

So by the devious route of a fashionable naturalist device—that usually described as ' presenting the character from the *inside* '—and the influence exercised on him by Miss Stein's technique of picturesque dementia— Mr. Joyce reaches the half-demented *crank* figure of traditional english humour.

CHAPTER VII

SKIN AND INTESTINES

I AM aware that the question of what is the suitable material for art, and then what art is, how constant its uses are, and so forth, would take us very far indeed : so far out of our way, in any case, that they cannot be followed here. What can be briefly said to some point is : The more art goes to science for its inspiration, the more of the *inside* of things, and the less of the *outside* of things, it will get into its shop. I have defined art as the science of the *outside* of things, and natural science as the science of the *inside* of things.

Further, the more it buries itself in and burrows into the vitals of things (by surrendering itself to psychoanalytic suggestion, with all the paraphernalia of neuroses, to the tester's and anthropometrist's obsessions), the less superficial shape and contour it will have. Its objective qualities, in which it is supreme and which is its unchallenged province, will be surrendered for more mixed and obscure issues. Again, the biological sciences, which usually attract it most, eventually hand it over to the doctor, psychiatrist, etc. The doctor's clients are the sick and imperfect, and they become the artist's clients too. That is how it may get its present bias for disease.

A preoccupation with the *vitals* of things is related to *vitalist* enthusiasms. ' Life ' (of the ' Up life ! down art ! ' cry) means invariably the smoking-hot *inside* of things, in contrast to the hard, cold, formal skull or carapace. The *emotional* of the bergsonian dogma is the heat, moisture, shapelessness, and tremor of the vitals of life. The *intellectual* is the ectodermic case, the ideality of the animal machine *with its skin on*.

Finally, the bergsonian (jamesesque, psycho-analytic, wagnerian Venusberg) philosophy of the hot *vitals*—of the blood-stream, of vast cosmic emotion, gush and flow— is that of a *blind* organism. There are no Eyes in that philosophy. It *sees* no more than the embryo : it is hardly yet male or female : it is sightless and neuter. It is the creed of a sightless, ganglionic mass, in short : and as such invites to that ' eternity of intoxication ' of the gibe of Plato.

A person living at large, not constrained in any way except by the constraint of existence (which is very great), self-controlled, you would expect to be more deliberate than the average demented person would be. But it is the *deliberation* of Miss Stein, for instance, that is the difficulty. For pretending to be a lunatic is the same order of thing as affecting to be a child. Miss Stein is probably a clever, sober, intelligent woman, who has her head screwed on straight and has been a pupil of William James. She is *amused* by the stammering and fumbling of the poor lunatic ; and, like an old child with a new toy, she imitates him. The comic juxtapositions and paradoxical features of the *nonsense-rhyme* continue to *amuse* this intelligent, leisured student. So she goes on playing her game of witty nonsense. Such a lady is, of course, the perfect ' highbrow ' of the press myth. She is also closely related, through her whimsical vein, to the doctrinaire *Amateur* of London art-circles.

Art, or rather tragic art and all religious or ritualistic art, has always threatened life or made the salutary pretence of doing so : that, as we started by saying, is its function. But it has not been its function formerly to mollify and fuse the crust on which we live : that, by its very insistence on shape and measure, objectivity, and delight in the symbols of strength and animal health, it has tended to stiffen. The Egyptians, for instance, composed in their art the most enduring shell imaginable. They were the greatest enemies of Death that have ever existed. We may come to be known as, above all, *the friends of Death*. When we think we should be styled the *friends of Life* par excellence, we may be its most notorious enemies. And in contemporary art by way of the lunatic we are flying off the board towards extinction ; by way of the child we are backing, or propelling ourselves backwards, into it ; by way of the diseased and corrupt organism we are embracing it ; by way of the strange dogma of the struggle for existence, for its own sake, we are glorifying it. Nietzsche was a death-snob (as Whitman was a life-snob) : and he was also a *madness-snob*. (This is a very ancient form of snob : but formerly the madness-snob never dreamt of going mad himself in his enthusiasm. *Zarathustra*, for all its splendid rhetoric, becomes ridiculous through the agency of this particular snobbery. Strindberg was a bad madness-snob (*cf.* the *Inferno*, etc.). The influence of these hysterical nineteenth-century mystico-materialists is far from extinct.

The plastic strength and composure that you get in a painting by Giotto, for what that is worth, could not be obtained from the most gifted lunatic. On the other hand, most lunatics can, and usually do, paint better pictures than you see in the Salon or in the illustrated papers : just as most children excel their elders in visual sensitiveness, and for a limited period paint better pictures.

Æsthetic expression, without being answerable to Tolstoy's simple peasant intelligence, has still somewhere *some* specimen person (normally functioning up to a point, not *too* constipated, myopic, or rheumatic, with a *few* teeth left, and just able to take care of himself without getting run over, or run in for indecent exposure, theft, or arbitrary behaviour on a bus) lying in wait for it, and able to discredit it—if *it*, in its turn, come to life, could do none of the things I have just enumerated.

Wherever a work of art happens to be of such a character that you can *bring it to life* in fancy without trouble, it has to bear in mind this ' specimen person.'

The goitrous torpid and squinting husks provided by Matisse in his sculpture are worthless except as tactful decorations for a mental home. It is the intelligence and not the body in them that essentially has been smashed or spoilt. It is this that makes them more repulsive than a picture showing the disembowelling of a horse in the bull-ring, for instance, an execution, or a slaughter-yard. The highly intellectual and methodic gibber of Miss Gertrude Stein is in the same situation. Even Dostoievsky as an epileptic fashion would be intolerable : he can only be borne because he was the *only* epileptic of that time, so he owes a great deal to Tolstoy and his other contemporaries for being so quiet.

Political revolution involves (1) destruction, and (2) reorganization : they are separate departments, but they necessarily work together, and sometimes get mixed up. Where they get thoroughly fused, as destruction is easier and more amusing than organization, it is that that gets the ascendency.   But all art must be a political expression to some extent, and science exists owing to its *usefulness.* Politically it is extremely *useful.*   And art to-day is more involved with science than at any former period.

From this rapid capitulation of facts it must follow, if they are correct, that art is in the nature of things not much less political than science : and that destructive factors, as well as factors of organization, come into it.   But in an intense revolutionary period it is inevitable, perhaps, that the destructive factors should predominate.   As, however, revolution is certainly an impulse to new life, no matter into whose hands it falls, and as automatically new and organizable elements come into existence every year, present themselves for valuation, and invite to new combinations, much of a not purely destructive nature must also be there.

Certain painting by Chirico or Picasso, for instance, music by Rimsky-Korsakov, mathematical theory of Einstein, contains a great vivifying force.   What is destructive— or, in the cases we have been considering, plainly *idiotic* or moronesque—is often absent from their work.   It is to save the purist revolutionary matter from contamination with the impure over-political matter with which it is carried along, in the midst of which it has to live, that, once more, this analysis has been undertaken.

CHAPTER VIII

SOREL, BERTH, ETC., *BAD* SYNDICALISTS
AS REGARDS THEIR OWN SYNDIC

WHERE Péguy is answering, in the time succeeding the *Affaire Dreyfus*, those people who accused *the intellectuals* of being at the bottom of that transaction of having *mounted* and *arranged* it, he bears down on them in one of his rushing waves of eloquence, and incidentally produces a very good plea for the *automatic* :—

> Si le parti intellectuel était assez malin, assez fort, assez pénétrant dans la réalité pour avoir monté, pour avoir su, pour avoir pu monter une aussi grosse affaire ; s'il avait été de taille et d'une profondeur à soulever ainsi un gros mouvement de la réalité, un aussi gros mouvement ; s'il avait été capable de malaxer ainsi, de triturer, de manier, d'élaborer, de pétrir un aussi gros morceau de la réalité ; justement alors, alors précisément ils ne seraient pas de ce que nous nommons le parti intellectuel, ils n'auraient point ces défauts, ces vices que nous nommons précisément du parti intellectuel, cette stérilité, cette incapacité, cette débilité, cette sécheresse, cet artificiel, ce superficiel, cet intellectuel. Ils seraient au contraire des gens qui auraient travaillé, connu, malaxé, pétri de la réalité. Ils seraient des gens qui auraient trempé dans la réalité même.

There are many people who are highly intellectual, well informed, possessing excellent taste, who are yet nothing, who are quite ineffective. The contrast between the extent of their intellectual possessions and the poorness of the use they make of them is striking and depressing. If that is what we could agree to call ' intellectual,' there would be little objection to the incessant use of the term to abuse and direct contempt with. And we can all agree with Péguy that if it was intellectuals who ' elaborated and shaped this great mass of reality ' of which he is speaking, then it would show a lack of judgment to regard them with contempt.

But unfortunately Benda's indictment of Sorel and the

407

rest for their use of this term in a sense deliberately aiming at the intellect, rather than at one of the crowd of its less satisfactory possessors or hangers-on, has much justification.   They were led to this by the exigencies of platform effect in their appeals to the crowd, and by such influences as that of Bergson's sensationalist philosophy.

It is especially strange that Sorel, Berth, and the syndicalists, with their great sense of reality where the *worker* was concerned—every worker, that is, except the intellectual worker—should have had so little sense and instinct where they themselves were concerned.   Indeed, they had so very little that they spent their time in abusing the intellectual—*themselves*—from morning till night.

Yet, if it is quite sound, as syndicalist doctrine had the honour of first emphasizing, that a baker or a miner must see and feel things as an average baker or miner : that you cannot set a baker to rule and legislate for a miner, or a miner for a baker, any more than you would ask an ant to take his orders from a moth or *vice versa*,—it is equally true that men writing pamphlets and books, and all that entails, like Sorel or Berth, also have *their* syndicalist *esprit de corps*, or should.   And why, in the name of all that is not insane, should they be ashamed of it ?   Why, as Sorel and a multitude of the ' intellectuals ' have done, should they repudiate each other with every resource of invective, and hold the ' intellect,' the instrument of all their life and power, up to scorn ?   What would you think of a baker who was always talking with an immense contempt of those half-naked, whitened figures who spend their horrible lives in the disgusting occupation of shovelling pieces of dough in and out of a filthy oven ? Or of a miner who never referred to the miner except as that black-faced devil, as malignant as despicable, who spends his life hitting his mother earth with a hammer ?

That is a mystery that I believe, in the foregoing pages, I have done something towards clearing up.

' Notre sujet n'est pas de discuter les doctrines de nos contemporains, mais de marquer les volontés qui s'y expriment.' (We are not discussing the doctrines of our contemporaries, but noting the will that finds expression in those doctrines.)   This could be used to describe in the main the object of this essay.   The difference no doubt would be that here, having laid bare the will concealed beneath the doctrine, we analyse it ; and that when the doctrine is seen to flow too deliberately from a not very beautiful will, by which it is pumped out by the gallon, the doctrine loses its importance automatically.   Hence, if we have succeeded in some instances in discrediting the will, it is to be hoped that indirectly we may have damaged the doctrine.

PART XIII

BEYOND ACTION AND REACTION

'*Premièrement le monde moderne est beaucoup
moins monté. Il est beaucoup plus une maladie
naturelle. Deuxièmement cette maladie naturelle
est beaucoup plus grave, beaucoup plus profonde,
beaucoup plus* universelle.
   '*Nul n'en profite et tout le monde en souffre.
Tout le monde en est atteint. Les modernes mêmes
en souffrent. Ceux qui s'en vantent, qui s'en glori-
fient, qui s'en réjouissent, en souffrent. Ceux qui
l'aiment le mieux, aiment leur mal. Ceux mêmes que
l'on croit qui n'en souffrent pas, en souffrent. Ceux
qui font les heureux sont aussi malheureux, plus malheureux que les autres, plus malheureux que nous.*
Dans le monde moderne, tout le monde souffre du
mal moderne. *Ceux qui font ceux que ça leur
profite, sont aussi malheureux, plus malheureux que
nous.* Tout le monde est malheureux dans le
monde moderne.'
                   Notre Jeunesse.   Charles Péguy.

'*Not that Adam that kept the paradise, but that
Adam that keeps the prison: . . . he that came
behind you, sir, like an evil angel, and bid you
forsake your liberty.'*
                   Comedy of Errors.   Shakespeare.

'*Why . . . monsieur, if you think your mystery in
stratagem can bring this instrument of honour again
into its native quarter . . . go on.'*
                   All's Well that ends Well.   Shakespeare.

CHAPTER I

IS 'EVERY ONE UNHAPPY IN THE MODERN WORLD'?

NO logical future has taken pictorial shape in these pages. All that has been done is to lay down a certain number of roads joining the present with something different from itself; yet something necessitated, it would appear, by its tendency. Both what is desirable and what is not in it contribute contradictorily to this impression. It is this *double* movement (proceeding from combined disgust and satisfaction) that must make the planning of these roads so difficult.

Like all engineers, we are of sanguine disposition. To build even a bridle-path across No Man's Land with the Trump of Doom sounding in our ears is evidence of that. But as far as possible this enviable cheerfulness has been concealed from the reader. *Tout le monde est malheureux dans le monde moderne*, Péguy, on the preceding page, chants. He is, of course, so wrong that his error can be neglected. It would be impossible to find a world in which *every one* was unhappy. First of all, a striking amount of unhappiness always means exceptional fortune for the few lucky ones that are not. In that sense it is an evidence of happiness, rather. Then Péguy himself is a living contradiction of his own statement. He was happy, for the noblest reasons, at the spectacle of so much misery. And for the most ignoble reasons there would always be plenty of others to be found whose satisfaction could be observed to grow as universal misfortune increased.

But in spite of all the evidences of deliberate maleficence in the modern world, when you have reckoned all that is deliberate, there still remains a great amount of *automatic* evil. In spite, similarly, of the small evidence of effort to produce any good, *automatically* a surplus of good comes into the world every year. For all the organization designed to convert it into evil with great despatch, there is still left over a respectable amount, which has either escaped attention or been found intractable to present methods. This brief statement must serve the purpose of an apology. The high-spirits implied by such a work as we have been engaged on does not signify the existence of a secret store of good, or as it were a secret still where high-spirits is manufactured. It is entirely the result of a prolonged contemplation of statistics.

The philosopher or the man of the type of Sir Thomas More is always accused of confusing the *possible* with the *desirable*. He is described as ' utopian ' or as ' a dreamer.' But he might, with some reason, retaliate that the emphatic ' practical ' man is guilty of that confusion. For his prudential prejudices have the same result educed from contrary impulses. His preoccupation with what is possible is apt to make the ' practical man ' describe that as desirable which usually is not.

Whether the Utopia I have been occupied in defining is possible, I do not know. You may consider it too much mixed up, in my exposition, with the real, to be a Utopia at all. Or you may think it entirely ' utopian ' to hope to devise a means of paralysing the dangerous forces of human life without injuring them, or without ' catastrophe.' Annihilation is Mr. Shaw's only solution (as it was Swift's) in his *Back to Methuselah*. Those Yahoos, Ozymandias, and Semiramis, after they have bitten and killed a promising sculptor, are destroyed. This appears to me too savage a doom. The destruction of any living thing involves the destruction of all, as is understood by the buddhist. It could, however, be castrated or otherwise treated, put to work and made innocuous, without involving one in vegetarian problems. Again, the spectator of this retribution (overtaking the historic puppets brought on the stage, and blasted by the shavian sages) will not perhaps see so much to choose as Mr. Shaw would have us believe between the bickering three-year-olds, conceived evidently by Mr. Shaw on some pseudo-classic, New Art, or Chelsea, pattern, and the dolls they make. The mesmerists that are called Elders, always sententiously rapt in thought, are no better. They seem to have no right to kill the dolls.

CHAPTER II

BEYOND ACTION AND REACTION

THIS essay is a statement of a position that would be entirely irreconcilable, but irreconcilable outside of the cadres and clichés of any recognized federated opinion. Above all, it would seek to dissociate from the pure revolutionary impulse of creative thought all those corrupt imitations which confuse so much the issue, in their over-night utilitarian travesties. The agency it naturally envisages is that of spiritual ascendency or persuasion, with the avoidance of all violence as an article of faith. It is nothing but a rough working system of thought for the wild time we live in.

Committed to one theory or another of revolution, to something radical and deliberate, that is: in capitulating about your divorce, in consequence, from the world of sentiment and quiet animal growth, it is well to remember that every one is ' a rebel ' to-day, to some extent. So your natural opponents will all be ' revolutionaries,' all ' modern.' A flag, a badge, or a uniform is, under these circumstances, no indication of friend or foe.

The statement of a position ' *beyond action and reaction* ' is our aim. That would be something as irreconcilable as primitive christianity, as radical as the truest speculative thought: which type of things are, as I have tried to show, the very source of revolution. I believe what I have outlined must in this sense be the attitude of the European of the future. He must be neither a ' good European ' nor a ' bad European '—but, in short, a ' beyond-the-good-and-bad European,' if anything at all. To parody another famous saying by a great phrase-maker, it could be said that you must *drive your plough over the bones of the unborn.* Use your revolutionary impulse as a magic carpet to transport you constantly into the future : this will act healthily on your present. You will fly back to your present to see how it is progressing, and will find it very slowly sprouting with less impatience than if you were unable to imagine its ever becoming anything else but what it is.

The naïvely conventional ' revolutionary ' is a stereotyped, routine protocol of a living activity, vulgarized for the purposes of mass use. It is really only put into the form of ' revolution ' to make it comprehensible. But what is asserted here is, further, that this vulgarized version is apt, by the religious tenacity with which it is held, to affect its original authors. Such extremely highly organized vulgarization as exists to-day is productive of that.

But all creative activity at the best of times must have been influenced, if not controlled, by political necessity. Von Hartmann finds it ' amazing that Locke's sensational-ism should have dominated the eighteenth century as it did.' The intellectual domination of certain schools of thought to-day would similarly seem ' amazing ' to some Von Hartmann of the future. What happens is, however, that in every epoch thinkers of different, opposite types occur : there is always a Leibniz and always a Locke. It has been the political tendencies of the time that make one or the other prevail.

The phenomenon noticed by Benda—namely, that to-day, in the intellectual world, there is no Opposition, is caused by the infinitely higher organization of our time. *This enables politics to dominate speculation and invention in a way it has never done before.* There is virtually no intel-lectual Opposition in Europe : Julien Benda, for instance, is a very marked exception. Similarly, there is no real *criticism* of existing society. Politics and the highly organized, deeply entrenched, dominant mercantile society has it all its own way. Proust, who may come to mind, is not a critic of the society he described. He is a partisan as much as is the novelist writing for the millionaire Mayfair public : he likes every odour that has ever reached him from the millionaire society he depicts, while, of course, thoroughly competent to appreciate its weak spots. Whether this is a good thing or a bad in principle, where pictures of contemporary habits are concerned, it is certainly crippling for more abstract activities.

The proof of this political ascendency over thought is not difficult to grasp. The history, geography, etc., that a child is taught are not conceived as science but as a political pabulum flavoured with this or that specialist truth, just so much truth as is politically safe. Useful and docile citizens, not learned ones or people trained to think for themselves, is what is desired.

But the press, which is an extension of the school on its political and informative side, is controlled by the same interests, naturally, as control the school curriculum. Science and philosophy, beyond this, invent and speculate somewhat to order. Neither the Lockes nor the Leibnizes can ever be said in their public teaching to be free. They are in a sense freest when most controlled.

I have already given you my reasons for not regarding an honest Inquisition as a bad thing. If it entirely abolished *the vulgarization of the best thought*—confining popular teaching to a routine in the hands of the small educational bureaucracy—it would have an excellent effect on the higher activities of the human mind, which should not be asked to turn teacher, but be left free to create.

The Zeitgeist has nothing to do with the workshop or laboratory, but is a phenomenon of the social world. Moving in millionaire circles, he hears to-day much talk of the *Méfaits des Intellectuels* (the Misdemeanours of the Intellectuals), naturally. At all times he is a *salon*-spirit, the spirit of fashion. And that sort of fashion has nothing to do with the creative intelligence, is a stranger to its habits, and lives in a different universe. If you are known to be of a ' revolutionary ' or of a ' pioneer ' complexion, a ' rebel,' as it is called, you will be expected to call the Zeitgeist by his christian name when you meet. But in fact you will hardly speak the same language.

Sorel encountered all these difficulties in the course of his revolutionary career. For instance, when he began (when he became a social revolutionary, that is), if there was one thing that was blindly accepted as part of the equipment of every revolutionary no matter of what shade of opinion, it was anti-clericalism. But Sorel, the most extreme of the french social revolutionaries of his time, was a very militant catholic, as was Péguy. Again, he was in all his tastes a doctrinaire classicist, with roman antiquity as his political anchor, in this resembling Machiavelli. But to the deceptions of the conventional (of those with minds composed of comfortable clichés) there is no end. The ' revolutionary ' will not even be ' revolutionary ' in the way you want him to be ; and is often ' revolutionary ' about things that no one ever dreamt a person could be ' revolutionary ' about !

CHAPTER III

THE GREAT DEVELOPMENT OF ASSOCIATIONAL LIFE

EVERYTHING assumes an increasingly associational form. A vast system of interlocking syndics— pleasure syndics, work syndics, sex and age syndics, vice and race syndics, health syndics, and valetudinarian syndics—is imposed. In *Sodome et Gomorrhe* Proust shows the working of this very well in his analysis of the powerful instinctive freemasonry of the pederast. But the Philatelist, the Anti-Semite, the Rollsite, or the Daimlerite, the Player of Chess or of Mah-Jong, can form equally well-cemented brotherhoods.

The associational habit in its present development is the result of mass production. It is fostered in the interests of economy in our overcrowded world, and people are encouraged to get as quickly as possible into the category that offers the nearest approach to what they require or what they can hope for, and there remain. The mass mind is required to gravitate to a standard size to receive the standard idea. The alternative is to go naked : the days of made-to-order and made-to-measure are past. The standardization of women's dress, which is effected by the absolutist machinery of fashion, is the type of all the other compulsions tending to a greater and greater uniformity and standardization. There a colour—' nigger-brown,' for instance—is imposed. The great syndic of the manufacturers, dressmakers, etc., agree on ' nigger-brown,' and so the world flowers universally in ' nigger-brown ' for a season, with perhaps a streak of mushroom-pink exuviæ from the last season. In the interest of great-scale industry and mass production the smaller the margin of diversity the better. The nearer the fashion is to a uniform the bigger the returns, the fewer dresses unsold—for where there is little difference in cut, colour, and fancy there is the less temptation to be individualistically fussy. When there is so little essential difference between one costume and another, the difference is so slight it is not worth holding out about.

418

This closer and closer enregimentation of women, with the rhythmic seasonal changes of sex-uniform, is effected without difficulty by simple fiats of fashion. The overpowering instinct for conformity, and the horror of antiquation or of the eccentric, sees to the rest. In all this vast smooth-running process you see the image of a political state in which no legislation, police, or any physical compulsion would be required : in which everything would be effected by public opinion, snobbery, and the magic of *fashion*. We have, historically, in the hebrew state, a type of non-executive state such as might be arrived at on those lines. The legislature, of the greek city-state sort, did not exist; of all coercive administrative machinery, only the judiciary was required. God did the rest, or rather the teachings of *righteousness*, the anxious fanatical conscience of the citizen, and a great system of ritual. That is an example of moral rule, or rule by opinion, as opposed to rule by physical force : of much more effective *interior*, mental, domination, in place of a less intelligent *exterior* form of government. Theocratic and theurgic forms of government are the highest form of democracy—a kind of super-democracy, in fact.

The ideas of a time are like the clothes of a season : they are as arbitrary, as much imposed by some superior will which is seldom explicit. They are utilitarian and political, the instruments of smooth-running government. And to criticize them seriously, especially to-day, *for themselves*, would be as absurd as to criticize the fashion in loofahs, bath-mats, bath-salts, or geysers, in children's frocks or soft felt hats.

Those who actually like uniformity are naturally open to an unflattering suspicion. If, for instance, you protest too much that ' all men are much the same '—does it not mean perhaps that you *wish* all men to be much the same ? You have no hope of benefiting by a general recognition of their being otherwise ? You see your interest best in a *degradation* of men, rather than in a belief in their potentialities and in the excelling of some ? If you reply that I or another are similarly arguing for privilege or discrimination because we have a personal interest in such an arrangement, that would have to be accepted by us. There would be no dishonour in such a conclusion to the argument.

At all events, that is the danger run by the person too emphatic for the uniform.   Again, the physical size of a living organism at any given moment of time is of the same value as the size of a stone.   A man six foot high and a stone six foot high are both six foot.   But since the man is living, goes on, and multiplies himself in space, there is no meaning in comparing them in that way.   By saying that the stone is alive, only living slower, you do not alter the matter on our plane, which is alone the plane on which we are conscious, and about which we are talking.   Outward uniformity is highly deceptive in any case.

The associational herd-instinct has one peculiarity that is very much to the point.   The higher up in the scale of intelligence and vitality people are found, the less do they care, or are they able, to associate with each other and lend each other help.   The inherent weakness of this natural isolation is the cause of all human misfortune, since the inventive individual is constantly exposed to destruction in a way that the uninventive, mechanical, associational man is not.   Had the best intelligences at any time in the world been able to combine, the result would have been a prodigy of power, and the result for men at large of the happiest.

What makes the present time, then, so hopeful a one is that in the ever closer and more mechanical association of the great masses of people into an ever more and more rigid system of clans, societies, clubs, syndics, and classes, the original man is more and more forced out of these groupings, since there is no play for the inventive or independent mind within them.   All these *odd men out* stand at present glaring at each other as usual, remarking perhaps to themselves that adversity brings them strange bedfellows.   But the time must arrive when *they*, too, in spite of themselves, form a sort of syndic.   That will be the moment of the renascence of our race, or will be the signal for a new biological transformation.   While the. philosopher of the sort of Mr. Russell, of the author of *The Anatomy of Melancholy*, or of Professor Richet, would be swept down into the underworld of subconscious automatism, wringing their hands, in attitudes of apocalyptic despair.

Earlier in this essay it was remarked that: ' Left at the

mercy of this vast average—its inertia, " creative hatred," and conspiratorial habits where the " new " is concerned— we shall always checkmate ourselves ; and the more we " advance," the more we shall lose ground.' But if this inertia (1) is *satisfied* by a businesslike organization of its desire (its *What the Public wants* requirement), and if (2) this inflexible organization severs it entirely from all the free intelligences in the world, which it more and more isolates, then a new duality of human life (introducing perhaps a new species, and issuing in biological transformation) would result. That is why, far from molesting or subjecting to damaging criticism (of a vulgarizing description) the processes of *stultification* which are occurring, everything should be done (publicly, and at large, of course) to hasten it. So it can be truly said with fullest good sense that whenever you see a particularly foolish play, read an especially idiotic article, full of that strident humbug to which we are so accustomed, you should rejoice. Mental food changes people in the same way as what they eat and the climate of their habitat. Those who like or can stomach what they are given in Western democracies to-day will change and separate themselves naturally from those who reject or vomit at that fare. A natural separation will then occur, and everybody will get what he wants. ' Nature's ethereal, human angel, Man,' will become segmented, and the divorce will be to the good of both these sections which are being forced apart.

CHAPTER IV

HOW MUCH TRUTH DOES A MAN REQUIRE ?

SOREL draws our attention to what he affirms is the importance of the *anticipatory* spirit by a quotation from von Hartmann :—

> The melancholy which is spread like a *presentiment* over all the masterpieces of greek art, in spite of the life with which they seem to overflow, is witness that individuals of genius, even in that period, were in a condition to penetrate the illusions of life, to which the genius of their age abandoned itself without experiencing the need to control them.

And Sorel comments on this to the effect that ' there are few doctrines more important for the understanding of history ' than that of *anticipation*, reminding us of Newman's use of it in his researches in the history of dogmas.

This melancholy presentiment of the truth, that the tragic drama possessed in Greece, enabling it to tear aside the veil of illusion, as Shakespeare did so terribly in our own time, was a possession (in both senses of that word) not shared by greek philosophy as a whole. Heraclitus, the ' dark,' the ' weeping,' philosopher, owned it. But the platonists were busy, as in their capacity of teachers and healers they were bound to be, with happier pictures. The artist's truth is in this way the deeper and more terrible. His classical tragic task of providing a *catharsis* —his diabolical rôle of getting as near to destruction and terror as that is possible without impairing the organism— requires of him a very different disposition to that of the philosopher.

When the tragic artist takes life in hand for representation, secondary characteristics disappear as he manipulates it. It is at life itself, rather than at our particular social life of the moment, that his terrible processes are directed. His ' truth,' if it were not deadened by a rhythmical enchantment, would annihilate us. But the philosopher, he who is responsible for the Utopias, although he may have

his ' presentiments ' as well, is typically engaged in be-
stowing life, not in pretending to take it away—however
salutary that threat may be in the event. He heals the
wounds inflicted by natural science, or tries to ; dovetails
his midwifery with the purges of the more terrible form of
artist ; investigates life's gentler and nobler possibilities
with the serener sort of artist. So he defines his discursive
functions : showing himself as indispensable as the dock
leaf is for the nettle, and claiming to stand between man
and the artist, as well as between man and the man of
science. He is the *lover*, his wisdom or system his carefully
collected nest.

That our contemporaries have an aversion, as Sorel says,
to ' every pessimistic idea ' is indisputable. But what
people have not had ? He means, however, that they
refuse to take on even so much of the harsh truth as is
necessary for life's bare preservation. But they get their
truth all right, in spite of themselves. Mechanically it
reaches them, without their knowing how, by way of the
vulgarization of scientific thought. They actually get
much too much, far more than what would be a suitable
ration. It is plainly the popularization of science that
is responsible for the fever and instability apparent on
all sides. To withhold knowledge from people, or to place
unassimilable knowledge in their hands, are both equally
effective, if you wish to render them helpless. As Einstein
is reported as saying in conversation, the characteristic
danger to human society is that the outstripping intellect
will destroy the backward mass of men by imposing a
civilization on it for which it is not ready.

The question, of course, remains if it will ever be ready.
That is the capital question where its destiny is concerned.
It is on the answer to that that all political thought must
repose. What has been suggested in the foregoing pages
is that ample evidence has been accumulated by now that
men, as a whole, will never be ready. Instead of sitting
down and abusing them as the man of the type of Robert
Burton does—or as Professor Richet has just done, and
as have numbers of other philosophers, ecclesiastics, etc.,
in the past,—and instead of fixing an eye of hatred on them,
and deciding that they must die, as Swift did, or coolly
blasting them (with the gesture, oddly enough, of bene-

diction), as Mr. Shaw does with Ozymandias, a quite different course, luckily, to-day presents itself.

In 1849 Lange wrote : ' Should it not be clear to every reasonable man that civilized Europe must enter into one great political community ? ' Earlier Goethe was a constant advocate of a world-state, and of the suppression of nationality. In other words, he was an ' internationalist.' To-day, in spite of very great efforts to artificially preserve ' national ' frontiers, these frontiers being a more disreputable farce than at any former period, *automatically*—the automatic defeating conscious strategy most plainly in this instance—internationalism is becoming a fact. The standardizing of giant industry and its international character will have it so, in spite of the international industrialists. When all Russians wore beards and all Americans were clean-shaven, it was much more easy to make them believe, respectively, that they were of different clay. But ' nationality ' is the one thing that cannot be manufactured. Once you have destroyed, or allowed to be destroyed, the ancient customs and arts of a country, you cannot reimpose them. The Maypole or Jack o' the Green in the Council-School festivity is too evident a lie : it is like a sphinx in St. Paul's, or a carthaginian galley on the Spree.

There is to-day a new reality ; it is its first appearance in terrestrial life—the fact of political world-control. To-day this may be said to be in existence, and to-morrow it will be still more of a fact. Neither can it be hidden—short of destroying everybody's sense of reality altogether. People no doubt could be persuaded that they did not see the sun and moon : but the effort to assimilate this gigantic lie would destroy their brains altogether, and universal imbecility would ensue.

Thereby the whole problem of government is altered. New methods are suggested that formerly circumstances did not allow people even to imagine. With a world-state and a recognized central world-control, argument about the ethics of war would become absurd. More profitable occupations could then be found for everybody. In a society organized on a world-basis, ' revolution ' would not be encouraged, either, any more than to-day it is encouraged in fascist Italy or soviet Russia.

The idea for which Professor Perry stands, that of the comparatively recent growth of war, and of the fundamentally pacific nature of man, when not trained or organized as a ' fighting machine ' (for it is only as a machine, even, that he can fight—by himself he is not very pugnacious or brave), is supported by a great deal of very good evidence. And there seems no reason at present why this period of chaotic wastefulness should not be regarded as drawing to a close. In order to wind it up, further wars and revolutions may occur. But they are not any longer necessary. There is no even political excuse for them. There may soon therefore no longer be any reason for the despairing philosopher to inquire, ' Who made so soft and peaceable a creature, born to love mercy, meekness, so to rave, rage like wild beasts, and run on to their own destruction? How may Nature expostulate with mankind, " I made thee a harmless, quiet, a divine creature ! ", etc.'

For we know quite well what makes such a soft and peaceable creature into a warrior—it is his rulers in the course of their competitive careers who effect this paradoxical transformation in their extremely soft subjects. If all competition were eliminated—both as between the small man and the big, and respectively between the several great ones of this earth—then this soft and peaceable, or ' mad, careless, and stupid,' creature would be spared the gymnastics required to turn him into a man-eating tiger. It is also absurd, and even wicked, to attempt to turn him into a philosopher. He should be left alone and allowed to lead a peaceful, industrious, and pleasant life, for we all as men belong to each other.

The optimism of socratic thought might even be rehabilitated, and not seem so aggravating as Sorel found it. His serene picture, without coming true, might no longer enrage : the ' presentiments ' of the prophets and artists could be taken or left—left by most people, who would hum and buzz as monotonously and peaceably through their life as even the most fortunate bee. Those who had a taste for other forms of life, or who were bred, by means of eugenics, to a different existence, would not rage against their soft and peaceable fellow-man as formerly. For every one would be perfectly satisfied.

CHAPTER V

DIFFERENT MAGICS

IN the Mind and Body war, the war of Sensation against Intellect, the war of the high and the low-brow, the war of women and men, you are expected to be obediently, conventionally, militant. If you agree, and if in the first, for instance, your occupation thrusts you into the ranks of the Mind, then you have imposed on you an attitude of artificial hostility to the Body. This may be against your nature, which disposes you to be friendly to both. The same through the whole list. The intolerance, the militancy-to-order, the savage partisanship imposed on you on every possible subject, is a conscription that, intellectually, you must learn to evade.

'Qui terre a, guerre a' is a French proverb. But without 'terre' it is apparently the same thing. Everything is done to make people wish to be animals rather than men. A writer in the *New Leader* recently quoted what purported to be a letter from a perplexed correspondent. It expresses very well the widespread discouragement of the moderately ambitious man:—

> 'What is the use of being told about books (he wrote) when I can't read them! I haven't the money to buy them, and nine times out of ten my local library hasn't got them; or if it has, there is a list as long as your arm of people waiting for them.'

Beginning on this personal note, his argument proceeded to wider considerations, raising the whole question of the value of civilization for the poor. A progress in culture, he said, meant a reduction in happiness; the more complicated a man's needs became, the more refined his tastes, the greater their liability to be outraged. The man who is used to good books is revolted by the sunday papers that satisfy his fellows; the man who likes good music is a martyr to noise and shudders every time a barrel-organ comes down his street; the man who recognizes a lovely building when he sees it, turns in loathing from the squalid ugliness of our towns.

If he be rich he can to some extent obtain compensation for the pain his cultivated tastes cause him, by spending

time and money on their satisfaction.   He can only shudder
away from a world of savages and hooligans and shrink into
himself in pride and disgust.

'Thus (my correspondent ended) if I had to choose to-day
between being a pig happy or being Socrates unhappy—
and wisdom seems to point to the necessity of being one or
the other—I should plump for the pig-stye every time.'

To be ' happy ' is the object of the person illustrated in
the letter.   If you want to be ' happy ' you must not be a
man, but a pig.   And that that is especially true to-day
is indisputable.   Well, the Circe of Capitalism is able to
achieve this for our shipwrecked world.   We can either
decide among ourselves, or draw lots, as to who shall be
happy and who unhappy.

There is a story that in the early days of socialism a
certain labour leader had organized a demonstration in
Trafalgar Square.   Thousands of strikers assembled, and
large forces of police were reported as approaching from
all directions.   The organizer of the demonstration passed
round the word that all the manifestants, at the first sign
of the police, should *sit down*.   In due course the police
appeared : they rushed furiously into Trafalgar Square
from Whitehall, Cockspur Street, and the Strand.   But a
non-resisting human carpet was spread out at their feet :
the entire crowd, as ordered, was *sitting down on the ground*.

Some of the revolutionary movements in full swing to-
day are an unconscious adoption of this method of meeting
the difficulties of the time.   It was a particularly good way,
and one that people cannot be blamed for adopting.   The
only magic that the ruled have at their command in face
of the demands of the ruler is such as balked the police
in the above story.   Complete industrial obedience would,
no doubt, absolve you from constant doses of war and
revolution.   The corrective of civil disobedience since
the world began has been military discipline, war, and
blood-letting.

Fourier refers to the *magical* effect of the capitalist
transformation of his day in words already quoted :—

One is ready to believe in magic on seeing kings and
empires thus circumvented by a few commercial sophisms,
and the race of monopolists, stockjobbers, *agioteurs* exalted
to the skies . . . who employ their influence in concentrating

masses of capital, in producing fluctuations in the price of products—ruining alternately all branches of industry.

We have got used to the money magicians. We are all under their spell. The Good European (perhaps Nietzsche's ' Good European ' was after all a mockery), the *Brave* European (*brave* as in german), is not very good at magic. He is very good at war, however. Of this he is very proud indeed : any time you ask him to fight and show how good he is at war, there is no holding him. What a pity he is not a better magician, and, on the other hand, a less remarkable fighter ! Oh, that ' fighting face ' of the novelette !

Celui qui sera mon curé, je serai son paroissien (Whoever will look after me can call me his client) is a *good* proverb for a good man, or ' Good European.' ' Whoever will be my Circe, I will be his swine ' would be the proverb for the writer of the letter quoted above. That argument turns on the question of the desirability of ' happiness,' which each man instinctively resolves for himself.

Happiness is the chief material also in the construction of Utopias. Christ's is the most famous and the nearest to socialism. And the Utopia of Christ can conveniently be compared with the Utopia of the Ford industrial colonies or the ideal working-class community of Port Sunlight.

Christ's millennium was the old jewish dream of a land of promise. The hard cash of suffering and enslavement that the Jew was willing to pay down, in vicarious atonement, through his long genealogical sequences, passed on to the sombreness of the puritan : the ' dogged old jewish optimism ' vanished : and the European must have a very imperfect notion of the dream of Jesus.

' However much, therefore, Christianity may have insisted on renouncing the world, the flesh, and the devil, it always kept in the background the perfectly jewish and pre-rational craving for a delectable promised land. The journey might be long and through a desert, but milk and honey were to flow in the oasis beyond.' Beyond the puritan's savage gloom there was no Valhalla, however, much less the delectable oasis indicated above by Santayana —the honey-pot of the hebrew faith.

However, whatever Christ's Kingdom of Heaven may have meant to his followers, there are certain elements in it that are accessible and generally understood. The difference between it and Port Sunlight, say, is this. Lord Leverhulme promised what he could perform, whereas Christ was in a very different position. The former was more honest, and, if allowed to, would, I think, in the fullness of time, have been a greater *benefactor* (measured by material cleanliness and comfort) than Christ. Port Sunlight is (in more senses than one, as I have suggested) a certainty. There is no *last shall be first* about it ; it is a dead level of sanitary life—sunlit, but not pretending to be Heaven. (It would be impossible for a man to say that he had Port Sunlight inside him, as he can say that he has Heaven within him.)

On the other hand, is Christ, promising what most likely can never come about, for that reason less of a benefactor than Lord Leverhulme or Henry Ford, promising what certainly can and will (most likely) come about ? Christ's perfection was full of impossibilities, on the mundane plane, and to stage them he had to take his audience *out of life* altogether. His doctrine was a drug : beneath its influence men saw their wrongs being righted, saw the ' oppressor's wrong, the proud man's contumely,' punished, and humble faith rewarded, the last first and the first last. Is it the action of an honourable man to give people these flattering visions ? Is not the modern benefactor of big business (possibly sometimes of the type against which Christ inveighed) really the eternal *rich man* justifying himself, stealing a march on the magician and so-called Saviour ? Even if this whitewashing of the whited sepulchre only resulted in a sanitary tiling such as we associate with lavatories and hospitals, is not perhaps this stone that the Builder rejected (namely, the *rich man*) becoming the headstone of the corner ?

But does he not also get much more out of it than Christ ? it might be objected. Even there it is not certain that Ford or Lord Leverhulme could not make good their claim for a bigger halo than Christ's. I have no means of knowing what exactly the author of Port Sunlight got out of life, or what Henry Ford is still enjoying ; but I should think that probably, on the model of most millionaires, they both must have led a harassed, frugal, lonely existence, full of distrust and indigestion. The experience of Christ—like a lyrical poet dying young, under romantic conditions, worshipped by throngs of people attracted by his personal magnetism, living to some extent the rosy dream that he recited daily—this experience sounds on the face of it more enviable than that of a modern millionaire.

' Malheur à celui qui en rit, il ne comprend pas l'esprit humain, sa fière originalité, petits esprits qui n'apprécient pas ce qui dépasse la vulgarité d'un salon, les étroites limites d'un bon sens vulgaire.'   So Renan writes of those who are apt to laugh at the holy passion of Sainte Thérèse, or other saints and madmen. ' Malheur ' indeed, and we must not be too hasty in taking Port Sunlight into our hearts in the place of the full christian or other dream.

But is not Christ's too exceptional a phantasy for the average of human desires ? The more discriminating arrangements of the hindu heaven—or system of heavens —respond probably more accurately to the reality of human wishes.

CHAPTER VI

THE POLITICS OF THE INTELLECT

THAT when I am speaking of the intellectual I evidently experience no shame (reflecting on the compromising nature of my own occupation), that I do not pretend to be ' a plain, blunt man,' is true.

Far from that, it is my effrontery to claim that men owe everything they can ever hope to have to an 'intellectual' of one sort or another. And that is true both of the business magnate and his meanest employee. I claim further that the intellectual is the only person in the world who is not a potential ' capitalist,' because his ' capital ' is something that cannot be bartered. What he deals in, even when it gives him power, gives him no money.

For this splendid and oppressed class nothing is done in the social revolution. But that it is a refuge for the scum of every other defeated class—or any class temporarily lying low—is true. And it is no doubt the great mass of pseudo-artists, writers, and so forth who discredit it. Therefore, when the agitator hurls his abuse at the intellectual, if he would be more specific and pick out the sort of figures that abuse the shelter of the too hospitable intellect, he would be doing a service.

The intelligence suffers to-day automatically in consequence of the attack on all authority, advantage, or privilege. These things are not done away with, it is needless to say, but numerous scapegoats are made of the less politically powerful, to satisfy the egalitarian rage awakened. The intellect, so exposed, so helpless in such a case, suffers most of any category, which is a danger to all of us. It is our own brain we are attacking—while the stomach looks on and laughs ' to see such sport.'

The possession and exercise of intellectual power in no way affects a person to a class enjoying political ascendency. There is nothing ' aristocratic ' about the intellect : its noticeable simplicity makes it unpromising to look for analogies to it in a complex society at all. An early society would offer better parallels, and indeed in many primitive communities the chief or leader is chosen as the man known

to have the best head.   But the word ' aristocratic,' with
its implication of a crowd within the bigger crowd, organized for the exploitation of the latter, is peculiarly inapt
for the essentially individual character of the intellect.

The intellect is more removed from the crowd than
is anything : but it is not a snobbish withdrawal, but a
going aside for the purposes of work, of work not without
its utility for the crowd.   The artificial barriers that
an aristocratic caste are forced to observe are upheld to
enhance a *difference* that is not a reality.   It is because
they are of the same stuff as their servants that they require
the disciplines of exclusiveness.   In the case where an
aristocratic régime represents a race ruling as the result of
conquest, as has generally been the case, often the aristocrat
is inferior in every respect to the subject population—
that is, except in organization for war.

The primitive, ' democratic,' picture of the intellectual
leader living his life simply among the people, with admirable simplicity and without fuss, has too many ready
illustrations in history to require specification.   But this
leader claims the authority of the function that he regards
as superior to any mechanical dominion of physical force
or wealth.   Also it is not for his own sake that he claims
it ; in this he resembles the king.   More than the prophet
or religious teacher he represents at his best the great
unworldly element in the world, and that is the guarantee
of his usefulness.   It is he and not the political ruler who
supplies the contrast of this something remote and *different*
that is the very stuff of which all living (not mechanical)
power is composed, and without whose incessant functioning men would rapidly sink back to their mechanical
origins.   The objectionable *difference* that is such an offence,
or can be made to look so, is the very sign by which he
should be known and accepted.

The life of the intelligence is the very incarnation of
freedom :   where it is dogmatic and harsh it is impure ;
where it is too political it is impure :   its disciplines are less
arbitrary and less *political* than those of religion :   and it is
the most inveterate enemy of unjust despotic power.   In
its operation it is less violent and more beneficent than
religion, with its customary intolerance of emotional
extremes.   It does not exercise power by terror or by

romantic pictures of the vast machinery of Judgment and Destruction.   It is more humane than are the programmes of the theological justiciary.   And its servants are not a sect nor an organized caste, like the priest or the hereditary aristocrat, but individuals possessing no concerted and lawless power, coming indifferently from all classes, and living simply among other people.   And their pride, if they have it, is because of something inside themselves which has been won at no one else's expense, and that no one can give them or remove from them.

But if you want to take him at his lowest, there is an intellectual who is the most valuable specialist in the service of capital.   The capitalist would have neither machine-guns nor aeroplanes nor bombs without this intellectual : for he could not invent these things or anything else himself.   The intellectual is thus a ' worker.'   What the capitalist does occasionally is to stir up the other workers against this highly salaried, specialist worker.

For the intellectual workman in general it is necessary to claim isolation and freedom from interference : that is, if the best intelligences of the race are to work for us and produce their best results.   This greatest and most valuable of all ' producers ' should be accommodated with conditions suitable to his maximum productivity.   He should not, if that were to be realized, be regarded (and hated) as the ' great man,' but regarded, more scientifically, as the chosen vessel of our human intelligence.   He should be no more the object of envy and dislike than Dempsey is because an unmatched gladiator.   And he should be relieved of the futile competition in all sorts of minor fields, so that his purest faculties could be free for the major tasks of intelligent creation.

It is easy to see how the passing of democracy and its accompanying vulgarities, owing to which any valuable discovery has to fight its way in the market-place—and the better it is, the bitterer the opposition—must facilitate this putting of the intelligence on a new basis.   The annihilation of industrial competition and the sweeping the board of the Small Man, commercially and socially, should have as its brilliant and beneficent corollary the freeing for its great and difficult tasks of intelligence of the first order.

Our minds are all still haunted by that Abstract Man, that enlightened abstraction of a common humanity, which had its greatest advertisement in the eighteenth century. That No Man in a No Man's Land, that phantom of democratic ' enlightenment,' is what has to be disposed for good in order to make way for higher human classifications, which, owing to scientific method, men could now attempt.

*' I wish to communicate this view
of the world to you exactly as it
manifests itself: and so no human
opinion will ever be able to get the
better of you.'*

Fragment viii. 61.
Parmenides.

EXTRACTS FROM PRESS NOTICES
OF 'TARR' AND OTHER WORKS BY
WYNDHAM LEWIS

*

THE method which produced Kreisler and Bertha [in *Tarr*] . . . are permanent for literature. In form, and in the actual writing, it [*Tarr*] is surpassed by *Cantelman's Spring Mate*. And *Inferior Religions* remains in my opinion the most indubitable evidence of genius, the most powerful piece of imaginative thought, of anything Mr. Lewis has written. . . .

Mr. Lewis is a magician who compels our interest in himself ; he is the most fascinating personality of our time. . . . The artist, I believe, is more primitive, as well as more civilized, than his contemporaries, his experience is deeper than civilization, and he only uses the phenomena of civilization in expressing it. . . . In the work of Mr. Lewis we recognize the thought of the modern and the energy of the cave-man.   T. S. ELIOT *in The Egoist.*

A BEAUTIFUL and serious work of art [*Tarr*] that reminds one of Dostoievsky only because it too is inquisitive about the soul, and because it contains one figure of vast moral significance which is worthy to stand beside Stavrogin. . . . The real achievement of the book which gives it both its momentary and permanent value is Kreisler. . . . We watch him turning life into blood-stained *charivari* exactly as we watched Germany during the war, until, having smirched every phenomenon within reach, he has to turn upon himself and pervert his own life unto death. . . . A work of art, of power, and distinction.
                    REBECCA WEST *in The Nation.*

MR. WYNDHAM LEWIS is a man of innumerable ideas . . . he can start more hares in a paragraph than most people can in a book. . . . Mr. Lewis is a keen psychologist, and one of the best living masters of English invective. . . . As against . . . feminine sensibility and irresponsibility he pleads the governing function of the intellect.

The art he pleads for is a masculine and austere art. It should have something of the severity of science and be quite as intelligent. . . .

This seriousness is Mr. Lewis's central passion. All his innumerable ideas on things in general have their roots here . . . he is one of the most serious writers of our time.   J. W. N. SULLIVAN *in The Times.*

Made in the USA
Monee, IL
19 May 2024

58646599R00261